NTC's
Dictionary
of
SPANISH
COGNATES

**Thematically
Organized**

NTC's
Dictionary
of
SPANISH
COGNATES

Thematically
Organized

Rose Nash, Ph.D.

New York   Chicago   San Francisco   Lisbon   London   Madrid   Mexico City
Milan   New Delhi   San Juan   Seoul   Singapore   Sydney   Toronto

The *McGraw·Hill* Companies

Library of Congress Cataloging-in-Publication Data

Nash, Rose.
    NTC's dictionary of Spanish cognates thematically organized / Rose Nash.
       p.   cm.
    ISBN 0-8442-7961-7 (hardcover) — ISBN 0-8442-7962-5 (paperback)
     1. Spanish language—Cognate words—English—Dictionaries.
  2. English language—Cognate words—Spanish—Dictionaries.
  I. National Textbook Company.   II. Title.
  PC4640.N35   1997
  468.2'421—dc21   97-16771
                                           CIP

10 11 12 13 14 15 16 17 18 19 20 21 22 23 24   HPC/HPC   0 9 8 7

ISBN-13: 978-0-8442-7961-9 (hardcover)
ISBN-10:   0-8442-7961-7 (hardcover)

ISBN-13: 978-0-8442-7962-6 (paperback)
ISBN-10:   0-8442-7962-5 (paperback)

Interior design by Terry Stone

This book is printed on acid-free paper.

Contents

Introduction

WHAT IS A COGNATE?

This is a book about true cognates—words in English and Spanish that (1) look alike and (2) have the same meanings. Its purpose is to enable you to learn a large amount of bilingual vocabulary very quickly, whether you are a beginning, intermediate, or advanced language student.

In written or printed form, cognates are easy to recognize. Any differences in spelling between the English and Spanish cognate words are minor compared to their striking similarities. In this sentence, there are three cognate pairs:

The computer is a modern invention.

La computadora es una invención moderna.

The cognate words in the sentence are:

English words	Spanish words
computer	computadora
modern	moderna
invention	invención

Differences in cognate spellings range from no difference to several letters. Let's look at more examples:

- Cognates with identical spellings

  color = color, legal = legal, crisis = crisis, radio = radio, usual = usual

- Cognates with a one-letter spelling difference

  author = autor, basic = básico, punctual = puntual, tomato = tomate

- Cognates with a more-than-one-letter spelling difference

  emphasis = énfasis, piece = pieza, office = oficina, system = sistema

- Cognates with different suffixes

  variety = variedad, civilize = civilizar, public = público, really = realmente

- Cognates with different prefixes

  abnormal = anormal, disarm = desarmar, unacceptable = inaceptable

Spelling differences between Spanish and English cognates are often repeated in other cognate pairs. These correspondence patterns help us to predict and remember the correct form of the word in the other language. In fact, one could say that, where cognates are concerned, even the differences are similar. Here are a few of the more common suffix patterns:

Nouns	Adjectives	Verbs	Adverbs
-ion = -ión	*-ous = -oso*	*-ate = -ar*	*-ly = -mente*
action = acción	curious = curioso	complicate = complicar	absolutely = absolutamente
nation = nación	delicious = delicioso	decorate = decorar	brutally = brutalmente
portion = porción	famous = famoso	eliminate = eliminar	exactly = exactamente
region = región	numerous = numeroso	graduate = graduar	legally = legalmente
section = sección	precious = precioso	penetrate = penetrar	partially = parcialmente

The similarities between the two languages become even more obvious if we compare sets of related words. Here are sets of English and Spanish cognates, each group based on the same word root:

Nouns	Adjectives	Verbs	Adverbs
alphabet	alphabetic	alphabetize	alphabetically
alfabeto	alfabético	alfabetizar	alfabéticamente
favor	favorable	favor	favorably
favor	favorable	favorecer	favorablemente
ideal	ideal	idealize	ideally
ideal	ideal	idealizar	idealmente
origin	original	originate	originally
origen	original	originar	originalmente
system	systematic	systematize	systematically
sistema	sistemático	sistematizar	sistemáticamente

Cognates like these are plentiful in English and Spanish. They account for one-third to one-half the average educated person's active vocabulary, estimated at 10,000 to 15,000 words. The percentage of cognates in the two languages is even higher if we add passive vocabulary, that is, specialized, literary, and obsolete words. However, not all cognates are true cognates like the examples given above. Out of the thousands and thousands of cognate pairs that exist in English and Spanish, a few hundred are *false* cognates—that is, words that look alike, but do *not* have the same meanings in the modern languages we use today. One common example is *library* (biblioteca) and *librería* (bookstore). These cases of "mistaken identity" are important in language learning because they may cause students to make errors in translation, and several books have been written about them. However, since this dictionary focuses on words that do have the same meanings, false cognates are not included.

Why do cognates, whether true or false, look so much alike? For the same reason that brothers and sisters often look alike—they are related by birth. Family members have shared genes. Spanish and English cognates have shared linguistic origins.

The cognates in this dictionary have many different origins. Some English words come from Spanish (*macho, enchilada, tango*), and some Spanish words come from English (*parking, zipper, knockout*). Both languages have borrowed words, not only from each other, but from other languages as well (English *karate* = Spanish *karate* from Japanese; English *amen* = Spanish *amén* from Hebrew; English *mammoth* = Spanish *mamut* from Russian). Geographical, historical, and personal names are also cognates (English *America* = Spanish *América*; English *Plato* = Spanish *Platón*; English *George* = Spanish *Jorge*). An important and ever-growing source of cognates is technical and scientific terminology, as words are constantly being created to deal with new concepts, discoveries, and inventions (English *quasar* = Spanish *cuásar*; English *robotics* = Spanish *robótica*; English *computer* = Spanish *computadora*).

Although all of these sources have contributed and continue to contribute to the vocabularies of English and Spanish, the largest number of cognates originated in ancient Latin and Greek, languages that flourished long before either English or Spanish even existed. How did this happen? It's an interesting story.

A LITTLE BIT OF HISTORY

Linguistically speaking, English and Spanish are cousins, members of the family of languages called *Indo-European*. However, they belong to different branches of this family. Spanish is one of the languages on the Romance branch, which also includes Italian, French, Portuguese, and Romanian. These modern languages developed from the local dialects of Latin spoken in ancient times by Roman soldiers who occupied various parts of Europe over a period of many centuries. Ancient Latin coexisted with ancient Greek, and had already borrowed much of its cultural vocabulary.

English is one of the languages on the Germanic branch, which also includes German, Dutch, Danish, Norwegian, and Swedish. Its history dates back to the Teutonic tribes that invaded England in the fourth and fifth centuries A.D. The most powerful of these tribes were the Angles and Saxons, and their speech, Anglo-Saxon, became the basis for modern English.

An event occurred in A.D. 1066 that had great influence on English, adding to its vocabulary a huge number of new words derived from Latin and Greek. This event was the invasion and occupation of England by William the Conqueror, king of the Normans. For the next three hundred years, French (one of the Romance languages) was imposed as the official language of the schools and law courts, and the English of the conquered people was kept alive only as a spoken language. Later, when English became a literary language, it was a blend of everyday speech and cultured French vocabulary.

Although English and Spanish changed in different ways throughout their histories, as all living languages do, the basic similarities in their shared Latin and Greek-derived vocabulary were never lost.

MEANING AND TRANSLATION

The great American linguist Leonard Bloomfield defined the meaning of a word as all the contexts in which it is used. A good monolingual dictionary distinguishes these contexts by describing the senses of the word separately and providing paraphrases, examples, labels, synonyms, and so on, all in the same language as the word being defined. If the word is part of the common everyday vocabulary and not a purely technical or scientific term, it is probably used in many different contexts with many different meanings. Webster's *New World College Dictionary*, Third Edition (1991), lists thirty-two main senses for the word *line* as a noun, not including its uses as a verb or adjective and in idioms.

The problem of dealing with multiple contexts is even more important in a bilingual dictionary, because the various meanings of a word may not have the same translation. For example, *line* = *línea* in geometry, but a *line* for hanging clothes is *cuerda*, a line for fishing is *sedal*, a line on the face is *arruga*, and one's line of work is *profesión*.

Bilingual dictionaries use various methods for distinguishing between the senses of words that have more than one meaning. Some bilingual dictionaries simply list all the possible translations, separating each sense-group with a semicolon. Others may number the senses, give labels, add associated words such as subjects or objects, or provide usage examples. In all these cases, the purpose is to identify the contexts in which the word appears so that the user can choose the correct translation.

In this dictionary, the contexts are defined by **topic**, and the meaning of every pair of cognates appearing in that particular list is identical. If cognates have the same meaning in more than one context, they will appear in more than one topic list. For example, *line* and *línea* are translational equivalents not only in Mathematics, the topic that includes geometry, but also in topics that deal with art, electricity, communications, defense, geography, and sports.

The Spanish cognate is not always the only translation of the English cognate, and in some cases it may not even be the most common translation, but it is certainly the one easiest for language learners to remember and use for communication. For example, in the topic Clothing, there is the entry "zipper = zíper *nm*." Some Spanish speakers refer to a zipper as *cremallera*, but they will always recognize and understand *zíper*.

Occasionally the cognate word is used only in a restricted formal or technical sense. For example, in the topic Law, there is the entry "insanity = insania *nf*." The Spanish word *insania* is primarily a legal term; the common translation for English *insanity* is *dementia* or *locura*.

A cognate dictionary is a very useful bridge between two languages, but it cannot give all possible translations. Noncognate synonyms of the words given in this dictionary, if they exist, can be found in a thesaurus.

WHAT KIND OF ENGLISH AND SPANISH?

English and Spanish are worldwide languages and both have several geographical varieties. In this book, the varieties used are general American English and general Latin-American Spanish. That means that the words listed in the topics are acceptable in the English- and Spanish-speaking countries of the Western hemisphere but not necessarily in European England and Spain.

The differences between American English and British English spelling patterns, on the other hand, are well established and widely used in Canadian English and other English-speaking areas of the world. Here are some common differences in spelling:

	American English	British English
-or = -our	color	colour
	favor	favour
	honor	honour
-er = -re	center	centre
	meter	metre
	theater	theatre
-se = -ce	defense	defence
	license	licence
	offense	offence
-e- = -ae-	anesthesia	anaesthesia
	archeology	archaeology
	orthopedic	orthopaedic

Many words have two possible spellings in American English, but only one of them is used in British English. Usually the longer spelling is the regular British English form, and the shorter spelling is preferred in American English, although both are acceptable. In such cases, both forms are indicated in the topic list, for example *dialog(ue)*, which means either *dialog* or *dialogue*.

English words with alternate spellings that are primarily or exclusively used in British English are marked Ⓐ for Appendix A, where the British English spellings are given.

In addition to these variant spellings, English has the problem of irregular noun plurals. They are called irregular because the plural forms cannot be predicted from the singular form by applying rules, but must be learned as exceptions. Many words still use their original Latin plurals (*crises, alumnae, media*) or the plural form from another language that was borrowed along with the word (*kibbutzim, literati, bureaux*). Some nouns even have *two* plural forms, one formed in the usual way and the other an irregular Latin plural (*aquariums* or *aquaria, indexes* or *indices, radiuses* or *radii*). Words ending with -*o* in the singular are especially problematic. As a rule, they form their plurals by adding -*s* (*radios, egos, tattoos*), but some words add -*es* (*echoes, heroes, potatoes*) and other words have two plural forms (*cargos* or *cargoes, halo* or *haloes, volcanos* or *volcanoes*).

In the topic lists, English words that have irregular or double plural forms are marked Ⓑ for Appendix B, where the plural forms are given.

Spanish nouns also have irregular plural forms, but to a much lesser extent than English. They usually involve words borrowed from English or other languages that do not fit the spelling patterns of Spanish and do not follow the regular rules for forming the plural. For example, most words that end in a consonant in Spanish add -*es* to form the plural (singular *acción*, plural *acciones*; singular *color*, plural *colores*; singular *realidad*, plural *realidades*). The plural form of Spanish *bistec*, however, is *bistecs* (English *beefsteak* and *beefsteaks*).

In the topic lists, Spanish words that have irregular plural forms are marked Ⓒ for Appendix C, where the plural forms are given.

Words that enter a language through contact with another language typically retain their original spelling at first, then change later, assimilating to the regular patterns of the language. Both forms coexist for a period of time. For example, *baseball* still has two spellings in Latin-American Spanish, *baseball* and *béisbol*; the second spelling is now preferred over the first.

Living languages do not remain static, and it would be both impossible and impractical to keep up with all the cognates that enter English and Spanish constantly. Words, like fashions, may come and go. New words, whether invented or borrowed, must stand the test of time before they become a permanent part of the language. When a word finally appears in a dictionary, it has already been used for some time, proved its usefulness and become generally accepted by the speech community. In this book there are many new cognate additions to English and Spanish, but all of them are documented in at least one standard bilingual dictionary.

There are also old cognates in the dictionary—words most of us no longer need in our contemporary language, but still recognize as part of our cultural history. In some cases, especially for geographical and political terms, the word refers to something that no longer exists, like the Roman Empire or the Soviet Union. In other cases the term has been replaced by another word. For example, the disease *tuberculosis* used to be called *consumption*.

Conventional dictionaries often add usage labels such as "archaic, historical, dated," to such word entries. In this dictionary, they are identified in two ways. If there are several of these cognates in a topic, they are grouped together under a separate subheading usually called Historical Terms; if there are only a few, they are included in the main list and labeled (obs).

The authority for American English plurals was Webster's *New World College Dictionary*, Third Edition (1995), and the authorities for British and Spanish spellings and usage were the *Oxford Spanish Dictionary* (Oxford University Press, 1994) and Simon and Schuster's *International Dictionary* (New York, 1973). It should be pointed out, however, that dictionaries disagree with each other. The aim of this dictionary is not to provide all variants, but to offer the most common acceptable forms.

WORDS AND ENTRIES

Every language has its own unique way of expressing meanings. The use of shared cognate vocabulary is one way that English and Spanish do this in a similar fashion, but the overlap is not complete, and sometimes a translation requires more than one word to be accurate. For example, Spanish *pera* = English *pear*, but Spanish *peral* = English *pear tree*. In the other direction, English *fiction* = Spanish *ficción*, but English *nonfiction* = Spanish *no ficción*.

Occasionally, the entries in both languages have more than one word. Multiword expressions important to the topic are included in this dictionary if at least one of the English words and one of the Spanish words are cognates. However, because English and Spanish have different rules for putting words together, the word order of the equivalent translations may not be the same, and more than one label may be necessary to indicate the part of speech, gender, number, etc., of the Spanish expression. Multiple labels apply to combinations of nouns, verbs, and/or adjectives in the order of their appearance. Here are some examples of multiword entries:

English words	Spanish words
acreage	medida en acres *nf, nmpl*
telephone directory	guía telefónica *nf*
press conference	conferencia de prensa *nf*
point of view	punto de vista *nm, nf*

For some single-word English entries, words or symbols have been added in parentheses. This additional information is not translated:

language (general)	lenguaje *nm*	
language (specific)	lengua *nf*	(clarification of meaning)
kilohertz (kHz)	kilohercio *nm*	(abbreviation)
sodium (Na)	sodio *nm*	(chemical symbol)

PARTS-OF-SPEECH LABELS

Note the following guidelines:

1. If the English and Spanish cognates are the same part of speech and number, labels are given only for the Spanish words. If there is a difference in usage, or the Spanish equivalent is a multiword expression, an English part-of-speech label is added for clarity:

vacation *nmsg*	vacaciones *nfpl*	(singular vs. plural usage)
archives *npl*	archivo *nm*	(plural vs. singular usage)
contrapuntal *aj*	de contrapunto *nm*	(adjective vs. prepositional phrase)

2. Spanish nouns that are used with the masculine definite article *el* in the singular and the feminine definite article *las* in the plural are labeled this way:

area	área *nf(el)*	(*el área*, but *las áreas*)

3. Spanish nouns referring to persons and animals that have different endings for masculine and feminine gender are shown in these ways:

biologist	biólogo, -a *nmf*	(el biólogo, la bióloga)
captain	capitán, -ana *nmf*	(el capitán, la capitana)
Berliner	berlinés, -esa *nmf*	(el berlinés, la berlinesa)
author	autor(a) *nmf*	(el autor, la autora)
mule	mulo, -a *nmf*	(el mulo, la mula)

4. Spanish adjectives that change form for masculine and feminine gender are shown in their masculine form:

clear	claro *aj*	(un día *claro* = a clear day)
		(una explicación *clara* = a clear explanation)
English	inglés *aj*	(un corno *inglés* = an English horn)
		(una palabra *inglesa* = an English word)
adoring	adorador *aj*	(un esposo *adorador* = an adoring husband)
		(una esposa *adoradora* = an adoring wife)

5. Spanish verbs that have only reflexive forms correspond to English intransitive verbs:

abstain	abstenerse *vr*	(to *abstain* from smoking = *abstenerse* de fumar)

If a Spanish verb has both a reflexive and a nonreflexive form, the reflexive ending is placed in parentheses. The Spanish verb without the reflexive ending corresponds to the English transitive verb (a) and the form with the reflexive ending corresponds to the English intransitive verb (b):

adapt	adaptar(se) *vt(r)*	(a) (to *adapt* a novel = *adaptar* una novela)
		(b) (to *adapt* to city life = *adaptarse* a la vida urbana)

6. If words function as more than one part of speech in both languages, all applicable labels are added. Here are some possible combinations:

horizontal	horizontal *aj, nf*	(adjective, feminine noun)
exterior	exterior *aj, nm*	(adjective, masculine noun)
activist	activista *aj, nmf*	(adjective, masculine or feminine noun)
American	americano, -a *aj, nmf*	(adjective, masculine or feminine noun)
alert	alerta *aj, av, nf*	(adjective, adverb, feminine noun)

The form of the cognate given in the topic list is the part of speech most frequently used in that context. As in most dictionaries, entries are primarily nouns, verbs, or adjectives. Parts of speech related to the entry word but not included in the topics are listed in Appendix D, including participial forms used as adjectives whose forms are irregular or cannot be easily predicted from the verb form such as *opuesto* from *oponer*.

ORGANIZATION OF THE LISTS

The dictionary has one hundred topics organized into twenty separate theme groups. The groups in the first part of the book deal with subjects of general interest, while the later groups are more specialized and technical. Each topic in the dictionary has its own appropriate format. A complex topic like Mathematics needs many headings and subheadings to properly organize all the specialized terms used in that field, while a simpler topic like Personal Names needs very few. However many headings and subheadings there are, they are arranged so that the general terms for that topic come first, followed by more specific categories. At the end of each topic list are cross-references to other topics or parts of topics that have related vocabulary. The topics within a theme group often share terminology, and to get a complete picture of the cognate vocabulary for that subject area, all the included topics should be consulted.

Here are translations for the most frequently used headings and subheadings:

General terms	Términos generales
Specializations	Especialidades
Aspects of . . .	Aspectos de . . .
Tools and equipment	Instrumentos y equipo
Measurements	Medidas
Persons	Personas
Supplementary vocabulary	Vocabulario adicional

HOW TO USE THIS BOOK

Here are two ways this dictionary can help you learn bilingual vocabulary quickly. Try both of them!

1. If you are primarily a language student, start at the beginning with the first topic, Everyday Vocabulary. Here you will find familiar, easy-to-remember words that you can put to use immediately, including a basic list of more than one hundred very high frequency cognates, common short-form words we use in informal speech, Latin expressions, greetings, and exclamations, and loanwords that English and Spanish have given to each other.

2. If you have a special interest, look at the table of Contents, which lists the topics by theme group in the order they are presented in the book. Immediately following this Introduction is an alphabetical list that gives the location of specific topics.

ACKNOWLEDGMENTS

Many experts contributed to the preparation of this dictionary. Their knowledge of the subject matter was indispensable in assuring that the terms included in the lists were complete and up-to-date. The author is especially grateful to the following for their invaluable help: Dr. Eugene Albert (mathematics, games), Dr. Richard M. de Andino (medicine and physical disorders), Anders E. Augustson (geology, minerals, gems), Dr. Joan Fayer (linguistics, sociology), Carl Victor Freedman (computers, communications, death), Marcie Guttman (plants), Milton Kaplan (economics, business, money, and finance), attorney Emilio Lopez Irrizary (law, politics, and government), Dan Knapp (urban life, geography), Professor Edith Lebed (entertainment, foods, beverages, literature, theater, magic), Dr. James McCoy (music), Dr. Eugene V. Mohr (visual arts), Professor Roberta Raymond (education, radio), Dr. Felix Schweizer (physics, chemistry, electricity, electronics, technology), Chris Roberts (fuels, metallurgy), and Stevens M. Wright (Bible, religion).

Alphabetical List of Topics

NTC's
Dictionary
of
SPANISH
COGNATES

Thematically
Organized

The Wide World of Words

EVERYDAY VOCABULARY

100-PLUS HIGH-FREQUENCY WORDS

accept	aceptar *vt*
action	acción *nf*
affect	afectar *vt*
air	aire *nm*
appear	aparecer *vi*
bank	banco *nm*
basic	básico *aj*
basis B	base *nf*
case	caso *nm*
cause	causa *nf*
center A	centro *nm*
central	central *aj*
character	carácter *nm*
class	clase *nf*
clear	claro *aj*
combine	combinar(se) *vt(r)*
common	común *aj*
condition	condición *nf*
contain	contener *vt*
contribute	contribuir *vti*
control	control *nm*
cooperate	cooperar *vi*
copy	copia *nf*
create	crear *vt*
day	día *nm*
decide	decidir *vti*
depend	depender *vi*
descend	descender *vi*
describe	describir *vt*
detail	detalle *nm*
difference	diferencia *nf*
different	diferente *aj*
difficult	difícil *aj*
direct	directo *aj*
double	doble *aj*
enter	entrar *vi*
equal	igual *aj*
error	error *nm*
exception	excepción *nf*
exist	existir *vi*
familiar	familiar *aj*
family	familia *nf*
famous	famoso *aj*
favor	favor *nm*
fine	fino *aj*

force	forzar *vt*
form	forma *nf*
general	general *aj*
group	grupo *nm*
hour	hora *nf*
human	humano, -a *aj, nmf*
idea	idea *nf*
important	importante *aj*
individual	individual *aj*
inform	informar *vt*
interest	interés *nm*
line	línea *nf*
list	lista *nf*
moment	momento *nm*
move	mover(se) *vt(r)*
name	nombre *nm*
necessary	necesario *aj*
new	nuevo *aj*
number	número *nm*
obtain	obtener *vt*
obvious	obvio *aj*
occupy	ocupar *vt*
operate	operar *vti*
opportunity	oportunidad *nf*
part	parte *nf*
pass	pasar *vti*
pause	pausa *nf*
perfect	perfecto *aj*
period	período, periodo *nm*
permit	permitir *vt*
person	persona *nf*
piece	pieza *nf*
plan	plan *nm*
point	punto *nm*
popular	popular *aj*
position	posición *nf*
possible	posible *aj*
practical	práctico *aj*
prefer	preferir *vt*
prepare	preparar *vt*
presence	presencia *nf*
present	presentar *vt*
price	precio *nm*
private	privado *aj*
probable	probable *aj*
problem	problema *nm*
produce	producir *vt*
program A	programa *nm*
progress	progreso *nm*

1

prove	probar *vt*	limo	limosina, limusina *nf*
public	público *aj, nm*	mayo	mayonesa *nf*
pure	puro *aj*	mike	micrófono *nm*
quality	calidad *nf*	phone	teléfono *nm*
quantity	cantidad *nf*	pop	popular *aj*
reality	realidad *nf*	prelims	preliminares *nmpl or*
reason	razón *nf*		*nfpl*
recognize	reconocer *vt*	prep	preparatorio *aj*
reduce	reducir *vt*	pro	profesional *nmf*
repeat	repetir *vt*	psycho	(p)sicópata *nmf*
rich	rico *aj*	recap	recapitular *vti*
secret	secreto *aj, nm*	rep	representante *nmf*
separate	separado *aj*	rhino ⃝B	rinoceronte *nm*
service	servicio *nm*	sci-fi	ciencia ficción *nf*
situation	situación *nf*	specs	especificaciones *nfpl*
social	social *aj*	sync	sincronización *nf*
special	especial *aj*		

— both languages —

state	estado *nm*	auto	auto *nm*
study	estudiar *vti*	bike	bici *nm*
style	estilo *nm*	cello	chelo *nm*
symbol	símbolo *nm*	fax	fax *nm*
system	sistema *nm*	isle	isla *nf*
time	tiempo *nm*	math *nsg*	mates *nfpl*
total	total *aj, nm*	memo	memo *nm*
type	tipo *nm*	mount	monte *nm*
typical	típico *aj*	polio	polio *nm*
unite	unir(se) *vt(r)*	porn, porno	porno *aj, nu*
united	unido *aj*	prof	profe *nm*
use	uso *nm*	sax	saxo *nm*
value	valor *nm*	schizo	esquizo, -a *nmf*
visit	visita *nf*	stereo	estéreo *aj, nm*
		taxi	taxi *nm*
		TV ⃝A	tele *nf*

CONVERSATIONAL FORMS

clipped words

— English only —

biotech	biotecnología *nf*		
chimp	chimpancé *nm*		
co-op	cooperativa *nf*		
coke	cocaína *nf*		
condo	condominio *nm*		
decaf	café descafeinado *nm*		
detox	desintoxicación *nf*		
ex-con	ex convicto *nm*		
exam	examen *nm*		
flu	influenza *nf*		
gas	gasolina *nf*		
grad	graduado, -a *nmf*		
gym ⃝B	gimnasio *nm*		
hippo	hipopótamo *nm*		
lab	laboratorio *nm*		
legit	legítimo *aj*		
lib	liberación *nf*		

greetings and exclamations

ah!	¡ah!
aha!	¡ajá!
ahem!	¡ejem!
ahoy!	¡ahó!
amen!	¡amén!
atchoo!	¡achís!
attention!	¡atención!
ay!	¡ay!
bah!	¡bah!
bingo!	¡bingo!
blah, blah, blah!	¡bla, bla, bla!
boo!	¡bú!
boo-hoo!	¡buuah!
bravo!	¡bravo!
brrr!	¡brrr!
ciao!	¡chao!
eh?	¿eh?
ha-ha!	¡ja-ja!

hallelujah!	¡aleluya!
halt!	¡alto!
hello!	¡hola!, ¡aló!
hey!	¡eh!
ho ho ho!	¡jo, jo!
no!	¡no!
oh no!	¡ay no!
OK!, okay!	¡okey!
sh!	¡sh!
ugh!	¡uf!
whoopee!, yippee!	¡yupi!
yah!	¡ja, ja!
yoo-hoo!	¡juju!
yum yum!	¡ñam ñam!

imitation and baby talk

bow-wow	guau-guau *nm*
choo-choo	chu-cu-chu(cu) *nm*
click	clic Ⓒ *nm*
crack (sound)	crac Ⓒ *nm*
ding-dong	din don *nm*
ticktock	tictac *nm*
zigzag	zigzag *nm*

LOANWORDS

from Spanish

banana	banana *nf*
barrio	barrio *nm*
bravado	bravata *nf*
burro	burro, -a *nmf*
cafeteria	cafetería *nf*
cocoa	cacao *nm*
fiesta	fiesta *nf*
flamenco	flamenco *nm*
gringo	gringo, -a *nmf*
hacienda	hacienda *nf*
lasso Ⓑ	lazo *nm*
machismo	machismo *nm*
mosquito Ⓑ	mosquito *nm*
mulatto Ⓑ	mulato, -a *aj, nmf*
patio	patio *nm*
pimiento	pimiento *nm*
pinto	pinto *nm*
poncho	poncho *nm*
potato Ⓑ	patata *nf*
rodeo	rodeo *nm*
siesta	siesta *nf*
taco	taco *nm*
tobacco	tabaco *nm*
tomato Ⓑ	tomate *nm*
tornado Ⓑ	tornado *nm*

from English

baseball	béisbol, baseball *nm*
clip	clip *nm*
cocktail	cóctel *nm*
hamburger	hamburguesa *nf*
hobby	hobby *nm*
jersey	jersey *nm*
jockey	jockey, yoquei Ⓒ *nmf*
junkie	yonqui *nmf*
knockout	nocaut, noqueo *nm*
leader	líder *nm*
meeting	mitin *nm*
microchip	microchip Ⓒ *nm*
pancake	panqueque *nm*
park	parquear *vt*
sandwich	sandwich *nm*
scooter	escúter *nm*
sexy	sexy *aj*
smog	esmog *nm*
snob	snob, esnob *nmf*
stop	stop *nm*
test (multiple-choice)	test *nm*
ticket	ticket *nm*
yuppie, yuppy	yupi Ⓒ *nmf*
zipper	ziper *nm*

LATIN EXPRESSIONS

a priori	a priori *av*
ad infinitum	ad infinitum *av*
alter ego	álter ego *nm*
curriculum vitae	curriculum vitae *nm*
et cetera	etcétera *av*
ex officio	ex oficio *aj*
in absentia	in absentia *av*
in situ	in situ *av*
in vitro	in vitro *aj*
ipso facto	ipso facto *av*
modus operandi	modus operandi *nm*
modus vivendi	modus vivendi *nm*
per capita	per cápita *av*
pro forma	pro forma *aj, av*
pro rata	prorrata *av*
sine qua non	sine qua non *aj*
status quo	statu quo *nm*
sui generis	sui generis *aj*

(*See also* **USING LANGUAGE**)

DICTIONARIES

GENERAL TERMS

alphabetical order	orden alfabético *nm*
dictionary	diccionario *nm*

entry	entrada *nf*
glossary	glosario *nm*
indicator	indicador *nm*
information	información *nf*
lexicography	lexicografía *nf*
lexicon (book) **B**	lexicón *nm*
lexicon (words) **B**	léxico *nm*
list	lista *nf*
specialized	especializado *aj*
standard	estándar *aj*
term	término *nm*
terminology	terminología *nf*
usage	uso *nm*
vocabulary	vocabulario *nm*

KINDS OF DICTIONARIES

standard

bilingual	bilingüe *aj*
monolingual	monolingüe *aj*
multilingual	multilingüe *aj*

specialized

biographical	biográfico *aj*
etymological	etimológico *aj*
frequency	de frecuencias *nfpl*
geographical	geográfico *aj*
phraseological	fraseológico *aj*
pronouncing	de pronunciación *nf*
rhetorical	retórico *aj*
rhyming	de rimas *nfpl*
technical	técnico *aj*
thematic	temático *aj*

DICTIONARY INFORMATION

type

grammatical	gramatical *aj*
orthographic	ortográfico *aj*
phonetic	fonético *aj*
semantic	semántico *aj*

phonetic and orthographic

accentuation	acentuación *nf*
pronunciation	pronunciación *nf*
syllabi(fi)cation	silabeo *nm*
variants	variante *nf*

grammatical and semantic

definition	definición *nf*
equivalent	equivalente *nm*
irregular form	forma irregular *nf*
part of speech	parte de la oración *nf*

word combinations

acronym	acrónimo *nm*
compound	compuesto *nm*
expression	expresión *nf*
idiomatic expression	expresión idiomática *nf*
locution	locución *nf*
phrasal verb	verbo con partícula *nm, nf*
proverb	proverbio *nm*
set phrase	frase hecha *nf*

usage labels

archaic	arcaico *aj*
colloquial	coloquial *aj*
dialectal	dialectal *aj*
diminutive	diminutivo *aj, nm*
euphemism	eufemismo *nm*
figurative	figurado *aj*
formal	formal *aj*
historical	histórico *aj*
humorous	humorístico *aj*
ironic	irónico *aj*
literary	literario *aj*
neologism	neologismo *nm*
obsolete	obsoleto *aj*
pejorative	peyorativo *aj, nm*
poetic	poético *aj*
rare	raro *aj*
technical	técnico *aj*
vulgar	vulgar *aj*

typographical indicators

italics *npl*	itálica *nf*
letter	letra *nf*
number	número *nm*
parentheses **B**	paréntesis **C** *nmpl*
symbol	símbolo *nm*

other information

abbreviation	abreviatura *nf*
antonym	antónimo *nm*
etymology	etimología *nf*
example in context	ejemplo en contexto *nm*
synonym	sinónimo *nm*

PERSONS

compiler	compilador(a), recopilador(a) *nmf*
etymologist	etimólogo, -a *nmf*
lexicographer	lexicógrafo, -a *nmf*
user	usuario, -a *nmf*

(*See also* TERMS IN SEMANTICS under **USING LANGUAGE**; *THE GREEK ALPHABET* under **WRITING**)

BOOKS AND LIBRARIES

GENERAL TERMS

collection	colección *nf*
copyright	copyright *nm*
edition	edición *nf*
publication	publicación *nf*
tome	tomo *nm*
volume	volumen *nm*

ASPECTS OF BOOKS

types of books

ABC-book	abecedario *nm*
almanac	almanaque *nm*
anecdote collection	anecdotario *nm*
annual	anuario *nm*
anthology	antología *nf*
atlas	atlas *nm*
catalog(ue)	catálogo *nm*
codex (obs) B	códice *nm*
compendium B	compendio *nm*
condensation	condensación *nf*
dictionary	diccionario *nm*
directory	directorio *nm*
dissertation	disertación *nf*
encyclopedia	enciclopedia *nf*
fable collection	fabulario *nm*
guidebook	guía *nf*
hymnal	himnario *nm*
manual	manual *nm*
pharmacopeia A	farmacopea *nf*
psalmody	salmodia *nf*
reference	referencia *nf*
reprint	reimpresión *nf*
schoolbook	libro escolar *nm*
telephone directory	guía telefónica *nf*
textbook	libro de texto *nm*
thesaurus B	tesauro *nm*
treatise	tratado *nm*

parts of books

addendum B	adenda *nf*
appendix B	apéndice *nm*
bibliography	bibliografía *nf*
chapter	capítulo *nm*
colophon (obs)	colofón *nm*
contents	contenido *nm*
cover	cubierta *nf*

dedication	dedicatoria *nf*
epigraph	epígrafe *nm*
errata *npl*	fe de erratas *nf, nfpl*
fascicle	fascículo *nm*
folio	folio *nm*
frontispiece	frontispicio *nm*
illustration	ilustración *nf*
index B	índice *nm*
introduction	introducción *nf*
margin	margen *nm*
notes	notas *nfpl*
page	página *nf*
passim	passim *av*
preface	prefacio *nm*
recto	recto *nm*
rubric	rúbrica *nf*
subtitle	subtítulo *nm*
text	texto *nm*
title	título *nm*
verso	verso *nm*

words describing books

absorbing	absorbente *aj*
best-seller	bestseller C *nm*
informative	informativo *aj*
interesting	interesante *aj*
rare	raro *aj*
valuable	valioso *aj*

book preparation

correction	corrección *nf*
formatting	formateado *nm*
galley	galerada *nf*
idea	idea *nf*
manuscript	manuscrito *nm*
pagination	paginación *nf*
printing	imprenta *nf*
word processor	procesador de palabras *nm, nfpl*

other terms

ex libris	ex libris *nm*
line	línea *nf*
paper	papel *nm*
royalties	royalties *nmpl*
trilogy	trilogía *nf*

ASPECTS OF LIBRARIES

types of libraries

circulating	circulante *aj*
community	comunitario *aj*

Library of Congress	Biblioteca del Congreso *nf, nm*
mobile	móvil, movible *aj*
private	privado *aj*
public	público *aj*
school	escolar *aj*
specialized	especializado *aj*

holdings

archives *npl*	archivo *nm*
audiovisual	audiovisual *aj*
microfiche	microficha *nf*
microfilm	microfilm(e) *nm*
video	video *nm*

tools and equipment

catalog(ue)	catálogo *nm*
cubicle	cubículo *nm*
photocopier	fotocopiadora *nf*

other terms

acquisition	adquisición *nf*
cataloging, cataloguing	catalogación *nf*
classification	clasificación *nf*
donation	donativo *nm*

PERSONS

archivist	archivero, -a, archivista *nmf*
author	autor(a) *nmf*
bibliographer	bibliógrafo, -a *nmf*
bibliomaniac	bibliómano, -a *nmf*
bibliophile	bibliófilo, -a *nmf*
cataloger, cataloguer	catalogador(a) *nmf*
coauthor	coautor(a) *nmf*
editor	editor, -a *nmf*
encyclopedist	enciclopedista *nmf*

(*See also* **PRINTING**)

JOURNALISM

GENERAL TERMS

article	artículo *nm*
bulletin	boletín *nm*
communiqué	comunicado *nm*
event	evento *nm*
information	información *nf*
media	medios *nmpl*
news *nsg*	noticias *nfpl*
news flash	flash informativo *nm*
press	prensa *nf*

press conference	conferencia de prensa *nf*
publication	publicación *nf*
Pulitzer Prize	Premio Pulitzer *nm*
reporting	reportaje *nm*
sensationalism	sensacionalismo *nm*

ASPECTS OF JOURNALISM

news media

daily (newspaper)	diario *nm*
pamphlet	panfleto *nm*
periodical	periódico *nm*
radio	radio *nm*
tabloid	tabloide *nm*
television	televisión *nf*

newspaper sections

classified (ads)	clasificado *aj*
comics, comic strip	tira cómica *nf*
employment	empleo *nm*
entertainment	entretenimiento *nm*
financial	financiero *aj*
obituaries	obituarios *nmpl*
personals	anuncios personales *nmpl*
sports	deportivo *aj*
TV listings *npl*	programación de TV *nf*

articles

column	columna *nf*
commentary	comentario *nm*
dispatch	despacho *nm*
documentary	documental *nm*
editorial	editorial *nm*
interview	entrevista *nf*
review	revista *nf*
testimonial	testimonial *nm*

news-gathering and reporting

censorship	censura *nf*
confidential	confidencial *aj*
coverage	cobertura *nf*
current	corriente *aj*
dateline	data *nf*
distortion	distorsión *nf*
divulge	divulgar *vt*
freelance	free-lance *aj*
illustration	ilustración *nf*
incident	incidente
libel	libelo *nm*
objectivity	objetividad *nf*
photograph	fotografía *nf*

privacy	privacidad *nf*
suppression	supresión *nf*

other terms

chronicle	crónica *nf*
circulation	circulación *nf*
concern	concernir *vt*
edition	edición *nf*
folio	folio *nm*
gazette	gaceta *nf*
newsprint	papel de prensa *nm, nf*
number	número *nm*
printed matter *nsg*	impresos *nmpl*
publicity	publicidad *nf*
serial	serial *nm*
subscription	su(b)scripción *nf*

PERSONS

article writer	articulista *nmf*
celebrity	celebridad *nf*
censor	censor *nmf*
columnist	columnista *nmf*
commentator	comentarista *nmf*
correspondent	corresponsal *nmf*
diarist	diarista *nmf*
editorial writer	editorialista *nmf*
interviewer	entrevistador(a) *nmf*
pamphleteer	panfletista *nmf*
paparazzi	paparazzi *nmpl*
photographer	fotógrafo, -a *nmf*
publicist	publicista *nmf*
reporter	reportero, -a *nmf*
subscriber	su(b)scriptor(a) *nmf*
distort	distorsionar *vt*

(*See also* **PRINTING**; **AMATEUR RADIO**; **TELEVISION AND VIDEO**)

LITERATURE

GENERAL TERMS

belles-lettres	bellas letras *nfpl*
criticism	crítica *nf*
expression	expresión *nf*
genre	género *nm*
humanities	humanidades *nfpl*
influence	influencia *nf*
license Ⓐ	licencia *nf*
literature	literatura *nf*
manner	manera *nf*
plagiarism	plagio *nm*
poem	poema *nm*
potpourri Ⓑ	popurrí *nm*

tetralogy	tetralogía *nf*
trilogy	trilogía *nf*

ASPECTS OF LITERATURE

genres

allegory	alegoría *nf*
drama	drama *nm*
epic	épica *nf*
erotica	literatura erótica *nf*
escapism	escapismo *nm*
fiction	ficción *nf*
juvenile	juvenil *aj*
narration	narración *nf*
nonfiction	no ficción *nf*
poetry	poesía *nf*
prose	prosa *nf*
scatology	escatología *nf*

elements

action	acción *nf*
anticlimax	anticlímax *nm*
character	carácter *nm*
climax	clímax Ⓒ *nm*
composition	composición *nf*
conflict	conflicto *nm*
description	descripción *nf*
dialog(ue)	diálogo *nm*
form	forma *nf*
hiatus Ⓑ	hiato *nm*
imagery *nsg*	imágenes *nfpl*
intrigue	intriga *nf*
location	localización *nf*
lyricism	lirismo *nm*
motivation	motivación *nf*
point of view	punto de vista *nm*
story	historia *nf*
structure	estructura *nf*
style	estilo *nm*
theme	tema *nm*
time	tiempo *nm*
treatment	tratamiento *nm*
unity	unidad *nf*

styles and themes

adventure	aventura *nf*
avant-garde	vanguardia *nf*
classicism	clasicismo *nm*
contemporary	contemporáneo *aj*
didactic	didáctico *aj*
epistolary	epistolario *nm*
esoteric	esotérico *aj*
Faustian	faustiano, fáustico *aj*

futurism	futurismo *nm*
Gothic (novel)	gótico *aj*
historical	histórico *aj*
Kafkaesque	kafkaiano, kafkiano *aj*
modernism	modernismo *nm*
naturalism	naturalismo *nm*
neoclassicism	neoclasicismo *nm*
pastoral	pastoral, pastoril *aj*
picaresque	picaresca *aj*
realism	realismo *nm*
romanticism	romanticismo *nm*
surrealism	surrealismo *nm*
symbolism	simbolismo *nm*
Utopian	utópico *aj*

parts of a work

canto	canto *nm*
epilog	epílogo *nm*
episode	episodio *nm*
extract	extracto *nm*
passage	pasaje *nm*
prologue	prólogo *nm*

humor in literature

caricature	caricatura *nf*
comedy	comedia *nf*
farce	farsa *nf*
humor	humor *nm*
irony	ironía *nf*
parody	parodia *nf*
sarcasm	sarcasmo *nm*
satire	sátira *nf*

FORMS OF FICTION

comic book	comic *nm*
detective novel	novela policial *nf*
fable	fábula *nf*
fantasy	literatura fantástica *nf*
folklore	folklore, folclore *nm*
legend	leyenda *nf*
mystery	misterio *nm*
narrative	narrativa *nf*
novel	novela *nf*
novelette	novela corta *nf*
parable	parábola *nf*
romance	romance *nm*
saga	saga *nf*
science fiction	ciencia ficción *nf*

FORMS OF DRAMA

melodrama	melodrama *nm*
miracle	milagro *nm*

morality	moralidad *nf*
passion	pasión *nf*
soliloquy	soliloquio *nm*
tragedy	tragedia *nf*
tragicomedy	tragicomedia *nf*

FORMS OF POETRY

ballad	balada *nf*
couplet	copla *nf*
elegy	elegía *nf*
epigram	epigrama *nm*
epode	epodo, epoda *nm, nf*
haiku	hai kai *nm*
idyll, idyl	idilio *nm*
octave	octava *nf*
ode	oda *nf*
paean	peán *nm*
quartrain	cuarteta *nf*
requiem	réquiem *nm*
rondel, rondelle	rondel *nm*
sonnet	soneto *nm*

FORMS OF FACTUAL PROSE

argument	argumento *nm*
autobiography	autobiografía *nf*
biography	biografía *nf*
commentary	comentario *nm*
critique	crítica *nf*
diary	diario *nm*
dissertation	disertación *nf*
essay	ensayo *nm*
exposition	exposición *nf*
history	historia *nf*
monograph	monografía *nf*
rhetoric	retórica *nf*
synopsis Ⓑ	sinopsis Ⓒ *nf*
thesis Ⓑ	tesis Ⓒ *nf*
treatise	tratado *nm*

SHORT FORMS OF WIT OR WISDOM

adage	adagio *nm*
anecdote	anécdota *nf*
aphorism	aforismo *nm*
apothegm	apotegma *nm*
epigram	epigrama *nm*
epigraph	epígrafe *nm*
epitaph	epitafio *nm*
epithet	epíteto *nm*
homily	homilia *nf*
maxim	máxima *nf*
proverb	proverbio *nm*

FICTIONAL CHARACTERS

generic characters

antagonist	antagonista *nmf*
antihero Ⓑ	antihéroe *nm*
hero Ⓑ	héroe *nm*
heroine	heroína *nf*
ingenue, ingénue	ingenua *nf*
innocent	inocentón *nm*
narrator	narrador(a) *nmf*
persona Ⓑ	persona *nf*
protagonist	protagonista *nmf*
romantic	romántico, -a *nmf*
superhero Ⓑ	superhéroe *nm*
villain	villano, -a *nmf*

science-fiction

alien	alienígena *nmf*
android	androide *nm*
humanoid	humanoide *nmf*
Martian	marciano, -a *nmf*
robot	robot *nm*

folklore and legend

elf	elfo, elfina *nm, nf*
genie Ⓑ	genio *nm*
gnome	gnomo, nomo *nm*
houri	hurí *nf*
incubus Ⓑ	incubo *nm*
jinn, jinni Ⓑ	genio *nm*
monster	monstruo *nm*
ogre	ogro *nm*
roc	rocho, ruc *nm*
vampire	vampiro, vampiresa *nm, nf*

famous fictional characters

Aladdin	Aladino *nm*
Faust	Fausto *nm*
Lilliputian	liliputiense *nmf*
Mephistopheles	Mefistófeles *nm*
Merlin the Magician	Merlín el Mago *nm*
Quasimodo	Cuasimodo *nm*
Scheherezade	Sherezade *nf*
Superman	Supermán *nm*

TERMS IN POETRY

basic terms

figure of speech	figura retórica *nf*
line	línea *nf*
meter Ⓐ	metro *nm*
metrics	métrica *nf*

pause	pausa *nf*
poetics	poética *nf*
rhythm	ritmo *nm*
scansion	escansión *nf*
verse	verso *nm*
verse (Bible)	versículo *nm*

major categories

dramatic	dramático *aj*
lyric	lírico *aj*
narrative	narrativo *aj*

kinds of verse

alexandrine	alejandrino *aj*
blank	blanco *aj*
free verse	verso libre *nm*
heroic	heroico *aj*
masculine	masculino *aj*
sestet	sextilla *nf*
strophe	estrofa *nf*
trope	tropo *nm*

kinds of rhythm

anapest	anapesto *nm*
dactyl	dáctilo *nm*
dimeter	dímetro *nm*
distich	dístico *nm*
heptameter	heptámetro *nm*
hexameter	hexámetro *nm*
iamb	yambo *nm*
monometer	monómetro *nm*
octometer	octómetro *nm*
pentameter	pentámetro *nm*
spondee	espondeo *nm*
tercet	terceto, tercerilla *nm, nf*
tetrameter	tetrámero *nm*
triplet	terceto *nm*
trochaic	trocaico *aj*
trochee	troqueo *nm*

figures of speech

allusion	alusión *nf*
hyperbole	hipérbole *nf*
metaphor	metáfora *nf*
metonymy	metonimia *nf*
personification	personificación *nf*
simile	símil *nm*

sound patterns

acrostic	acróstico *nm*
alliteration	aliteración *nf*
anacrusis	anacrusis *nf*
anaphora	anáfora *nf*

assonance	asonancia *nf*
caesura **B**	cesura *nf*
consonance	consonancia *nf*
echo **B**	eco *nm*
hemistich	hemistiquio *nm*
onomatopoeia	onomatopeya *nf*
rhyme	rima *nf*

classical poems

Aeneid	Eneida *nf*
Iliad	Ilíada *nf*
Odyssey	Odisea *nf*
hyperbolic(al)	hiperbólico *aj*
metaphoric(al)	metafórico *aj*

PERSONS

writers

author	autor(a) *nmf*
biographer	biógrafo, -a *nmf*
coauthor	coautor(a) *nmf*
critic	crítico, -a *nmf*
diarist	diarista *nmf*
dramatist	dramaturgo, -a *nmf*
essayist	ensayista *nmf*
fabulist	fabulista *nmf*
folklorist	folklorista, folclorista *nmf*

humorist **A**	humorista *nmf*
imagist	imaginista *nmf*
ironist	ironista *nmf*
literati	literatos *nmpl*
novelist	novelista, novelador, -a *nmf*
parodist	parodista *nmf*
plagiarist	plagiario, -a *nmf*
poet	poeta *nmf*
poet laureate	poeta laureado, -a *nmf*
poetaster	poetastro, -a *nmf*
poetess (obs)	poetisa *nf*
rhymester	rimador(a) *nmf*
romanticist	romántico, -a *nmf*
satirist	satírico, -a *nmf*
stylist	estilista *nmf*
surrealist	surrealista *nmf*
symbolist	simbolista *nmf*
versifier	versificador(a) *nmf*

historical storytellers

bard	bardo *nm*
skald	escaldo *nm*
troubadour	trovador *nm*

(*See also* **writers** *and* **artists** under **ANCIENT CIVILIZATIONS**)

Pleasures and Pastimes

ENTERTAINMENT

GENERAL TERMS

buffoonery	bufonería *nf*
celebration	celebración *nf*
distraction	distracción *nf*
diversion	diversión *nf*
entertainment	entretenimiento *nm*
festivity	festividad *nf*
frivolity	frivolidad *nf*
hilarity	hilaridad *nf*
humor Ⓐ	humor *nm*
joking	jocoso *aj*
jovial	jovial *aj*
pastime	pasatiempo *nm*
pleasure	placer *nm*
recreation	recreación, recreo *nf, nm*
relax	relajarse *vr*
spectacle	espectáculo *nm*

FORMS OF ENTERTAINMENT

participatory

banquet	banquete *nm*
camping	camping *nm*
cards	cartas *nfpl*
collection	colección *nf*
computer	computadora *nf*
crossword	crucigrama *nm*
excursion	excursión *nf*
feast	festín *nm*
fiesta	fiesta *nf*
gag	gag Ⓒ *nm*
gardening	jardinería *nf*
hobby	hobby *nm*
jigsaw puzzle	puzzle *nm*
masquerade	mascarada *nf*
miniature golf	minigolf *nm*
numismatics	numismática *nf*
origami	origami *nm*
philately	filatelia *nf*
photography	fotografía *nf*
picnic	picnic *nm*
tourism	turismo *nm*

spectator

acrobatics	acrobacia *nf*

attraction	atracción *nf*
ballet	ballet *nm*
burlesque	burlesco *nm*
cinema	cíne *nm*
circus	circo *nm*
comedy	comedia *nf*
comics, comic strip	tira cómica *nf*
concert	concierto *nm*
farce	farsa *nf*
hypnotism	hipnotismo *nm*
imitation	imitación *nf*
magic	magia *nf*
mimicry	mímica *nf*
pantomime	pantomima *nf*
parade (military)	parada *nf*
parody	parodia *nf*
pyrotechnics	pirotenia *nf*
retrospective	retrospectiva *nf*
revue	revista *nf*
rodeo	rodeo *nm*
show	show Ⓒ *nm*
striptease	striptease *nm*
television	televisión *nf*
trick	truco *nm*
variety show *nsg*	variedades *nfpl*
vaudeville	vodevil *nm*
ventriloquism, ventriloquy	ventriloquia *nf*
video	video *nm*

participatory or spectator

art	arte *nf(el)*
dance	danza *nf*
dramatics	arte dramático *nm*
music	música *nf*
radio	radio *nm*
sports	deportes *nmpl*

events and celebrations

carnival	carnaval *nm*
cavalcade	cabalgata *nf*
centennial	centenario *nm*
exhibition	exhibición *nf*
exposition	exposición *nf*
fair	feria *nf*
festival	festival *nm*
function	función *nf*
gala	gala *nf*
jubilee	jubileo *nm*

PLACES

cabaret	cabaret *nm*
casino	casino *nm*
club	club *nm*
discoteque	discoteca *nf*
fairground	ferial *nm*
hippodrome	hipódromo *nm*
museum	museo *nm*
nightclub	club nocturno *nm*
park	parque *nm*
theater Ⓐ	teatro *nm*
zoo	zoo *nm*

TOOLS AND EQUIPMENT

binoculars	binoculares *nmpl*
camcorder	camcórder *nm*
camera	cámara *nf*
carousel, carrousel	carrusel *nm*
confetti	confeti *nm*
festoon	festón *nm*
giant (in a parade)	gigantón *nm*
kaleidoscope	caledoscopio *nm*
marionette	marioneta *nf*
mask	máscara *nf*
tent	tienda *nf*
trampoline	trampolín *nm*
trapeze	trapecio *nm*

PERSONS

acrobat	acróbata *nmf*
amateur	amateur *nmf*
artist	artista *nmf*
buffoon	bufón *nm*
chorine, chorus singer	corista *nmf*
clown	clown *nm*
collector	coleccionista *nmf*
comedian, comedienne	comediante *nmf*
comic	cómico, -a *nmf*
contortionist	contorsionista *nmf*
geisha	geisha *nf*
Harlequin	Arlequín *nm*
humorist Ⓐ	humorista *nmf*
illusionist	ilusionista *nmf*
imitator	imitador(a) *nmf*
magician	mágico, -a *nmf*
master of ceremonies	maestro de ceremonias *nm, nfpl*
mime	mimo *nm*
musician	músico, -a *nmf*
numismatist	numismatista *nmf*

parodist	parodista *nmf*
philatelist	filatelista *nmf*
radio ham	radioaficionado, -a *nmf*
spectator	espectador(a) *nmf*
trapeze artist	trapecista *nmf*
troupe	troupe *nf*
ventriloquist	ventríloquo, -a *nmf*

(*See also* **DANCING**; *entertainment* under **MAGIC**; **MUSIC**; **THEATER PERFORMANCE**; **VISUAL ARTS**)

SPORTS

GENERAL TERMS

athlete	atleta *nmf*
athletics	atletismo *nm*
competition	competencia *nf*
Olympics	Olimpiada *nf*
sport	deporte *nm*
sports	deportismo *nm*
sportsmanship	deportividad *nf*

ASPECTS OF SPORTS

types of sport

amateur	amateur *aj*
intramural	intramuros *aj*
martial	marcial *aj*
professional	profesional *aj*

places

arena	arena *nf*
astrodome	astródomo *nm*
bowling alley	bowling *nm*
camp, encampment	campamento *nm*
casino	casino *nm*
coliseum	coliseo *nm*
golf course	cancha de golf *nf*
gym, gymnasium Ⓑ	gimnasio *nm*
hippodrome	hipódromo *nm*
ring	ring *nm*
stadium Ⓑ	estadio *nm*
tennis court	cancha de tenis *nf, nm*
velodrome	velódromo *nm*

contests

beat (record)	batir *vt*
championship	campeonato *nm*
cup	copa *nf*
derby	derby *nm*
equal (record)	igualar *vt*
favorite Ⓐ	favorito *aj*
match	match *nm*

photo finish	fotofinish *nf*
record	récord *nm*
set	set *nm*
tournament	torneo *nm*
trophy	trofeo *nm*

other terms

disqualification	descalificación *nf*
encampment	campamento *nm*
league	liga *nf*
prelims	preliminares *nmpl or nfpl*
rally	rally *nm*
sponsorship	esponsorización *nf*
training	entrenamiento *nm*

COMMON SPORTS

ball/racket sports

badminton	bádminton *nm*
baseball	béisbol *nm*
basketball	básquetbol *nm*
bowling *nsg*	bolos *nmpl*
cricket	criquet *nm*
croquet	croquet *nm*
football	fútbol *nm*
golf, golfing	golf *nm*
handball	handball *nm*
hockey	hockey *nm*
jai alai	jai alai *nm*
lacrosse	lacrosse *nm*
miniature golf	minigolf *nm*
polo	polo *nm*
rugby	rugby *nm*
tennis	tenis *nm*
volleyball	vóleibol, voleibol *nm*

water sports

aquatics	deportes acuáticos *nmpl*
boating	paseo en bote *nm*
canoeing	canotaje *nm*
regatta	regata *nf*
yachting	navegación en yate *nf, nm*

other sports

acrobatics	acrobacia *nf*
alpinism	alpinismo *nm*
archery	tiro de arco *nm*
camping	camping *nm*
chase (hunting)	caza *nf*
cross-country	cross-country *nm*

curling	curling *nm*
cycling	ciclismo *nm*
equitation	equitación *nf*
falconry	halconería *nf*
mountaineering	montañismo *nm*
obstacle race	carrera de obstáculos *nf, nmpl*
skiing	esquí Ⓒ *nm*
sprint	sprint, esprint Ⓒ *nm*

Olympic events

decathlon	decatlón *nm*
hepathlon	hepatlón *nm*
marathon	maratón *nm*
pentathlon	pentatlón *nm*

martial arts

boxing	boxeo *nm*
jousting *npl*	justas *nfpl*
judo	judo *nm*
jujitsu	jiu-jitsu *nm*
karate	karate *nm*
kung fu	kung fu *nm*
pugilism	pugilato *nm*

fitness

aerobics	aeróbica *nf*
calisthenics	calistenia *nf*
exercise	ejercicio *nm*
gymnastics	gimnasia, gimnástica *nf*
isometrics	isometría *nf*
isotonics	isotonía *nf*
tai chi	tai ji *nm*
yoga	yoga *nm*

RULES AND ACTIONS IN SPORTS

specific actions

base	base *nf*
batting	bateo *nm*
block	bloqueo *nm*
dribble	drible *nm*
inning	inning *nm*
knockout	nocaut, noqueo *nm*
parry	parar *vt*
pass	pase *nm*
service	servicio *nm*
slalom	slalom *nm*
strategy	estrategia *nf*
tierce	tercera *nf*
tumble	tumbo *nm*
volley	volea *nf*

other terms

concede	conceder *vt*
conversion	conversión *nf*
count	cuenta *nf*
defense Ⓐ	defensa *nf*
doubles (tennis)	dobles *nmpl*
fault	falta *nf*
foul	foul Ⓒ *nm*
goal	gol *nm*
intercept	interceptar *vt*
line	línea *nf*
lineup	alineación *nf*
offense Ⓐ	ofensiva *nf*
par	par *nf*
penalty	penalty *nm*
quarterfinal	cuarto de final *nm*
time out	tiempo muerto *av*

EQUIPMENT

boats

canoe	canoa *nf*
caravel	carabela *nf*
catamaran	catamarán *nm*
kayak	kayac *nm*
motorboat	motora *nf*
sailboat	bote de vela *nm, nf*
yacht	yate *nm*

vehicles

bicycle	bicicleta *nf*
motorcycle	moto, motocicleta *nf*
racing car	carro de carreras *nm, nfpl*
skilift	telesquí *nm*

other equipment

apparatus	aparatos *nmpl*
baseball (object)	pelota de béisbol *nf, nm*
bat	bate *nm*
boat	bote *nm*
bunker	búnker *nm*
discus	disco *nm*
football (object)	balón de fútbol *nm*
golf club	palo de golf *nm*
javelin	jabalina *nf*
mashie	mashie *nm*
mask	máscara *nf*
monoski	monoesquí *nm*
muleta	muleta *nf*
parallel bars	barras paralelas *nfpl*
plastron	plastrón *nm*
puck	puck *nm*

putter	putter *nm*
racket	raqueta *nf*
ski	esquí Ⓒ *nm*
snorkel	esnórquel *nm*
tee	tee *nm*
tent	tienda *nf*
toboggan	tobogán *nm*
trampoline	trampolín *nm*
trapeze	trapecio *nm*
volleyball (object)	balón de voleibol *nm*

PERSONS

athletes

acrobat	acróbata *nmf*
alpinist	alpinista *nmf*
archer	arquero *nm*
batter	bateador *nm*
bowler	jugador(a) de bolos *nmf, nmpl*
boxer	boxeador *nm*
canoeist	canoero, -a *nmf*
cyclist	ciclista *nmf*
discus thrower	discóbolo *nm*
golfer	golfista *nmf*
gymnast	gimnasta *nmf*
jockey	jockey, yoquei Ⓒ *nmf*
linesman	juez de línea *nm, nf*
matador	matador *nm*
party (hunting)	partida *nf*
pro	profesional *nmf*
pugilist	pugilista *nmf*
skier	esquiador(a) *nmf*
sportsman, sportswoman	deportista *nmf*
sprinter	esprínter *nmf*
surfer	surfista *nmf*
tennis player	tenista *nmf*

competitors

ace	as *nmf*
champion	campeón, -ona *nmf*
competitor	competidor(a) *nmf*
contender	contendiente *nmf*
entrant	entrante *nmf*
finalist	finalista *nmf*
medalist Ⓐ	medallista *nmf*
opponent	oponente *nmf*
quarterfinalist	cuartofinalista *nmf*
semifinalist	semifinalista *nmf*

other persons

amateur	amateur *nmf*

baseball fan	beisbolista *nmf*
camper	campista, acampador(a) *nmf*
captain	capitán, -ana *nmf*
fan	fan Ⓒ *nmf*
football fanatic	futbolero, -a *nmf*
lottery ticket seller	lotero, -a *nmf*
manager	manager *nm*
referee	réferi *nmf*
sponsor	espónsor *nmf*
sportcaster	comentarista deportivo, -a *nmf*
trainer	entrenador(a) *nmf*

(*See also* **GAMES**)

GAMES

GENERAL TERMS

championship	campeonato *nm*
competition	competencia *nf*
match	match *nm*
tournament	torneo *nm*
trophy	trofeo *nm*

NAMES OF GAMES

board and table games

backgammon	backgammon *nm*
bagatelle	bagatela *nf*
billiards	billar *nm*
bingo	bingo *nm*
Chinese checkers *nsg*	damas chinas *nfpl*
darts	dardos *nmpl*
lotto	lotería *nf*
mah-jongg	ma-jong *nm*
Monopoly	monópolis *nm*
parcheesi	parchís *nm*
ping-pong	ping-pong *nm*
pool	pool *nm*
Scrabble	Scrabble *nm*
table tennis	tenis de mesa *nm*

casino games

baccarat	bacará *nm*
blackjack	black-jack *nm*
craps	crap *nm*
croupier	crupier, croupier *nmf*
keno	keno *nm*
roulette	ruleta *nf*

other card games

| bridge | bridge *nm* |

canasta	canasta *nf*
gin rummy	gin rummy *nm*
pinochle	pinacle *nm*
poker	póquer *nm*
rummy	rummy, rami *nm*
solitaire	solitario *nm*

word games

acrostic	acróstico *nm*
anagram	anagrama *nm*
charades	charadas *nfpl*
crossword puzzle	crucigrama *nm*
cryptogram	criptograma *nm*

other games and toys

computer game	juego de computadora *nm, nf*
dominoes	dominó *nm*
Frisbee	Frisbee *nm*
jigsaw puzzle	puzzle *nm*
lottery	lotería *nf*
TV game	juego de TV *nm*
video game	videojuego *nm*
yo-yo	yoyo, yoyó *nm*

RULES AND ACTIONS IN GAMES

general

move	movida *nf*
pass	pase *nm*
strategy	estrategia *nf*
turn	turno *nm*

chess

capture	capturar *vt*
check	jaque *nm*
checkmate	jaque y mate *nm*
gambit	gambito *nm*
mate	mate *nm*
pawn	peón *nm*
piece	pieza *nf*
rook	roque *nm*

cards

ace	as *nm*
bank	banca *nmf*
card	carta *nf*
deuce	dos *nm*
diamond	diamante *nm*
discard	descartar *vt*
honors Ⓐ	honores *nmpl*
spade	espada *nf*
trey	trés *nm*

bridge terms

contract	contrato *nm*
declaration	declaración *nf*
double	doblar *vt*
duplicate	duplicado *aj*
pass	pasar *vti*
redouble	redoble, redoblo *nm*
slam	slam *nm*

billiards

carom	carambola *nf*
cue ball	bola blanca *nf*

(*See also* **SPORTS**)

TELEVISION AND VIDEO

GENERAL TERMS

audio	audio *nm*
channel	canal *nm*
guide	guía *nf*
kinescope	cinescopio *nm*
lineup	alineación *nf*
medium Ⓑ	medio *nm*
program Ⓐ	programa *nm*
programming, programing	programación *nf*
reception	recepción *nf*
selection	selección *nf*
studio	estudio *nm*
television	televisión, tele *nf*
transmission	tra(n)smisión *nf*
TV	TV *nf*
VCR	VCR *nm*
video	video *nm*

ASPECTS OF TELEVISION

types of television stations

adult	adulto *aj*
cable	cable *nm*
closed-circuit	por circuito cerrado *nm*
commercial	comercial *aj*
educational	educativo *aj*
ethnic	étnico *aj*
independent	independiente *aj*
local	local *aj*
national	nacional *aj*
Pay-Per-View	Pay-Per-View *nm*
public	público *aj*
satellite	satélite *nm*
sports	deportivo *aj*

telemarketing	telemárketing *nm*
UHF	UHF *nf*

programs and programming

adaptation	adaptación *nf*
audience participation	participación del público *nf, nm*
biography	biografía *nf*
comedy	comedia *nf*
commentary	comentario *nm*
commercial	comercial *nm*
credits	créditos *nmpl*
docudrama	docudrama *nf*
documentary	documental *nm*
dramatization	dramatización *nf*
episode	episodio *nm*
interview	entrevista *nf*
miniseries	miniserie *nf*
production	producción *nf*
serial	serial *nm*
situation comedy, sitcom	comedia de la vida diaria *nf*
special events	eventos especiales *nmpl*
TV movie	telefilm(e) *nm*
TV soap opera	telenovela *nf*
variety	variedad *nf*

transmission and reception

antenna Ⓑ	antena *nf*
coaxial	coaxial *aj*
contrast	contraste *nm*
definition	definición *nf*
dial	dial *nm*
direction	dirección *nf*
iconoscope	iconoscopio *nm*
installation	instalación *nf*
interference	interferencia *nf*
readjust	reajustar *vt*
reconnection	reconexión *nf*
selector	selector *nm*
service	servicio *nm*
static	estático *aj, nm*

TOOLS AND EQUIPMENT

remote control	control remoto *nm*
videocamera	videocámara *nf*
videocassette	videocasete *nm*
videodisc, videodisk	videodisco *nm*
videotape	videocinta *nf*
suppressor	supresor *nm*
camcorder	camcórder *nm*
camera	cámara *nf*
converter	convertidor *nm*

decoder	decodificador, descodificador *nm*
receiver	receptor *nm*
teleprompter	teleprompter *nm*
television set	televisor *nm*
transmitter	tra(n)smisor *nm*
tube	tubo *nm*
video library	videoteca *nf*

PERSONS

audience	audiencia *nf*
cameraman Ⓑ	cameraman, camarágrafo, -a *nmf*
commentator	comentarista *nmf*
dialog writer	dialoguista *nmf*
director	director(a) *nmf*
distributor	distribuidor(a) *nmf*
producer	productor(a) *nmf*
subscriber	suscriptor(a), subscriptor(a) *nmf*
talent	talento *nm*
television viewer	televidente *nmf*

(*See also* ASPECTS OF FILM-MAKING under **MOVIES**; ASPECTS OF PERFORMANCE ART under **THEATER PERFORMANCE**)

MOVIES

GENERAL TERMS

cinema	cine *nm*
cinematography	cinematografía *nf*
distribution	distribución *nf*
editing	edición *nf*
festival	festival *nm*
filming	filmación *nf*
matinee, matinée	matiné *nf*
nomination	nominación *nf*
Oscar	Oscar *nm*
studio	estudio *nm*

ASPECTS OF FILM-MAKING

elements of a film

action	acción *nf*
background music	música de fondo *nf, nm*
characterization	caracterización *nf*
dialog(ue)	diálogo *nm*
narration	narración *nf*
scene	escena *nf*
sound	son, sonido *nm*
suspense	suspenso *nm*
title	título *nm*

filming and editing techniques

animation	animación *nf*
flashback	flashback Ⓒ *nm*
interruption	interrupción *nf*
montage	montaje *nm*
panorama	panorama *nm*
sequence	secuencia *nf*
special effects	efectos especiales *nmpl*
strobe lighting	iluminación estroboscópica *nf*
trick photography	trucaje *nm*
voice-over	voz superpuesta *nf*

screen processes

CinemaScope	CinemaScope *nm*
cinerama	cinerama *nm*
Technicolor	tecnicolor *nm*

popular characters

cowboy	cowboy Ⓒ *nm* vaqueros
detective	detective *nmf*
gangster	gángster *nm*
mad scientist	científico loco *nm*
sex symbol	sex symbol *nmf*

popular genres

adventure	aventura *nf*
biography	biografía *nf*
fantasy	fantasía *nf*
farce	farsa *nf*
horror	horror *nm*
musical	musical *nm*
romance	romance *nm*

other terms

adaptation	adaptación *nf*
censorship	censura *nf*
projection	proyección *nf*
subtitles	subtítulos *nmpl*
version	versión *nf*

TOOLS AND EQUIPMENT

camera	cámara *nf*
dolly	dolly *nm*
film	filme *nm*
film library	filmoteca *nm*
projector	proyector *nm*
telephoto (lens)	telefoto *nm*
wide-angle lens	gran angular *nm*

PERSONS

actor	actor *nmf*

actress (obs)	actriz *nf*
animator	animador(a) *nmf*
cameraman Ⓑ	cameraman, camarágrafo, -a *nmf*
censor	censor *nmf*
cinema buff	cinéfilo, -a *nmf*
cinematographer	cinematógrafo, -a *nmf*
composer	compositor(a) *nmf*
critic	crítico, -a *nmf*
decorator	decorador(a) *nmf*
designer	diseñador(a) *nmf*
director	director(a) *nmf*
distributor	distribuidor(a) *nmf*
editor	editor, -a *nmf*
exhibitor	exhibidor(a) *nmf*
extra	extra *nmf*
idol	ídolo *nm*
producer	productor(a) *nmf*
projectionist	proyeccionista *nmf*
talent scout	cazatalentos *nmf*

(*See also* **LITERATURE**; **PHOTOGRAPHY**; **TELEVISION AND VIDEO**; **THEATER PERFORMANCE**)

PHOTOGRAPHY

GENERAL TERMS

camera	cámara *nf*
exposure	exposición *nf*
film	filme *nm*
photograph	fotografía *nf*
photographer	fotógrafo, -a *nmf*
photography	fotografía *nf*
subject	sujeto *nm*

ASPECTS OF PHOTOGRAPHY

types of still photography

aerial photo	aerofoto, áereofoto *nf*
daguerrotype (obs)	daguerrotipo *nm*
hologram	holograma *nm*
microfilm	microfilm(e) *nm*
photo	foto *nf*
photomontage	fotomontaje *nm*
tintype (obs)	ferrotipo *nm*
transparency	transparencia *nf*

taking photographs

advance (film)	avanzar *vt*
angle	ángulo *nm*
aperture	abertura *nf*
color Ⓐ	color *nm*

composition	composición *nf*
direction	dirección *nf*
distance	distancia *nf*
focus Ⓑ	foco *nm*
image	imagen *nf*
line	línea *nf*
overexposure	sobreexposición *nf*
photocomposition	fotocomposición *nf*
photogenic	fotogénico *aj*
pose	pose *nf*
time	tiempo *nm*
underexposure	subexposición *nf*

tools and equipment

airbrush	aerógrafo *nm*
album	álbum *nm*
box camera	cámara de cajón *nf, nm*
carrousel	carrusel *nm*
diaphragm	diafragma *nm*
exposure meter	exposímetro *nm*
filter	filtro *nm*
flash	flash *nm*
lens Ⓑ	lente *nm or nf*
panchromatic (film)	pancromático *aj*
photometer	fotómetro *nm*
projector	proyector *nm*
reflex (camera)	reflejo *aj*
roll (of film)	rollo *nm*
stereoscope	estereoscopio *nm*
stroboscope	estroboscopio *nm*
tripod	trípode *nm*
zoom lens	zoom *nm*

processing film

actinic (rays)	actínico *aj*
contrast	contraste *nm*
definition	definición *nf*
densitometer	densitómetro *nm*
desensitizer	desensibilizador *nm*
detail	detalle *nm*
emulsifier	emulsor *nm*
emulsion	emulsión *nf*
fixer, fixative	fijador *nm*
fixing bath	baño fijador *nm*
grain	grano *nm*
latent (image)	latente *aj*
matte	mate *aj*
negative	negativo *nm*
paper	papel *nm*
pellicle	película *nf*
positive	positivo *nm*
proof	prueba *nf*
reducer	reductor *nm*
reproduction	reproducción *nf*

retouching — retoque *nm*
solution — solución *nf*
thermometer — termómetro *nm*
tone — tono *nm*
unexposed — no expuesto *aj*

(*See also* **MOVIES**; **TELEVISION AND VIDEO**)

AMATEUR RADIO

GENERAL TERMS

AM — AM *nf*
amateur — amateur *aj*
band — banda *nf*
emergency — emergencia *nf*
FM — FM *nf*
license Ⓐ — licencia *nf*
message — mensaje *nm*
radio — radio *nm*
radio broadcasting — radiodifusión *nf*
radio station — radioemisora *nf*
radiotelephone — radioteléfono *nm*
signal — señal *nf*
station — estación *nf*
transmission — tra(n)smisión *nf*

ASPECTS OF AMATEUR RADIO

types of licenses

expert — experto *aj*
general — general *aj*
novice — novato *aj*
technician — técnico, -a *nmf*

components

amplifier — amplificador *nm*
antenna Ⓑ — antena *nf*
circuit — circuito *nm*
converter — convertidor *nm*
dial — dial *nm*
dipole — dipolo *nm*
dynode — dinodo *nm*
microphone — micrófono *nm*
modulator — modulador *nm*
oscillator — oscilador *nm*
receiver — receptor *nm*
rectifier — rectificador *nm*
resistor — resistencia *nf*
selector — selector *nm*
suppressor — supresor *nm*
transformer — tra(n)sformador *nm*
transistor — transistor *nm*
transmitter — tra(n)smisor *nm*
transponder — transpondedor *nm*

measurements

audiofrequency — audiofrecuencia *nf*
hertz Ⓑ — hertz, hertzio, hercio *nm*
kilocycle (obs) — kilociclo *nm*
kilohertz (kHz) Ⓑ — kilohercio *nm*
megahertz (MHz) Ⓑ — megahertzio *nm*

other terms

amplitude — amplitud *nf*
antistatic — antiestático *aj*
audio — audio *nm*
bandwidth — amplitude de banda *nf*
diplex — diplex, díplex *aj*
directional — direccional *aj*
echo Ⓑ — eco *nm*
fidelity — fidelidad *nf*
frequency — frecuencia *nf*
heterodyne — heterodino *nm*
interference — interferencia *nf*
modulation — modulación *nf*
multiband — multibanda *nf*
multiplex — multiplex *nm*
omnidirectional — omnidireccional *aj*
radiofrequency — radiofrecuencia *nf*
radiolocation — radiolocalización *nf*
reception — recepción *nf*
response — respuesta *nf*
static — estático *nm*
volume — volumen *nm*

PERSONS

audience — audiencia *nf*
disc-jockey — disc-jockey *nmf*
operator — operador(a) *nmf*
radio ham — radioaficionado, -a *nmf*
radio listener — radioescucha, radioyente *nmf*

(*See also* *FORMS OF TELECOMMUNICATION* under **COMMUNICATIONS**; *programs and programming* under **TELEVISION AND VIDEO**)

PERSONAL COMPUTERS

GENERAL TERMS

application — aplicación *nf*
code — código *nm*
communications — comunicaciones *nfpl*
computer — computadora *nf*
cybernetics — cibernética *nf*
electronic — electrónico *aj*

hardware	hardware *nm*
information	información *nf*
interface	interface, interfaz *nf*
listing	listado *nm*
logic	lógica *nf*
PC	PC *nm or nf*
program Ⓐ	programa *nm*
software	software *nm*
system	sistema *nm*

TYPES OF COMPUTERS

analog(ue)	análogo *nm*
dedicated	dedicado *aj*
digital	digital *aj*
hybrid	híbrido *aj*
laptop	laptop *nm*
microcomputer	microcomputadora *nf*
minicomputer	minicomputadora *nf*
multimedia	multimedia *aj*
personal	personal *aj*
portable	portátil *aj*
robot	robot *nm*
supercomputer	supercomputadora *nf*

HARDWARE TERMS

accelerator	acelerador *nm*
access (time)	acceso *nm*
accessory	accesorio *nm*
adapter	adaptador *nm*
architectura	arquitectura *nf*
auxiliary (memory)	auxiliar *aj*
bus Ⓑ	bus *nm*
cache	cache *nm*
cartridge	cartucho *nm*
CD	CD *nm*
chip	chip Ⓒ *nm*
circuit	circuito *nm*
compact disc	disco compacto *nm*
compatible	compatible *aj*
connector	conector *nm*
console	consola *nf*
converter	convertidor *nm*
CPU	CPU *nf*
cursor	cursor *nm*
disk drive	unidad de disco *nf, nm*
disk, diskette	disco *nm*
display	display *nm*
dot-matrix printer	imprimador matricial *nm*
expand	expandir *vt*
external (modem)	externo *aj*
floppy disk	floppy Ⓒ *nm*

font	fuente *nf*
format	formatear *vt*
function (key)	función *nf*
hard disk	disco duro *nm*
integrated (circuit)	integrado *aj*
intelligent (terminal)	inteligente *aj*
interpreter	intérprete *nm*
inverter	inversor *nm*
laser (printer)	láser *nm*
memory	memoria *nf*
microchip	microchip Ⓒ *nm*
microcircuit	microcircuito *nm*
microprocessor	microprocesadora *nf*
miniaturization	miniaturización *nf*
modem	modem Ⓒ *nm*
monitor	monitor *nm*
optical (scanner)	óptico *aj*
peripheral	equipo periférico *nm*
port	puerto *nm*
printer	impresor *nm*
processor	procesador *nm*
RAM	RAM *nf*
real time	tiempo real *nm*
register	registro *nm*
resolution	resolución *nf*
ROM	ROM *nf*
scanner	escáner Ⓒ *nm*
semiconductor	semiconductor *nm*
synthesizer	sintetizador *nm*
terminal	terminal *nm*
touch-sensitive (screen)	sensible al tacto *aj, nm*
tower	torre *nf*
tractor	tractor *nm*
transducer	transductor *nm*
unit	unidad *nf*

SOFTWARE TERMS

algorithm	algoritmo *nm*
alphanumeric	alfanumérico *aj*
ASCII	ASCII *nm*
assembler (language)	ensamblador *nm*
BASIC	BASIC *nm*
binary	binario *aj*
block	bloque *nm*
calculation	cálculo *nm*
character	carácter *nm*
COBOL	COBOL *nm*
compiler	compilador *nm*
configuration	configuración *nf*
corrupt	corromper *vt*
counter	contador *nm*

data *nsg* or *npl*	datos *nmpl*
database	base de datos *nf*
decimal	decimal *nm*
decode	descodificar *vt*
delimiter	símbolo delimitador *nm*
descriptor	descriptor *nm*
DOS	DOS *nm*
error	error *nm*
formatting	formateado *nm*
FORTRAN	FORTRAN *nm*
graphics	gráficos *nmpl*
hex, hexadecimal	hexadecimal *nm*
icon	icono *nm*
index ▣	índice *nm*
initialize	inicializar *vt*
install	instalar *vt*
instruction	instrucción *nf*
interrogation	interrogación *nf*
iteration	iteración *nf*
language	lenguaje *nm*
macro	macro, macroinstrucción *nm, nf*
macrocode	macrocodificación *nf*
message	mensaje *nm*
module	módulo *nm*
numeric(al)	numérico *aj*
parameter	parámetro *nm*
procedure	procedimiento *nm*
processing	procesamiento *nm*
programming, programing	programación *nf*
quantifier	cuantificador *nm*
routine	rutina *nf*
sequence	secuencia *nf*
signal	señal *nf*
simulation	simulación *nf*
symbol	símbolo *nm*
syntax	sintaxis *nf*
tabulation	tabulación *nf*
validate	validar *vt*
variable	variable *aj, nf*
virtual	virtual *aj*
word processing	procesamiento de palabras *nm, nfpl*

COMMUNICATIONS

cyberspace	ciberespacio *nm*
fax	fax *nm*
interactive	interactivo *aj*
interconnect	interconectar *vt*
Internet	Internet *nm*

local (network)	local *aj*
on-line, on line	en línea *aj, av*
parity	paridad *nf*
protocol	protocolo *nm*
remote	remoto *aj*
server	servidor *nm*
time sharing	tiempo compartido *nm*

MEASUREMENTS

baud	baudio *nm*
bit	bitio *nm*
byte	byte *nm*
gigabyte	gigabyte *nm*
hertz ▣	hertz, hertzio, hercio *nm*
kilobaud	kilobaudio *nm*
kilobit	kilobitio *nm*
kilobyte	kilobyte *nm*
kilohertz (kHz) ▣	kilohercio *nm*
megabyte	megabyte *nm*
megahertz (mHz) ▣	megahercio *nm*
nanosecond	nanosegundo *nm*

PERSONS

analyst	analista *nmf*
codifier	codificador *nmf*
operator	operador(a) *nmf*
programmer, programer	programador(a) *nmf*
user	usuario, -a *nmf*

(*See also* **ELECTRICITY AND ELECTRONICS**)

TRAVEL AND TOURISM

GENERAL TERMS

attraction	atracción *nf*
class	clase *nf*
destination	destino *nm*
exploration	exploración *nf*
line	línea *nf*
tourism	turismo *nm*
transit	tránsito *nm*
transportation	tra(n)sportación *nf*
vacation *nsg*	vacaciones *nfpl*

ASPECTS OF TOURISM

types of vacations

cruise	crucero *nm*
excursion	excursión *nf*
expedition	expedición *nf*

odyssey	odisea *nf*
peregrination	peregrinación *nf*
safari	safari *nm*
transatlantic ocean liner	transatlántico *nm*
trekking	trekking *nm*
visit	visita *nf*
voyage	viaje *nm*

lodging

hostel	hostería *nf*
hotel	hotel *nm*
motel	motel *nm*
pension	pensión *nf*
reception	recepción *nf*
suite	suite *nf*

long-distance transportation

airline	aerolínea *nf*
auto, automobile	auto *nm*
boat	bote *nm*
car	carro *nm*
caravan	caravana *nf*
express (train, mail)	expreso *aj, nm*
omnibus	ómnibus *nm*
train	tren *nm*

local transportation

air taxi	aerotaxi *nm*
auto, automobile	automóvil *nm*
bus, autobus 🅱	bus, autobús *nm*
funicular	funicular *nm*
gondola	góndola *nf*
limousine	limusina *nf*
metro	metro *nm*
monorail	monorriel *nm*
taxi, taxicab	taxi, taxímetro *nm*
tramway	tranvía *nf*
trolley	trole *nm*

travel arrangements

agency	agencia *nf*
cancellation	cancelación *nf*
charter	chárter *nm*
itinerary	itinerario *nm*
lodging	alojamiento *nm*
pack	empacar *vt*
passage	pasaje *nm*
reservation	reservación *nf*
tariff	tarifa *nf*

classes of travel

deluxe	de lujo *aj*
first-class	de primera clase *aj*
luxury	de lujo *aj*
second-class	de segunda clase *aj*
third-class	en tercera clase *aj*
tourist	de turista *aj*

documents

passport	pasaporte *nm*
ticket (baggage)	ticket *nm*
traveler's check	cheque de viajero *nm*
visa	visa *nf*

starting and ending

airport	aeropuerto *nm*
carousel, carrousel	carrusel *nm*
disembark	desembarcarse *vr*
embark	embarcarse *vr*
excess (baggage)	exceso *nm*
port	puerto *nm*
station	estación *nf*
terminal	terminal *nm*
terminus 🅱	terminal *nm*

seeing the sights

guidebook	guía *nf*
map	mapa *nm*
route	ruta *nf*
ruins	ruinas *nfpl*

PERSONS

chauffeur	chófer *nm*
cicerone 🅱	cicerone *nmf*
coachman	cochero *nm*
conductor	conductor(a) *nmf*
globetrotter	trotamundos *nmf*
gondolier	gondolero *nm*
guide	guía *nmf*
hotelkeeper	hotelero, -a *nmf*
passenger	pasajero, -a *nmf*
porter	portero *nm*
taxi driver	taxista *nmf*
tourist	turista *nmf*
transient	transeúnte *aj, nmf*
vagabond	vagabundo, -a *aj, nmf*
visitor	visitante *nmf*
voyager	viajero, -a *nmf*

(*See also* **AVIATION AND SPACE TRAVEL**; **BOATS AND SHIPS**; **LAND TRANSPORTATION**)

The Arts

ART AND AESTHETICS

GENERAL TERMS

aesthetics, esthetics	estética *nf*
creation	creación *nf*
criterion Ⓑ	criterio *nm*
flowering	florecimiento *nm*
formalism	formalismo *nm*
genre	género *nm*
ideal	ideal *aj, nm*
influence	influencia *nf*
manner	manera *nf*
masterpiece	obra maestra *nf*
patronage	patrocinio *nm*
purism	purismo *nm*
quality	calidad *nf*
realism	realismo *nm*
style	estilo *nm*
symbolism	simbolismo *nm*
technique	técnica *nf*

PRINCIPLES OF BEAUTY

contrast	contraste *nm*
design, designing	diseño *nm*
form	forma *nf*
harmony	armonía *nf*
proportion	proporción *nf*
symmetry	simetría *nf*
unity	unidad *nf*

ATTRIBUTES OF THE ARTIST

artistry	talento artístico *nm*
creativity	creatividad *nf*
imagination (inventiveness)	imaginativa *nf*
inspiration	inspiración *nf*
inventiveness	inventiva *nf*
originality	originalidad *nf*
prolific	prolífico *aj*
talent	talento *nm*

THE ENJOYMENT OF ART

appreciation	apreciación *nf*
contemplation	contemplación *nf*
criticism	crítica *nf*
effect	efecto *nm*
experience	experiencia *nf*
idealism	idealismo *nm*
interpretation	interpretación *nf*
pleasure	placer *nm*
satisfaction	satisfacción *nf*
sensation	sensación *nf*
sensibility	sensibilidad *nf*
subjectivism	subjetivismo *nm*
value	valor *nm*

MAJOR STYLES

baroque	barroco *aj*
classicism	clasicismo *nm*
contemporary	contemporáneo *aj*
expressionism	expresionismo *nm*
futurism	futurismo *nm*
impressionism	impresionismo *nm*
modern	moderno *aj*
neoclassicism	neoclasicismo *nm*
postimpressionism	postimpresionismo *nm*
rococo	rococó *aj, nm*
romanticism	romanticismo *nm*

PERSONS

aesthete, esthete	esteta *nmf*
artist	artista *nmf*
connoisseur	conocedor(a) *nmf*
dilettante	diletante *nmf*
formalist	formalista *aj, nmf*
genius	genio *nm*

MUSIC

GENERAL TERMS

acoustics	acústica *nf*
classical	clásico *aj*
composition	composición *nf*
dynamics	dinámica *nf*
execution	ejecución *nf*
instrument	instrumento *nm*
instruments *npl*	instrumental *nmsg*
literature	literatura *nf*
music	música *nf*
musicology	musicología *nf*
percussion	percusión *nf*
piece	pieza *nf*
popular	popular *aj*
potpourri Ⓑ	popurrí *nm*

practice **A**	practicar *vt*
repertory	repertorio *nm*
sacred	sacro *aj*
symbol	símbolo *nm*
talent	talento *nm*
temperament	temperamento *nm*
theory	teoría *nf*
vocal	vocal *aj*

COMPOSITIONS

religious forms

cantata	cantata *nf*
chorale	coral *nm*
Gregorian chant	canto gregoriano *nm*
hymn	himno *nm*
mass	misa *nf*
motet	motete *nm*
oratorio	oratorio *nm*
passion	pasión *nf*
requiem	réquiem *nm*
spiritual	espiritual *nm*

dance forms

arabesque	arabesco *nm*
bourrée	bourrée *nm*
danza	danza *nf*
galop	galopa *nf*
gavotte	gavota *nf*
gigue	giga *nf*
mazurka	mazurca *nf*
minuet	minué, menueto *nm*
polka	polca *nf*
polonaise	polonesa *nf*
saraband(e)	zarabanda *nf*
tango	tango *nm*
tarantella	tarantela *nf*
waltz	vals *nm*

theatrical forms

ballet	ballet *nm*
grand opera	gran ópera *nf*
musical comedy	comedia musical *nf*
opera	ópera *nf*
opera buffa	ópera bufa *nf*
operetta	opereta *nf*
zarzuela	zarzuela *nf*

other forms

— vocal —

air	aire *nm*
aria	aria *nf(el)*
madrigal	madrigal *nm*

recitative	recitativo *nm*
round	ronda *nf*

— instrumental —

bagatelle	bagatela *nf*
barcarole, barcarolle	barcarola *nf*
canon	canon *nm*
capriccio	capricho *nm*
chaconne	chacona *nf*
chamber music	música de cámara *nf*
concerto	concierto *nm*
divertimento **B**	divertimento *nm*
etude, étude	estudio *nm*
fantasia	fantasía *nf*
fugue	fuga *nf*
improvisation	improvisación *nf*
impromptu	impromptu *nm*
interlude	interludio *nm*
intermezzo **B**	intermezzo *nm*
invention	invención *nf*
lament	lamento *nm*
march	marcha *nf*
nocturne	nocturno *nm*
overture	obertura *nf*
partita	partita *nf*
passacaglia	pasacalle *nm*
prelude	preludio *nm*
rhapsody	rapsodia *nf*
rondo	rondó *nm*
scherzo **B**	scherzo *nm*
sonata	sonata *nf*
sonatina	sonatina *nf*
suite	suite *nf*
symphony	sinfonía *nf*
theme and variations	tema y variaciones *nm, nfpl*
toccata	tocata *nf*

— vocal or instrumental —

ballad	balada *nf*
folk music (modern)	música folk *nf*
folk music (traditional)	música folclórica *nf*
serenade	serenata *nf*
tune	tonada *nf*

INSTRUMENTS

sound sources

acoustic(al)	acústico *aj*
digital	digital *aj*
electric	eléctrico *aj*
electronic	electrónico *aj*

keyboard instruments

accordion	acordeón *nm*
celesta	celesta *nf*
clavichord	clavicordio *nm*
organ	órgano *nm*
piano	piano *nm*
spinet	espineta *nf*

string instruments

autoharp	autoarpa *nf*
balalaika	balalaica *nf*
banjo Ⓑ	banjo *nm*
cello	chelo *nm*
contrabass	contrabajo *nm*
dulcimer	dulcémele *nm*
guitar	guitarra *nf*
harp	arpa *nf*
mandolin	mandolina *nf*
ukulele	ukelele *nm*
viola	viola *nf*
violin	violín *nm*
violoncello	violonc(h)elo *nm*
zither	cítara *nf*

wind instruments

bassoon	bajón *nm*
bugle	bugle *nm*
clarinet	clarinete *nm*
contrabassoon	contrabajón *nm*
cornet	corneta *nf*
flute	flauta *nf*
harmonica	armónica *nf*
oboe	oboe *nm*
ocarina	ocarina *nf*
piccolo	piccolo *nm*
saxophone	saxófono *nm*
trombone	trombón *nm*
trumpet	trompeta *nf*
tuba	tuba *nf*

percussion instruments

– drums and cymbals –

bongo Ⓑ	bongó, bongo *nm*
conga *nsg*	congas *nfpl*
cymbal	címbalo *nm*
gong	gong Ⓒ *nm*
timbal	timbal *nm*
timpani	tímpanos *nmpl*
tom-tom	tam-tam *nm*
tympani	tímpanos *nmpl*

– keyboard-related –

concertina	concertina *nf*
marimba	marimba *nf*

melodeon	melodión, melodina *nm, nf*
vibraphone	vibráfono *nm*
xylophone	xilófono *nm*

– small instruments –

castanet	castañeta, castañuela *nf*
maracas	maracas *nfpl*
triangle	triángulo *nm*

Asian instruments

gamelan	gamelán *nm*
koto	koto *nm*
samisen	samisén *nm*
sitar	sitar *nm*

other instruments

barrel organ	organillo *nm*
carillon	carillón *nm*
clarion	clarín *nm*
harmonium	armonio *nm*
synthesizer	sintetizador *nm*
theramin	teramín *nm*

MUSIC THEORY

basic concepts

atonality	atonalidad *nf*
chord	acorde *nm*
harmony	armonía *nf*
interval	intervalo *nm*
melody	melodía *nf*
modality	modalidad *nf*
mode	modo *nm*
notation	notación *nf*
note	nota *nf*
polyphony	polifonía *nf*
polytonality	politonalidad *nf*
rhythm	ritmo *nm*
scale	escala *nf*
tempo Ⓑ	tempo *nm*
texture	textura *nf*
tonality	tonalidad *nf*
tone	tono *nm*

kinds of scales

chromatic	cromático *aj*
diatonic	diatónico *aj*
major	mayor *aj*
minor	menor *aj*
modal	modal *aj*
pentatonic	pentatónico *aj*

notes of the diatonic scale

do	do *nm*
fa Ⓐ	fa *nm*
la	la *nm*
mi	mi *nm*
re	re *nm*
sol	sol *nm*
ti	si *nm*
dominant	dominante *aj, nf*
subdominant	subdominante *aj, nf*
supertonic	supertónica *nf*
tonic	tónica *nf*

intervals

augmented	aumentado *aj*
diminished	disminuido *aj*
octave	octava *nf*
perfect	perfecto *aj, nm*
semitone	semitono *nm*
unison	unísono *nm*

chords

arpeggio	arpegio *nm*
augmented	aumentado *aj*
consonant	consonante *aj*
diminished	disminuido *aj*
dissonant	disonante *aj*
major	mayor *aj*
minor	menor *aj*
triad	tríada *nf*

textures

homophonic	homofónico *aj*
monophonic	monofónico *aj*
polyphonic	polifónico *aj*

harmonic devices

cadence	cadencia *nf*
consonance	consonancia *nf*
dissonance	disonancia *nf*
modulation	modulación *nf*
progression	progresión *nf*
resolution	resolución *nf*
suspension	suspensión *nf*

polyphonic devices

contrary (motion)	contrario *aj*
counterpoint	contrapunto *nm*
imitation	imitación *nf*
inversion	inversión *nf*
parallel (motion)	paralelo *aj*
retrograde (motion)	retrógrado *aj*

melodic devices

augmentation	aumento *nm*
diminution	diminución *nf*
figure	figura *nf*
leitmotif, leitmotiv	leitmotivo *nm*
motif	motivo *nm*
obbligato Ⓑ	obligado *nm*
pause	pausa *nf*
repetition	repetición *nf*
sequence	secuencia *nf*
syncopation	síncopa *nf*
theme	tema *nm*
transposition	transporte *nm*

notation

accidental	accidental *nm*
enharmonic	enharmónico *nm*
natural	nota natural *nf*
septuplet	septillo *nm*
sextuplet	sextillo *nm*
triplet	tresillo *nm*

parts of compositions

coda	coda *nf*
exposition	exposición *nf*
finale	final *nm*
introduction	introducción *nf*
movement	movimiento *nm*
part	parte *nf*
passage	pasaje *nm*
transition	transición *nf*

other terms

alto (instrument)	alto *aj*
bass (register)	bajo *aj*
binary (form)	binario *aj*
clef	clave *nf*
contrapuntal	de contrapunto
diapason	diapasón *nm*
discordant	discordante, discorde *aj*
gamut	gama *nf*
harmonization	armonización *nf*
orchestration	orquestación *nf*
register	registro *nm*
sol-fa, solfeggio	solfeo *nm*
tessitura	tesitura *nf*
transcription	tra(n)scripción *nf*

PERFORMANCE TERMS

dynamics

crescendo	crescendo *nm*
decrescendo	descrescendo *nm*

diminuendo	diminuendo *av, nm*
forte	forte *av, nm*
fortissimo	fortísimo *aj, av*
pianissimo	pianísimo *av*
piano	piano *av, nm*

tempo

adagio	adagio *nm*
agitato	agitado *aj*
allegretto	alegreto *aj, av*
allegro	alegro *aj, av, nm*
andante	andante *av, nm*
duple (time)	duplo *aj*
largo	largo *aj, av*
lento	lento *aj, nm*
moderato	moderato *av*
presto	presto *aj, av, nm*

execution

a capella	a capella *aj, av*
arrangement	arreglo *nm*
brio	brío *nm*
cantabile	cantábile *nm*
entrance	entrada *nf*
falsetto	falsete *nm*
intonation	entonación *nf*
legato	ligado *aj, av*
ligature	ligadura *nf*
monotone	monótono *aj*
phrasing	fraseo *nm*
pizzicato	pizzicato *aj, av*
sotto voce	sotto voce *av*
staccato	staccato *aj*
vibrato	vibrato *nm*

embellishment

anticipation	anticipación *nf*
appoggiatura	apoyatura *nf*
flourish	floreo *nm*
mordent	mordente *nm*
tremolo	trémolo *nm*
trill	trino *nm*

places and events

concert	concierto *nm*
concert hall	sala de conciertos *nf, nmpl*
conservatory	conservatorio *nm*
recital	recital *nm*
studio	estudio *nm*

other terms

accompaniment	acompañamiento *nm*
antiphonal	antifonal *aj*

bel canto	bel canto, canto bello *nm*
instrumentation	instrumentación *nf*
interpretation	interpretación *nf*
libretto Ⓑ	libreto *nm*
selection	selección *nf*
solo	solo *nm*
timbre	timbre *nm*
vocalization	vocalización *nf*

POPULAR MUSIC TERMS

blues	blues *nm*
boogie-woogie	bugui-bugui *nm*
bop	bop *nm*
calypso	calipso *nm*
discoteque	discoteca *nf*
jazz	jazz *nm*
ragtime	ragtime *nm*
rap	rap *nm*
reggae	reggae *nm*
rock	rock *nm*
rock'n'roll	rocanrol *nm*
salsa	salsa *nf*
swing	swing *nm*

MUSICAL ACOUSTICS

absolute (pitch)	absoluto *aj*
amplify	amplificar *vt*
fundamental	tono fundamental *nm*
harmonic	armónico *aj, nm*
harmonics *npl*	armonía *nfsg*
partial	tono parcial *nm*
quadraphonic	cuadrifónico *aj*
resonance	resonancia *nf*
stereophonic	estereofónico *aj*
sympathetic (vibration)	simpático *aj*
vibrate	vibrarse *vr*

TOOLS AND EQUIPMENT

baton	batuta *nf*
cassette	cassete, casete *nm or nf*
CD	CD *nm*
compact disc	disco compacto *nm*
component	componente *nm*
console	consola *nf*
metronome	metrónomo *nm*
music cabinet	musiquero *nm*
pedal	pedal *nm*
piston	pistón *nm*
plectrum Ⓑ	plectro *nm*
podium Ⓑ	podio *nm*

resonator   resonador *nm*
stereo   estéreo *nm*
stylus B   estilo *nm*

PERSONS

vocal performers

alto (female)   contralto *nf*
alto (male)   alto *nm*
baritone   barítono *nm*
basso   bajo *nm*
basso profundo   bajo profundo *nm*
chorister   corista *nmf*
coloratura   coloratura *nf*
contralto   contralto *nf*
diva   diva *nf*
folk singer   cantante de música folk *nmf*
opera singer   operista *nmf*
serenader   él que da serenatas *nm*
soprano   soprano *nm, nmf*
tenor   tenor *nm*

instrumental performers

accompanist   acompañante *nmf*
accordionist   acordeonista *nmf*
bassoonist   bajonista *nmf*
cellist   chelista, violoncelista *nmf*
clarinetist   clarinete, clarinetista *nmf*
cornetist   corneta *nmf*
flutist A   flautista *nmf*
guitarrist   guitarrista *nmf*
harpist   arpista *nmf*
oboist   oboísta *nmf*
organist   organista *nmf*
percussionist   músico de percusión *nmf, nf*
pianist   pianista *nmf*
saxophonist   saxofonista *nmf*
timpanist   timbalero, -a *nmf*
trombonist   trombón *nm*
tympanist   timbalero, -a *nmf*
violinist   violinista *nmf*
violist   viola *nmf*
violoncellist   violonc(h)ista *nmf*
xylophonist   xilofonista *nmf*

performance groups

band   banda *nf*
chamber orchestra   orquesta de cámara *nf*

choir   coro *nm*
chorus   coro *nm*
duet   dueto *nm*
duo   dúo *nm*
octet   octeto *nm*
orchestra   orquesta *nf*
philharmonic   orquesta filarmónica *nf*
quartet, quartette   cuarteto *nm*
quintet, quintette   quinteto *nm*
septet   septeto *nm*
sextet, sextette   sexteto *nm*
trio   trío *nm*

other persons

arranger   arreglista *nmf*
choirmaster   director(a) de coro *nmf, nm*
composer   compositor(a) *nmf*
concert artist   concertista *nmf*
concertmaster   concertino *nm*
director   director(a) *nmf*
instrumentalist   instrumentista *nmf*
interpreter   intérprete *nmf*
librettist   libretista *nmf*
maestro B   maestro *nm*
musician   músico, -a *nmf*
musicologist   musicologista *nmf*
protégé(e)   protegido, -a *nmf*
soloist   solista *nmf*
virtuoso B   virtuoso, -a *nmf*
vocalist   vocalista *nmf*

OBSOLETE AND HISTORICAL TERMS

gramophone   gramófono *nm*
lyre   lira *nf*
phonograph   fonógrafo *nm*
psaltery   salterio *nm*
tabor, tabour   tamboril *nm*
virginal   virginal *nm*

(*See also* **ART AND AESTHETICS**; *historical storytellers* under **LITERATURE**)

DANCING

GENERAL TERMS

gesture   gesto *nm*
line   línea *nf*
movement   movimiento *nm*
music   música *nf*
rhythm   ritmo *nm*

TYPES OF DANCE

theatrical

acrobatic	acrobático *aj*
ballet	ballet *nm*
exhibition	exhibición *nf*
modern	moderno *aj*

social

ballroom	salón de baile *nm*
folkloric	folklórico, folclórico *aj*
popular	popular *aj*
recreational	recreativo *aj*

other classifications

aerobic	aeróbico *aj*
ceremonial	ceremonial *aj*
narrative	narrativo *aj*
religious	religioso *aj*
ritual	ritual *aj*

NAMES OF DANCES

modern dances

bolero	bolero *nm*
break dancing	break *nm*
cancan	cancán *nm*
cha-cha-cha	cha-cha-chá *nm*
conga	conga *nf*
contredanse	contradanza *nf*
danza	danza *nf*
fandango	fandango *nm*
flamenco	flamenco *nm*
foxtrot	foxtrot *nm*
galop	galopa *nf*
go-go	gogó *nf*
habanera	habanera *nf*
horah	hora *nf*
hula	hula *nf*
jig	giga *nf*
limbo	limbo *nm*
mambo	mambo *nm*
maxixe	machicha *nf*
mazurka	mazurca *nf*
merengue	merengue *nm*
one-step	one-step *nm*
polka	polca *nf*
polonaise	polonesa *nf*
quadrille	cuadrilla *nf*
rumba, rhumba	rumba *nf*
samba	samba *nm or nf*
shimmy	shimmy *nm*
tango	tango *nm*

tarantella	tarantela *nf*
waltz	vals *nm*

historical dances

allemande	alemanda *nf*
bourrée	bourrée *nm*
chaconne	chacona *nf*
cotillion	cotillón *nm*
galliard	gallarda *nf*
gavotte	gavota *nf*
minuet	minué, minuete *nm*
passepied	paspié *nm*
pavan(e)	pavana *nf*
saraband(e)	zarabanda *nf*

TERMS IN BALLET

arabesque	arabesco *nm*
attitude	actitud *nf*
choreography	coreografía *nf*
corps de ballet	cuerpo de baile *nm*
pas	paso *nm*
pirouette	pirueta *nf*
points	puntas de pie *nfpl*
position	posición *nf*
tutu	tutú *nm*

PERSONS

ballerina	bailarina *nf*
balletomane	aficionado, -a al ballet *nmf*
choreographer	coreógrafo, -a *nmf*
dancer	danzante *nmf*

(*See also* **ENTERTAINMENT**; **MUSIC**; **THEATER PERFORMANCE**)

THEATER PERFORMANCE

GENERAL TERMS

acting	actuación *nf*
audition	audición *nf*
cancellation	cancelación *nf*
dramatics	arte dramático *nm*
histrionics *npl*	histrionismo *nm*
mount	montar *vt*
piece	pieza *nf*
production	producción *nf*
program Ⓐ	programa *nm*
represent	representar *vt*
stellar (role, performance)	estelar *aj*
theatricals	funciones teatrales *nfpl*

ASPECTS OF PERFORMANCE ART

types of theater art

amateur	amateur *aj*
avant-garde	vanguardista *aj*
classical	clásico *aj*
community	comunitario *aj*
experimental	experimental *aj*
marionette	marioneta *nf*
professional	profesional *aj*
repertory	repertorio *nm*
Shakespearean, Shakespearian	shakesperiano *aj*
theater of the absurd	teatro del absurdo *nm*

kinds of productions

adaptation	adaptación *nf*
burlesque	burlesco *nm*
comedy	comedia *nf*
drama	drama *nm*
dramatization	dramatización *nf*
farce	farsa *nf*
improvisation	improvisación *nf*
melodrama	melodrama *nm*
musical	comedia musical *nf*
opera	ópera *nf*
operetta	opereta *nf*
pantomime	pantomima *nf*
pastiche	pastiche *nm*
revue	revista *nf*
spectacle	espectáculo *nm*
variety	variedad *nf*
vaudeville	vodevil *nm*

elements of performance

act	acto *nm*
choreography	coreografía *nf*
cyclorama	ciclorama *nm*
declamation	declamación *nf*
decor, décor	decorado *nm*
entrance	entrada *nf*
epilog	epílogo *nm*
intermission	intermedio *nm*
interpretation	interpretación *nf*
mask	máscara *nf*
matinee, matinée	matiné *nf*
prologue	prólogo *nm*
scene	escena *nf*

places

amphitheater Ⓐ	anfiteatro *nm*

arch	arco *nm*
arena	arena *nf*
auditorium Ⓑ	auditorio *nm*
gallery	galería *nf*
open-air theater	teatro al aire libre *nm*
opera house	ópera *nf*
proscenium	proscenio *nm*
theater Ⓐ	teatro *nm*
theater-in-the-round	teatro circular *nm*

audience response

acclaim	aclamación *nf*
applause	aplauso *nm*
boo	abuchear *vti*
bravo!	¡bravo! *intj*
ovation	ovación *nf*

PERSONS

individuals

actor	actor *nm*
actress	actriz *nf*
agent	agente *nmf*
character	carácter *nm*
declaimer	declamador(a) *nmf*
designer	diseñador(a) *nmf*
director	director(a) *nmf*
dramatist	dramaturgo, -a *nmf*
dramaturge	dramaturgo *nmf*
impresario	empresario *nm*
ingénue	ingenua *nf*
interpreter	intérprete *nmf*
mime	mimo *nmf*
protagonist	protagonista *nmf*
technician	técnico, -a *nmf*
tragedian	trágico *nm*
tragedienne	trágica *nf*

groups

chorus	coro *nm*
claque	claque *nf*
company	compañía *nf*
duo	dúo *nm*
public	público *nm*
spectator	espectador(a) *nmf*
applaud	aplaudir *vti*
electrify	electrizar *vt*

(*See also* **spectator** under **ENTERTAINMENT**; **FORMS OF DRAMA** under **LITERATURE**)

VISUAL ARTS

GENERAL TERMS

art	arte *nf(el)*
arts and crafts	artes y oficios *nfpl,* *nmpl*
authentic	auténtico *aj*
collection	colección *nf*
color **A**	color *nm*
copy	copia *nf*
design, designing	diseño *nm*
expression	expresión *nf*
figure	figura *nf*
genuine	genuino *aj*
materials	materiales *nmpl*
medium **B**	medio *nm*
object	objeto *nm*
original	original *aj, nm*
piece	pieza *nf*
representation	representación *nf*
style	estilo *nm*
symbol	símbolo *nm*

FORMS OF VISUAL ART

calligraphy	caligrafía *nf*
ceramics	cerámica *nf*
cloisonné	cloisonné *nm*
decor, decoration	decoración *nf*
graphics	diseño gráfico *nm*
lithography	litografía *nf*
origami	origami *nm*
painting	pintura *nf*
photography	fotografía *nf*
sculpture	escultura *nf*
tapestry	tapiz *nm*
xylography	xilografía *nf*

CREATING AND DISPLAYING ART

art objects

adornment	adorno *nm*
antiques	antigüedades *nfpl*
aquarelle (watercolor)	acuarela *nf*
aquatint	acuatinta *nf*
arabesque	arabesco *nm*
bas-relief	bajorrelieve *nm*
bronze	bronce *nm*
bust	busto *nm*
caricature	caricatura *nf*
china	china *nf*
collage	collage *nm*
curio	curiosidad *nf*

diorama	diorama *nm*
diptych	díptico *nm*
engraving	grabado *nm*
figurine	figura *nf*
filigree	filigrana *nf*
flower arrangement	arreglo floral *nm*
fresco	fresco *nm*
icon, ikon	icono *nm*
illustration	ilustración *nf*
inscription	inscripción *nf*
lithograph	litografía *nf*
Madonna	Madona
mask	máscara *nf*
medallion	medallón *nm*
mezzotint	mezzotinto *nm*
miniature	miniatura *nf*
mobile	móvil *nm*
molding **A**	molde *nm*
montage	montaje *nm*
monument	monumento *nm*
mosaic	mosaico *nm*
mural	mural *nm*
nude	desnudo *nmf*
obelisk	obelisco *nm*
ornament	ornamento *nm*
pedestal	pedestal *nm*
photograph	fotografía *nf*
porcelain	porcelana *nf*
poster	póster *nm*
pot	pote *nm*
relief	relieve *nm*
replica	réplica *nf*
rosette	roseta *nf*
sculpture	escultura *nf*
statuary	estatuaria *nf*
statue	estatua *nf*
statues *npl*	estatuaria *nf*
statuette	estatuilla *nf*
study	estudio *nm*
tapestry	tapicería *nf*
tattoo	tatuaje *nm*
triptych	tríptico *nm*
urn	urna *nf*
xylograph (woodcut)	xilografía *nf*

design

asymmetry	asimetría *nf*
composition	composición *nf*
contour	contorno *nm*
contrast	contraste *nm*
delineation	delineación *nf*
dissymmetry	disimetría *nf*
figuration	figuración *nf*

illumination	iluminación *nf*
image	imagen *nf*
imagery	imaginería *nf*
line	línea *nf*
mannerism	manerismo *nm*
mass	masa *nf*
motif	motivo *nm*
movement	movimiento *nm*
ornamentation	ornamentación, ornato *nf, nm*
perspective	perspectiva *nf*
plane	plano *nm*
profile	perfil *nm*
repetition	repetición *nf*
silhouette	silueta *nf*
space	espacio *nm*
symmetry	simetría *nf*
texture	textura *nf*
tonality	tonalidad *nf*
volume	volumen *nm*

tools, materials, techniques

abrasive	abrasivo *aj, nm*
acrylic	acrílico *aj*
adhesive	adhesivo *aj, nm*
airbrush	aerógrafo *nm*
alabaster	alabastro *nm*
armature	armazón *nf*
brushstroke	brochazo *nm*
chisel	cincel *nm*
color	colorido *nm*
colorant	colorante *nm*
fixative	fijador *nm*
gesso	yeso *nm*
glazed	glaseado *aj*
gouache	gouache *nm*
graphite	grafito *nm*
gum arabic	goma arábiga *nf*
gutta-percha	gutapercha *nf*
lac, lacquer	laca *nf*
latex	látex *nm*
linseed	linaza *nf*
macrame, macramé	macramé *nm*
mannequin, manikin	maniquí *nmf*
marble	mármol *nm*
matte	mate *aj*
metal	metal *nm*
modeling Ⓐ	modelado *nm*
mold Ⓐ	molde *nm*
mucilage	mucílago *nm*
muffle	mufla *nf*
ocher Ⓑ	ocre *nm*
oil	óleo *nm*

paint	pintura *nf*
palette	paleta *nf*
paste	pasta *nf*
pastel	pastel *nm*
patina	pátina *nf*
pigment	pigmento *nm*
plastic	plástico *aj, nm*
pose	pose *nf*
solvent	solvente *nm*
spatula	espátula *nf*
stencil	esténcil *nm*
stylus Ⓑ	estilo *nm*
talc	talco *nm*
taxidermy	taxidermia *nf*
tempera	témpera *nf*
terra-cotta	terracota *nf*
touch	toque *nm*
varnish	barniz *nm*

places

gallery	galería *nf*
museum	museo *nm*
salon	salón *nm*
studio	estudio *nm*

COLOR TERMS

general

colorant	colorante *nm*
coloration Ⓐ	coloración *nf*
coloring Ⓐ (substance)	colorante *nm*
coloring Ⓐ (design)	colorido *nm*
discoloration Ⓐ	descoloración, decoloramiento *nf, nm*
polychromy	policromía *nf*
prism	prisma *nm*
spectrum Ⓑ	espectro *nm*
Technicolor	tecnicolor *nm*

classifications

complementary	complementario *aj*
monochrome	monocromo *aj, nm*
polychrome	policromo *aj*
primary	primario *aj*
secondary	secundario *aj*

qualities

contrast	contraste *nm*
intensity	intensidad *nf*
purity	pureza *nf*
tint	tinte *nm*

pigments and dyes

anil	añil *nm*
carmine	carmín *nm*
sienna	siena *nm*
vermilion, vermillion	bermellón *nm*

other color names

amber	ámbar *nm*
aquamarine	aguamarina *nf*
azure	azul celeste *nm*
beige	beige *nm*
canary-yellow	amarillo canario *aj*
cerise	(color) cereza *nf*
chocolate	(color) chocolate *nm*
coffee	(color) café *nm*
copper	(color) cobre *nm*
cream	(color) crema *nf*
ebony	(color de) ébano *nm*
emerald	verde esmeralda *nf*
garnet	granate *nm*
henna	henna, alheña *nf*
indigo B	azul índigo *nm*
jade	verde jade *nm*
khaki	caqui, kaki *nm*
lemon	amarillo limón *nm*
lilac	lila *nf*
magenta	magenta *nf*
mauve	malva *nf*
mustard	mostaza *nf*
ocher A	ocre *nm*
olive	(color) verde olivo *nm*
orange	(color) naranja *nf*
purple	púrpura *nf*
ruby	rojo rubí *nm*
sapphire	azul zafiro *nm*
scarlet	rojo escarlata *nm*
sepia	sepia *nf*
tobacco	atabacado *aj*
turquoise	turquesa *aj, nf*
ultramarine	ultramarino *aj, nm*
violet	violeta *aj, nm*

description

amber	ambarino *aj*
chromatic	cromático *aj*
colored	coloreado *aj*
colorful	lleno de colorido *aj*
colorless	incoloro *aj*
coppery	cobrizo *aj*
delicate	delicado *aj*
discolored	descolorido *aj*
emerald	esmeraldino *aj*
mixed	mixto *aj*

monochromatic	monocromático *aj*
multicolored A	multicolor *aj*
neutral	neutro *aj*
olive-colored	oliváceo *aj*
opalescent	opalescente *aj*
pastel	pastel *aj*
polychromatic	policromado *aj*
purple, purplish	purpúreo *aj*
rose-colored A	rosado *aj*
vibrant	vibrante *aj*

STYLES AND GENRES

abstract	abstracto *aj*
Art Deco	Art Decó *nm*
avant-garde	vanguardia *nf*
baroque	barroco *aj*
bucolic	bucólico *aj*
Byzantine	bizantino *aj*
Chinese	chinesco *aj*
contemporary, contemporaneous	contemporáneo *aj*
cubism	cubismo *nm*
Dadaism	dadaísmo *nm*
dexterous, dextrous	diestro *aj*
elaborate	elaborado *aj*
erotica	arte erótico *nm*
Fauvism	fauvismo *nm*
Gothic	gótico *aj, nm*
Greco-Roman, Graeco-Roman	grecorromano *aj*
grotesque	grotesco *aj*
kitsch	kitsch *nm*
minimalism	minimalismo *nm*
modernism	modernismo *nm*
Moorish	morisco *aj*
naturalism	naturalismo *nm*
op art	op-art *nm*
ornate	ornado *aj*
pastoral	pastoral, pastoril *aj*
photorealism	fotorealismo *nm*
pointillism	puntillismo *nm*
pop art	arte popular *nf(el)*
pre-Columbian	pre-colombino *aj*
Pre-Raphaelite	prerrafaelita *aj, nmf*
primitive	primitivo *aj*
realism	realismo *nm*
Renaissance	Renacimiento *nm*
rococo	rococó *aj, nm*
surrealism	surrealismo *nm*

PERSONS

animator	animador(a) *nmf*

artisan	artesano, -a *nmf*
artist	artista *nmf*
Bohemian	bohemio, -a *aj, nmf*
calligrapher	calígrafo, -a *nmf*
caricaturist	caricaturista *nmf*
ceramicist, ceramist	ceramista *nmf*
classicist	clasicista *nmf*
colorist Ⓐ	colorista *nmf*
cubist	cubista *nmf*
decorator	decorador(a) *nmf*
designer	diseñador(a) *nmf*
engraver	grabador(a) *nmf*
illuminator	iluminador(a) *nmf*
illustrator	ilustrador(a) *nmf*
impressionist	impresionista *nmf*
lithographer	litógrafo, -a *nmf*
maestro Ⓑ	maestro *nm*
miniaturist	miniaturista *nmf*
model	modelo *nmf*
modeler Ⓐ	modelador(a) *nmf*
painter	pintor(a) *nmf*
postimpressionist	postimpresionista *nmf*
realist	realista *nmf*
sculptor	escultor(a) *nmf*
stylist	estilista *nmf*
surrealist	surrealista *nmf*
symbolist	simbolista *nmf*

(*See also* **ART AND AESTHETICS**)

ARCHITECTURE

GENERAL TERMS

architectura	arquitectura *nf*
complex	complejo *nm*
construction	construcción *nf*
edifice	edificio *nm*
engineering	ingeniería *nf*
erect	erigir *vt*
exterior	exterior *nm*
facilities	facilidades *nfpl*
foundation	fundamento *nm*
front	frente *nm*
interior	interior *nm*
mass	masa *nf*
materials	materiales *nmpl*
model	modelo *nm*
order	orden *nm*
plan	plan *nm*
plane	plano *nm*
remodelling	remodelación *nf*
renovation	renovación *nf*

scale	escala *nf*
site	sitio *nm*
space	espacio *nm*
structure	estructura *nf*
style	estilo *nm*
texture	textura *nf*

TYPES OF CONSTRUCTION

dwellings

bungalow	bungalow *nm*
castle	castillo *nm*
chalet	chalé, chalet *nm*
condominium	condominio *nm*
hacienda	hacienda *nf*
igloo	iglú *nm*
palace	palacio *nm*
residence	residencia *nf*
teepee	tipi *nm*
villa	villa *nf*
yurt	yurt *nm*

religious

basilica	basílica *nf*
cathedral	catedral *nf*
cloister	claustro *nm*
convent	convento *nm*
hermitage	ermita *nf*
monastery	monasterio *nm*
mosque	mezquita *nf*
oratory	oratorio *nm*
pagoda	pagoda *nf*
priory	priorato *nm*
synagog(ue)	sinagoga *nf*
temple	templo *nm*
tomb	tumba *nf*

military and penal

citadel	ciudadela *nf*
fort	fuerte *nm*
fortress	fortaleza *nf*
penitentiary	penitenciaría *nf*
prison	prisión *nf*

public use

auditorium Ⓑ	auditorio *nm*
hospital	hospital *nm*
hotel	hotel *nm*
motel	motel *nm*
museum	museo *nm*
observatory	observatorio *nm*
planetarium	planetario *nm*
school	escuela *nf*

other construction

aquaduct	acueducto *nm*
astrodome	astródomo *nm*
campanile	campanario *nm*
catacombs	catacumbas *nfpl*
cenotaph	cenotafio *nm*
cistern	cisterna *nf*
dike	dique *nm*
garage	garaje *nm*
monument	monumento *nm*
obelisk	obelisco *nm*
palisade	palizada *nf*
pyramid	pirámide *nf*
silo	silo *nm*
sphinx	esfinge *nf*
terrace	terraza *nf*
viaduct	viaducto *nm*

ARCHITECTURAL FEATURES

parts of buildings

alcove	alcoba *nf*
annex	anexo *nm*
anteroom	antesala *nf*
corridor	corredor *nm*
duct	conducto *nm*
elevator	elevador *nm*
entrance	entrada *nf*
lavatory	lavatorio *nm*
patio	patio *nm*
salon	salón *nm*
veranda	veranda *nf*
vestibule	vestíbulo *nm*

structural

abacus Ⓑ	ábaco *nm*
apse	ábside *nm*
arcade	arcada *nf*
arch	arco *nm*
architrave	arquitrabe *nm*
atrium	atrio *nm*
balcony	balcón *nm*
balustrade	balaustrada *nf*
base	base *nf*
campanile	campanario *nm*
chimney	chimenea *nf*
colonnade	columnata *nf*
column	columna *nf*
crossing	crucero *nm*
cupola	cúpula *nf*
dado	dado *nm*
dome	domo *nm*
entablature	entablamento *nm*

gallery	galería *nf*
geodesic dome	domo geodésico *nm*
jamb	jamba *nf*
loggia	logia *nf*
mansard	mansarda *nf*
mastaba	mastaba *nf*
minaret	minarete *nm*
monolith	monolito *nm*
narthex	nartex *nm*
nave	nave *nf*
patio	patio *nm*
pavilion	pabellón *nm*
peristyle	peristilo *nm*
pillar	pilar *nm*
porch	porche *nm*
portal	portal *nm*
portico Ⓑ	pórtico *nm*
pylon	pilón *nm*
rotunda	rotonda *nf*
stela, stele Ⓑ	estela *nf*
tower	torre *nf*
transept	transepto *nm*
turret	torreón *nm*
veranda	veranda *nf*
ziggurat	zigurat *nm*

decorative

acanthus	acanto *nm*
arabesque	arabesco *nm*
archivolt	archivolta *nf*
attic	ático *nm*
baluster	balaustre *nm*
capital	capitel *nm*
cartouche	cartucho *nm*
caryatid	cariátide *nf*
cornice	cornisa *nf*
corona Ⓑ	corona *nf*
dentil	dentículo, dentellón *nm*
echinus	equino *nm*
entasis	éntasis *nf*
facade	fachada *nf*
festoon	festón *nm*
fountain	fuente *nf*
fresco	fresco *nm*
frieze	friso *nm*
frontispiece	frontispicio *nm*
gable	gableta *nf*
gargoyle	gárgola *nf*
girandole	girándula *nf*
helix Ⓑ	hélice *nf*
lantern	linterna *nf*
listel	listel, listón *nm*
mantel	manto *nm*

metope	métopa, metopa *nf*
molding **A**	moldura *nf*
mosaic	mosaico *nm*
motif	motivo *nm*
mural	mural *nm*
niche	nicho *nm*
ogive	ojiva *nf*
parapet	parapeto *nm*
pedestal	pedestal *nm*
pergola	pérgola *nf*
pilaster	pilastra *nf*
pinnacle	pináculo *nm*
plinth	plinto *nm*
prostyle	próstilo *aj*
quatrefoil	cuatrifolio *nm*
relief	relieve *nm*
rose window	rosetón *nm*
socle	zócalo *nm*
soffit	sofito *nm*
tracery	tracería *nf*
trefoil	trifolio *nm*
triglyph	tríglifo *nm*
tympanum **B**	tímpano *nm*
volute	voluta *nf*

MAJOR ARCHITECTURAL STYLES

baroque	barroco *aj*
Byzantine	bizantino *aj*
colonial	colonial *aj*
Corinthian	corintio *aj*
Doric	dórico *aj*
Georgian	georgiano *aj*
Gothic	gótico *aj*
Ionic	jónico *aj*
Islamic	islámico *aj*
Modernism	modernismo *nm*
post-Modernism	posmodernismo *nm*
Renaissance	Renacimiento *nm*
rococo	rococó *aj, nm*
Romanesque	románico *aj*
Tudor	tudor *aj*

MATERIALS, TOOLS, EQUIPMENT

adhesive	adhesivo *aj, nm*
adobe	adobe *nm*
aluminum **A**	aluminio *nm*
angle iron	angular *nm*
asphalt	asfalto *nm*
block	bloque *nm*
brush	brocha *nf*
bulldozer	bulldozer *nm*
cement	cemento *nm*

cementite	cementita *nf*
ceramics	cerámica *nf*
chisel	cincel *nm*
concrete	concreto *aj, nm*
cork	corcho *nm*
creosote	creosota *nf*
excavator	excavadora *mf*
fiberglass **A**	fibra de vidrio *nf*
granite	granito *nm*
gravel	grava *nf*
insulation	aislamiento *nm*
latex	látex *nm*
macadam	macadán *nm*
marble	mármol *nm*
masonry	masonería *nf*
mastic	mástique *nm*
mortar	mortero *nm*
mortise	mortaja *nf*
oxyacetylene (torch)	oxiacetilénico *aj*
paint	pintura *nf*
panel	panel *nm*
paneling **A**	paneles *nmpl*
pickax **A**	piqueta *nf*
pile	pilar *nm*
pincer	pinza *nf*
plastic	plástico *aj, nm*
plumb	plomo *nm*
plumbing	plomería *nf*
plummet	plomada *nf*
post	poste *nm*
pulley	polea *nf*
punch	punzón *nm*
rock chips	rocalla *nf*
sandpaper	papel de lija *nm*
stake	estaca *nf*
stucco	estuco *nm*
terra-cotta	terracota *nf*
terrazzo	terrazo *nm*

TERMS IN CONSTRUCTION

air conditioning	aire acondicionado *nm*
carpentry	carpintería *nf*
conduit	conducto *nm*
excavation	excavación *nf*
generator	generador *nm*
installation	instalación *nf*
joint	junta *nf*
lamination	laminación *nf*
lot	lote *nm*
occupancy	ocupación *nf*
painting	pintura *nf*
permit	permiso *nm*
prefabrication	prefabricación *nf*

reinforce	reforzar *vt*	constructor	constructor(a) *nmf*
specification	especificación *nf*	contractor	contratista *nmf*
support	soporte *nm*	decorator	decorador(a) *nmf*
suspension	suspensión *nf*	electrician	electricista *nmf*
vacant	vacante *aj*	engineer	ingeniero, -a *nmf*
ventilation	ventilación *nf*	master	maestro, -a *aj, nmf*
zoning	zonificación *nf*	occupant	ocupante *nmf*
		painter	pintor(a) *nmf*
		plumber	plomero *nm*

PERSONS

architect	arquitecto, -a *nmf*
carpenter	carpintero, -a *nmf*

(*See also* **buildings and monuments** under **ANCIENT CIVILIZATIONS**; **TECHNOLOGY OVERVIEW**)

Knowledge, Faith, and the Paranormal

PHILOSOPHY

GENERAL TERMS

abstraction	abstracción *nf*
causality	causalidad *nf*
concept	concepto *nm*
doctrine	doctrina *nf*
ethic	ética *nf*
existence	existencia *nf*
fate	fatalidad *nf*
form	forma *nf*
hypostasis	hipóstasis *nf*
ism	ismo *nm*
medieval, mediaeval	medieval *aj*
modern	moderno *aj*
monad	mónada *nf*
morality	moralidad *nf*
object	objeto *nm*
philosophy	filosofía *nf*
postulate	postulado *nm*
reality	realidad *nf*
Socratic	socrático *aj*
universal	universal *aj, nm*

BRANCHES OF PHILOSOPHY

major fields

aesthetics, esthetics	estética *nf*
epistemology	epistemología *nf*
ethics	ética *nf*
logic	lógica *nf*
metaphysics	metafísica *nf*

other fields

cosmology	cosmología *nf*
etiology	etiología *nf*
ontology	ontología *nf*
semiotics	semiótica *nf*
teleology	teleología *nf*

WESTERN PHILOSOPHIES

ancient philosophy

Aristotelianism	aristotelismo *nm*
atomism	atomismo *nm*
cynicism	cinismo *nm*
Epicureanism	epicureísmo *nm*
hedonism	hedonismo *nm*
logos	logos *nm*
Neoplatonism	neoplatonismo *nm*
peripatetic	peripatético *aj*
Platonism	platonismo *nm*
skepticism Ⓐ	escepticismo *nm*
stoicism	estoicismo *nm*

medieval philosophy

Gnosticism	(g)nosticismo *nm*
scholasticism	escolasticismo *nm*

modern philosophy

constructivism	constructivismo *nm*
empiricism	empirismo *nm*
existentialism	existencialismo *nm*
materialism	materialismo *nm*
mentalism	mentalismo *nm*
nihilism	nihilismo *nm*
obscurantism	oscurantismo *nm*
phenomenology	fenomenología *nf*
positivism	positivismo *nm*
pragmatics	pragmática *nf*
pragmatism	pragmatismo *nm*
rationalism	racionalismo *nm*
transcendentalism	tra(n)scendentalismo *nm*
utilitarianism	utilitarismo *nm*

political philosophies

anarchism	anarquismo *nm*
authoritarianism	autoritarismo *nm*
conservatism	conservadurismo, conservatismo *nm*
liberalism	liberalismo *nm*
nonviolence	no violencia *nf*
pluralism	pluralismo *nm*

other philosophical theories

animalism	animalismo *nm*
determinism	determinismo *nm*
dualism	dualismo *nm*
idealism	idealismo *nm*
individualism	individualismo *nm*

instrumentalism	instrumentalismo *nm*
mechanism	mecanismo *nm*
monism	monismo *nm*
moralism	moralismo *nm*
nativism	nativismo *nm*
naturalism	naturalismo *nm*
objectivism	objetivismo *nm*
parallelism	paralelismo *nm*
realism	realismo *nm*
relativism	relativismo *nm*
solipsism	solipsismo *nm*
spiritualism	espiritualismo *nm*
subjectivism	subjetivismo *nm*
vitalism	vitalismo *nm*

ORIENTAL PHILOSOPHIES

Buddhism	budismo *nm*
Confucianism	confucianismo *nm*
Hinduism	hinduismo *nm*
Islam	islam *nm*
Jainism	jainismo, yainismo *nm*
nirvana	nirvana *nf*
Taoism	taoísmo *nm*
yang	yang *nm*
yin	yin *nm*

TERMS IN LOGIC

general

analytics	analítica *nf*
argument	argumento *nm*
category	categoría *nf*
cause	causa *nf*
consequence	consecuencia *nf*
copula Ⓑ	cópula *nf*
dialectics	dialéctica *nf*
effect	efecto *nm*
fallacy	falacia *nf*
figure	figura *nf*
genus Ⓑ	género *nm*
logic	lógica *nf*
method	método *nm*
modality	modalidad *nf*
mode	modo *nm*
proposition	proposición *nf*
quantifier	cuantificador *nm*
rationality	racionalidad *nf*
reason	razón *nf*
relationship	relación *nf*
sophism	sofisma *nm*
species Ⓑ	especie *nf*
symbol	símbolo *nm*
system	sistema *nm*

validity	validez *nf*

operations

connection Ⓐ	conexión *nf*
contradiction	contradicción *nf*
conversion	conversión *nf*
deduction	deducción *nf*
disjunction	disyunción *nf*
implication	implicación *nf*
induction	inducción *nf*
nexus Ⓑ	nexo *nm*
opposition	oposición *nf*
predication	predicación *nf*
rationalization	racionalización *nf*
reasoning	razonamiento *nm*

statements

antecedent	antecedente *nm*
assertion	aserción, aserto *nf, nm*
axiom	axioma *nm*
conclusion	conclusión *nf*
corollary	corolario *nm*
formula Ⓑ	fórmula *nf*
homology	homología *nf*
inference	inferencia *nf*
lemma	lema *nm*
paradox	paradoja *nf*
particular	particular *aj, nm*
precept	precepto *nm*
predicate	predicado *nm*
premise	premisa *nf*
syllogism	silogismo *nm*
tautology	tautología *nf*

other terms

analyze Ⓐ	analizar *vt*
apparent	aparente *aj*
coherence	coherencia *nf*
coherent	coherente *aj*
conditional	condicional *aj*
construct	constructo *nm*
contrary	contrario *aj, nm*
convert	convertir *vt*
erroneous	erróneo *aj*
formal	formal *aj*
implicit	implícito *aj*
incompatible	incompatible *aj*
invalid	inválido *aj*
negative	negativo *aj*
ramification	ramificación *nf*
relational	relacional *aj*
spurious	espurio *aj*

PERSONS

Aristotelian	aristotélico *aj, nm*
Cartesian	cartesiano, -a *aj, nmf*
casuist	casuista *nmf*
constructivist	constructivista *aj, nmf*
dialectician	dialéctico, -a *nmf*
empiricist	empírico, -a *nmf*
Epicurean	epicureo, -a *nmf*
existentialist	existentialista *nmf*
fatalist	fatalista *nmf*
hedonist	hedonista *nmf*
Hegelian	hegeliano, -a *aj, nmf*
iconoclast	iconoclasta *nmf*
instrumentalist	instrumentista *nmf*
Kantian	kantiano, -a *aj, nmf*
logician	lógico, -a *nmf*
moralist	moralista *nmf*
nihilist	nihilista *nmf*
philosopher	filósofo *nmf*
positivist	positivista *nmf*
pragmatist	pragmatista *nmf*
rationalist	racionalista *nmf*
realist	realista *nmf*
skeptic Ⓐ	escéptico, -a *nmf*
sophist	sofista *nmf*
spiritualist	espiritista *nmf*
stoic	estoico, -a *nmf*
superman	superhombre *nm*
utilitarian	utilitarista *aj, nmf*

(*See also philosophers* under **ANCIENT CIVILIZATIONS**; *beliefs* and *doctrines* under **RELIGION**)

RELIGION

GENERAL TERMS

adoration	adoración *nf*
celebration	celebración *nf*
ceremony	ceremonia *nf*
charity	caridad *nf*
conscience	conciencia *nf*
credo, creed	credo *nm*
cult	culto *nm*
deity	deidad *nf*
dissent	disenso *nm*
divinity	divinidad *nf*
doctrine	doctrina *nf*
ecstasy	éxtasis *nm*
ex cathedra	ex cátedra *av*
faith	fe *nf*
glory	gloria *nf*
intolerance	intolerancia *nf*

martyrdom	martirio *nm*
morality	moralidad *nf*
mystery	misterio *nm*
observance	observancia *nf*
pardon	perdón *nm*
persecution	persecución *nf*
piety	piedad *nf*
religion	religión *nf*
rite	rito *nm*
ritual	ritual *aj, nm*
sacred	sagrado, sacro *aj*
spiritual	espiritual *aj*
supernatural	sobrenatural *aj*
theology	teología *nf*

ASPECTS OF RELIGION

types of religion

animism	animismo *nm*
atheism	ateísmo *nm*
demonism	demonismo *nm*
monotheism	monoteísmo *nm*
pantheism	panteísmo *nm*
polytheism	politeísmo *nm*

doctrines

agnosticism	agnosticismo *nm*
anabaptism	anabaptismo *nm*
apologetics	apologética *nf*
asceticism	ascetismo *nm*
caste	casta *nf*
celibacy	celibato *nm*
clericalism	clericalismo *nm*
creationism	creacionismo *nm*
deism	deísmo *nm*
dispensation	dispensa *nf*
dogma Ⓑ	dogma *nm*
dualism	dualismo *nm*
ecumenism	ecumenismo *nm*
ethics	ética *nf*
evangelism	evangelismo *nm*
fetishism	fetichismo *nm*
fundamentalism	fundamentalismo *nm*
Gnosticism	(g)nosticismo *nm*
heterodoxy	heterodoxia *nf*
humanism	humanismo *nm*
karma	karma *nf*
messianism	mesianismo *nm*
monasticism	monaquismo, monacato *nm*
Mosaic law	ley mosaica *nf*
mysticism	misticismo *nm*
omnipotence	omnipotencia *nf*

orthodoxy	ortodoxia *nf*
paganism	paganismo *nm*
Pietism	pietismo *nm*
ritualism	ritualismo *nm*
Satanism	satanismo *nm*
schism	cisma *nm*
scholasticism	escolasticismo *nm*
sectarianism	sectarismo *nm*
secularism	secularismo *nm*
spiritism	espiritismo *nm*
spiritualism	espiritualismo *nm*
syncretism	sincretismo *nm*
theocracy	teocracia *nf*
theosophy	teosofía *nf*

beliefs

Assumption	Asunción *nf*
destiny	destino *nm*
exoneration	exoneración *nf*
expiation	expiación *nf*
immanence, immanency	inmanencia *nf*
immortality	inmortalidad *nf*
incarnation	encarnación *nf*
inferno	infierno *nm*
limbo	limbo *nm*
nirvana	nirvana *nf*
perdition	perdición *nf*
predestination	predestinación *nf*
providence	providencia *nf*
purgatory	purgatorio *nm*
redemption	redención *nf*
reincarnation	reencarnación *nf*
resurrection	resurrección *nf*
salvation	salvación *nf*
sanctity	santidad *nf*
savior Ⓐ	salvador(a) *nmf*
superstition	superstición *nf*
theism	teísmo *nm*
transcendence	tra(n)scendencia *nf*
transfiguration	tra(n)sfiguración *nf*
transmigration	tra(n)smigración *nf*
trinity	trinidad *nf*

holy places

abbey	abadía *nf*
altar	altar *nm*
baptistery, baptistry	baptisterio, bautisterio *nm*
cathedral	catedral *nf*
chapel	capilla *nf*
cloister	claustro *nm*
confessional	confesionario *nm*

convent	convento *nm*
mission	misión *nf*
monastery	monasterio *nm*
mosque	mezquita *nf*
pagoda	pagoda *nf*
paradise	paraíso *nm*
priory	priorato *nm*
sacristy	sacristía *nf*
sanctuary	santuario *nm*
synagog(ue)	sinagoga *nf*
temple	templo *nm*

religious titles

abbess	abadesa *nf*
abbot	abad *nm*
archbishop	arzobispo *nm*
archdeacon	archidiácono *nm*
bishop	obispo *nm*
chaplain	capellán *nm*
Dalai Lama	Dalai Lama *nm*
deacon	diácono *nm*
deaconess	diaconisa *nf*
dervish	derviche *nm*
fakir	faquir *nm*
friar	fraile *nm*
imam	imán *nm*
lama	lama *nm*
mahatma	mahatma *nm*
metropolitan	metropolitano *nm*
ordinary	ordinario *nm*
pastor	pastor *nm*
pontiff	pontífice *nm*
Pope	papa *nm*
prelate	prelado *nm*
primate	primado *nm*
prior	prior *nm*
prioress	priora *nf*
rabbi	rabí *nm*
rector	rector *nm*
reverend	reverendo *nm*
vicar	vicario *nm*

organizations and offices

archdiocese	archidiócesis, arquidiócesis *nf*
benefice	beneficio *nm*
bishopric	obispado *nm*
college	colegio *nm*
consistory	consistorio *nm*
deaconry	diaconado, diaconato *nm*
diocese	diócesis Ⓒ *nf*
episcopate	episcopado *nm*

order	orden *nf*
papacy, popedom	papado *nm*
parish	parroquía *nf*
prelacy	prelacia *nf*
rabbinate	rabinato *nm*
synod	sínodo *nm*
Vatican	Vaticano *nm*
vicarage	vicaría *nf*

scholarship and translation

alteration	alteración *nf*
concordance	concordancia *nf*
demonology	demonología *nf*
emendation	enmienda *nf*
eschatology	escatología *nf*
hagiography	hagiografía *nf*
index Ⓑ	índice *nm*
martyrology	martirologio *nm*
midrash Ⓑ	midrash *nm*
seminary	seminario *nm*
yeshiva	yeshiva *nf*

other terms

apostasy	apostasía *nf*
celestial	celestial *aj*
devout	devoto *aj*
interdict, interdiction	interdicto *nm*
octave	octava *nf*
omniscient	omnisciente *aj*
practice Ⓐ	practicar *vt*
prebend	prebenda *nf*
temporal	temporal *aj*

NAMES

founders of religions

Abraham	Abrahán *nm*
Buddha	Buda *nm*
Christ	Cristo *nm*
Confucius	Confucio *nm*
Jesus Christ	Jesucristo *nm*
Luther	Lutero *nm*
Mohammed, Muhammad	Mahoma *nm*
Moses	Moisés *nm*
Zarathustra	Zaratustra *nm*
Zoroaster	Zoroastro *nm*

major world religions

Buddhism	budismo *nm*
Christianity	cristiandad *nf*
Confucianism	confucianismo *nm*
Hinduism	hinduismo *nm*
Islam	islam *nm*
Judaism	judaísmo *nm*
Shinto	sintoísmo *nm*
Taoism	taoísmo *nm*

other religions and groups

Anglicanism	anglicanismo *nm*
Bahaism	bahaísmo *nm*
Brahmanism	brahmanismo *nm*
Calvinism	calvinismo *nm*
Catholicism	catolicismo *nm*
Congregationalism	congregationalismo *nm*
Jansenism	jansenismo *nm*
Lutheranism	luteranismo *nm*
Methodism	metodismo *nm*
Mormonism	mormonismo *nm*
Orthodox Church	Iglesia ortodoxa *nf*
Protestantism	protestantismo *nm*
Quakerism	cuaquerismo *nm*
Scientology	cientología *nf*
Sikhism	sikhismo *nm*
Unification Church	Iglesia de la Unificación *nf*
Unitarianism	unitarismo *nm*
Voodoo	vudú *nm*
Zoroastrianism	zoroastrismo *nm*

deities

Allah	Alá *nm*
Brahma	Brahma *nm*
Creator	Creador *nm*
Jehovah	Jehová *nm*
Krishna	Krisna *nm*
Messiah	Mesías *nm*
Redeemer	Redentor *nm*
Shiva	Siva *nm*
Vishnu	Visnú, Vishnú *nm*
Yahweh, Yahveh	Jahvé *nm*

holy cities

Bethlehem	Belén *nm*
Jerusalem	Jerusalén *nf*
Mecca	Meca *nf*
Rome	Roma *nf*
Zion (obs)	Sión *nm*

sacred books

Bhagavad-Gita	Bhagavad-Gita *nf*
Bible	Biblia *nf*
Kamasutra	Kama-Sutra
Koran	Corán, Alcorán *nm*
Talmud	Talmud *nm*
Torah	Tora *nm or nf*
Veda	Veda *nm*

holidays and celebrations

Advent	Adviento *nm*
Chanukah, Hanukkah	Janucá *nm*
Epiphany	Epifanía *nf*
Pentecost	Pentecostés *nm*
Purim	purim *nm*
Ramadan	Ramadán *nm*
Yom Kippur	Yom Kippur *nm*

PRACTICES AND TRADITIONS

rites and ceremonies

ablutions	ablución *nf*
absolution	absolución *nf*
apotheosis Ⓑ	apoteosis Ⓒ *nf*
baptism	bautismo, bautizo *nm*
bar mitzvah	bar mitzvah *nm*
bat mitzvah	bat mitzvah *nm*
beatification	beatificación *nf*
canonization	canonización *nf*
catechism	catecismo *nm*
circumcision	circuncisión *nf*
communion	comunión *nf*
confession	confesión *nf*
confirmation	confirmación *nf*
consecration	consagración *nf*
contemplation	contemplación *nf*
conversion	conversión *nf*
deification	deificación *nf*
diabolism	diabolismo *nm*
excommunication	excomunión *nf*
festival	festival *nm*
flagellation	flagelación *nf*
funeral	funeral *nm*
genuflection Ⓐ	genuflexión *nf*
glorification	glorificación *nf*
idolatry	idolatría *nf*
immersion	inmersión *nf*
indulgence	indulgencia *nf*
invocation	invocación *nf*
jubilee	jubileo *nm*
liturgy	liturgia *nf*
mass	misa *nf*
meditation	meditación *nf*
mortification	mortificación *nf*
occultism	ocultismo *nm*
offering	ofrenda *nf*
Offertory	ofertorio *nm*
ordination	ordenación *nf*
penitence	penitencia *nf*
procession	procesión *nf*
propitiation	propiciación *nf*
purification	purificación *nf*

repentance	arrepentimiento *nm*
response	respuesta *nf*
Sabbath	sábado *nm*
sacrament	sacramento *nm*
sacrifice	sacrificio *nm*
sanctification	santificación *nf*
service	servicio *nm*
supplication	súplica, suplicación *nf*
vespers	vísperas *nfpl*

eating and drinking

abstinence	abstinencia *nf*
dietary (laws)	dietético *aj*
feast	fiesta *nf*
kosher	kosher *aj*
libation	libación *nf*
renunciation	renuncia *nf*
seder	seder *nm*
vegetarianism	vegetarianismo *nm*

birth and death

cremation	cremación *nf*
extreme unction	extremaunción *nf*
reliquary	relicario *nm*
vigil	vigilia *nf*

objects, charms, symbols

calix Ⓑ	cáliz *nm*
chalice	cáliz *nm*
cross	cruz *nf*
crucifix	crucifijo *nm*
Eucharist	eucaristía *nf*
fetish	fetiche *nm*
Holy Grail (obs)	Santo Grial *nm*
Host	hostia *nf*
hyssop (obs)	hisopo *nm*
icon, ikon	icono *nm*
idol	ídolo *nm*
incense	incienso *nm*
menorah	menorá *nf*
oblation	oblación *nf*
paschal	pascual *aj*
paten	patena *nf*
phallus Ⓑ	falo *nm*
pulpit	púlpito *nm*
pyx	píxide *nf*
rosary	rosario *nm*
tabernacle (on altar)	tabernáculo *nm*
talisman	talismán *nm*
torii	torii *nm*
totem	tótem *nm*

clothing and appearance

alb	alba *nf(el)*

44

habit	hábito *nm*
miter	mitra *nf*
mozetta, muzetta	muceta *nf*
pallium	palio *nm*
phylactery	filacteria *nf*
scapular	escapulario *nm*
tallit, tallith	taled *nm*
tiara	tiara *nf*
tonsure	tonsura *nf*
vestment	vestidura, vestimenta *nf*

sins and crimes

adultery	adulterio *nm*
anathema	anatema *nm*
attrition	atrición *nf*
blasphemy	blasfemia *nf*
corruption	corrupción *nf*
deicide (god killing)	deicidio *nm*
envy	envidia *nf*
fornication	fornicación *nf*
gluttony	glotonería *nf*
heresy	herejía *nf*
impenitence	impenitencia *nf*
impiety	impiedad *nf*
infidelity	infidelidad *nf*
nonobservance	inobservancia *nf*
offense Ⓐ	ofensa *nf*
peccadillo Ⓑ	pecadillo *nm*
profanation	profanación *nf*
sacrilege	sacrilegio *nm*
sodomy	sodomía *nf*
temptation	tentación *nf*
transgression	tra(n)sgresión *nf*

prayers

amen	amén *intj*
benediction	bendición *nf*
breviary	breviario *nm*
doxology	doxología *nf*
grace	gracia *nf*
Hallelujah	aleluya *nf*
litany	letanía *nf*
mantra	mantra *nm*
paternoster	paternóster *nm*

other language uses

allegory	alegoría *nf*
bull	bula *nf*
encyclical	encíclica *nf*
homily	homilia *nf*
parable	parábola *nf*
scripture	escritura *nf*
sermon	sermón *nm*

music and art

canon	canon *nm*
chant	canto *nm*
choir	coro *nm*
Gregorian (chant)	gregoriano *aj*
halo Ⓑ	halo *nm*
hymn	himno *nm*
hymnal	himnario *nm*
intone	entonar *vt*
introit	introito *nm*
Kyrie	kirie *nm*
Madonna	Madona
oratorio	oratorio *nm*
passion	pasión *nf*
psalm	salmo *nm*
psalmody	salmodia *nf*
recessional	himno recesional *nm*
spiritual	espiritual *nm*

supernatural beings

angel	ángel *nm*
cherub Ⓑ	querubín *nm*
Christ	Cristo *nm*
Creator	Creador *nm*
demon	demonio *nm*
devil	diablo *nm*
seraph Ⓑ	serafín *nm*
spirit	espíritu *nm*

MEMBERS OF RELIGIOUS GROUPS

larger groups

Bahai	bahai *nmf*
Buddhist	budista *aj, nmf*
Catholic	católico, -a *aj, nmf*
Christian	cristiano, -a *aj, nmf*
Confucianist	confucianista, confuciano, -a *aj, nmf*
Hindu	hindú *aj, nmf*
Islamite	islamita *nmf*
Jew	judío, -a *nmf*
Mohammedan	mahometano, -a *aj, nmf*
Moslem, Muslim	musulmán, -ana *aj, nmf*
Protestant	protestante *aj, nmf*

Protestants

Adventist	adventista *aj, nmf*
Anabaptist	anabaptista *aj, nmf*
Anglican	anglicano, -a *aj, nmf*
Baptist	bautista *aj, nmf*
Calvinist	calvinista *aj, nmf*

Congregationalist	congregacionalista *aj, nmf*
Coptic	copto, -a *aj, nmf*
Episcopalian	episcopalista *aj, nmf*
Huguenot (obs)	hugonote *aj, nmf*
Lutheran	luterano, -a *aj, nmf*
Mennonite	menonita *aj, nmf*
Methodist	metodista *aj, nmf*
Pentecostal	pentecostal *aj, nmf*
Presbyterian	presbiteriano, -a *aj, nmf*
Puritan (obs)	puritano, -a *aj, nmf*
Quaker	cuáquero, -a *aj, nmf*

Jews

Ashkenazi 🅱	askenazi *aj, nmf*
Conservative	conservador(a) *aj, nmf*
Hasidism	hasidismo, jasidismo *nm*
Orthodox	ortodoxo *aj*
Reconstructionist	reconstruccionista *aj*
Reform, Reformed	reformado *aj*
Sephardi	sefardí, sefardita *nmf*

Muslims

Hizbollah	hezbolá *nmf*
mujaheddin, mujahedeen	mujahedín, muyahidin *nmpl*
Shiite	chiíta, shií *aj, nmf*
Sufi	sufí *nm*
Sunni	suní, sunita *aj, nmf*

Catholic orders

Augustinian	agustino, -a *nmf*
Benedictine	benedictino *nm*
Capuchin	capuchino *nm*
Carmelite	carmelita *nmf*
Dominican	dominico *nm*
Franciscan	franciscano *aj, nm*
Jacobin	jacobino *nm*
Jesuit	jesuita *nf*
Trappist	trapense *nm*

other groups

Brahman, Brahmin	brahmán, brahmín *nm*
Druse, Druze	druso, -a *aj, nmf*
Mormon	mormón, -ona *aj, nmf*
Rastafarian	rastafariano, -a *aj, nmf*
Rosicrucian	rosacruz *aj, nmf*
Scientologist	cientolólogo, -a *nmf*
Sephardim	sefardíes *nmfpl*
Sikh	Sikh *aj, nmf*
Unitarian	unitario, -a *aj, nmf*
Universalist	universalista *aj, nmf*

Zen (Buddhist)	zen *nm*
Zoroastrian	zoroástrico, -a *nmf*

HISTORICAL TERMS

persecution against Jews

anti-Semitism	antisemitismo *nm*
Diaspora	diáspora *nf*
ghetto 🅱	gueto, ghetto *nm*
Holocaust	Holocausto *nm*
Inquisition	Inquisición *nf*
pogrom	pogromo *nm*

other terms

Counter-Reformation	Contrarreforma *nf*
Crusade	cruzada *nf*
Puritanism (obs)	puritanismo *nm*
Reformation	Reforma *nf*

PERSONS

groups

clergy	clero *nm*
congregation	congregación *nf*
denomination	denominación *nf*
laity	laicado *nm*
sect	secta *nf*

scholars

acolyte	acólito *nm*
cabalist	cabalista *nmf*
catechumen	catecúmeno, -a *nmf*
hagiographer	hagiógrafo, -a *nmf*
novitiate	noviciado, -a *nmf*
seminarian	seminarista *nmf*
Talmudist	talmudista *nmf*
theologian	teólogo *nm*

special-purpose practitioners

baptizer	bautista *nmf*
cantor	cantor(a) *nmf*
clergyman	clérigo *nm*
clergywoman 🅱	clériga *nf*
cleric	clérigo, -a *nmf*
confessor	confesor(a) *nmf*
curate	cura *nm*
ecclesiastic	eclesiástico, -a *nmf*
evangelist	evangelista, evangelizador(a) *nmf*
exorcist	exorcista *nmf*
guardian	guardián, -ana *nmf*
guru	gurú, guru 🅲 *nmf*
inquisitor (obs)	inquisidor(a) *nmf*

lector	lector *nm*
legate	legado *nm*
liturgist	liturgista *nmf*
Magus (obs) 🅱	mago *nm*
minister	ministro, -a *nmf*
missionary	misionero, -a *nmf*
monk	monje *nm*
muezzin	muecín *nm*
nuncio	nuncio *nm*
officiant	oficiante *nm*
patron saint	patrono, -a *nmf*
prophet	profeta *nm*
psalmist	salmista *nmf*
rabbi	rabino *nm*
shaman	shamán, chamán *nm*
spiritualist	espiritista *nmf*
yogi	yogui *nmf*

other persons

agnostic	agnóstico, -a *aj, nmf*
anti-Christian	anticristiano, -a *aj, nmf*
anti-Semite	antisemita *nmf*
ascetic	asceta *nmf*
atheist	ateo, -a *nmf*
blasphemer	blasfemador(a) *nmf*
celebrant	celebrante *nmf*
celibate	célibe *aj, nmf*
convert	converso, -a *nmf*
creationist	creacionista *nmf*
Crusader (obs)	cruzado *nmf*
deist	deísta *nmf*
devotee	devoto, -a *nmf*
disciple	discípulo, -a *nmf*
dissenter	disidente *nmf*
dogmatist	dogmatista *nmf*
fetishist	fetichista *nmf*
flagellant	flagelador(a) *nmf*
fornicator	fornicador(a) *nmf*
fundamentalist	fundamentalista *nmf*
gentile	gentil *aj, nmf*
heretic	hereje *nmf*
iconoclast	iconoclasta *nmf*
idolater	idólatra *nmf*
impenitent	impenitente *aj, nmf*
infidel	infiel *nmf*
Jacobin	jacobino, -a *nmf*
latitudinarian	latitudinario, -a *aj, nmf*
martyr	mártir *nmf*
mendicant	mendicante *nmf*
neophyte	neófito, -a *nmf*
novice	novicio, -a *nmf*
oblate	oblato *nm*
pagan	pagano, -a *aj, nmf*

papist	papista *nmf*
patron	patrón, -ona *nmf*
penitent	penitente *nmf*
proselyte	prosélito, -a *nmf*
religious person	religioso, -a *nmf*
sacrilegious person	sacrílego, -a *nmf*
saint	santo, -a *nmf*
supplicant	suplicante *aj, nmf*
tempter	tentador(a) *nmf*
temptress	tentadora *nf*
theist	teísta *nmf*
theosophist	teósofo, -a *nmf*
transgressor	tra(n)sgresor(a) *nmf*
untouchable	intocable *aj, nmf*
Zionist	sionista *aj, nmf*

RELATED TERMS

Ashkenazi	askenazita *aj*
Biblical	bíblico *aj*
Christianize	acristianizar *vt*
Hasidic	hasídico *aj*
Islamic	islámico *aj*
Jewish	judío *aj*
Judaic	judaico *aj*
Judaica *nsg*	cosas judaicas *nfpl*
Judeo-Christian	judeocristiano *aj*
Mormon	mormónico *aj*
Sephardic	sefardí *aj*
Talmudic	talmúdico *aj*

(*See also* **ANCIENT CIVILIZATIONS**; **THE BIBLE**; *religious phenomena* under **MAGIC**; *OTHER ANCIENT DEITIES* under **MYTHOLOGY**)

MAGIC

GENERAL TERMS

arcane	arcano *aj*
extrasensory	extrasensorial *aj*
fantasy	fantasía *nf*
magic	mágico *aj, nm*
occult	oculto *aj*
paranormal	paranormal *aj*
prediction	predicción *nf*
pseudoscience	pseudociencia *nf*
supernatural	sobrenatural *aj*
superstition	superstición *nf*
surreal	surrealista *aj*

FORMS OF MAGIC

pseudosciences

alchemy	alquimia *nf*

astrology	astrología *nf*
chiromancy	quiromancia *nf*
graphology	grafología *nf*
parapsychology	parasicología *nf*
phrenology	frenología *nf*
physiognomy	fisionomía *nf*
psychokinesis	psicocinesis *nf*
telekinesis	telequinesis *nf*
telepathy	telepatía *nf*
theosophy	teosofía *nf*

entertainment

cards	cartas *nf*
disappearance	desaparición *nf*
escape	escape *nm*
hypnosis Ⓑ	hipnosis *nf*
illusion	ilusión *nf*
levitation	levitación *nf*
mentalism	mentalismo *nm*
prestidigitation	prestidigitación *nf*
trick	truco *nm*

prediction

aeromancy	aeromancia *nf*
augur (obs)	augur *nm*
augury	augurio *nm*
clairvoyance	clarividencia *nf*
divination	adivinación *nf*
geomancy	geomancia *nf*
numerology	numerología *nf*
oracle (obs)	oráculo *nm*
precognition	precognición *nf*
premonition	premonición *nf*
presage	presagio *nm*
prescience	presciencia *nf*
presentiment	presentimiento *nm*
prevision	previsión *nf*
pyromancy	piromancia *nf*
vaticination	vaticinio *nm*

religious phenomena

apparition	aparición *nf*
astral (spirit)	astral *aj*
avatar	avatar *nm*
cabala	cábala *nf*
charisma	carisma *nm*
exorcism	exorcismo *nm*
manifestation	manifestación *nf*
metempsychosis	metempsicosis *nf*
miracle	milagro *nm*
mystery	misterio *nm*
mysticism	misticismo *nm*
occultism	ocultismo *nm*

possession	posesión *nf*
reincarnation	reencarnación *nf*
taboo	tabú Ⓒ *nm*
theurgy	teurgia *nf*
trance	trance *nm*
transubstantiation	transubstanciación *nf*
vision	visión, vista *nf*
visitation	visitación *nf*
voodoo	vudú *nm*

prediction in religion

preordination	preordinación *nf*
prophecy	profecía *nf*
revelation	revelación *nf*
sign	señal *nf*

communication with the dead

evocation	evocación *nf*
necromancy	nigromancía *nf*
Ouija board	tablera de ouija *nf*
spiritism	espiritismo *nm*

other terms

black magic	magia negra *nf*
enchantment	encantamiento *nm*
enigma	enigma *nm*
metamorphosis Ⓑ	metamorfosis Ⓒ *nf*
phantasmagoria	fantasmagoria *nf*
vampirism	vampirismo *nm*

TOOLS AND EQUIPMENT

words and actions

abracadabra!	¡abracadabra! *nm*
hex	hechizo *nm*
invocation	invocación *nf*
open sesame!	¡ábrete sésame! *nm*
ritual	ritual *nm*

objects and symbols

amulet	amuleto *nm*
crystal ball	bola de cristal *nf, nm*
fetish	fetiche *nm*
pentacle	pentáculo *nm*
periapt	periapto *nm*
swastika	esvástica *nf*
talisman	talismán *nm*
tarot	tarot *nm*
tea leaves	hojas de té *nfpl, nm*

substances

aura	aura *nf(el)*
ectoplasm	ectoplasma *nm*

elixir	elíxir *nm*
incense	incienso *nm*
philter Ⓐ	filtro *nm*
potion	poción *nf*

supernatural beings

genie Ⓑ	genio *nm*
incubus Ⓑ	incubo *nm*
jinn, jinni Ⓑ	genio *nm*
phantasm, phantom	fantasma *nm*
poltergeist	poltergeist *nm*
specter Ⓐ	espectro *nm*
spirit	espíritu *nm*
vampire	vampiro, vampiresa *nm, nf*
zombie, zombi	zombie, zombi *nmf*

TERMS IN ASTROLOGY

signs of the Zodiac

Aquarius	Acuario *nm*
Aries	Aries *nm*
Cancer	Cáncer *nm*
Capricorn	Capricornio *nm*
Gemini	Géminis *nmpl*
Leo	Leo *nm*
Libra	Libra *nf*
Pisces	Piscis *nm*
Sagittarius	Sagitario *nm*
Scorpio	Escorpio *nm*
Taurus	Tauro *nm*
Virgo	Virgo *nm*

other terms

ascendant, ascendent	ascendente *aj*
aspect	aspecto *nm*
astral	astral *aj*
horoscope	horóscopo *nm*
juxtaposition	yuxtaposición *nf*
opposition	oposición *nf*
sign	signo *nm*
vanish	desvanecerse *vr*

PERSONS

astrologer	astrólogo, -a *nmf*
chiromancer	quiromantico, -a *nmf*
clairvoyant	clarividente *nmf*
enchanter/enchantress	encantador(a) *nmf*
exorcist	exorcista *nmf*
fakir	faquir *nm*
illusionist	ilusionista *nmf*
magician	mágico, -a *nmf*
magus (obs) Ⓑ	mago *nm*
medium	médium *nmf*
mentalist	mentalista *nmf*
mystic	místico, -a *nmf*
occultist	ocultista *nmf*
parapsychologist	parasicólogo, -a *nmf*
phrenologist	frenólogo *nmf*
prophet	profeta/profetisa *nmf*
shaman	shamán, chamán *nm*
spiritualist	espiritista *nmf*
visionary	visionario, -a *aj, nmf*

(*See also* creatures under **THE BIBLE**; *folklore and legend* under **LITERATURE**; **MYTHOLOGY**; *supernatural beings* under **RELIGION**)

Daily Living

THE CITY

GENERAL TERMS

city	ciudad *nf*
county	condado *nm*
district	distrito *nm*
diversity	diversidad *nf*
location	localización *nf*
megalopolis	megalópolis *nf*
metropolis	metrópoli *nf*
municipality	municipio *nm*
ordinance	ordenanza *nf*
population	población *nf*
suburbia *nsg*	suburbios *nmpl*
urban	urbano *aj*

URBAN PROBLEMS

congestion	congestión *nf*
crime	crimen *nm*
delinquency	delincuencia *nf*
density (population)	densidad *nf*
education	educación *nf*
graffiti *nsg* or *npl*	graffiti *nmpl*
illumination	iluminación *nf*
planning	planificación *nf*
pollution	polución *nf*
poverty	pobreza *nf*
privacy	privacidad *nf*
prostitution	prostitución *nf*
race relations	relaciones raciales *nfpl*
recreation	recreación, recreo *nf, nm*
recycling	reciclaje *nm*
smog	esmog *nm*
traffic	tráfico *nm*
transportation	tra(n)sportación *nf*
unemployment	desempleo *nm*
urban renewal	renovación urbana *aj*
zoning	zonificación *nf*

SECTIONS OF THE CITY

major categories

commercial	comercial *aj*
industrial	industrial *aj*
residential	residencial *aj*

nonspecific locations

locale	local *nm*
locality	localidad *nf*
site	sitio *nm*
subterranean	subterráneo *aj*

particular sections

barrio	barrio *nm*
center 🅐	centro *nm*
Chinatown	barrio chino *nm*
ethnic (neighborhood)	étnico *aj*
ghetto 🅑	gueto, ghetto *nm*
plaza	plaza *nf*
private (property)	privado *aj*
public (property)	público *aj*
subdivision	subdivisión *nf*
suburb	suburbio *nm*

PLACES

streets and traffic

alley	callejón *nm*
avenue	avenida *nf*
boulevard	bulevar *nm*
crossing	cruce *nm*
crossover	cruzamiento *nm*
crossroads	encrucijada *nf*
island	isleta *nf*
passage	pasaje *nm*
tunnel	túnel *nm*

business

airport	aeropuerto *nm*
barbershop	barbería *nf*
bazaar, bazar	bazar *nm*
casino	casino *nm*
florist shop	floristería *nf*
hotel	hotel *nm*
laundromat	lavadoras automáticas *nfpl*
market	mercado *nm*
marketplace	plaza del mercado *nf, nm*
motel	motel *nm*
restaurant	restaurante *nm*
supermarket	supermercado *nm*

education

college	colegio *nm*
kindergarten	kindergarten *nm*
school	escuela *nf*
university	universidad *nf*

recreation

aquarium Ⓑ	acuario *nm*
club	club *nm*
gym, gymnasium Ⓑ	gimnasio *nm*
museum	museo *nm*
nightclub	club nocturno *nm*
park	parque *nm*
pavilion	pabellón *nm*
stadium Ⓑ	estadio *nm*
theater Ⓐ	teatro *nm*
zoo	zoo *nm*

dwellings

apartment	apartamento *nm*
apartment hotel	apart(h)otel, apartotel *nm*
bungalow	bungalow *nm*
condominium	condominio *nm*
dormitory	dormitorio *nm*
duplex	dúplex *nm*
hacienda	hacienda *nf*
lodge	logia *nf*
mansion	mansión *nf*
orphanage	orfanato, orfelinato *nm*
palace	palacio *nm*
penthouse	penthouse *nm*
residence	residencia *nf*

religion

chapel	capilla *nf*
mosque	mezquita *nf*
synagog(ue)	sinagoga *nf*
temple	templo *nm*

beautification

fountain	fuente *nf*
monument	monumento *nm*
tomb	tumba *nf*

other places

cemetery	cementerio *nm*
clinic	clínica *nf*
funeral home	funeraria *nf*
garage	garaje *nm*
hospital	hospital *nm*
station	estación *nf*
viaduct	viaducto *nm*

PUBLIC TRANSPORTATION

bus Ⓑ	autobús, bus *nm*
express (train)	expreso *aj*
interurban (train)	interurbano *aj*
local (train)	local *aj*
metro	metro *nm*
taxicab, taxi	taxi *nm*
train	tren *nm*
tramway	tranvía *nf*
trolley	trole *nm*
trolleybus	trolebús *nm*
monorail	monorriel *nm*

PERSONS

individuals

cosmopolite	cosmopolita *nmf*
councilman Ⓑ	concejal *nm*
councilwoman Ⓑ	consejala *nf*
guard (museum, park)	guarda *nmf*
indigent	indigente *nmf*
inhabitant	habitante *nmf*
policeman Ⓑ	policía *nm*
policewoman	policía *nf*
prostitute	prostituta *nf*
resident	residente *aj, nmf*
suburbanite	suburbano, -a *nmf*
taxi driver	taxista *nmf*
tourist	turista *nmf*
vagrant	vago, -a *nmf*

groups

council (municipal govt.)	concejo *nm*
minority	minoría *nf*
police	policía *nf*
underclass	clase marginada *nf*
planner	planificador(a) *nmf*

(*See also* **ARCHITECTURE**; **AUTOMOBILES**)

HOME FURNISHINGS

GENERAL TERMS

color scheme Ⓐ	combinación de colores *nf, nmpl*
decor, decoration	decoración *nf*
exterior	exterior *aj, nm*
interior	interior *aj, nm*
ornamentation	ornamentación *nf*
style	estilo *nm*

KINDS OF FURNITURE

colonial	colonial *aj*
comfortable	confortable *aj*
functional	funcional *aj*
metal	metal *nm*
modern	moderno *aj*
plastic	plástico *aj*
rattan	rota *nf*
sectional *aj*	por secciones *nfpl*
varnished	barnizado *aj*

ITEMS

living room

console	consola *nf*
convertible sofa	sofá-cama *nm*
cushion	cojín *nm*
divan	diván *nm*
music cabinet	musiquero *nm*
ottoman	otomana *nf*
sofa	sofá *nm*
television	televisión *nf*

bedroom and bathroom

bidet	bidé *nm*
cabinet	gabinete *nm*
clock radio	radiodespertador *nm*
commode (chest)	cómoda *nf*
eiderdown (quilt)	edredón *nm*
towel	toalla *nf*
towel rack	toallero *nm*
urinal	orinal, urinario *nm*

windows and lighting

candelabrum	candelabro *nm*
candlestick	candelero *nm*
curtain	cortina *nf*
jalousie	celosía *nf*
lamp	lámpara *nf*

floors and walls

flowered (wallpaper, drapes)	floreado *aj*
linoleum	linóleo *nm*
painting	pintura *nf*
paneling Ⓐ *nsg*	paneles *nmpl*
paper (walls)	empapelar *vt*
parquet	parqué *nm*
plaque	placa *nf*
tapestry	tapiz *nm*
vinyl	vinilo *nm*

outdoors

barbecue	barbacoa *nf*
grill	grill *nm*
hammock	hamaca *nf*

appliances

air conditioner	acondicionador de aire *nm*
coffeepot	cafetera *nf*
dehumidifier	deshumedecedor *nm*
freezer	freezer *nm*
humidifier	humedecedor, humectador *nm*
microwave	microonda *nf*
stove	estufa *nf*
washing machine	máquina de lavar *nf*

PERSONS

carpenter	carpintero *nm*
domestic	doméstico, -a *nmf*
electrician	electricista *nmf*
interior decorator	interiorista *nmf*
plumber	plomero *nm*

(*See also* **ARCHITECTURE**; *tools and equipment* under **FOOD AND NUTRITION**)

FOOD AND NUTRITION

ASPECTS OF FOOD CONSUMPTION

places to buy or eat food

cafeteria	cafetería *nf*
canteen	cantina *nf*
commissary	comisario *nm*
fruit store/stand	frutería *nf*
oyster bar	ostrería *nf*
pizzeria	pizzería *nf*
refectory	refectorio *nm*
restaurant	restaurante *nm*
supermarket	supermercado *nm*

tastes, textures, quality

acerb	acerbo *aj*
acrid	acre *aj*
contaminated	contaminado *aj*
creamy	cremoso *aj*
delicious	delicioso *aj*
exotic	exótico *aj*
fresh	fresco *aj*
fruity	afrutado, frutoso *aj*
grainy, granular	granulado *aj*

greasy	grasiento *aj*
insipid	insípido *aj*
juicy	jugoso *aj*
lemony	a limón *aj*
mentholated	mentolado *aj*
pap *nsg*	papilla, papas *nf, nfpl*
piquant	picante *aj*
pure	puro *aj*
rancid	rancio *aj*
saccharine	sacarino *aj*
salty, salted	salado *aj*
savory Ⓐ	sabroso *aj*
seasoned	sazonado *aj*
spicy	especiado *aj*
succulent	suculento *aj*
sugary	azucarado *aj*
tutti-frutti	tutti-frutti *nm*
vinegary	avinagrado, vinagroso *aj*

other general terms

additive	aditivo *aj, nm*
ambiance, ambience	ambiente *nm*
appetite	apetito *nm*
comestibles	comestibles *nmpl*
culinary	culinario *aj*
digestion	digestión *nf*
gastronomy	gastronomía *nf*
menu	menú *nm*
nutrition	nutrición *nf*
provisions	provisiones *nfpl*
savor Ⓐ	sabor *nm*
tempting	tentador *aj*

KINDS OF FOOD

meals

banquet	banquete *nm*
barbecue	barbacoa *nf*
buffet	buffet, bufet, bufé *nm*
feast	festín *nm*
picnic	picnic *nm*

major categories

casserole	cacerola *nf*
cereal	cereal *nm*
condiment	condimento *nm*
confection	confección *nf*
dressing	aderezo *nm*
extract	extracto *nm*
fruit	fruta *nf*
grain	grano *nm*
legume	legumbre *nf*

omelet Ⓐ	omelette *nf*
organic	orgánico *aj*
pasta	pasta *nf*
produce	producto *nm*
salad	ensalada *nf*
sandwich	sandwich *nm*
sauce	salsa *nf*
seasoning	sazón *nf*
soup	sopa *nf*
spice	especia *nf*
vegetable	vegetal *nm*
vegetarian	vegetariano *aj*

soups

bouillabaisse	bullabesa *nf*
condensed soup	sopa condensada *nf*
consommé	consomé *nm*
gazpacho	gazpacho *nm*
goulash	gulash *nm*
gumbo	quingombó *nm*
potage	potaje *nm*
puree, purée	puré *nm*

meat and poultry

beefsteak	biftec, bistec *nm*
capon	capón *nm*
corned beef	corned beef *nm*
croquette	croqueta *nf*
entrecote	entrecot *nm*
fricassee	fricasé *nm*
ham	jamón *nm*
hamburger	hamburguesa *nf*
pastrami	pastrami *nm*
pemican, pemmican	pemicán *nm*
pork	puerco *nm*
ragout	ragú *nm*
salami	salami *nm*
scallop	escalope *nm*
taco	taco *nm*
tournedos	turnedó *nm*

seafood

albacore	albacora *nf*
anchovy	ancho(v)a *nf*
carp Ⓑ	carpa *nf*
caviar	caviar *nm*
halibut	halibut *nm*
oyster	ostra *nf*
perch Ⓑ	perca *nf*
pompano	pámpano *nm*
salmon Ⓑ	salmón *nm*
sardine	sardina *nf*
sturgeon	esturión *nm*

trout Ⓑ	trucha *nf*
tuna	atún *nm*

dairy

brie	brie *nm*
Camembert	camembert *nm*
cheese	queso *nm*
condensed milk	leche condensada *nf*
cream	crema *nf*
evaporated milk	leche evaporada *nf*
fondue	fondue *nf*
Gruyère	gruyere *nm*
homogenized milk	leche homogeneizada *nf*
mozzarella	mozzarella *nf*
pasteurized milk	leche past(e)urizada *nf*

pasta

lasagna, lasagne	lasaña *nf*
macaroni *nsg*	macarrones *nmpl*
ravioli *nsg*	ravioles *nmpl*
rissotto	risotto *nm*
spaghetti *nsg*	espaguetis *nmpl*

bread and cereal

brioche	brioche *nm*
croissant	croissant *nm*
crouton	crutón *nm*
farina	harina *nf*
pabulum	pábulo *nm*
pumpernickle	pumpernickel *nm*
rice	arroz *nm*
semolina	sémola *nf*
toast	tostada *nf*
tortilla	tortilla *nf*

vegetables

asparagus	espárrago *nm*
bamboo	bambú Ⓒ *nm*
broccoli	brécol, brócoli *nm*
cauliflower	coliflor *nf*
chayote	chayote, cayote *nm*
endive	endibia, endivia *nf*
escarole	escarola *nf*
jicama	jícama *nf*
kohlrabi Ⓑ	colirrábano *nm*
lentil	lenteja *nf*
potato Ⓑ	patata *nf*
salsify	salsifí *nm*
shallot	chalote *nm*
soybean	soja *nf*
spinach *nsg*	espinacas *nfpl*
taro	taro *nm*

tofu	tofu *nm*
tomato Ⓑ	tomate *nm*

fruits

acerola	acerola *nf*
banana	banana *nf*
bergamot	bergamota *nf*
calabash	calabaza *nf*
cantaloupe, cantaloup	cantalupo *nm*
chayote	chayote *nm*
cherry	cereza *nf*
citron	cidra *nf*
citrus	cítrico *aj*
coconut, cocoanut	coco *nm*
date	dátil *nm*
fig	higo *nm*
guava	guayaba *nf*
kiwi	kiwi *nm*
kumquat	kuncuat *nm*
lemon	limón *nm*
lime	lima *nf*
mandarine	mandarina *nf*
mango Ⓑ	mango *nm*
melon	melón *nm*
nectarine	nectarina *nf*
olive	oliva *nf*
orange	naranja *nf*
papaya	papaya *nf*
pear	pera *nf*
pineapple	piña *nf*
plantain	plátano *nm*
pomegranate	granada *nf*
rhubarb	ruíbarbo *nm*
tamarind	tamarindo *nm*

nuts

almond	almendra *nf*
betel	betel *nm*
Brazil	brasil *nm*
litchi Ⓐ	lichi *nm*
macadamia	macadamia *nf*
pecan	pacana *nf*
pine nut	piñón *nm*
pistachio	pistacho *nm*
sesame	sésamo *nm*

sweet foods

bonbon	bombón *nm*
caramel	caramelo *nm*
chocolate	chocolate *nm*
compote	compota *nf*
crepe, crêpe	crep, crêpe *nm*
doughnut	dona, donut Ⓒ *nf, nm*

mushroom (s)   champiñon (es)   55

flan	flan *nm*
frangipani	franchipaniero *nm*
halva, halvah	halva *nf*
jelly	jalea *nf*
macaroon	macarrón *nm*
marmalade	mermelada *nf*
marzipan	mazapán *nm*
meringue	merengue *nm*
mousse	mousse *nf*
pancake	panqueque *nm*
penuche	panocha *nf*
praline	praliné *nm*
pudding	pudín, budín *nm*
sugar	azúcar *nm or nf*
tapioca	tapioca *nf*
tart	tarta *nf*
torte	torta *nf*
truffle	trufa *nf*

sauces, spices, syrups

anise	anís *nm*
bechamel	bechamel, besamel *nf*
bolognese	boloñesa *nf*
caraway	alcaravea *nf*
cardamom	cardamomo *nm*
cayenne	cayena *nf*
chickory	achicoria *nf*
chutney	chutney *nm*
clove	clavo *nm*
coriander	coriandro *nm*
cumin	comino *nm*
curry	curry, cari *nm*
ginger	jengibre *nm*
hollandaise	holandesa *nf*
ketchup, catsup Ⓐ	catsup *nm*
mace	macis *nf*
marjoram	mejorana *nf*
mint	menta *nf*
molasses	melaza *nf*
mustard	mostaza *nf*
oregano	orégano *nm*
paprika	paprika *nf*
pimento, pimiento	pimiento *nm*
roux	roux *nm*
saccharin	sacarina *nf*
saffron	azafrán *nm*
salt	sal *nf*
sassafras	sasafrás *nm*
sorghum	sorgo *nm*
tarragon	estragón *nm*

vanilla	vainilla *nf*
vinegar	vinagre *nm*

fats and oils

lard	lardo *nm*
margarine	margarina *nf*
oleo, oleomargarine	oleomargarina *nf*

dressings

mayonnaise	mayonesa *nf*
vinaigrette	vinagreta *nf*

popular ethnic dishes

chili, chilli	chile *nm*
chop suey	chop suey *nm*
chow mein	chow mein *nm*
couscous	cuscús, couscous *nm*
gnocchi	ñoquis *nmpl*
moussaka	mousaka, moussaka *nf*
pizza	pizza *nf*
soufflé	suflé *nm*
tamale	tamal *nm*

other foods

canapé	canapé *nm*
chicle	chicle *nm*
filet, fillet	filete *nm*
fritter	fritada, fritura *nf*
granulated (sugar)	granulado *aj*
menthol	mentol *nm*
paste	pasta *nf*
peel	peladura *nf*
pulp	pulpa *nf*

PROCESSED FOODS

additives

agar, agar-agar	agar, agar-agar *nm*
antioxidant	antioxidante *nm*
coloring	colorido *nm*
emulsifier	emulsor *nm*
gelatin, gelatine	gelatina *nf*
pectin	pectina *nf*
stabilizer	estabilizante *nm*
supplement	suplemento *nm*

processes

curing	curación *nf*
dehydration	deshidratación *nf*
fermentation	fermentación *nf*
hydrogenation	hidrogenación *nf*
irradiation	irradiación *nf*
packaging	empaque *nm*

pasteurization	past(e)urización *nf*
reconstitution	reconstitución *nf*

PREPARATION AND CONSUMPTION

tools and equipment

beater	batidora *nf*
bottle-opener	abrebotellas Ⓒ *nm*
brazier	brasero *nm*
caldron	calderón *nm*
colander	colador *nm*
food processor	procesador de alimentos *nm*
freezer	freezer *nm*
grill	grill *nm*
jar	jarra *nf*
kebab, kebob	kebab *nm*
liquefier	licuadora *nf*
microwave	microonda *nf*
mold Ⓐ	molde *nm*
pot	pote *nm*
pressure cooker	olla a presión *nf*
recipe	receta *nf*
refrigerator	refrigerador *nm*
sandwich toaster	sandwichera, sandwichero *nf, nm*
separator	separador *nm*
spatula	espátula *nf*
spice rack	especiero *nm*
stove	estufa *nf*
toaster	tostadora *nf*
utensil	utensilio *nm*
yogurt maker	yogurtera *nf*

recipe instructions

base	base *nf*
beat	batir *vt*
blanch	blanquear *vt*
clarify	clarificar *vt*
consistency	consistencia *nf*
dress	aderezar *vt*
eviscerate	eviscerar *vt*
fillet	cortar en filetes *vt, nmpl*
fry	freír *vt*
garnish	guarnecer *vt*
glaze	glasear *vt*
ingredient	ingrediente *nm*
leaven, leavening	levadura *nf*
macerate	macerar *vt*
peel	pelar *vt*
puree, purée	hacer un puré con *vt*
refrigerate	refrigerar *vt*

salt	salar *vt*
scald	escaldar *vt*
season	sazonar *vt*
toast	tostar *vt*

food service

china	china *nf*
china closet	chinero *nm*
fruit bowl	frutero *nm*
plate	plato *nm*
platter	platón *nm*
porcelain	porcelana *nf*
portion	porción *nf*
salad bowl	ensaladera *nf*
saltcellar, saltshaker	salero *nm*
self-service	autoservicio *nm*
soup plate/tureen	sopera *nf*
sugar bowl	azucarera *nf*

eating and digestion

aroma	aroma *nm*
consumption	consumo *nm*
devour	devorar *vt*
famished	famélico *aj*
gustatory	gustativo *aj*
mastication	masticación *nf*
metabolism	metabolismo *nm*
satiation	saciedad *nf*
subsistence	subsistencia *nf*
voracious (appetite)	voraz *aj*

religious and historical terms

ambrosia	ambrosía *nf*
kosher	kosher *aj*
manna	maná *nm*
paschal	pascual *aj*
victuals (obs)	vituallas *nfpl*

NUTRITION

general terms

amino acid	aminoácido *nm*
calorie	caloría *nf*
carbohydrate	carbohidrato *nm*
casein	caseína *nf*
diet	dieta *nf*
dietetics	dietética *nf*
gluten	gluten *nm*
glycogen	glicógeno *nm*
malnutrition	desnutrición *nf*
mineral	mineral *nm*
nutrient	nutriente *nm*
nutriment	nutrimiento *nm*

protein	proteína *nf*
vanillin	vainillina *nf*
vitamin	vitamina *nf*

vitamins

ascorbic (acid)	ascórbico *aj*
niacin (Vitamin B)	niacina *nf*
retinol (Vitamin A)	retinol *nm*
riboflavin	riboflavina *nf*
thiamine, thiamin	tiamina *nf*

minerals

calcium	calcio *nm*
iodine	yodo *nm*
magnesium	magnesio *nm*
phosphorus	fósforo *nm*
potassium	potasio *nm*
sodium	sodio *nm*

sugars

dextrose	dextrosa *nf*
fructose	fructosa *nf*
glucose	glucosa *nf*
lactose	lactosa *nf*
maltose	maltosa *nf*
sucrose	sacarosa *nf*

fats

cholesterol	colesterol *nm*
glycerol	glicerol *nm*
lecithin	lecitina *nf*
lipid, lipide	lípido *nm*
triglyceride	triglicérido *nm*
balanced (diet)	balanceado *aj*
macrobiotic	macrobiótico *aj*
polyunsaturated (fat)	poliinsaturado *aj*

PERSONS

chef	chef, jefe *nmf*
connoisseur	conocedor(a) *nmf*
dietician	dietista *nmf*
Epicurean	epicureo, -a *nmf*
gastronome	gastrónomo, -a *nmf*
glutton	glotón, -ona *nmf*
gourmet	gourmet *nmf*
nutritionist	nutricionista *nmf*
oyster vender	ostrero, -a *nmf*
picnicker	participante del picnic *nmf*
vegetarian	vegetariano, -a *nmf*

(*See also major food crops* under **AGRICULTURE**; **BEVERAGES**)

BEVERAGES

GENERAL TERMS

alcohol	alcohol *nm*
beverage	bebida *nf*
distillery	destilería *nf*
elixir	elíxir *nm*
libation	libación *nf*
liquor	licor *nm*
potion	poción *nf*
prohibition (obs)	prohibición *nf*

ALCOHOLIC BEVERAGES

kinds of drinks

aperitif, apéritif	aperitivo *nm*
cordial	cordial *nm*
liqueur	licor *nm*
wine	vino *nm*

wines

Burgundy	borgoña *nf*
cabernet	cabernet *nm*
cava	cava *nf*
champagne	champán, champaña *nm, nf*
Chianti	quianti *nm*
claret	clarete *nm*
Madeira	madeira *nf*
Malaga	málaga *nf*
moselle	vino del Mosela *nm*
muscatel	moscatel *nm*
must	mosto *nm*
port	oporto *nm*
Riesling	riesling *nm*
rosé	rosado *nm*
sherry	jerez *nm*
vermouth	vermut, vermú *nm*

liqueurs

absinth(e)	absenta *nf*
anisette	licor de anís *nm*
brandy	brandy Ⓒ *nm*
cognac	coñac, coñá *nm*
curaçao	curasao, curazao *nm*
grenadine	granadina *nf*
julep	julepe *nm*
kirsch	kirsch *nm*
kümmel	kummel, cúmel *nm*
maraschino	marrasquino *nm*

mixed drinks

cocktail	cóctel *nm*

daiquiri	daikiri, daiquiri *nm*
manhattan	manhattan *nm*
margarita	margarita *nf*
martini	martini *nm*
punch	ponche *nm*
sangria	sangría *nf*

other alcoholic beverages

gin	ginebra *nf*
ginger beer	cerveza de jengibre *nf, nm*
kvass	kwas, kvas *nm*
mescal	mezcal *nm*
ouzo	ouzo *nm*
rum	ron *nm*
sake	sake, saki *nm*
Scotch	whisky escocés *nm*
tequila	tequila
vodka	vodka *nf*
whiskey, whisky Ⓑ	whisky, whiski, güisqui *nm*

drinking practices

abstinence	abstinencia *nf*
intemperance	intemperancia *nf*
moderation	moderación *nf*
sobriety	sobriedad *nf*

public places

bar	bar *nm*
cafe, café	café *nm*
coffee bar	cafetín *nm*
tavern	taberna *nf*

TERMS RELATING TO WINE

aroma	aroma *nf*
bouquet	bouquet, buqué *nm*
enology Ⓐ	enología *nf*
fortified	fortificado *aj*
sec	seco *aj*
select	selecto *aj*
vineyard	viña, viñedo *nf, nm*
wine merchant	vinatero, -a *nmf*
wine shop/trade	vinatería *nf*
winery	vinería *nf*

NON-ALCOHOLIC BEVERAGES

cappuccino	capuchino *nm*
chocolate	chocolate *nm*
cider	sidra *nf*
cocoa	cacao *nm*

cocoa	cocoa *nf*
coffee	café *nm*
coke	coque, Coca-cola *nm*
cola	cola *nf*
espresso	café exprés *nm*
ginger ale	refresco de jengibre *nm*
juice	jugo *nm*
lemonade	limonada *nf*
malted	malteado *aj*
mineral water	agua mineral *nm*
mocha	moca *nf*
nectar	néctar *nm*
orangeade	naranjada *nf*
punch	ponche *nm*
quinine (water)	quinina *nf*
sarsparilla (tea)	zarzaparrilla *nf*
seltzer	agua de Seltz *nf(el)*
soda, soda water	soda *nf*
tea	té *nm*

DESCRIPTIVE TERMS

adulterated	adulterado *aj*
alcoholic	alcohólico *aj*
carbonated	carbonatado *aj*
decaffeinated	descafeinado *aj*
diluted	diluido *aj*
distilled	destilado *aj*
effervescent	efervescente *aj*
fermented	fermentado *aj*
nonalcoholic	no alcohólico *aj*
potable	potable *aj*
refreshing	refrescante *aj*
spumy	espumoso *aj*
tepid	tibio *aj*

CONTAINERS AND ACCESSORIES

barrel	barril *nm*
bottle	botella *nf*
carafe	garrafa *nf*
chalice	cáliz *nm*
cocktail shaker	coctelera *nf*
coffeepot, coffee maker	cafetera *nf*
cork	corcho *nm*
corkscrew	sacacorchos *nm*
decanter	decantador *nm*
extractor	extractor *nm*
ice cube	cubito de hielo *nm*
punchbowl	ponchera *nf*
samovar	samovar *nm*
teapot	tetera *nf*
thermos	termo *nm*
wineglass	copa para vino *nf, nm*

PERSONS

abstainer	abstemio, -a *nmf*
designated driver	conductor designado *nmf*
dipsomaniac	dipsómano, -a *nmf*
distiller	destilador(a) *nmf*
enologist	enólogo, -a *nmf*
vintner	vinatero, -a *nmf*

(*See also* **FOOD AND NUTRITION**)

AUTOMOBILES

GENERAL TERMS

auto, automobile	auto, automóvil *nm*
automotive (industry)	automotor, automotriz *aj*
automotive (vehicles)	automovilístico *aj*
car	carro *nm*
gas, gasoline	gasolina *nf*
luxury	de lujo *aj*
maintenance	mantenimiento *nm*
model	modelo *nm*
repair	reparación *nf*
traffic	tráfico *nm*
vehicle	vehículo *nm*

ASPECTS OF AUTOMOBILES

models

compact	coche compacto *nm*
convertible	convertible *nm*
coupe, coupé	cupé *nm*
Jeep	jeep *nm*
new	nuevo *aj*
sedan	sedán *nm*
sports	deportivo *aj*
used	usado *aj*

parts and equipment

accelerator	acelerador *nm*
battery	batería *nf*
block (engine)	bloque *nm*
cable	cable *nm*
carburetor	carburador *nm*
catalytic converter	catalizador *nm*
chassis Ⓑ	chasis Ⓒ *nm*
controls	controles *nmpl*
cylinder	cilindro *nm*
differential	diferencial *nm*
disk	disco *nm*
emergency (brake)	emergencia *nf*
generator	generador *nm*

glove compartment	guantera *nf*
hubcap	tapacubos *nm*
hydraulic (brake)	hidráulico *aj*
ignition	ignición *nf*
indicator	indicador *nm*
instrument	instrumento *nm*
manual (gearshift)	manual *aj*
motor	motor *nm*
odometer	odómetro *nm*
panel	panel *nm*
pedal	pedal *nm*
piston	pistón *nm*
pump	bomba *nf*
radial (tire)	radial *aj*
radiator	radiador *nm*
silencer	silenciador *nm*
thermostat	termostato *nm*
transmission	transmisión *nf*
valve	válvula *nf*

maintenance and repairs

adjustment	ajuste *nm*
air	aire *nm*
alignment	alineación *nf*
antifreeze	anticongelante *nm*
charge (battery)	carga *nf*
check (brakes)	chequear *vt*
compression	compresión *nf*
garage	garaje *nm*
gas station	gasolinera *nf*
grease	grasa *nf*
inflate (tires)	inflar *vt*
lubrication	lubricación *nf*
performance	performance *nf*
pressure	presión *nf*

driving

acceleration	aceleración *nf*
accident	accidente *nm*
avenue	avenida *nf*
bifurcation	bifurcación *nf*
block (street)	bloquear *vt*
bottleneck	embotellamiento *nm*
circular (route)	circular *aj*
collision	colisión *nf*
congestion	congestión *nf*
crossing	cruce *nm*
crossroads	encrucijada *nf*
curve	curva *nf*
deceleration	deceleración *nf*
direct (route)	directo *aj*
direction	dirección *nf*
intersection	intersección *nf*

island	isla *nf*
kilometer distance	kilometraje *nm*
license Ⓐ	licencia *nf*
median	mediana *nf*
mileage	distancia en millas *nf,* *nfpl*
obstruction	obstrucción *nf*
overpass	paso superior *nm*
parking lot	parking *nm*
parking meter	parquímetro *nm*
pavement	pavimento *nm*
ramp	rampa *nf*
route	ruta *nf*
second gear	segunda *nf*
signal	señal *nf*
speed limit	límite de velocidad *nm,* *nf*
stop (sign)	stop *nm*
traction	tracción *nf*
traffic island	isleta *nf*
tunnel	túnel *nm*
underpass	paso inferior *nm*

PERSONS

accident victim	accidentado, -a *nmf*
garage attendant	garajista *nmf*
motorist	motorista *nmf*
passenger	pasajero, -a *nmf*

(*See also* **streets and traffic** under **THE CITY**; **LAND TRANSPORTATION**; **TRAVEL AND TOURISM**)

WORK

GENERAL TERMS

career	carrera *nf*
employ, employment	empleo *nm*
equipment	equipo *nm*
ergonomics	ergonomía *nf*
industry	industria *nf*
labor Ⓐ	labor *nf*
NAFTA	NAFTA *nm*
occupation	ocupación *nf*
pension	pensión *nf*
permit	permiso *nm*
post	puesto *nm*
profession	profesión *nf*
retirement	retiro *nm*
Social Security	Seguro Social *nm*
speciality, specialty	especialidad *nf*
syndicalism	sindicalismo *nm*
vacation *nsg*	vacaciones *nfpl*

vocation	vocación *nf*
working class	clase obrera *nf*

ASPECTS OF EMPLOYMENT

leading fields of work

agriculture	agricultura *nf*
commerce	comercio *nm*
manufacturing	manufactura *nf*
services	servicios *nmpl*
transportation	tra(n)sportación *nf*

factors affecting work

absenteeism	absentismo *nm*
automation	automación, automatización *nf*
economy	economía *nf*
experience	experiencia *nf*
recession	recesión *nf*
retirement plan	plan de retiro *nm*
technology	tecnología *nf*
vacancy	vacante *nf*

labor relations

arbitration	arbitraje *nm*
conciliation	conciliación *nf*
contract	contrato *nm*
incentive	incentivo *nm*
negotiation	negociación *nf*
nepotism	nepotismo *nm*
pact	pacto *nm*
removal	remoción *nf*
supervision	supervisión *nf*
working conditions	condiciones de trabajo *nfpl, nm*

wages

honorarium Ⓑ *nsg*	honorarios *nmpl*
minimum wage	sueldo mínimo *nm*
net income	ingreso neto *nm*
pay	paga *nf*
payday	día de paga *nm, nf*
remuneration	remuneración *nf*
salary	salario *nm*
stipend	estipendio *nm*

places

department	departamento *nm*
office	oficina *nf*
plant	planta *nf*

basis of employment

daily *aj*	por día *nm*

full-time *aj*	a tiempo completo *nm*
hourly *aj*	por horas *nfpl*
part-time *aj*	a tiempo parcial *nm*
permanent *aj*	permanente *aj*
temporary *aj*	temporal *aj*

terms describing workers

capable	capaz *aj*
competent	competente *aj*
efficient	eficiente *aj*
experienced *aj*	con experiencia *nf*
industrious	industrioso *aj*
qualified	calificado *aj*
salaried	asalariado *aj*
undocumented	indocumentado *aj*
unqualified	no calificado *aj*

terms describing work

arduous	arduo *aj*
fatiguing	fatigoso *aj*
interesting	interesante *aj*
remunerative	remunerador *aj*
routine	rutinario *aj*
sedentary	sedentario *aj*

other terms

apprenticeship	aprendizaje *nm*
assumption (duties)	asunción *nf*
collaboration	colaboración *nf*
sinecure	sinecura *nf*
sustenance	sustento *nm*
uniform	uniforme *nm*

PERSONS

groups

administration	administración *nf*

personnel	personal *nm*
picket line	piquete *nm*

individuals

apprentice	aprendiz, -iza *nmf*
arbitrator	árbitro, -a *nmf*
collaborator	colaborador(a) *nmf*
colleague	colega *nmf*
conciliator	conciliador(a) *nmf*
coordinator	coordinador(a) *nmf*
director	director(a) *nmf*
employee	empleado, -a *nmf*
employer	empleador, -a *nmf*
factotum (handyman)	factótum *nm*
functionary	funcionario, -a *nmf*
inferior	inferior *nmf*
inspector	inspector(a) *nmf*
itinerant worker	obrero, -a itinerante *nmf*
negotiator	negociador(a) *nmf*
office worker	oficinista *nmf*
officer	oficial *nmf*
operative	operario, -a *nmf*
pensioner	pensionado, -a, pensionista *nmf*
professional	profesional *aj, nmf*
specialist	especialista *nmf*
subordinate	subordinado, -a *nmf*
superintendent	superintendente *nmf*
superior	superior *nmf*
supervisor	supervisor(a) *nmf*

(*See also* **BUSINESS**; **ECONOMICS**)

Keeping the Body Beautiful

CLOTHING

GENERAL TERMS

accessory	accesorio *nm*
design	diseño *nm*
dictates (of fashion)	dictados *nmpl*
mode	moda *nf*
ornament	ornamento *nm*
pair	par *nm*
style	estilo *nm*
vogue	boga *nf*

ASPECTS OF CLOTHING

functions of clothing

communication	comunicación *nf*
decoration	decoración *nf*
entertainment	entretenimiento *nm*
modesty	modestia *nf*
protection	protección *nf*

types of clothing

appropriate	apropiado *aj*
ceremonial	ceremonial *aj*
formal	formal *aj*
informal	informal *aj*
maternity *aj*	de maternidad *nf*
sports	deportivo *aj*
theatrical	teatral *aj*
traditional	tradicional *aj*

cleaning

air out	airear *vt*
detergent	detergente *aj, nm*
laundry	lavandería *nf*
ticket (laundry)	ticket *nm*

ARTICLES OF CLOTHING

headwear

crown	coronilla *nf*
fez Ⓑ	fez Ⓒ *nm*
helmet	yelmo *nm*
kepi	quepis, kepis *nm*
mantilla	mantilla *nf*
plumed	con plumas *aj*
shako	chacó *nm*
toque	toca *nf*

turban	turbante *nm*
visor	visera *nf*

footwear

boot	bota, botín *nf, nm*
bootee	botita *nf*
laces	lazos *nmpl*
moccasin	mocasín *nm*
platform	plataforma *nf*
sandal	sandalia *nf*

undergarments and sleepwear

corselet, corslet	coselete *nm*
corset	corsé *nm*
lingerie	lencería *nf*
negligee, negligée, negligé	negligé *nm*
pajamas Ⓐ	pijama, piyama *nm*
pantyhose	medias panti(e)s *nmpl, nfpl*

outerwear

blazer	blazer *nm*
blouse	blusa *nf*
blouse (long)	blusón *nm*
bolero	bolero *nm*
caftan	caftán *nm*
cape	capa *nf*
cardigan	cárdigan Ⓒ *nm*
domino Ⓑ	dominó *nm*
guayabera	guayabera *nf*
jacket	chaqueta *nf*
mantle	manto *nm*
miniskirt	minifalda *nf*
mitten	mitón *nm*
pants	pantalones *nmpl*
parka	parka *nf*
poncho	poncho *nm*
sweater	suéter *nm*
uniform	uniforme *nm*

other garments

bikini	bikini, biquini *nm or nf*
coordinates	coordinados *nmpl*
jeans	jeans *nmpl*
jellabah	chilaba *nf*
kimono	kimono, quimono *nm*
leotard	leotardo *nm*
overalls	overol *nm*

sari	sari *nm*
sarong	sarong *nm*
tunic	túnica *nf*
tutu	tutú *nm*

historical clothing

armor Ⓐ	armadura *nf*
brassard	brazal *nm*
chiton	quitón *nm*
mail	malla *nf*
pantaloons	pantalones *nmpl*
tabard	tabardo *nm*
toga	toga *nf*
tricorne (hat)	tricornio *nm*

ACCESSORIES AND ORNAMENTS

bandoleer, bandolier	bandolera *nf*
boa	boa *nf*
bracelet	brazalete *nm*
brooch	broche *nm*
clip-on (earrings)	de clip *nm*
coronet	corona *nf*
diadem	diadema *nf*
laces	lazos *nmpl*
mask	máscara *nf*
monocle	monóculo *nm*
parasol	parasol *nm*
pendant	pendiente *nm*
serape	sarape *nm*
shawl	chal *nm*
stole	estola *nf*
veil	velo *nm*

SEWING TERMS

stitches

basting	baste *nm*
bias	bies *nm*
double	doble *aj*
zigzag	zigzag *nm*

design features

appliqué	aplicación *nf*
band	banda *nf*
button	botón *nm*
filigree	filigrana *nf*
fringe	franja *nf*
miter	mitra *nf*
peplum	peplo *nm*
pleat	pliegue *nm*
raglan	raglán *aj, nm*
zipper	zíper *nm*

tools and equipment

bobbin	bobina *nf*
elastic	elástico *aj, nm*
mannequin, manikin	maniquí *nmf*
pattern	patrón *nm*
sewing machine	máquina de coser *nf*
stiletto Ⓑ	estilete *nm*
Velcro	velcro *nm*

measurements and sizes

centimeter Ⓐ	centímetro *nm*
cup	copa *nf*
meter Ⓐ	metro *nm*
yard	yarda *nf*
yardage	medida en yardas, tela *nf*

fabric patterns

flowered	floreado *aj*
geometric	geométrico *aj*
intricate	intrincado *aj*

other terms

crochet	crochet, croché *nm*
knot	nudo *nm*
palm (glove)	palma *nf*
reverse (side of fabric)	revés *nm*
roll (of fabric)	rollo *nm*
texture	textura *nf*
button shop	botonería *nf*

PERSONS

arbiter	árbitro *nm*
button dealer	botonero, -a *nmf*
designer	diseñador(a) *nmf*
model	modelo *nmf*
modiste	modista *nmf*
transvestite	transvestido, -a *nmf*

(*See also* **clothing fabrics** under ASPECTS OF TEXTILES; **GEMS AND JEWELRY**; *uniform* under **THE MILITARY ESTABLISHMENT**; *clothing and appearance* under **RELIGION**)

COSMETICS AND GROOMING

GENERAL TERMS

barbershop	barbería *nf*
beauty salon	salón de belleza *nm, nf*
cosmetic	cosmético *aj, nm*
cosmetology	cosmética *nf*
substance	sustancia *nf*
treatment	tratamiento *nm*

ASPECTS OF SKIN AND HAIR CARE

treatments

coloring Ⓐ	coloración *nf*
depilation	depilación *nf*
douche	ducha *nf*
electrolysis	electrólisis *nf*
face lift	lifting *nm*
facial	tratamiento facial *nm*
laser	láser *nm*
liposuction	liposucción *nf*
manicure	manicura *nf*
massage	masaje *nm*
pedicure	pedicura *nf*
peeling	peeling *nm*
permanent	permanente *nf*
sauna	sauna *nf*
shiatsu	shiatsu *nm*
styling	estilización *nf*
tattoo	tatuaje *nm*

substances

aloe	áloe, aloe *nm*
antiperspirant	antisudoral *nm*
astringent	astringente *aj, nm*
balm	bálsamo *nm*
brilliantine	brillantina *nf*
calamine (lotion)	calamina *nf*
camphor ice	cerato de alcanfor *nm*
citronella	citronela *nf*
cologne	colonia *nf*
conditioner	acondicionador *nm*
cream	crema *nf*
deodorant	desodorante *nm*
depilatory	depilatorio *nm*
emollient	emoliente *nm*
eucalyptus (oil)	eucalipto *nm*
gargle	gargarismo *nm*
gel	gel *nm*
glycerin(e)	glicerina *nf*
henna	alheña *nf*
humectant	humectante *nm*
lanolin	lanolina *nf*
lavender	lavanda *nf*
lotion	loción *nf*
lubricant	lubricante *nm*
mask	máscara *nf*
mousse	mousse *nf*
perfume	perfume *nm*
peroxide	peróxido *nm*
petrolatum	petrolato *nm*
pomade	pomada *nf*
shampoo	champú *nm*

spray	espray Ⓒ *nm*
talcum powder	talco *nm*
tint	tinte *nm*
unguent	ungüento *nm*

tools and equipment

roller	rulo, rulero *nm*
toupee	tupé *nm*
towel	toalla *nf*

other terms

Afro	afro *nm*
apply (makeup)	aplicar *vt*
hypoallergenic	hipoalergénico *aj*
manageable (hair)	manejable *aj*
medicated	medicinal *aj*
retouch	retocarse *vt*

PERSONS

barber	barbero, -a *nmf*
cosmetologist	cosmetólogo, -a *nmf*
hair stylist	estilista *nmf*
manicurist	manicuro, -a *nmf*
masseur	masajista *nm*
masseuse	masajista *nf*
plastic surgeon	cirujano plástico *nmf*

(*See also* NUTRITION under **FOOD AND NUTRITION**; *fitness* under **SPORTS**)

GEMS AND JEWELRY

GENERAL TERMS

facet	faceta *nf*
gem	gema *nf*
glyptography	gliptografía *nf*
jewelry	joyería *nf*
mounting	montura *nf*
precious	precioso *aj*
semiprecious	semiprecioso *aj*

TYPES OF GEMS

precious

diamond	diamante *nm*
emerald	esmeralda *nf*
ruby	rubí *nm*
sapphire	zafiro *nm*

semiprecious

agate	ágata *nf*
carnelian	carniola, cornalina *nf*
garnet	granate *nm*

jade	jade *nm*
jasper	jaspe *nm*
lapis lazuli	lapislázuli *nm*
onyx	ónice, ónix, ónique *nm*
opal	ópalo *nm*
pearl	perla *nf*
sardonyx	sardónica, sardónice *nf*
turquoise	turquesa *nf*

other jewelry materials

alabaster	alabastro *nm*
amber	ámbar *nm*
amethyst	amatista *nf*
aquamarine	aguamarina *nf*
coral	coral *nm*
nacre	nácar *nm*
topaz	topacio *nm*
tourmaline	turmalina *nf*
zircon	circón, zircón *nm*

other terms

artificial	artificial *aj*
brillant	brillante *nm*
cameo	camafeo *nm*
carbuncle (ruby)	carbúnculo, carbunclo *nm*
cultured (pearl)	cultivado *aj*
iridescence	iridescencia *nf*
natural (pearl)	natural *aj*
opalescence	opalescencia *nf*
solitaire	solitario *nm*
transparent	tra(n)sparente *aj*

PERSONS

diamond cutter	diamantista *nmf*
glyptographer	gliptógrafo, -a *nmf*
jeweler, jeweller	joyero, -a *nmf*
lapidary	lapidario, -a *nmf*

(*See also* ACCESSORIES AND ORNAMENTS under **CLOTHING**; **GEOLOGY**; **MINERALS AND MINING**)

The Inner Self

FEELINGS AND EMOTIONS

EMOTIONAL STATES

happy

anxious (eager)	ansioso *aj*
content, contented	contento *aj*
euphoric	eufórico *aj*
excited	excitado *aj*
exuberant	exuberante *aj*
gratified	gratificado *aj*
jovial	jovial *aj*
jubilant	jubiloso *aj*
satisfied	satisfecho *aj*

unhappy

anguished	angustiado *aj*
contrite	contrito *aj*
depressed	deprimido *aj*
desolate	desolado *aj*
despairing	desesperanzado *aj*
desperate	desesperado *aj*
disconsolate	desconsolado *aj*
discontented	descontento *aj*
dissatisfied	insatisfecho *aj*
envious	envidioso *aj*
inconsolable	inconsolable *aj*
lugubrious	lúgubre *aj*
melancholic, melancholy	melancólico *aj*
miserable	miserable *aj*
somber Ⓐ	sombrío *aj*
tormented	atormentado *aj*

afraid

alarmed	alarmado *aj*
apprehensive	aprensivo, aprehensivo *aj*
horror-stricken	horrorizado *aj*
panicky	pánico *aj*
terrified	aterrorizado *aj*
timorous	timorato *aj*
vulnerable	vulnerable *aj*

upset, annoyed

confused	confundido *aj*
disconcerted	desconcertado *aj*
disoriented	desorientado *aj*
distracted	distraído *aj*

frustrated	frustrado *aj*
impatient	impaciente *aj*
irritated	irritado *aj*
perplexed	perplejo *aj*
tense	tenso *aj*

angry

exasperated	exasperado *aj*
furious	furioso *aj*
indignant	indignado *aj*
infuriated	enfurecido *aj*
irate	iracundo *aj*
jealous	celoso *aj*
livid	lívido *aj*
offended	ofendido *aj*
provoked	provocado *aj*
rabid	rabioso *aj*
resentful	resentido *aj*

FEELINGS

pleasant

affection	afecto *nm*
amity	amistad *nf*
animation	animación *nf*
calmness	calma *nf*
camaraderie	camaradería *nf*
certainty	certeza, certidumbre *nf*
composure	compostura *nf*
confidence	confianza *nf*
consolation	consuelo *nm*
contentment	contento *nm*
delight	deleite *nm*
desire	deseo *nm*
effusion	efusión *nf*
enchantment	encanto *nm*
enthusiasm	entusiasmo *nm*
euphoria	euforia *nf*
exaltation	exaltación *nf*
excitement	excitación *nf*
expectation *nsg*	expectativas *nfpl*
exuberance	exuberancia *nf*
exultation	exultación *nf*
fascination	fascinación *nf*
felicity	felicidad *nf*
fervor	fervor *nm*
gratification	gratificación *nf*

gratitude	gratitud *nf*
hilarity	hilaridad *nf*
intimacy	intimidad *nf*
joviality	jovialidad *nf*
jubilation	júbilo *nm*
nostalgia	nostalgia *nf*
passion	pasión *nf*
pensive	pensativo *aj*
pleasure	placer *nm*
satisfaction	satisfacción *nf*
serenity	serenidad *nf*
solace	solaz *nm*
solemnity	solemnidad *nf*
solitude	soledad *nf*
surprise	sorpresa *nf*
tranquility Ⓐ	tranquilidad *nf*
zeal	celo *nm*

unpleasant

abandonment	abandono *nm*
abhorrence	aborrecimiento *nm*
abnegation	abnegación *nf*
abomination	abominación *nf*
acrimony	acrimonia *nf*
alarm	alarma *nf*
ambivalence	ambivalencia *nf*
anguish	angustia *nf*
animadversion	animadversión *nf*
animosity	animosidad *nf*
antagonism	antagonismo *nm*
antipathy	antipatía *nf*
anxiety	ansiedad *nf*
apathy	apatía *nf*
apprehension	aprensión *nf*
aversion	aversión *nf*
boredom	aburrimiento *nm*
confusion	confusión *nf*
consternation	consternación *nf*
contrition	contrición *nf*
depression	depresión *nf*
desolation	desolación *nf*
despair, desperation	desesperación *nf*
detestation	detestación *nf*
disaffection	desafecto *nm*
discontent	descontento *nm*
disdain	desdén *nm*
disenchantment	desencanto *nm*
disorientation	desorientación *nf*
displeasure	desplacer *nm*
disquiet, disquietude	inquietud *nf*
dissatisfaction	insatisfacción *nf*
distraction	distracción *nf*
doubt	duda *nf*

enmity	enemistad *nf*
envy	envidia *nf*
exacerbation	exacerbación *nf*
exasperation	exasperación *nf*
frenzy	frenesí *nm*
frustration	frustración *nf*
fury	furia *nf*
futility	futilidad *nf*
horror	horror *nm*
hostility	hostilidad *nf*
humiliation	humillación *nf*
impatience	impaciencia *nf*
indecision	indecisión *nf*
indignation	indignación *nf*
inferiority	inferioridad *nf*
inhibition	inhibición *nf*
insecurity	inseguridad *nf*
intimidation	intimidación *nf*
ire	ira *nf*
irritation	irritación *nf*
jealousy	celosía *nf*
malevolence	malevolencia *nf*
malice	malicia *nf*
melancholy	melancolía *nf*
misery	miseria *nf*
monotony	monotonía *nf*
nervousness	nerviosidad *nf*
odium	odio *nm*
panic	pánico *nm*
provocation	provocación *nf*
rage	rabia *nf*
rancor Ⓐ	rencor *nm*
recrimination	recriminación *nf*
repentance	arrepentimiento *nm*
repugnance	repugnancia *nf*
repulsion	repulsión *nf*
resentment	resentimiento *nm*
resignation	resignación *nf*
revenge	venganza *nf*
revulsion	revulsión *nf*
rivalry	rivalidad *nf*
strangeness	extrañeza *nf*
tedium	tedio *nm*
tension	tensión *nf*
terror	terror *nm*
torment	tormento *nm*
uncertainty	incertidumbre *nf*
unreality	irrealidad *nf*
vacillation	vacilación *nf*
vehemence	vehemencia *nf*
vengeance	venganza *nf*

(*See also* **PSYCHOLOGY**)

CHARACTER TRAITS

ELEMENTS OF PERSONALITY

aptitude	aptitud *nf*
attitude	actitud *nf*
attribute	atributo *nm*
character	carácter *nm*
emotion	emoción *nf*
habit	hábito *nm*
idiosyncrasy	idiosincrasia *nf*
intellect	intelecto *nm*
morale	moral *nf*
preconception	preconcepción *nf*
predilection	predilección *nf*
predisposition	predisposición *nf*
self-expression	autoexpresión *nf*
self-image	autoimagen *nf*
sentiments	sentimientos *nmpl*
talent	talento *nm*
temperament	temperamento *nm*
tendencies	tendencias *nfpl*
volition	volición *nf*

QUALITIES

desirable

affability	afabilidad *nf*
altruism	altruismo *nm*
amiability	amabilidad *nf*
aplomb	aplomo *nm*
ardor Ⓐ	ardor *nm*
aspiration	aspiración *nf*
avidity	avidez *nf*
benevolence	benevolencia *nf*
charisma	carisma *nm*
circumspection	circunspección *nf*
civic-mindedness	civismo, civilidad *nm, nf*
commiseration	conmiseración *nf*
compassion	compasión *nf*
cordiality	cordialidad *nf*
courage	coraje *nm*
courtesy	cortesía *nf*
credibility	credibilidad *nf*
curiosity	curiosidad *nf*
decency	decencia *nf*
dedication	dedicación *nf*
deference	deferencia *nf*
determination	determinación *nf*
dexterity	destreza *nf*
dignity	dignidad *nf*
diligence	diligencia *nf*
discretion	discreción *nf*

dynamism	dinamismo *nm*
effervescence	efervescencia *nf*
elegance	elegancia *nf*
empathy	empatía *nf*
ethics	ética *nf*
expressivity	expresividad *nf*
fidelity	fidelidad *nf*
fortitude	fortaleza *nf*
gallantry	galantería *nf*
generosity	generosidad *nf*
heroism	heroísmo *nm*
honesty	honestidad, honradez *nf*
honor Ⓐ	honor, honra *nm, nf*
hospitality	hospitalidad *nf*
humanitarianism	humanitarismo *nm*
humility	humildad *nf*
humor Ⓐ	humor *nm*
idealism	idealismo *nm*
imagination (inventiveness)	imaginativa *nf*
impartiality	imparcialidad *nf*
imperturbability	imperturbabilidad *nf*
individuality	individualidad *nf*
infallibility	infalibilidad *nf*
ingenuity	ingenio *nm*
integrity	integridad *nf*
inventiveness	inventiva *nf*
invulnerability	invulnerabilidad *nf*
judgment	juicio *nm*
largess(e)	largueza *nf*
leadership	liderazgo, liderato *nm*
loyalty	lealtad *nf*
magnanimity	magnanimidad *nf*
maturity	madurez *nf*
mercy	merced *nf*
modesty	modestia *nf*
munificence	munificencia *nf*
naturalness	naturalidad *nf*
nobility	nobleza *nf*
obedience	obediencia *nf*
objectivity	objetividad *nf*
optimism	optimismo *nm*
patience	paciencia *nf*
perseverance	perseverancia *nf*
persistence	persistencia *nf*
perspicacity	perspicacia *nf*
persuasiveness	persuasiva *nf*
philanthropy	filantropía *nf*
pity	piedad *nf*
placidity	placidez *nf*
precociousness, precocity	precocidad *nf*

promptness	prontitud *nf*	disloyalty	deslealtad *nf*
prudence	prudencia *nf*	disobedience	desobediencia *nf*
rectitude	rectitud *nf*	docility	docilidad *nf*
refinement	refinamiento *nm*	duplicity	duplicidad *nf*
respect	respeto *nm*	egocentrism	egocentrismo *nm*
respectability	respetabilidad *nf*	egoism	egoísmo *nm*
reverence	reverencia *nf*	egotism	egotismo *nm*
sagacity	sagacidad *nf*	elitism	elitismo *nm*
self-criticism	autocrítica *nf*	excitability	excitabilidad *nf*
self-determination	autodeterminación *nf*	exclusivism	exclusivismo *nm*
self-discipline	autodisciplina *nf*	exhibitionism	exhibicionismo *nm*
self-sufficiency	autosuficiencia *nf*	fallibility	falibilidad *nf*
sensibility	sensibilidad *nf*	falsity	falsedad, falsía *nf*
sincerity	sinceridad *nf*	fanaticism	fanatismo *nm*
sociability	sociabilidad *nf*	ferocity	ferocidad *nf*
solicitude	solicitud *nf*	frankness	franqueza *nf*
sophistication	sofisticación *nf*	hypocrisy	hipocresía *nf*
spontaneity	espontaneidad *nf*	ignorance	ignorancia *nf*
stability	estabilidad *nf*	immaturity	inmadurez *nf*
subtlety	sutileza *nf*	immodesty	inmodestia *nf*
tact	tacto *nm*	immorality	inmoralidad *nf*
tenacity	tenacidad *nf*	impassivity	impasibilidad *nf*
tolerance	tolerancia *nf*	impersonality	impersonalidad *nf*
urbanity	urbanidad *nf*	impertinence	impertinencia *nf*
valor Ⓐ	valentía, valor *nf, nm*	impetuosity	impetuosidad *nf*
values	valores *nmpl*	implacability	implacabilidad *nf*
veracity	veracidad *nf*	impracticability	impracticabilidad *nf*
vigilance	vigilancia *nf*	imprudence	imprudencia *nf*
virtue	virtud *nf*	impudence	impudencia *nf*
virtuosity	virtuosismo *nm*	inaccessibility	inaccesibilidad *nf*
		inadaptability	inadaptabilidad *nf*
		inadequacy	inadecuación *nf*

undesirable

		inconstancy	inconstancia *nf*
affectation	afectación *nf*	incorrigibility	incorregibilidad *nf*
aggression,	agresividad *nf*	incredibility	incredibilidad *nf*
aggressiveness		incredulity	incredulidad *nf*
amorality	amoralidad *nf*	indecency	indecencia *nf*
arbitrariness	arbitrariedad *nf*	indecorum	indecoro *nm*
arrogance	arrogancia *nf*	indelicacy	falta de delicadeza *nf*
audacity	audacia *nf*	indifference	indiferencia *nf*
avarice	avaricia *nf*	indiscretion	indiscreción *nf*
banality	banalidad *nf*	indolence	indolencia *nf*
belligerence	beligerancia *nf*	inefficiency	ineficacia *nf*
brusqueness	brusquedad *nf*	inelegance	inelegancia *nf*
brutality	brutalidad *nf*	ineptitude	ineptitud *nf*
capriciousness	capricho *nm*	ineptness	inepcia, ineptitud *nf*
condescension	condescendencia *nf*	inexperience	inexperiencia *nf*
cowardice	cobardía *nf*	ingenuousness	ingenuidad *nf*
cruelty	crueldad *nf*	(naivete)	
cynicism	cinismo *nm*	ingratitude	ingratitud *nf*
defiance	desafío *nm*	inhumanity	inhumanidad *nf*
depravity	depravación *nf*	insincerity	insinceridad *nf*
discourtesy	descortesía *nf*	insolence	insolencia *nf*
dishonesty	deshonestidad *nf*		

T

instability	inestabilidad *nf*
intemperance	intemperancia *nf*
intolerance	intolerancia *nf*
intransigence	intransigencia *nf*
irrationality	irracionalidad *nf*
irresolution	irresolución *nf*
irresponsibility	irresponsabilidad *nf*
irreverence	irreverencia *nf*
masochism	masoquismo *nm*
mediocrity	mediocridad *nf*
obstinacy	obstinación *nf*
opportunism	oportunismo *nm*
partiality	parcialidad *nf*
passivity	pasividad *nf*
pedantry	pedantería *nf*
perversity	perversidad *nf*
pessimism	pesimismo *nm*
pomposity	pomposidad *nf*
pretense, pretension Ⓐ	pretensión *nf*
provincialism	provincialismo *nm*
pugnacity	pugnacidad *nf*
pusillanimity	pusilanimidad *nf*
racism Ⓐ	racismo *nm*
rapacity	rapacidad *nf*
rebelliousness	rebeldía *nf*
reticence	reticencia *nf*
self-destruction	autodestrucción *nf*
servility	servilismo *nm*
sexism	sexismo *nm*
snobbery, snobbishness	snobismo, esnobismo *nm*
stupidity	estupidez *nf*
subjectivity	subjetividad *nf*
submissiveness	sumisión *nf*
superficiality	superficialidad *nf*
timidity	timidez *nf*
vainglory	vanagloria *nf*
vanity	vanidad *nf*
villainy	villanía *nf*
voracity	voracidad *nf*
vulgarity	vulgaridad *nf*
vulnerability	vulnerabilidad *nf*

depends on point of view

acquiescence	aquiescencia *nf*
ambition	ambición *nf*
austerity	austeridad *nf*
conformity	conformidad *nf*
eccentricity	excentricidad *nf*
eclecticism	eclecticismo *nm*
frugality	frugalidad *nf*
inflexibility	inflexibilidad *nf*
innocence	inocencia *nf*

intellectualism	intelectualismo *nm*
intrepidity	intrepidez *nf*
introspection	introspección *nf*
lenience, leniency	lenidad *nf*
liberality	liberalidad *nf*
nonconformity	disconformidad *nf*
normalcy, normality	normalidad *nf*
permissiveness	permisividad *nf*
propensity	propensión *nf*
reserve	reserva *nf*
sentimentalism	sentimentalismo *nm*
suggestibility	sugestibilidad *nf*
temerity	temeridad *nf*

(*See also* **PSYCHOLOGY**)

SENSE IMPRESSIONS
GENERAL TERMS

acuity	acuidad *nf*
audible	audible *aj*
auditory	auditivo *aj*
discernment	discernimiento *nm*
discriminate	discriminar *vt*
distinguish	distinguir *vti*
emotion	emoción *nf*
olfactory	olfatorio *aj*
palate	paladar *nm*
perception	percepción *nf*
sensation	sensación *nf*
sensory	sensorial, sensorio *aj*
sensual, sensuous	sensual *aj*
sentiment	sentimiento *nm*
sound	son, sonido *nm*
tactile	táctil *aj*
touch	toque *nm*
vision	visión, vista *nf*
visual	visual *aj*

THE SENSE OF VISION
common light sources

candle	candela *nf*
lamp	lámpara *nf*
lantern	linterna *nf*
neon	neón *nm*
torch	antorcha *nf*

light associations

brilliant	brillante *aj*
clear	claro *aj*
incandescent	incandescente *aj*
invisible	invisible *aj*

iridescent	iridescente, irisado *aj*
lucid	lúcido *aj*
luminescent	luminescente *aj*
luminous	luminoso *aj*
opalescent	opalescente *aj*
opaque	opaco *aj*
phosphorescent	fosforescente *aj*
visible	visible *aj*

pleasant sights

art	arte *nf(el)*
decoration	decoración *nf*
garden	jardín *nm*
panorama	panorama *nm*
scene	escena *nf*
spectacle	espectáculo *nm*
splendor	esplendidez, esplendor *nf, nm*
vista	vista *nf*

unpleasant sights

chaos	caos *nm*
commotion	conmoción *nf*
disorder	desorden *nm*
monstrosity	monstruosidad *nf*
sordidness	sordidez *nf*
squalor	escualidez *nf*

other terms

appearance	aparición *nf*
color Ⓐ	color *nm*
evanescent	evanescente *aj*
illumination	iluminación *nf*
illusion	ilusión *nf*
luster Ⓐ	lustre *nm*
obscure	oscuro *aj*
reflection	reflejo *nm*
semitransparent	semitransparente *aj*
silhouette	silueta *nf*
translucent	tra(n)slúcido *aj*
transparent	tra(n)sparente *aj*

THE SENSE OF HEARING

pleasant sounds

euphonious	eufónico *aj*
harmonious	armonioso *aj*
mellifluous	melifluo *aj*
melodious	melodioso *aj*
murmur	murmullo *nm*
musical	musical *aj*
resonant	resonante *aj*
sonorous	sonoro *aj*

unpleasant sounds

alarm	alarma *nf*
cacophony	cacofonía *nf*
clamor	clamor *nm*
crack	crac *nm*
pandemonium	pandemonio, pandemónium *nm*
rasping	raspadura *nf*
stentorian	estentóreo *aj*
strident	estridente *aj*

imitative sounds

choo-choo	chu-cu-chu(ca) *nm*
click	clic Ⓒ *nm*
ding dong	din don *nm*
echo Ⓑ	eco *nm*
ticktock	tictac *nm*
tintinabulation	tintineo *nm*

other terms

acoustic(al)	acústico *aj*
inaudible	inaudible *aj*
megaphone	megáfono *nm*
repercussion	repercusión *nf*
reverberation	reverberación, reverbero *nf, nm*
silence	silencio *nm*
sound	sonar *vi*
subsonic	subsónico *aj*
supersonic	supersónico *aj*
tone	tono *nm*
tumult	tumulto *nm*
tumultuous	tumultuoso *aj*
ululate	ulular *vi*
voice	voz *nf*

THE SENSE OF TOUCH

kinds of touch

breeze	brisa *nf*
caress	caricia *nf*
embrace	abrazo *nm*
gummy	gomoso *aj*
manipulation	manipulación, manipuleo *nf, nm*
palpation	palpación *nf*

other terms

balm	bálsamo *nm*
mastic	mástique *nm*
mucilage	mucílago *nm*
tangible	tangible *aj*
voluptuous	voluptuoso *aj*

SMELL

pleasant

aroma	aroma *nm*
bouquet	bouquet, buqué *nm*
essence	esencia *nf*
fragrance	fragancia *nf*
perfume	perfume *nm*
potpourri Ⓑ	popurrí *nm*
sandalwood	sándalo *nm*
tuberose	tuberosa *nf*
violet	violeta *nf*

unpleasant

acrid	acre *aj*
fetid, foetid	fétido *aj*
fetidness	fetidez *nf*
nauseating	nauseabundo *aj*
putrid	pútrido, putrefacto *aj*
rancid	rancio *aj*

other terms

deodorant	desodorante *nm*
odor Ⓐ	olor *nm*
pungent	pungente *aj*

GENERAL PHYSICAL SENSATIONS

agility	agilidad *nf*
comfort	confort *nm*
energetic	enérgico *aj*
inactivity	inactividad *nf*
languid	lánguido *aj*
languor	languidez *nf*
lassitude	lasitud *nf*
lethargy	letargo, aletargamiento *nm*
phlegmatic	flemático *aj*
relaxation	relajación *nf*
robustness	robustez *nf*
sensuousness	sensualidad *nf*
stress	estrés *nm*
stupefaction	estupefacción *nf*
stupor	estupor *nm*
tension	tensión *nf*
trembling	temblor *nm*
vigor Ⓐ	vigor *nm*
vitality	vitalidad *nf*
vivacity	vivacidad, viveza *nf*

(*See also tastes, textures, quality,* under **FOOD AND NUTRITION**; *TERMS IN WAVE PHYSICS* under **PHYSICS**; *PHYSIOLOGY* under **THE HUMAN BODY**)

ACTIONS AND ACTORS

DESIRABLE

adaptable	adaptable *aj*
admirable	admirable *aj*
adorable	adorable *aj*
adventurous	aventurero *aj*
agreeable	agradable *aj*
altruistic	altruista *aj*
ambitious	ambicioso *aj*
amiable	amable *aj*
amicable	amigable *aj*
attentive	atento *aj*
attractive	atractivo, atrayente *aj*
benevolent	benévolo *aj*
calm	calmo *aj*
capricious	caprichoso *aj*
captivating	cautivador *aj*
cautious	cauteloso, cauto *aj*
charitable	caritativo *aj*
communicative	comunicativo *aj*
compassionate	compasivo *aj*
competent	competente *aj*
conciliatory	conciliador *aj*
conscientious	concienzudo *aj*
considerate	considerado *aj*
cooperative	cooperativo *aj*
cordial	cordial *aj*
cosmopolitan	cosmopolita *aj*
courteous	cortés *aj*
creative	creativo *aj*
credible	creíble *aj*
cultivated, cultured	culto *aj*
curious	curioso *aj*
decent	decente *aj*
deferential	deferente *aj*
deliberate	deliberado *aj*
devoted	devoto *aj*
dignified	digno *aj*
diligent	diligente *aj*
diplomatic	diplomático *aj*
discreet	discreto *aj*
distinguished	distinguido *aj*
dynamic	dinámico *aj*
efficient	eficiente *aj*
elegant	elegante *aj*
enchanting	encantador *aj*
experienced	experimentado *aj*
expert	experto, -a *aj, nmf*
faithful	fiel *aj*
fascinating	fascinador, fascinante *aj*
flexible	flexible *aj*

gallant	galante *aj*	permissive	permisivo *aj*
generous	generoso *aj*	perspicacious	perspicaz *aj*
grateful	agradecido *aj*	persuasive	persuasivo *aj*
gregarious	gregario *aj*	philanthropic	filantrópico *aj*
heroic	heroico *aj*	philosophical	filosófico *aj*
honest	honesto, honrado *aj*	placid	plácido *aj*
honorable Ⓐ	honorable, honrado *aj*	pleasant, pleasing	placentero *aj*
hospitable	hospitalario *aj*	precocious	precoz *aj*
humane	humano *aj*	presentable	presentable *aj*
humanitarian	humanitario *aj*	prestigious	prestigioso *aj*
humble	humilde *aj*	prudent	prudente *aj*
humorous	humorístico *aj*	punctilious	puntilloso *aj*
idealistic	idealista *aj*	quixotic	quijotesco *aj*
illustrious	ilustre *aj*	rational	racional *aj*
imaginative	imaginativo *aj*	reasonable	razonable *aj*
impartial	imparcial *aj*	receptive	receptivo *aj*
incorruptible	incorruptible *aj*	refined	refinado *aj*
indefatigable	infatigable *aj*	reflective	reflexivo *aj*
indulgent	indulgente *aj*	respectful	respetuoso *aj*
influential	influyente *aj*	responsible	responsable *aj*
informed	informado *aj*	reverent	reverente *aj*
ingratiating	congraciador *aj*	romantic	romántico, -a *aj, nmf*
innovative	innovador *aj*	sagacious	sagaz *aj*
inquisitive (mind)	inquisitivo *aj*	scrupulous	escrupuloso *aj*
intellectual	intelectual *aj*	selective	selectivo *aj*
intelligent	inteligente *aj*	self-directed	autodirigido *aj*
interested	interesado *aj*	self-sufficient	autosuficiente *aj*
intrepid	intrépido *aj*	serene	sereno *aj*
intuitive	intuitivo *aj*	serious	serio *aj*
inventive	inventivo *aj*	sociable	sociable *aj*
irreproachable	irreprochable *aj*	solicitous	solícito *aj*
just	justo *aj*	spontaneous	espontáneo *aj*
laudable	laudable *aj*	stable	estable *aj*
laudatory	laudatorio *aj*	stimulating	estimulante *aj*
logical	lógico *aj*	tactful *aj*	de mucho tacto *nm*
loyal	leal *aj*	tolerant	tolerante *aj*
magnanimous	magnánimo *aj*	tranquil	tranquilo *aj*
methodical	metódico *aj*	unconventional	poco convencional *aj*
meticulous	meticuloso *aj*	unpretentious *aj*	sin pretenciones *nfpl*
model	modelo *aj*	urbane	urbano *aj*
modest	modesto *aj*	valiant	valiente *aj*
moral	moral *aj*	valorous	valeroso *aj*
motivated	motivado *aj*	versed	versado *aj*
munificent	munificente, munífico *aj*	vigilant	vigilante *aj*
		virtuous	virtuoso *aj*
noble	noble *aj*		
normal	normal *aj*		
obedient	obediente *aj*		

UNDESIRABLE

objective	objetivo *aj*
observant	observador *aj*
passionate	apasionado *aj*
patient	paciente *aj*
peaceful	pacífico *aj*

aberrant	aberrante *aj*
abhorrent	aborrecible *aj*
abnormal	anormal *aj*
absurd	absurdo *aj*
affected	afectado *aj*
aggressive	agresivo *aj*

alarming	alarmante *aj*	false	falso *aj*
antisocial	antisocial *aj*	flagrant	flagrante *aj*
atrocious	atroz *aj*	frenetic	frenético *aj*
audacious	audaz *aj*	frivolous	frívolo *aj*
belligerent	beligerante *aj*	frugal	frugal *aj*
boring	aburrido, aburridor *aj*	furtive	furtivo *aj*
brusque	brusco *aj*	gluttonous	glotón *aj*
brutal, brutish	brutal *aj*	horrendous	horrendo *aj*
calculating	calculador *aj*	horrible	horrible *aj*
compulsive	compulsivo *aj*	hostile	hostil *aj*
condescending	condescendiente *aj*	humorless *aj* 🅐	sin sentido del humor
contumacious	contumaz *aj*		*nm*
conventional	convencional *aj*	hypercritical	hipercrítico *aj*
corrupt	corrupto, corrompido	hypocritical	hipócrita *aj*
	aj	ignoble	innoble *aj*
counterproductive	contraproducente *aj*	ignominious	ignominioso *aj*
cowardly	cobarde *aj*	ignorant	ignorante *aj*
crass	craso *aj*	illogical	ilógico *aj*
criminal	criminal *aj, nmf*	immature	inmaduro *aj*
critical	crítico *aj*	immoderate	inmoderado *aj*
cruel	cruel *aj*	immodest	inmodesto *aj*
cynical	cínico *aj*	immoral	inmoral *aj*
decadent	decadente *aj*	imperious	imperioso *aj*
defiant	desafiante *aj*	impertinent	impertinente *aj*
degenerate	degenerado, -a *aj, nmf*	impetuous	impetuoso *aj*
denigrating	denigrante *aj*	impractical	impráctico *aj*
deplorable	deplorable *aj*	improper	impropio *aj*
depraved	depravado *aj*	imprudent	imprudente *aj*
destructive	destructor *aj*	impulsive	impulsivo *aj*
detestable	detestable *aj*	inane	inano *aj*
diabolic(al)	diabólico *aj*	incapable	incapaz *aj*
dictatorial	dictatorial *aj*	incautious	incauto *aj*
disagreeable	desagradable *aj*	incompetent	incompetente *aj*
disciplined	disciplinado *aj*	inconsiderate	desconsiderado *aj*
discourteous	descortés *aj*	inconsistent	inconsistente *aj*
disdainful	desdeñoso *aj*	incorrigible	incorregible *aj*
dishonorable	deshonroso *aj*	indecent	indecente *aj*
disloyal	desleal *aj*	indefensible	indefendible *aj*
disobedient	desobediente *aj*	indelicate	indelicado *aj*
disorganized	desorganizado *aj*	indiscreet	indiscreto *aj*
disrespectful	irrespetuoso *aj*	indolent	indolente *aj*
dissolute	disoluto *aj*	indomitable	indomable, indómito *aj*
docile	dócil *aj*	inefficient	ineficaz *aj*
dogmatic	dogmático *aj*	inept	inepto *aj*
domineering	dominante *aj*	inexcusable	inexcusable *aj*
eccentric	excéntrico, -a *aj, nmf*	infantile	infantil *aj*
effusive	efusivo *aj*	ingenuous	ingenuo *aj*
egocentric	egocéntrico *aj*	inhibited	inhibido *aj*
egoistic(al),	egoísta, egotista *aj*	inhospitable	inhospitalario *aj*
egotistic(al)		inhumane	inhumano *aj*
exasperating	exasperante *aj*	iniquitous	inicuo *aj*
extravagant	extravagante *aj*	insatiable	insaciable *aj*
extremist	extremista *aj, nmf*	insecure	inseguro *aj*

insidious	insidioso *aj*	provocative	provocador *aj*
insincere	insincero *aj*	puerile	pueril *aj*
insolent	insolente *aj*	pugnacious	pugnaz *aj*
insubordinate	insubordinado *aj*	puritanical	puritano *aj*
insufferable	insufrible *aj*	pusillanimous	pusil nime *aj*
insulting	insultante *aj*	questionable	cuestionable *aj*
intolerable	intolerable *aj*	racist Ⓐ	racista *aj, nmf*
intolerant	intolerante *aj*	rancorous	rencoroso *aj*
intractable	intratable *aj*	rapacious	rapaz *aj*
intransigent	intransigente *aj*	rebellious	rebelde *aj*
irrational	irracional *aj*	repellent	repelente *aj*
irresponsible	irresponsable *aj*	reprehensible	reprensible *aj*
irritable	irritable *aj*	reproachful	reprobador *aj*
irritating	irritante *aj*	repugnant	repugnante *aj*
lascivious	lascivo *aj*	repulsive	repulsivo *aj*
malevolent	malévolo *aj*	reserved	reservado *aj*
malicious	malicioso *aj*	reticent	reticente *aj*
manipulative	manipulador *aj*	ridiculous	ridículo *aj*
mannered	amanerado *aj*	rigid	rígido *aj*
masochistic	masoquista *aj*	sadistic	sádico *aj*
materialistic	materialista *aj*	sanctimonious	santurrón *aj*
menacing	amenazador *aj*	sarcastic	sarcástico *aj*
moralizing	moralizador *aj*	sardonic	sardónico *aj*
morbid	mórbido *aj*	satanic	satánico *aj*
nefarious	nefario *aj*	savage	salvaje *aj, nmf*
neurotic	neurótico, -a *aj, nmf*	scandalous	escandaloso *aj*
objectionable	objetable *aj*	self-destructive	autodestructor *aj*
obsequious	obsequioso *aj*	senseless	insensato *aj*
obsessive	obsesivo *aj*	servile	servil *aj*
obstinate	obstinado *aj*	sexist	sexista *aj, nmf*
odious	odioso *aj*	shocking	chocante *aj*
offensive	ofensivo *aj*	simplistic	simplista *aj*
officious	oficioso *aj*	sinister	siniestro *aj*
opprobious	oprobioso *aj*	snobbish	esnobista *aj*
ostentatious	ostentoso *aj*	solitary	solitario *aj*
otiose	ocioso *aj*	strange	extraño *aj*
overcritical	criticón *aj*	strict	estricto *aj*
parasitic	parásito *aj*	stupid	estúpido *aj*
parsimonious	parsimonioso *aj*	submissive	sumiso *aj*
partial	parcial *aj*	subnormal	subnormal *aj*
passionless	poco apasionado *aj*	subversive	subversivo, -a *aj, nmf*
pedantic	pedante, pedantesco *aj*	superficial	superficial *aj*
pedestrian	pedestre *aj*	surreptitious	subrepticio *aj*
perfidious	pérfido *aj*	suspicious	sospechoso *aj*
persistent	persistente *aj*	tactless	falto de tacto *aj, nm*
perverse	perverso *aj*	timid	tímido *aj*
pessimistic	pesimista *aj*	tormenting	atormentador *aj*
pitiless	despiadado *aj*	tyrannical	tiránico, tirano *aj*
pompous	pomposo *aj*	ultraconservative	ultraconservador(a) *aj, nmf*
possessive	posesivo *aj*		
pretentious	pretencioso *aj*	unacceptable	inaceptable *aj*
promiscuous	promiscuo *aj*	unceremonious	inceremonioso *aj*
provincial	provincial *aj*	uncivil	incivil *aj*

uncivilized	incivilizado *aj*
uncontrollable	incontrolable *aj*
uncultured	inculto *aj*
uncuous	untuoso *aj*
undesirable	indeseable *aj*
undisciplined	indisciplinado *aj*
uneducated	ineducado *aj*
ungovernable	ingobernable *aj*
ungrateful	ingrato *aj*
unimaginative	poco imaginativo *aj*
unintelligent	ininteligente *aj*
unjust	unjusto *aj*
unlettered	iletrado *aj*
unpardonable	imperdonable *aj*
unscrupulous	inescrupuloso *aj*
unsociable	insociable *aj*
unsocial	insocial *aj*
unsportsmanlike [A]	antideportivo *aj*
vacuous	vacuo *aj*
vain	vanidoso *aj*
vainglorious	vanaglorioso *aj*
vengeful	vengativo *aj*
vicious	vicioso *aj*
vile	vil *aj*
villainous	villano *aj*
vindictive	vindicativo *aj*
violent	violento *aj*

(*See also* **ROLES AND RELATIONSHIPS**)

EXPERIENCES

BENEFICIAL

acclaim	aclamación *nf*
accolade	acolada *nf*
admiration	admiración *nf*
adulation	adulación *nf*
advantage	ventaja *nf*
affection	afecto *nm*
amenity	amenidad *nf*
applause	aplauso *nm*
approbation	aprobación *nf*
approval	aprobación *nf*
assent	asentimiento, asenso *nm*
benefit	beneficio *nm*
caprice	capricho *nm*
celebrity	celebridad *nmf*
compliment	cumplido *nm*
cooperation	cooperación *nf*
eminence	eminencia *nf*
encomium [B]	encomio *nm*
esteem	estima *nf*
eulogy	elogio *nm*
fame	fama *nf*
glamour, glamor	glamour *nm*
homage	homenaje *nm*
honors [A]	honores *nmpl*
laurels	laureles *nmpf*
popularity	popularidad *nf*
prestige	prestigio *nm*
recognition	reconocimiento *nm*
recommendation	recomendación *nf*
reconciliation	reconciliación *nf*
renown	renombre *nm*
respect	respeto *nm*
tribute	tributo *nm*
veneration	veneración *nf*

HARMFUL

abuse	abuso *nm*
accident	accidente *nm*
adversity	adversidad *nf*
affront	afrenta *nf*
altercation	altercado *nm*
calamity	calamidad *nf*
confinement	confinamiento *nm*
confrontation	confrontación *nf*
connivance	connivencia *nf*
debacle	debacle *nf*
defamation	difamación *nf*
degradation	degradación *nf*
demoralization	desmoralización *nf*
denigration	denigración *nf*
deprivation	privación *nf*
deterioration	deterioro *nm*
detriment	detrimento *nm*
difficulty	dificultad *nf*
dilemma	dilema *nm*
disadvantage	desventaja *nf*
disapproval	desaprobación *nf*
discord	discordia *nf*
discredit	descrédito *nm*
discrimination	discriminación *nf*
disfigurement	desfiguración *nf*
dishonor [A]	deshonra *nf*
disillusion	desilusión *nf*
disorganization	desorganización *nf*
dispossession	desposeimiento *nm*
dispute	disputa *nf*
disservice	deservicio *nm*
domination	dominación *nf*
enslavement	esclavización *nf*
expropriation	expropiación *nf*
falsification	falsificación *nf*
favoritism	favoritismo *nm*

fiasco Ⓑ	fiasco *nm*
furor	furor *nm*
ignominy	ignominia *nf*
inconvenience	inconveniente *nm*
indignity	indignidad *nf*
indoctrination	adoctrinamiento *nm*
inequity	inequidad *nf*
infamy	infamia *nf*
iniquity	iniquidad *nf*
injustice	injusticia *nf*
insistence	insistencia *nf*
intrusion	intrusión *nf*
lamentation	lamentación *nf*
limitation	limitación *nf*
machination	maquinación *nf*
maltreatment	maltrato,
	maltratamiento *nm*
menace	amenaza *nf*
misfortune	infortunio *nm*
mistreatment	maltrato *nm*
mutilation	mutilación *nf*
neglect, negligence	negligencia *nf*
obscurity	o(b)scuridad *nf*
obsession	obsesión *nf*
oppression	opresión *nf*
opprobrium	oprobio *nm*
ostracism	ostracismo *nm*
palliative	paliativo *nm*

paperwork	papeleo *nm*
perfidy	perfidia *nf*
persecution	persecución *nf*
prejudice	prejuicio *nm*
preoccupation (worry)	preocupación *nf*
pretext	pretexto *nm*
protestation	protestación *nf*
reprimand	reprimenda *nf*
reproach	reproche *nm*
repudiation	repudiación, repudio
	nf, nm
restriction	restricción *nf*
ridicule	ridículo *nm*
ruin	ruina *nf*
scandal	escándalo *nm*
servitude	servidumbre *nf*
stigma Ⓑ	estigma *nm*
subjugation	subyugación *nf*
subterfuge	subterfugio *nm*
suffering	sufrimiento *nm*
suppression	supresión *nf*
suspicion	sospecha *nf*
temptation	tentación *nf*
tribulation	tribulación *nf*
ultimatum Ⓑ	ultimátum *nm*
unpopularity	impopularidad *nf*

(*See also* CULTURAL ANTHROPOLOGY under
ANTHROPOLOGY AND ARCHEOLOGY)

Forms of Address

PERSONAL NAMES

FEMININE NAMES

Biblical origin

Deborah	Debora *nf*
Esther	Éster *nf*
Eve	Eva *nf*
Josephine	Josefa *nf*
Judith	Judit *nf*
Mary	María *nf*
Rachel	Raquel *nf*
Ruth	Rut *nf*
Sarah	Sara *nf*

Greek or Latin origin

Alexandra	Alejandra *nf*
Barbara	Bárbara *nf*
Beatrice	Beatriz *nf*
Catherine	Catalina *nf*
Cecily	Cecilia *nf*
Clara	Clara *nf*
Clementine	Clementina *nf*
Constance	Constanza *nf*
Daphne	Dafne *nf*
Diana	Diana *nf*
Dorothy	Dorotea *nf*
Ellen	Elena *nf*
Emily	Emilia *nf*
Florence	Florencia *nf*
Gloria	Gloria *nf*
Helen	Helena *nf*
Inez	Inés *nf*
Irene	Irena *nf*
Julia	Julia *nf*
Juliana	Juliana *nf*
Juliet	Julieta *nf*
Lucy	Lucía *nf*
Madeline	Magdalena *nf*
Margaret	Margarita *nf*
Patricia	Patricia *nf*
Pauline	Paulina *nf*
Regina	Regina *nf*
Rose	Rosa *nf*
Sophia	Sofía *nf*
Theresa	Teresa *nf*
Veronica	Verónica *nf*
Victoria	Victoria *nf*
Virginia	Virginia *nf*

Germanic origin

Adele	Adela *nf*
Alice	Alicia *nf*
Amelia	Amalia *nf*
Bridgit	Brígida *nf*
Caroline	Carolina *nf*
Edith	Edita *nf*
Ernestine	Ernestina *nf*
Frances	Francisca *nf*
Frieda	Frida *nf*
Gertrude	Gertrudís *nf*
Henrietta	Enriqueta *nf*
Louise	Luisa *nf*
Matilda	Matilde *nf*

other origins

Ann, Anne, Anna	Ana *nf*
Bernadette	Bernarda *nf*
Charlotte	Carlota *nf*
Christine	Cristina *nf*
Elizabeth	Isabela *nf*
Isabella	Isabel *nf*
Joan	Juana *nf*
Leonore	Leonora *nf*
Lorraine	Lorena *nf*
Martha	Marta *nf*
Rosalind	Rosalinda *nf*
Susan	Susana *nf*

MASCULINE NAMES

Biblical origin

Aaron	Arón *nm*
Abraham	Abrahán *nm*
Adam	Adán *nm*
Benjamin	Benjamín *nm*
Daniel	Daniel *nm*
David	David *nm*
Emmanuel, Imanuel	Emanuel, Imanuel *nm*
Ezekiel	Ezequiel *nm*
Ezra	Esdras *nm*
Gabriel	Gabriel *nm*
Isaac	Isaac *nm*
Jacob	Jacobo *nm*
James	Jaime *nm*
John	Juan *nm*
Joseph	José *nm*

Joshua	Josué *nm*
Luke	Lucas *nm*
Mark	Marcos *nm*
Matthew	Mateo *nm*
Michael	Miguel *nm*
Nathan	Natán *nm*
Noah	Noé *nm*
Paul	Pablo *nm*
Peter	Pedro *nm*
Raphael	Rafael *nm*
Samuel	Samuel *nm*
Saul	Saúl *nm*
Simon	Simón *nm*
Solomon	Salomón *nm*
Thomas	Tomás *nm*
Timothy	Timoteo *nm*

Greek or Latin origin

Alexander	Alejandro *nm*
Ambrose	Ambrosio *nm*
Andrew	Andrés *nm*
Anthony	Antonio *nm*
Bartholomew	Bartolomé *nm*
Benedict	Benito *nm*
Cecil	Cecilio *nm*
Christopher	Cristóbal *nm*
Claud, Claude	Claudio *nm*
Clement	Clemente *nm*
Dennis	Dionisio *nm*
Emil	Emilio *nm*
Eugene	Eugenio *nm*
George	Jorge *nm*
Giles	Gil *nm*
Gregory	Gregorio *nm*
Hadrian	Adriano *nm*
Horace	Horacio *nm*
Ignatius	Ignacio *nm*
Jerome	Jerónimo *nm*
Julian	Julián *nm*
Julius	Julio *nm*
Laurence, Lawrence	Lorenzo *nm*
Leo	Leo *nm*
Leonard	Leonardo *nm*
Lucius	Lucio *nm*
Marcus	Marcos *nm*
Martin	Martín *nm*
Nicholas	Nicolás *nm*
Patrick	Patricio *nm*
Philip	Felipe *nm*
Stephen	Esteban *nm*
Theodore	Teodoro *nm*
Victor	Victor *nm*
Vincent	Vicente *nm*

Germanic origin

Adolf	Adolfo *nm*
Albert	Alberto *nm*
Alphonso	Alfonso *nm*
Bernard	Bernardo *nm*
Charles	Carlos *nm*
Ernest	Ernesto *nm*
Ferdinand	Fernando *nm*
Francis	Francisco *nm*
Frederick	Federico *nm*
Gerald	Geraldo *nm*
Gerard	Gerardo *nm*
Godfrey	Godofredo *nm*
Harold	Haroldo *nm*
Henry	Enrique *nm*
Lewis, Louis	Luis *nm*
Ralph	Raúl *nm*
Raymond	Ramón, Raimundo *nm*
Reginald	Reginaldo *nm*
Richard	Ricardo *nm*
Robert	Roberto *nm*
Rudolph	Rudolfo *nm*
Walter	Gualterio *nm*
William	Guillermo *nm*

other origins

Adrian	Adriano *nm*
Alan	Alano *nm*
Alfred	Alfredo *nm*
Arthur	Arturo *nm*
Augustine	Agustín *nm*
Calvin	Calvino *nm*
Edward	Eduardo *nm*
Ellis	Elías *nm*
Herbert	Herberto *nm*
Hugh	Hugo *nm*
Maurice	Moricio *nm*
Oliver	Oliverio *nm*
Stanley	Estanislao *nm*

RELATED TERMS

alias	alias *av, nm*
anonymity	anonimato *nm*
autograph	autógrafo *nm*
eponym	epónimo *nm*
family name	nombre de familia *nm, nf*
fictitious name	nombre ficticio *nm*
first name	nombre de pila *nm*
identity	identidad *nf*
incognito	incógnito *aj, av*

nom de plume	nombre de pluma *nm, nf*
onomastics	onomástica *nf*
patronymic	patronímico *nm*
pseudonym	(p)seudónimo *nm*

(*See also* **THE BIBLE**; **HISTORY**; **RELIGION**)

TITLES

GENERAL TERMS

designation	designación *nf*
domain	dominio *nm*
honorific	honorífico *aj*
rank	rango *nm*
title	título *nm*

KINDS OF TITLES

political

ambassador	embajador(a) *nmf*
Chancellor	canciller *nm*
congressman Ⓑ	congresista *nm*
congresswoman Ⓑ	congresista *nf*
consul	cónsul *nm*
emir	emir *nm*
emperor	emperador *nm*
empress	emperatriz *nf*
Excellency	Excelencia *nmf*
governor	gobernador(a) *nmf*
khan	kan *nm*
minister	ministro, -a *nmf*
premier	primer ministro *nmf*
president	presidente *nmf*
prime minister	primer ministro *nm*
prime minister	primera ministra *nf*
regent	regente *nmf*
secretary	secretario, -a *nmf*
senator	senador(a) *nmf*
sultan	sultán *nm*
sultana	sultana *nf*
vice-president	vicepresidente *nmf*

military

admiral	almirante *nm*
brigadier general	general de brigada *nm*
captain	capitán, -ana *nmf*
colonel	coronel(a) *nmf*
general	general(a) *nmf*
generalissimo	generalísimo *nm*
lieutenant	teniente *nmf*
major	mayor *nm*

marshall	mariscal *nm*
sergeant	sargento *nm*

religious

abbess	abadesa *nf*
abbot	abad *nm*
archbishop	arzobispo *nm*
archdeacon	archidiácono *nm*
ayatollah	ayatolah *nm*
bishop	obispo *nm*
cardinal	cardenal *nm*
deacon	diácono *nm*
deaconess	diaconisa *nf*
dervish	derviche *nm*
Eminence	Eminencia *nf*
fakir	faquir *nm*
friar	fraile *nm*
imam	imán *nm*
lama	lama *nm*
mahatma	mahatma *nm*
metropolitan	metropolitano *nm*
minister	ministro, -a *nmf*
monk	monje *nm*
patriarch	patriarca *nm*
pontiff	pontífice *nm*
pope	papa *nm*
prelate	prelado *nm*
presbyter	presbítero *nm*
primate	primado *nm*
prior	prior *nm*
prioress	priora *nf*
rabbi	rabí *nm*
reverend	reverendo *nm*
vicar	vicario *nm*

royal

archduchess	archiduquesa *nf*
archduke	archiduque *nm*
baron	barón *nm*
baroness	baronesa *nf*
baronet	baronet *nm*
count	conde *nm*
countess	condesa *nf*
duchess	duquesa *nf*
duke	duque *nm*
Lord	lord *nm*
Majesty	Majestad *nmf*
marquis	marqués *nm*
marquise	marquesa *nf*
noble, nobleman Ⓑ	noble *nm*
noble, noblewoman Ⓑ	noble *nf*
peer	par *nmf*

peeress	paresa *nf*
prince	príncipe *nm*
princess	princesa *nf*
raja(h)	rajá *nm*
rani	rani *nf*
sheik(h)	jeque *nm*

historical

boyar	boyar, boyardo *nm*
burgomaster	burgomaestre *nm*
cacique	cacique *nm*
caliph	califa *nm*
centurion	centurión *nm*
commissar	comisario *nmf*
consul	cónsul *nm*
czar, tsar	zar *nm*
czarevitch, tsarevitch	zarevitz *nm*
czarevna, tzarevna	zarevna *nf*
czarina, czaritza	zarina *nf*
dauphin	delfín *nm*
dauphine	delfina *nf*
doge	dux *nm*
Kaiser	káiser *nm*
khedive	jedive *nm*
Levite	levita *nm*
maharaja(h)	maharajá, marajá *nm*
maharani, maharanee	maharani *nf*
Mandarin	mandarín *nm*
margrave	margrave *nm*
mikado	micado *nm*
pasha	pachá *nm*
Pharaoh	faraón *nm*
praetor	pretor *nm*
satrap	sátrapa *nm*
shah	sha, cha *nm*
shogun	shogún *nm*
tribune	tribuno *nm*
viscount	vizconde *nm*
viscountess	vizcondesa *nf*
vizier	visir *nm*

professional

counselor Ⓐ	consejero, -a *nmf*
doctor	doctor(a) *nmf*
emeritus	emérito *aj*
professor	profesor(a) *nmf*

other titles

chamberlain	chambelán *nm*
comrade	camarada *nf*
dame	dama *nf*
majordomo	mayordomo *nm*

OFFICES, RANKS, DOMAINS

ambassadorship	embajada *nf*
barony	baronía *nf*
caliphate	califato *nm*
captaincy	capitanía *nf*
chancellery	cancillería *nf*
commissariat	comisariato *nm*
consulship	consulado *nm*
duchy	ducado *aj*
dukedom	ducado *aj*
emirate	emirato *nm*
empire	imperio *nm*
generalship	generalato *nm*
governorship	gobierno *nm*
khanate	kanato *nm*
ministry	ministerio *nm*
peerage	paría *nf*
presidency	presidencia *nf*
princedom	principado *nm*
professorship	profesorado *nm*
rabbinate	rabinato *nm*
regency	regencia *nf*
secretariat	secretaría *nf*
senatorship	senaduría *nf*
sergeancy	sargentía *nf*
sheikdom	principado de jeque *nm*
sultanate	sultanato *nm*
vice-presidency	vicepresidencia *nmf*

(*See also* PERSONS under **LAW**; PERSONS under **RELIGION**; PERSONS under **THE MILITARY ESTABLISHMENT**)

ROLES AND RELATIONSHIPS

GENERAL TERMS

companionship	compañerismo *nm*
company	compañía *nf*
comradeship	camaradería *nf*
individual	individuo *nm*
personality	personalidad *nf*
relationship	relación *nf*
role, rôle	rol *nm*

RELATIONSHIPS

friendly

admirer	admirador(a) *nmf*
ally	aliado, -a *nmf*
associate	asociado, -a *nmf*
benefactor	benefactor(a) *nmf*
collaborator	colaborador(a) *nmf*
colleague	colega *nmf*

companion	compañero, -a *nmf*	conciliator	conciliador(a) *nmf*
comrade	camarada *nmf*	coordinator	coordinador(a) *nmf*
confidant	confidente *nmf*	intermediary	intermediario, -a
consoler	consolador(a) *nmf*		*nmf*
disciple	discípulo, -a *nmf*	judge	juez *nmf*
emulator	emulador(a) *nmf*	mediator	mediador(a) *nmf*
fan	fan C *nmf*	moderator	moderador, -a *nmf*
liberator	liberador, libertador	negotiator	negociador(a) *nmf*
	nm	pacifier	pacificador(a) *nmf*
protector	protector(a) *nmf*		
protégé(e)	protegido, -a *nmf*		

trouble-makers

provider	proveedor(a) *nmf*
receiver	recibidor(a) *nmf*
recipient	receptor(a) *nmf*
redeemer	redentor(a) *nmf*
spouse	esposo, -a *nmf*
sympathizer	simpatizante *nmf*
visitor	visitante *nmf*

agitator	agitador(a) *nmf*
alarmist	alarmista *nmf*
instigator	instigador(a) *nmf*
intruder	intruso, -a *nmf*
malcontent	malcontento, -a *nmf*
obstructionist	obstruccionista *nmf*
rebel	rebelde *nmf*
renegade	renegado, -a *nmf*
subversive	subversivo, -a *nmf*
traitor	traidor(a) *nmf*

unfriendly

accuser	acusador(a) *nmf*
adversary	adversario, -a *nmf*
antagonist	antagonista *nmf*
attacker	atacante *nmf*
avenger	vengador(a) *nmf*
competitor	competidor(a) *nmf*
contender	contendiente *nmf*
critic	crítico, -a *nmf*
defamer	difamador(a) *nmf*
denigrator	denigrador(a),
	denigrante *nmf*
detractor	detractor(a) *nmf*
enemy	enemigo, -a *nmf*
exploiter	explotador(a) *nmf*
expropriator	expropiador(a) *nmf*
flagellator	flagelador(a) *nmf*
manipulator	manipulador(a) *nmf*
opponent	oponente *nmf*
oppressor	opresor(a) *nmf*
persecutor	perseguidor(a) *nmf*
rival	rival *nmf*
tormenter, tormentor	atormentador(a) *nmf*
victim	víctima *nf*

advisers

arbiter	árbitro *nm*
counselor A	consejero, -a *nmf*
guide	guía *nmf*
instructor	instructor(a) *nmf*
leader	líder *nm*
mentor	mentor(a) *nmf*
monitor	monitor(a) *nmf*
trainer	entrenador(a) *nmf*
tutor	tutor(a) *nmf*

jokesters

buffoon	bufón *nm*
comedian	comediante *nmf*
comedienne	comedianta *nf*
comic	cómico, -a *nmf*
humorist A	humorista *nmf*
master of ceremonies	maestro de ceremonias
	nm, nfpl
parodist	parodista *nmf*

same status

double	doble *nmf*
equal	igual *nmf*
peer	par *nmf*
substitute	sustituto, -a *nmf*

thinkers

analyzer	analizador(a) *nmf*
genius B	genio *nm*
intellectual	intelectual *nmf*
pragmatist	pragmatista *nmf*
prodigy	prodigio *nm*
rationalist	racionalista *nmf*
skeptic A	escéptico, -a *nmf*
strategist	estratega *nmf*
visionary	visionario, -a *nmf*

ROLES

peacemakers

arbitrator	árbitro, -a *nmf*

doers

adventurer	aventurero, -a *nmf*
creator	creador(a) *nmf*
designer	diseñador(a) *nmf*
initiator	iniciador(a) *nmf*
innovator	innovador(a) *nmf*
inventor	inventor(a) *nmf*
organizer	organizador(a) *nmf*
originator	originador(a) *nmf*
pioneer	pionero, -a *nmf*
planner	planificador(a) *nmf*
producer	productor(a) *nmf*

givers

altruist	altruista *nmf*
contributor	contribuyente *nmf*
donor	donador(a), donante *nmf*
humanitarian	humanitario, -a *nmf*
philanthropist	filántropo, -a *nmf*
volunteer	voluntario, -a *nmf*

mavericks

disputant, disputer	disputador(a) *nmf*
dissident, dissenter	disidente *nmf*
independent	independiente *nmf*
individualist	individualista *nmf*
nonconformist	anticonformista *nmf*
objector	objetor(a) *nmf*

advocates

activist	activista *nmf*
apologist	apologista *nmf*
champion	campeón, -ona *nmf*
defender	defensor(a) *nmf*
enthusiast	entusiasta *nmf*
partisan	partidario, -a *nmf*
patron	patrocinador(a) *nmf*
promoter	promotor(a) *nmf*
propagandist	propagandista *nmf*

PERSONALITY TYPES

eccentric

bohemian	bohemio, -a *nmf*
eccentric	excéntrico, -a *nmf*
eclectic	ecléctico, -a *nmf*
fanatic	fanático, -a *nmf*
hermit	ermitaño, -a *nmf*

haters

homophobe	homofóbo, -a *nmf*
misanthrope	misántropo, -a *nmf*
misogynist	misógino *nm*
neo-Nazi	neonazi *nmf*
racist Ⓐ	racista *nmf*
supremacist	supremacista *nmf*
xenophobe	xenófobo, -a *nmf*

pleasure-seekers

aesthete, esthete	esteta *nmf*
connoisseur	conocedor(a) *nmf*
cosmopolitan, cosmopolite	cosmopolita *nmf*
epicure	epicúreo, -a *nmf*
esthete, aesthete	esteta *nmf*
gourmet	gourmet *nmf*
hedonist	hedonista *nmf*
libertine	libertino, -a *nmf*
sensualist	sensualista *nmf*
sybarite	sibarita *nmf*
voluptuary	voluptuoso, -a *nmf*

self-centered

egotist	egotista *nmf*
exhibitionist	exhibicionista *nmf*
megalomaniac	megalómano, -a *nmf*
opportunist	oportunista *nmf*

bullies

brute	bruto, -a *nmf*
masochist	masoquista *nmf*
mutilator	mutilador(a) *nmf*
ruffian	rufián *nm*
sadist	sádico, -a *nmf*
savage	salvaje *nmf*
vandal	vándalo, -a *nmf*
villain	villano, -a *nmf*

narrow-minded

chauvinist	chovinista *nmf*
dogmatist	dogmatista *nmf*
extremist	extremista *nmf*
ideologue	ideólogo, -a *nmf*
jingo, jingoist	jingoísta *nmf*
moralizer	moralizador(a) *nmf*
purist	purista *nmf*
radical	radical *nmf*
reactionary	reaccionario, -a *nmf*

liars

adulator	adulador(a) *nmf*
charlatan	charlatán, -ana *nmf*
defrauder	defraudador(a) *nmf*
falsifier	falsificador(a) *nmf*
hypocrite	hipócrita *nmf*
impostor	impostor(a) *nmf*

prevaricator   prevaricador(a) *nmf*
sycophant   sicofante *nm*

immoral

corrupter   corruptor(a) *nmf*
decadent   decadente *nmf*
degenerate   degenerado, -a *nmf*
pervert   pervertido, -a *nmf*
reprobate   réprobo, -a *nmf*
seducer   seductor(a) *nmf*
sociopath   sociópata *nmf*
tempter   tentador(a) *nmf*

martinets

authoritarian   autoritario, -a *nmf*
autocrat   autócrata *nmf*
demagog(ue)   demagogo, -a *nmf*
despot   déspota *nmf*
dictator   dictador(a) *nmf*
tyrant   tirano, -a *nmf*

other persons—good

expert   experto, -a *nmf*
hero B   héroe *nm*
heroine   heroína *nf*
idealist   idealista *nmf*
notable   notable *nmf*
optimist   optimista *nmf*
perfectionist   perfeccionista *nmf*
personage   personaje *nm*

realist   realista *nmf*
reformer   reformador(a) *nmf*
restorer   restaurador(a) *nmf*

other persons—bad

boob   bobo, -a *nmf*
conformist   conformista *nmf*
coward   cobarde *nmf*
cynic   cínico, -a *nmf*
dilettante   diletante *nmf*
idiot   idiota *nmf*
ignoramus   ignorante *nmf*
monopolizer   monopolizador(a) *nmf*
offender   ofensor(a) *nmf*
pariah   paria *nmf*
pessimist   pesimista *nmf*
sexist   sexista *nmf*
snob   snob, esnob *nmf*
vagabond   vagabundo, -a *nmf*

(*See also* PERSONS under **ENTERTAINMENT**; PERSONS under **FAMILY**; PERSONS under **JOURNALISM**; PERSONS under **USING LANGUAGE**; PERSONS under **LAW**; PERSONS under **MAGIC**; PERSONS under **MONEY AND FINANCE**; PERSONS under **ORGANIZATIONS AND MEETINGS**; PERSONS under **POLITICS AND GOVERNMENT**; PERSONS under **PSYCHOLOGY**; *real persons* under **SEXUALITY**; PERSONS under **THE MILITARY ESTABLISHMENT**; *individuals* under **WORK**)

Society and Culture

FAMILY

GENERAL TERMS

family	familia *nf*
generation	generación *nf*
lineage	linaje *nm*
matrimony	matrimonio *nm*

CLASSIFICATION

marriage terms

ceremony	ceremonia *nf*
certificate	certificado *nm*
conjugal	conyugal *aj*
connubial	connubial *aj*
courting	cortejo *nm*
domesticity	domesticidad *nf*
marital	marital *aj*
marriage of convenience	matrimonio de conveniencias *nm, nfpl*
matrimonial	matrimonial *aj*
mixed	mixto *aj*
morganatic	morganático *aj*
nubile	núbil *aj*
nuptials	nupcias *nfpl*
plural	plural *aj*
prenuptial	prenupcial *aj*
proposal	propuesta *nf*

types of families

communal	comunal *aj*
equalitarian	igualitario *aj*
extended	extendido *aj*
interracial	interracial *aj*
matriarchal	matriarcal *aj*
nuclear	nuclear *aj*
patriarchal	patriarcal *aj*
polygamous, polygynous	polígamo *aj*
traditional	tradicional *aj*

family groups

clan	clan *nm*
dynasty	dinastía *nf*
tribe	tribu *nf*

marriage practices

consanguinity	consanguinidad *nf*
endogamy	endogamia *nf*
exogamy	exogamia *nf*
monogamy	monogamia *nf*
polyandry	poliandria *nf*
polygamy	poligamia *nf*
polygyny	poliginia *nf*

lineage terms

extraction	extracción *nf*
genealogy	genealogía *nf*
heredity, heritage	herencia *nf*
matrilineal *aj*	por línea materna *nf*
mulatto B	mulato, -a *aj, nmf*
origin	origen *nm*
patrilineal	patrilineal *aj*
primogeniture	primogenitura *nf*
putative	putativo *aj*

parents

adoptive	adoptivo *aj*
biological	biológico *aj*
maternal	materno *aj*
paternal	paterno *aj*

children

adopted	adoptado *aj*
fraternal (twins)	fraternal *aj*
identical (twins)	idéntico *aj*
natural	natural *aj*
progeny	progenie *nf*
quadruplet	cuatrillizo, -a *nmf*
quintuplet	quintillizo, -a *nmf*
septuplet	septillizo, -a *nmf*
sextuplet	séxtuple *nmf*
triplet	trillizo, -a *nmf*

other terms

affinity	afinidad *nf*
cohabitation	cohabitación *nf*
collateral	colateral *aj*
concubinage	concubinato *nm*
consort	consorte *nmf*
filial	filial *aj*
harem	harén *nm*
seraglio	serrallo *nm*

LEGAL ASPECTS

possible grounds for divorce

abandonment	abandono *nm*
abuse	abuso *nm*
addiction	adicción *nf*
adultery	adulterio *nm*
alcoholism	alcoholismo *nm*
alienation	alienación *nf*
bigamy	bigamia *nf*
cruelty	crueldad *nf*
impotence	impotencia *nf*
incest	incesto *nm*
incompatibility	incompatibilidad *nf*
insanity	insania *nf*
neglect	negligencia *nf*
separation	separación *nf*

family crimes

fratricide (act)	fratricidio *nm*
infanticide (act)	infanticidio *nm*
matricide (act)	matricidio *nm*
parricide (act)	parricidio *nm*

other terms

adoption	adopción *nf*
alimony *nsg*	alimentos *nmpl*
annulment	anulación *nf*
custody	custodia *nf*
disinherit	desheredar *vt*
divorce	divorcio *nm*
illegitimacy	ilegitimidad *nf*
inheritance	herencia *nf*
intestate	intestado *aj*
legitimate	legítimo *aj*
patrimony	patrimonio *nm*
repudiation	repudio *nm*
succession	sucesión *nf*
surviving	sobreviviente *aj*

SEXUAL ASPECTS

consummation	consumación *nf*
extramarital	extramatrimonial *aj*
family planning	planificación familiar *nf*
fidelity	fidelidad *nf*
incestuous	incestuoso *aj*
infidelity	infidelidad *nf*
misogamy	misogamia *nf*
pair	pareja *nf*
pair off	emparejarse *vr*
paternity	paternidad *nf*
premarital	premarital *aj*

refuge	refugio *nm*
sex	sexo *nm*

PERSONS

adulterer	adúltero, -a *nmf*
adultress	adúltera *nf*
bastard	bastardo, -a *aj, nmf*
bigamist	bígamo, -a *nmf*
concubine	concubina *nf*
descendant	descendiente *nmf*
divorcé	divorciado *nm*
divorcée	divorciada *nf*
family member	familiar *nmf*
fratricide (killer)	fratricida *nm*
genealogist	genealogista *nmf*
heir	heredero, -a *nmf*
infanticide (killer)	infanticida *nmf*
ma, mama, momma	mamá *nf*
matriarch	matriarca *nf*
matricide (killer)	matricida *nmf*
matron	matrona *nf*
mom, mommy	mamita *nf*
orphan	huérfano, -a *nmf*
pa, papa, pop, poppa	papá, papi, papito *nm*
parricide (killer)	parricida *nmf*
paterfamilias Ⓑ	paterfamilias *nm*
patriarch	patriarca *nm*
polygamist	polígamo, -a *nmf*
primogenitor	primogenitor *nm*
progenitor	progenitor(a) *nmf*
second-born	segundogénito, -a *aj, nmf*
second son	segundón *nm*
spouse	esposo, -a *nmf*
successor	sucesor(a) *nmf*
widow	viuda *nf*
widower	viudo *nm*

(*See also* **SEXUALITY**)

EDUCATION

GENERAL TERMS

academe	mundo académico *nm*
academic	académico *aj*
calendar	calendario *nm*
class	clase *nf*
course	curso *nm*
curriculum Ⓑ	currículo *nm*
discipline	disciplina *nf*
edification	edificación *nf*
education	educación *nf*
erudition	erudición *nf*

examination	examen *nm*
graduation	graduación *nf*
institution	institución *nf*
instruction	instrucción *nf*
lesson	lección *nf*
materials	materiales *nmpl*
matriculation	matrícula *nf*
method	método *nm*
program 🅐	programa *nm*
school	escuela *nf*
specialization	especialización *nf*
study	estudio *nm*
test	test *nm*

SPECIALIZATIONS

didactics	didáctica *nf*
heuristics	heurística *nf*
methodology	metodología *nf*
pedagogy	pedagogía *nf*

ASPECTS OF EDUCATION

general types

adult	adulto *aj*
alternative	alternativo *aj*
bilingual	bilingüe *aj, nmf*
formal	formal *aj*
general	general *aj*
informal	informal *aj*
liberal	liberal *aj, nmf*
physical	físico *aj*
preschool	preescolar *aj*
special	especial *aj*
vocational	vocacional *aj*

types of schools

academy	academia *nf*
accredited	acreditado *aj*
coeducational	coeducacional *aj*
college	colegio *nm*
correspondence	correspondencia *nf*
elementary	elemental *aj*
extension	de extensión *nf*
graduate	graduado *aj*
institute	instituto *nm*
intermediate	intermedio *aj*
kindergarten	kindergarten *nm*
laboratory	laboratorio *nm*
medical	de medicina
military	militar *aj*
normal (obs)	normal *aj*
postgraduate	pos(t)graduado *aj*
preparatory	preparatorio *aj*

primary	primario *aj*
private	privado *aj*
professional	profesional *aj, nmf*
progressive	progresivo *aj*
public	público *aj, nm*
reform	reforma *nf*
religious	religioso *aj*
secondary	secundario *aj*
seminary	seminario *nm*
technological	tecnológico *aj*
university	universidad *nf*

major disciplines

arts	artes *nfpl*
humanities	humanidades *nfpl*
languages	lenguas *nfpl*
literature	literatura *nf*
mathematics	matemática(s) *nf(pl)*
sciences	ciencias *nfpl*

kinds of courses

advanced	avanzado *aj*
computer-assisted	asistido por computadora *aj, nf*
interdisciplinary	interdisciplinario *aj*
introductory	introductorio *aj*
prerequisite	requisito *nm*
programmed, programed 🅐	programado *aj*
repeated	repetido *aj*
seminar	seminario *nm*
short course	cursillo *nm*

methods of learning

analysis 🅑	análisis 🅒 *nm*
conditioning	condicionamiento *nm*
demonstration	demostración *nf*
memorize	memorizar *vt*
repetition	repetición *nf*
Socratic	socrático *aj*
transfer, transference	tra(n)sferencia *nf*
trial and error	ensayo y error *nm*

school calendar

grade	grado *nm*
sabbatical	sabático *aj*
semester	semestre *nm*
trimester	trimestre *nm*
vacation *nsg*	vacaciones *nfpl*

degrees and graduation

baccalaureate	bachillerato *nm*
cum laude	cum laude *av*
diploma	diploma *nm*

dissertation	disertación *nf*
doctorate	doctorado *nm*
honorary	honorario *aj*
magna cum laude	magna cum laude *av*
master's degree	maestría *nf*
summa cum laude	summa cum laude *av*
thesis Ⓑ	tesis Ⓒ *nf*

other terms

absent	ausente *aj*
credit	crédito *nm*
department	departamento *nm*
extracurricular	extracurricular *aj*
extramural	extramural *aj*
faculty	facultad *nf*
honorarium Ⓑ *nsg*	honorarios *nmpl*
intramural	intramuros *aj*
objective	objetivo *nm*
orientation	orientación *nf*
place	plaza *nf*
Sorbonne	Sorbona *nf*
stipend	estipendio *nm*
unit	unidad *nf*

TESTS AND EXAMINATIONS

kinds of tests

aptitude	aptitud *nf*
competency	competencia *nf*
diagnostic	diagnóstico *aj*
evaluation	evaluación *nf*
intelligence	inteligencia *nf*
interest	interés *nm*
multiple-choice *aj*	de opción múltiple *nf*
personality	personalidad *nf*
predictive *aj*	que predice
reasoning	razonamiento *nm*
recognition	reconocimiento *nm*
standardized	estandarizado *aj*
subjective	subjetivo *aj*
true-or-false	cierto o falso *aj*

kinds of exams

doctoral	doctoral *aj*
final	final *aj*
oral	oral *aj*
preliminary	preliminar *aj*
semifinal	semifinal *aj*

other terms

admission	admisión *nf*
demerit	demérito *nm*
norm	norma *nf*
percentile	percentil *nm*

psychometrics	(p)sicometría *nf*
validation	convalidación *nf*
validity	validez *nf*

TOOLS AND MATERIALS

atlas	atlas *nm*
audiovisual	audiovisual *aj*
calculator	calculadora *nf*
compass	compás *nm*
computer	computadora *nf*
dictionary	diccionario *nm*
exercises	ejercicios *nmpl*
map	mapa *nm*
pointer	puntero *nm*
schoolbook	libro escolar *nm*
textbook	libro de texto *nm*
transparency	transparencia *nf*

PERSONS

groups

professors *npl*	profesorado *nm*
student body	estudiantado *nm*

individuals

academician	académico, -a *nmf*
bachelor	bachiller *nm*
collegian	colegiado, -a *nmf*
consultant	consultor(a) *nmf*
counselor	consejero, -a *nmf*
dean	decano *nm*
doctor	doctor(a) *nmf*
educator	educador(a) *nmf*
examinee	examinando, -a *nmf*
examiner	examinador, -a *nmf*
graduate	graduado, -a *nmf*
instructor	instructor(a) *nmf*
matriculant	matriculador(a) *nmf*
mentor	mentor(a) *nmf*
monitor	monitor(a) *nmf*
pedagog(ue)	pedagogo *nm*
postgraduate	pos(t)graduado, -a *nmf*
professor	profesor(a) *nmf*
professor emeritus	profesora emérita *nf*
professor emeritus	profesor emérito *nm*
rector	rector *nm*
registrar	registrador(a) *nmf*
seminarian	seminarista *nmf*
student	estudiante *nmf*
tutor	tutor(a) *nmf*

(*See also* **PSYCHOMETRIC TESTS** under **PSYCHOLOGY**)

ORGANIZATIONS AND MEETINGS

GENERAL TERMS

election	elección *nf*
group	grupo *nm*
invitation	invitación *nf*
membership	membresía *nf*
organization	organización *nf*
parliamentary law	reglamento parlamentario *n*
participation	participación *nf*
procedure	procedimiento *nm*
voting	votación *nf*

ASPECTS OF ORGANIZATIONS

establishment

auspices	auspicios *nmpl*
charter	carta *nf*
constitution	constitución *nf*
found	fundar *vt*

types

affiliation	afiliación, afiliada *nf*
association	asociación *nf*
circle	círculo *nm*
club	club *nm*
commission	comisión *nf*
committee	comité *nm*
consortium Ⓑ	consorcio *nm*
council (advisory)	consejo *nm*
delegation	delegación *nf*
foundation	fundación *nf*
fraternal	fraternal *aj*
legislature	legislatura *nf*
lodge	logia *nf*
parliament	parlamento *nm*
senate	senado *nm*
society	sociedad *nf*
subcommittee	subcomité *nm*

procedures

action	acción *nf*
agenda	agenda *nf*
amendment	enmienda *nf*
approve	aprobar *vti*
clarification	aclaración *nf*
declaration	declaración *nf*
deliberation	deliberación *nf*
disband	desbandar(se) *vt(r)*
discussion	discusión *nf*
dissolution	disolución *nf*

inauguration	inauguración *nf*
initiate	iniciar *vt*
introduce	introducir *vt*
memo, memorandum	memorándum *nm*
motion	moción *nf*
mutatis mutandis	mutatis mutandis *av*
objection	objeción *nf*
officiate	oficiar *vt*
pending	pendiente *aj*
point of order	cuestión de orden *nf, nm*
present (a motion)	presentar *vt*
preside	presidir *vti*
privilege	privilegio *nm*
proposal	propuesta *nf*
ratification	ratificación *nf*
recess	receso *nm*
resolution	resolución *nf*
second (the motion)	secundar *vt*
suspend	suspender *vt*

voting

abstention	abstención *nf*
acclamation	aclamación *nf*
plenum	pleno *nm*
plurality	pluralidad *nf*
quorum	quórum *nm*
unanimous	unánime *aj*

other terms

auditorium Ⓑ	auditorio *nm*
congregate	congregarse *vr*
disunity	desunión *nf*
exclusivist	exclusivista *aj*
factious (groups)	faccioso *aj*
platform	plataforma *nf*
tribune	tribuna *nf*

KINDS OF MEETINGS

small groups

colloquy	coloquio *nm*
consultation	consulta, consultación *nf*
encounter	encuentro *nm*
interview	entrevista *nf*
tête-à-tête	tête-à-tête *nm*
visit	visita *nf*

large groups

assembly	asamblea *nf*
colloquium Ⓑ	coloquio *nm*
conclave	cónclave *nm*

congress	congreso *nm*
convention	convención *nf*
convocation	convocatoria *nf*
debate	debate *nm*
meeting (political)	mitin *nm*
plenary	plenario *aj*
rally	rallye Ⓒ *nm*
reception	recepción *nf*
session	sesión *nf*
symposium Ⓑ	simposio *nm*

small or large

class	clase *nf*
conference	conferencia *nf*
reunion	reunión *nf*
seminar	seminario *nm*

TERMS IN DEBATING

affirmative	afirmativo *nm*
argue	argumentar *vi*
decision	decisión *nf*
moderate	moderar *vt*
negative	negativo *nm*
opposing	opuesto *aj*
opposition	oposición *nf*
proposition	proposición *nf*
question	cuestión *nf*
resolve	resolver *vt*

PERSONS

officers

president	presidente *nmf*
secretary	secretario, -a *nmf*
treasurer	tesorero, -a *nmf*
vice-president	vicepresidente *nmf*

members

associate member	miembro no numerario *nmf*
founding member	fundador(a) *nmf*
full member	miembro de número *nmf*
honorary member	miembro honorario *nmf*
lifetime member	miembro vitalicio *nmf*

other persons

abstainer	abstencionista *nmf*
conventioneer	convencionista *nmf*
delegate	delegado, -a *nf*
founder	fundador(a) *nmf*
initiate	iniciado, -a *nmf*
mason, Mason	masón *nm*

member	miembro *nm*
moderator (debate)	moderador, -a *nmf*
objector	objetor(a) *nmf*
observer	observador(a) *nmf*
opponent	oponente *nmf*
organizer	organizador(a) *nmf*
panelist Ⓐ	miembro del panel *nm*
parliamentarian	parlamentario, -a *nmf*
participant	participante, partícipe *nmf*
representative	representante *nmf*
Rotarian	rotario, -a *nmf*

(*See also* **POLITICS AND GOVERNMENT**)

SOCIOLOGY

GENERAL TERMS

caste	casta *nf*
class	clase *nf*
community	comunidad *nf*
culture	cultura *nf*
group dynamics *npl*	dinámica de grupo *nf, nm*
institution	institución *nf*
population	población *nf*
social change	cambio social *nm*
social welfare	bienestar social *nm*
socialization	socialización *nf*
society	sociedad *nf*
sociology	sociología *nf*
status	estatus *nm*
status symbol	símbolo de estatus *nm*
stratum Ⓑ	estrato *nm*
structure	estructura *nf*

SPECIALIZATIONS

criminology	criminología *nf*
demography	demografía *nf*
deviance	desviación *nf*
economics	economía *nf*
psychology	(p)sicología *nf*
social work	asistencia social *nf*
sociobiology	sociobiología *nf*
sociolinguistics	sociolingüística *nf*
statistics	estadística *nf*

ASPECTS OF SOCIOLOGY

social studies

civics	educación cívica *nf*
geography	geografía *nf*
history	historia *nf*

population statistics

census	censo *nm*
control	control *nm*
ethnicity	identidad étnica *nf*
explosion	explosión *nf*
immigration	inmigración *nf*
marital status	estado civil *nm*
minority	minoría *nf*
race	raza *nf*
rural	rural *aj*
urban	urbano *aj*
vital statistics	estadísticas demográficas *nfpl*

factors in social status

celebrity	celebridad *nf*
fame	fama *nf*
family	familia *nf*
fortune	fortuna *nf*
image	imagen *nf*
influence	influencia *nf*
possessions	posesiones *nfpl*
power	poder *nm*
prestige	prestigio *nm*
reputation	reputación *nf*
role, rôle	rol *nm*

conducting surveys

data *nsg or npl*	datos *nmpl*
estimate	estimado *nm*
interview	entrevista *nf*
map	mapa *nm*
margin of error	margen de error *nm*
norm	norma *nf*
opinion poll	encuesta de opinión *nf*
prediction	predicción *nf*
preference	preferencia *nf*
questionnaire	cuestionario *nm*
study	estudio *nm*
subject	sujeto *nm*

frequent survey topics

abuse	abuso *nm*
crime	crimen *nm*
drugs	drogas *nfpl*
government	gobierno *nm*
lifestyle	estilo de vida *nm, nf*
politics	política *nf*
prejudice	prejuicio *nm*
race relations	relaciones raciales *nfpl*
sex	sexo *nm*
treatment	trato *nm*

unemployment	desempleo *nm*
violence	violencia *nf*

PERSONS

high status

cosmopolite	cosmopolita *nmf*
debutante, débutante	debutante *nf*
elite, élite	élite *nf*
socialite	persona de alta sociedad
yuppie, yuppy	yupi Ⓒ *nmf*

low status

beatnik (obs)	beatnik *nmf*
hippy, hippie (obs)	hippy *nmf*
homeless person	persona sin hogar *nf, nm*
sociopath	sociópata *nmf*

other persons

demographer	demógrafo, -a *nmf*
informant	informante *nmf*
interviewer	entrevistador(a) *nmf*
social scientist	científico, -a social *nmf*
sociologist	sociólogo, -a *nmf*
statistician	estadístico, -a *nmf*

(*See also* URBAN PROBLEMS under **THE CITY**)

ANTHROPOLOGY AND ARCHEOLOGY

GENERAL TERMS

anthropology	antropología *nf*
civilization	civilización *nf*
culture	cultura *nf*
humanity, humankind	humanidad *nf*
race	raza *nf*
society	sociedad *nf*

SPECIALIZATIONS

anthropometry	antropometría *nf*
archeology Ⓐ	arqueología *nf*
ethnography	etnografía *nf*
ethnology	etnología *nf*
linguistics	lingüística *nf*
sociology	sociología *nf*

PHYSICAL ANTHROPOLOGY

human development

adaptation	adaptación *nf*
cephalic index	índice cefálico *nm*

evolution	evolución *nf*
hominid	homínido, -a *aj, nmf*
homo sapiens	homo sapiens *nm*
mammal	mamífero *nm*
primate	primate *nm*
vertebrate	vertebrado *aj, nm*

prehistoric humans

Cro-Magnon	cromañón *nm*
Neanderthal	neandertal *nm*
pithecanthropus	pitecántropo, -a *nmf*

living races

Caucasoid	caucasoide *aj*
Mongoloid	mongoloide *aj*
Negroid	negroide *aj*

CULTURAL ANTHROPOLOGY

basic concepts

conformity	conformidad *nf*
diversity	diversidad *nf*
ethnocentrism	etnocentrismo *nm*
functionalism	funcionalismo *nm*
migration	migración *nf*
multiculturalism	multiculturalismo *nm*
orthogenesis (obs)	ortogénesis *nf*
relativism	relativismo *nm*
stereotype	estereotipo *nm*

kinds of culture

advanced	avanzado *aj*
contemporary	contemporáneo *aj*
counterculture	contracultura *nf*
decadent	decadente *aj*
ethnic	étnico *aj*
indigenous	indígena *aj*
international	internacional *aj*
material	material *aj*
matriarchal	matriarcal *aj*
national	nacional *aj*
nonmaterial	no material *aj*
patriarchal	patriarcal *aj*
popular	popular *aj*
primitive	primitivo *aj*
subculture	subcultura *nf*
tribal	tribal *aj*

elements of developed cultures

arts	artes *nfpl*
conventions	convenciones *nfpl*
customs	costumbres *nfpl*
decorum	decoro *nm*

education	educación *nf*
etiquette	etiqueta *nf*
family	familia *nf*
folklore	folklore, folclore *nm*
government	gobierno *nm*
institution	institución *nf*
invention	invención *nf*
language	lenguaje *nm*
religion	religión *nf*
symbols	símbolos *nmpl*
technology	tecnología *nf*
tradition	tradición *nf*
values	valores *nmpl*

cultures in contact

acculturation	aculturación *nf*
Americanization	americanización *nf*
assimilation	asimilación *nf*
culture shock	choque de culturas *nm*
diffusion	difusión *nf*
Europeanization	europeización *nf*
exodus	éxodo *nm*
insularity	insularidad *nf*
latinize	latinizar *vt*
xenophilia	afición a lo extranjero *nf*
xenophobia	xenofobia *nf*

TERMS IN ARCHEOLOGY
general terms

artifact Ⓐ	artefacto *nm*
chronology	cronología *nf*
dating	datación *nf*
discovery	descubrimiento *nm*
excavation	excavación *nf*
interpretation	interpretación *nf*
preservation	preservación *nf*
site	sitio *nm*

methods of dating

dendochronology	dendocronologia *nf*
geochronology	geocronología *nf*
radiocarbon	radiocarbono *nm*
reconstruction	reconstrucción *nf*
stratigraphy	estratigrafía *nf*

artifacts and structures

ammonite	amonita *nf*
caryatid	cariátide *nf*
eolith	eolito *nm*
fossil	fósil *aj, nm*
glyph	glifo *nm*

gnomon	gnomon *nm*
hieroglyph	jeroglífico *nm*
megalith	megalito *nm*
menhir	menhir *nm*
necropolis	necrópolis *nf*
petroglyph	petroglifo *nm*
Rosetta stone	piedra de Roseta *nf*
tomb	tumba *nf*

other terms

aerial photo	aerofoto, áereofoto *nf*
Egyptology	egiptología *nf*
fragile	frágil *aj*
hieratic	hierático *aj*
ruins	ruinas *nfpl*
Sinology	sinología *nf*
stratum Ⓑ	estrato *nm*

ETHNIC GROUPS AROUND THE WORLD

cross-cultural terms

Afro-American	afroamericano, -a *aj, nmf*
Afro-Asian	afroasiático, -a *aj, nmf*
Anglo-American	angloamericano, -a *aj, nmf*
French-Canadian	francocanadiense *aj, nmf*
Hispanic-American	hispanoamericano *aj, nmf*
Latin-American	latinoamericano, -a *aj, nmf*

North and South America

Amerind, Amerindian	amerindio, -a *aj, nmf*
Cherokee	cheroquí *nm, nmf*
Creole	criollo, -a *aj, nmf*
Eskimo	esquimal *aj, nmf*
Guarani	guaraní *aj, nmf*
Hispanic	hispano, -a *aj, nmf*
Latin, Latino	latino, -a *aj, nmf*
Quechua	quechua, quichua *aj, nmf*
Sioux	siux, sioux *aj, nmf*
Yankee	yanqui *aj, nmf*

Europe

Basque	vasco, -a *aj, nmf*
Lapp, Laplander	lapón, -ona *nmf*
Magyar	magiar *aj, nmf*
Saxon	sajón, -ona *aj, nmf*
Slavic, Slav	eslavo, -a *aj, nmf*
Tartar, Tatar	tártaro, -a *aj, nmf*
Walloon	valón, -ona *aj, nmf*

Africa

Afrikaner	afrikaner *nmf*
Arab	árabe *aj, nmf*
Bantu	bantú *aj, nmf*
Bedouin	beduino, -a *aj, nmf*
Berber	beréber, berberisco, -a *aj, nmf*
Boer	bóer *aj, nmf*
Coptic	copto, -a *aj, nmf*
Hottentot	hotentote *nmf*
Pygmy Ⓑ	pigmeo, -a *aj, nmf*
Zulu	zulú *aj, nmf*

Asia and the Pacific

Aborigine	aborigen *nmf*
Dravidian	dravidiano, -a, drávida *aj, nmf*
Khmer Ⓑ	kmer *nmf*
Kurd, Kurdish	kurdo, -a, curdo, -a *aj, nmf*
Maori	maorí *aj, nmf*
Mogul	mogol(a) *nmf*
Sinhalese, Singhalese	cingalés, -esa *aj, nmf*
Tagalog	tagalo, -a *aj, nmf*
Tamil	tamil, tamul *aj, nmf*
Teutonic	teutónico *aj*

historical groups

Anglo-Saxon	anglosajón, -ona *aj, nmf*
Aztec	azteca *aj, nmf*
Cossack	cosaco, -a *aj, nm*
Frank	franco *nm*
Gallic	galo *aj*
Goth	godo, -a *nmf*
Hun	huno, -a *nmf*
Inca	inca *aj, nmf*
Mayan Ⓑ	maya *aj, nmf*
Moor	moro, -a *aj, nmf*
Norman	normando, -a *aj, nmf*
Pict	picto, -a *nmf*
Saracen	sarraceno, -a *aj, nmf*
Sumerian	sumerio, -a *aj, nmf*
Teuton	teutón, -ona *aj, nmf*
Toltec	tolteca *nmf*
Viking	vikingo *nm*
Visigoth	visigodo *nm*

PERSONS

primitive

barbarian	bárbaro, -a *nmf*
cannibal	caníbal *nmf*
cave dweller	cavernícola *nmf*
nomad	nómada *nmf*
nudist	nudista *nmf*
savage	salvaje *nmf*
troglodyte	troglodita *nmf*

racially mixed

Afro-Asian	afroasiático, -a *aj, nmf*
Amerasian	amerasiático, -a *aj, nmf*
Creole	criollo, -a *aj, nm*
Eurasian	eurasiático, -a *aj, nmf*
mestizo	mestizo, -a *aj, nmf*
mulatto Ⓑ	mulato, -a *aj, nmf*
quadroon	cuarterón, -ona *aj, nmf*

haters

misanthrope, misanthropist	misántropo, -a *nmf*
neo-Nazi	neonazi *aj, nmf*

supremacist	supremacista *nmf*
xenophobe	xenófobo, -a *nmf*

groups

clan	clan *nm*
gens Ⓑ	gens *nf*
horde	horda *nf*
tribe	tribu *nf*

other persons

aborigine	aborigen *nmf*
Africanist	africanista *nmf*
anthropologist	antropólogo, -a *nmf*
Caucasian	caucásico, -a *aj, nmf*
ethnographer	etnógrafo, -a *nmf*
excavator	excavador(a) *nmf*
folklorist	folklorista, folclorista *nmf*
Negro	negro, -a *aj, nmf*
Nordic	nórdico, -a *aj, nmf*
Oriental	oriental *aj, nmf*
Sinologist	sinólogo, -a *nmf*
xenophile	xenófilo, -a *nmf*

(*See also* **peoples and tribes** under **THE BIBLE**)

Affairs of State

LAW

GENERAL TERMS

appeal	apelación *nf*
argument	argumento *nm*
attestation	atestación, atestado *nf, nm*
bar	barra *nf*
capacity	capacidad *nf*
case	caso *nm*
cause	causa *nf*
charge	cargo *nm*
circumstance	circunstancia *nf*
claim	reclamación, reclamo *nf, nm*
code	código *nm*
codex Ⓑ	códice *nm*
codification	codificación *nf*
competence	competencia *nf*
compliance	cumplimiento *nm*
contingency	contingencia *nf*
costs	costas *nfpl*
counsel	consejo *nm*
court	corte *nf*
crime	crimen *nm*
decision	decisión *nf*
decree	decreto *nm*
defense Ⓐ	defensa *nf*
deposition	deposición *nf*
dictum Ⓑ	dictamen *nm*
discovery	descubrimiento *nm*
document	documento *nm*
documentation	documentación *nf*
domain, dominion	dominio *nm*
domicile	domicilio *nm*
equity	equidad *nf*
expenses	expensas *nfpl*
forum Ⓑ	foro *nm*
habeas corpus	habeas corpus *nm*
ignorance (of the law)	ignorancia *nf*
impediment	impedimento *nm*
injustice	injusticia *nf*
innocence	inocencia *nf*
instance	instancia *nf*
intent	intención *nm*
interpretation	interpretación *nf*
judicature	judicatura *nf*
jurisdiction	jurisdicción *nf*
jurisprudence	jurisprudencia *nf*
justice	justicia *nf*
law	ley *nf*
legal	legal *aj*
legitimate	legítimo *aj*
licit	lícito *aj*
litigation	litigio *nm*
majority (age)	mayoría *nf*
malice	malicia *nf*
mandate	mandato *nm*
motive	motivo *nm*
noncompliance	incumplimiento *nm*
null	nulo *aj*
obligation	obligación *nf*
occupancy	ocupación *nf*
offer	oferta *nf*
opinion	opinión *nf*
order	orden *nf*
ordinance	ordenanza *nf*
practice	práctica *nf*
process	proceso *nm*
promulgation	promulgación *nf*
proof	prueba *nf*
protection	protección *nf*
public domain	dominio público *nm*
recourse	recurso *nm*
regulations	reglamento *nmsg*
rehabilitation	rehabilitación *nf*
representation	representación *nf*
statute	estatuto *nm*
technicality	tecnicismo *nm*
tribunal	tribunal *nm*
violation	violación *nf*
violence	violencia *nf*

TYPES OF LAW

public

administrative	administrativo *aj*
constitutional	constitucional *aj*
criminal	criminal *aj*
international	internacional *aj*
maritime	marítimo *aj*
martial	marcial *aj*
mercantile	mercantil *aj*
penal	penal *aj*

civil

canon	canónico *aj*

civil	civil *aj*
commercial	comercial *aj*
contract	de contrato *nm*
corporation	de corporación *nf*
family	de familia *nf*
labor	laboral *aj*
patent	de patente *nf*
property	de propiedad *nf*

historical

Justinian	justiniano *aj*
Mosaic	mosaico *aj*
Napoleonic	napoleónico *aj*
Roman	romano *aj*
instigation	instigación *nf*

ASPECTS OF LEGAL PRACTICE

kinds of courts

appellate	de apelación *nf*
circuit	circuito *nm*
district	distrito *nm*
federal	federal *aj*
municipal	municipal *aj*
Supreme Court	Corte Suprema *nf*
traffic	de tráfico *nm*

rights

access	acceso *nm*
consortium Ⓑ	consorcio *nm*
constitutional	constitucional *aj*
herbage	herbaje *nm*
inalienable	inalienable *aj*
prerogative	prerrogativa *nf*
privacy	privacidad *nf*
privilege	privilegio *nm*
proprietary	propietario *aj*
reversion	reversión *nf*
riparian	ribereño *aj*
suffrage	sufragio *nm*
tenancy	tenencia *nf*
use	uso *nm*
usufruct	usufructo *nm*

terms in law enforcement

apprehend (a criminal)	aprehender *vt*
arrest	arresto *nm*
clandestine (operation)	clandestino *aj*
cordon	cordón *nm*
criminology	criminología *nf*
dactylography	dactilografía *nf*
detection	detección *nf*

felony	felonía *nf*
Interpol	Interpol *mf*
investigation	investigación *nf*
patrol	patrulla *nf*
polygraph	polígrafo *nm*
reconstruct (a crime)	reconstruir *vt*
secret (police)	secreto *aj*

judicial actions

adoption	adopción *nf*
amnesty	amnistía *nf*
annulment	anulación *nf*
asylum	asilo *nm*
citation	citación *nf*
detainer	orden de detención *nf*
expropriation	expropiación *nf*
extradition	extradición *nf*
immunity	inmunidad *nf*
inquest	encuesta *nf*
interdict, interdiction	interdicto *nm*
interlocutory (decree)	interlocutorio *aj*
judgment	orden judicial *nf*
legalization	legalización *nf*
moratorium Ⓑ	moratoria *nf*
naturalization	naturalización *nf*
novation	novación *nf*
nullification	anulación *nf*
prescription	prescripción *nf*
prohibition	prohibición *nf*
proscription	proscripción *nf*
replication (reply)	réplica *nf*
requisition	requisitoria *nf*
rescission	rescisión *nf*
revocation	revocación *nf*
sanctuary	santuario *nm*
subrogation	subrogación *nf*
transfer, transference	tra(n)sferencia *nf*
validation	validación *nf*
vitiate	viciar *vt*

documents

affidavit	afidávit *nm*
article	artículo *nm*
certificate	certificado *nm*
clause	cláusula *nf*
codicil	codicilo *nm*
covenant	convenio *nm*
holograph	(h)ológrafo *nm*
instrument	instrumento *nm*
license Ⓐ	licencia *nf*
memorandum	memorándum *nm*
petition	petición *nf*
power of attorney	poder notarial *nm*

title	título *nm*
verification	verificación *nf*

legal argumentation

adduce	aducir *vt*
allegation	alegato *nm*
confutation	confutación *nf*
objection	objeción *nf*
protest	protesta *nf*
refutation	refutación *nf*

evidence

admissible	admisible *aj*
conclusive	concluyente *aj*
corroboration	corroboración *nf*
cumulative	cumulativo *aj*
fraudulent	fraudulento *aj*
irrelevance, irrelevancy	irrelevancia *nf*
moral	moral *aj*
pertinence	pertinencia *nf*
preponderance	preponderancia *nf*
prima facie	prima facie *av*
probative, probatory	probatorio *aj*
relevant	relevante *aj*
stipulation	estipulación *nf*
testimony	testimonio *nm*

other terms

abjure	abjurar *vt*
abolish	abolir *vt*
abrogate	abrogar *vt*
abuse	abusar *vi*
alienate (property)	alienar *vt*
appropriate	apropiar(se) *vt(r)*
arbitration	arbitraje *nm*
attenuating	atenuante *aj*
authority	autoridad *nf*
contravene	contravenir *vt*
desist	desistir *vi*
exempt	exento *aj*
exert (authority)	ejercer *vt*
fictitious (name)	ficticio *aj*
forensic	forense *aj*
fungible	fungible *aj*
inoperative	inoperante *aj*
instruct (the jury)	instruir *vt*
intention	intencionalidad *nf*
interrogatory	interrogatorio *nm*
invalid	inválido *aj*
mandamus	mandamiento *nm*
mediation	mediación *nf*
pending	pendiente *aj*
peremptory	perentorio *aj*

precedent	precedente *nm*
prejudicial	perjudicial *aj*
proceeding	procedimiento *nm*
quasi contract	cuasicontrato *nm*
ratify (a contract)	ratificar *vt*
receivership	receptoría *nf*
reclaim (rights)	reclamar *vt*
renunciation (of a claim)	renuncia *nf*
sequestration	secuestración *nf*
summary (judgment)	sumario *aj*

CRIMES AND MISDEMEANORS

kinds of crimes

capital	capital *aj*
financial	financiero *aj*
military	militar *aj*
nonviolent	no violento *aj*
political	político *aj*
premeditated	premeditado *aj*
sex	de sexo
violent	violento *aj*

violent

aggravated (assault)	con agravante *nm*
assassination	asesinato *nm*
banditry	bandidaje *nm*
cannibalism	canibalismo *nm*
fratricide (act)	fratricidio *nm*
gangsterism	gangsterismo *nm*
genocide	genocidio *nm*
homicide (act)	homicidio *nm*
infanticide (act)	infanticidio *nm*
lynching	linchamiento *nm*
robbery	robo *nm*
terrorism	terrorismo *nm*
vandalism	vandalismo *nm*

financial

bankruptcy	bancarrota *nf*
connivance	connivencia *nf*
extortion	extorsión *nf*
tax evasion	evasión fiscal *nf*
usury	usura *nf*

sex crimes

bestiality	bestialidad *nf*
incest	incesto *nm*
pedophilia 🅐	pedofilia *nf*
prostitution	prostitución *nf*
seduction	seducción *nf*
sodomy	sodomía *nf*

political and military

assassination	asesinato *nm*
collaboration (with enemy)	colaboracionismo *nm*
desertion	deserción *nf*
espionage	espionaje *nm*
insubordination	insubordinación *nf*
insurrection	insurrección *nf*
misconduct	mala conducta *nf*
sabotage	sabotaje *nm*
sedition	sedición *nf*
treason	traición *nf*

language crimes

calumny	calumnia *nf*
defamation	difamación *nf*
libel	libelo *nm*
obscenity	obscenidad *nf*
perjury	perjurio *nm*
plagiarism	plagio *nm*
subornation	soborno *nm*

crimes on the high seas

mutiny	motín *nm*
piracy	piratería *nf*

miscellaneous crimes

collusion	colusión *nf*
complicity	complicidad *nf*
conspiracy	conspiración *nf*
contumacy	contumacia *nf*
delinquency	delincuencia *nf*
discrimination	discriminación *nf*
fraud	fraude *nm*
incitement	incitación *nf*
infraction	infracción *nf*
kleptomania	cleptomanía *nf*
negligence	negligencia *nf*
obstruction	obstrucción *nf*
possession	posesión *nf*
slavery	esclavitud *nf*
suicide (act)	suicidio *nm*
vagrancy	vagancia *nf*

legal defenses

accident	accidente *nm*
alibi	alibí *nm*
coercion	coerción *nf*
consent	consentimiento *nm*
incapacity	incapacidad *nf*
incompetence	incompetencia *nf*
insanity	insania *nf*
insolvency	insolvencia *nf*

justification	justificación *nf*
necessity	necesidad *nf*
prevention	prevención *nf*
reasonable (doubt)	razonable *aj*
self-defense 🅰	autodefensa *nf*

other terms

accusation	acusación *nf*
admission	admisión *nf*
brutal	brutal *aj*
coercive	coercitivo *aj*
commit	cometer *vt*
confession	confesión *nf*
conviction	convicción *nf*
culpability	culpabildad *nf*
exculpation	exculpación *nf*
forced (entry)	forzado *aj*
incendiary	incendiario *aj*
incrimination	incriminación *nf*
indemnity	indemnidad *nf*
infringe	infringir *vi*
interrogation	interrogación *nf*
involuntary (manslaughter)	involuntario *aj*
justifiable (homicide)	justificable *aj*
perpetration	perpetración *nf*
plot	complot *nm*
presumption	presunción *nf*
punishable	punible *aj*
responsibility	responsabilidad *nf*
self-incrimination	autoincriminación *nf*
transgression	tra(n)sgresión *nf*
verdict	veredicto *nm*
vindication	vindicación *nf*

PUNISHMENT

kinds of punishment

compensation	compensación *nf*
condemnation	condena *nf*
confiscation	confiscación *nf*
corporal	corporal *aj*
damages	daños *nmpl*
deportation	deportación *nf*
detention	detención *nf*
electrocution	electrocución *nf*
execution	ejecución *nf*
exile	exilio *nm*
incapacitation	privación de la capacidad *nf*
incarceration	encarcelación *nf*
internment	internamiento *nm*
penalty	pena *nf*

punitive	punitivo *aj*
reprimand	reprimenda *nf*
sanction	sanción *nf*
sentence	sentencia *nf*
torture	tortura *nf*

places of punishment

calaboose	calabozo *nm*
cell	celda *nf*
correctional institution	correccional *nm or nf*
penitentiary	penitenciaría *nf*
prison	prisión *nf*
reformatory	reformatorio *nm*
stockade	estacada *nf*

other terms

clemency	clemencia *nf*
commutation	conmutación *nf*
corrective	correctivo *aj, nm*
impunity	impunidad *nf*

PERSONS

offenders

accomplice	cómplice *nmf*
accused	acusado, -a *nmf*
assassin	asesino, -a *nmf*
bandit	bandido, -a *nmf*
bigamist	bígamo, -a *nmf*
collaborationist	colaboracionista *nmf*
conspirator	conspirador(a) *nmf*
convict	convicto, -a *nmf*
criminal	criminal *nmf*
culprit	culpable *nmf*
defrauder	defraudador(a) *nmf*
delinquent	delincuente *nmf*
deportee	deportado, -a *nmf*
detainee	detenido, -a *nmf*
extortionist	autor(a) de extorsiones *nmf, nfpl*
felon	felón *nm*
fratricide (killer)	fratricida *nmf*
fugitive	fugitivo, -a *nmf*
gangster	gángster *nm*
homicide (killer)	homicida *nmf*
insurrectionist	insurrecto, -a *nmf*
kleptomaniac	cleptómano, -a *nmf*
libeler, libelist	libelista *nmf*
Mafioso **B**	mafioso *nm*
offender	ofensor(a) *nmf*
pedophile **A**	pedofilo, -a *nmf*
perjurer	perjuro, -a *nmf*
perpetrator	perpetrador(a) *nmf*

pirate	pirata *nmf*
plagiarist	plagiario, -a *nmf*
prisoner	prisionero, -a *nmf*
saboteur	saboteador(a) *nmf*
suborner	sobornador(a) *nmf*
suspect	sospechoso, -a *nmf*
terrorist	terrorista *aj, nmf*
trafficker	traficante *nmf*
transgressor	tra(n)sgresor(a) *nmf*
vagrant	vago, -a *nmf*
vandal	vándalo, -a *nmf*

law enforcement personnel

agent	agente *nmf*
commissioner	comisionado, -a *nmf*
criminalist	criminalista *nmf*
criminologist	criminalista *nmf*
custodian	custodio, -a *nmf*
deputy	diputado, -a *nmf*
detainer	detentador(a) *nmf*
detective	detective *nmf*
inspector	inspector(a) *nmf*
interrogator	interrogador(a) *nmf*
investigator	investigador(a) *nmf*
judge	juez *nmf*
jurist	jurista *nmf*
juror	jurado *nmf*
Justice of the Peace	juez/jueza de paz *nmf, nf*
magistrate	magistrado *nmf*
matron	matrona *nf*
penologist	penalista *nmf*
policeman/ policewoman **B**	policía *nmf*
public defender	defensor(a) de oficio *nmf, nm*

other individuals

accuser	acusador(a) *nmf*
adjuster	ajustador(a) *nmf*
administrator	administrador(a) *nmf*
adversary	adversario, -a *nmf*
advocate	abogado, -a *nmf*
arbitrator	árbitro, -a *nmf*
beneficiary	beneficiario, -a *nmf*
claimant	reclamante *nmf*
client	cliente *nmf*
codifier	codificador(a) *nmf*
cosignatory	cosignatario, -a *nmf*
deponent	deponente *nmf*
divorcé	divorciado *nm*
divorcée	divorciada *nf*
executor	ejecutor(a) *nmf*

expert	experto, -a *nmf*
heir	heredero, -a *nmf*
juvenile	juvenil *nmf*
legatee	legatario *nm*
legislator	legislador(a) *nmf*
litigant, litigator	litigante *nmf*
mediator	mediador(a) *nmf*
minor	menor *nmf*
notary	notario, -a *nmf*
occupant	ocupador(a) *nmf*
official	oficial *nmf*
ombudsman	ombudsman *nm*
party (legal person)	parte *nf*
person	persona *nf*
petitioner	peticionario, -a *nmf*
possessor	poseedor(a) *nmf*
principal	principal *nm*
promulgator	promulgador(a) *nmf*
registrar	registrador(a) *nmf*
sheriff	sheriff *nmf*
victim	víctima *nf*
vigilante	vigilante *nmf*

groups

appellant	apelante *nmf*
clientele	clientela *nf*
corroborator	corroborante *nmf*
informant	informante *nmf*
instigator	instigador(a) *nmf*
judiciary	judicatura *nf*
jury	jurado *nm*
Mafia	Mafia *nf*
militia	milicia *nf*
police	policía *nf*

(*See also LEGAL TERMS* under **BUSINESS**; *legal aspects* under **DEATH**; *LEGAL ASPECTS* under **FAMILY**)

THE MILITARY ESTABLISHMENT

GENERAL TERMS

action	acción *nf*
ally	aliado *nm*
combat	combate *nm*
command	mando, comando *nm*
conflict	conflicto *nm*
defense Ⓐ	defensa *nf*
enemy	enemigo *nm*
equipment	equipo *nm*
hostilities	hostilidades *nfpl*
martial	marcial *aj*

military	militar *aj*
offense Ⓐ	ofensiva *nf*
order	orden *nf*
protocol	protocolo *nm*
rank	rango *nm*
service	servicio *nm*
uniform	uniforme *nm*

FIELDS IN MILITARY SCIENCE

ballistics	balística *nf*
communications	comunicaciones *nfpl*
counterespionage	contraespionaje *nm*
counterintelligence	contrainteligencia *nf*
cryptography	criptografía *nf*
electrothermics	electrotermia *nf*
engineering	ingeniería *nf*
espionage	espionaje *nm*
intelligence	inteligencia *nf*
logistics	logística *nf*
strategy	estrategia *nf*
tactics	táctica *nf*

ASPECTS OF MILITARY LIFE

groups

armada	armada *nf*
auxiliaries	tropas auxiliares *nfpl*
battalion	batallón *nm*
battery	batería *nf*
brigade	brigada *nf*
cadre	cuadro *nm*
cavalry	caballería *nf*
Coastguard, the *nsg*	guardacostas, los *nmpl*
company	compañía *nf*
contingent	contingente *nm*
corps Ⓑ	cuerpo *nm*
detachment	destacamento *nm*
division	división *nf*
echelon	escalón *nm*
escort	escolta *nf*
file	fila *nf*
fleet	flota *nf*
forces	fuerzas *nfpl*
group	grupo *nm*
infantry	infantería *nf*
junta	junta *nf*
legion	legión *nf*
military police	policía militar *nf*
military, the *nsg*	militares, los *nmpl*
militia	milicia *nf*
National Guard	Guardia Nacional *nf*
party (reconaissance)	partida *nf*
patrol	patrulla *nf*

regiment	regimiento *nm*
section	sección *nf*
squadron	escuadrón *nm*
troop	tropa *nf*
unit	unidad *nf*
vanguard	vanguardia *nf*

places

armory Ⓐ	armería *nf*
banquette	banqueta *nf*
barracks	barraca *nf*
base	base *nf*
bastion	bastión *nm*
blockhouse	blocao *nm*
camp, encampment	campamento *nm*
citadel	ciudadela *nf*
command post/area	comandancia *nf*
commissary	comisario *nm*
concentration camp	campo de concentración *nm*
emplacement	emplazamiento *nm*
fort	fuerte *nm*
fortification	fortificación *nf*
fortress	fortaleza *nf*
front	frente *nm*
garrison	guarnición *nf*
guardhouse (guards' quarters)	cuartel de la guardia *nm, nf*
latrine	letrina *nf*
parade	parada *nf*
parapet	parapeto *nm*
park	parque *nm*
Pentagon	Pentágono *nm*
perimeter	perímetro *nm*
post	puesto *nm*
prison	prisión *nf*
prison camp	campo de prisioneros *nm, nmpl*
quarters *npl*	cuartel *nm*
sector	sector *nm*
silo (missile)	silo *nm*
stockade	estacada *nf*
tent	tienda *nf*
trench	trinchera *nf*

ranks and titles

admiral	almirante *nm*
aide-de-camp Ⓑ	edecán *nm*
brigadier	brigadier *nm*
captain	capitán, -ana *nmf*
chaplain	capellán *nm*
Chief-of-Staff	jefe del estado mayor *nmf, nm*

colonel	coronel(a) *nmf*
commodore	comodoro *nm*
degrade	degradar *vt*
general	general(a) *nmf*
generalissimo	generalísimo *nm*
lieutenant	teniente *nmf*
major	mayor *nm*
marshall	mariscal *nm*
rear admiral	contraalmirante *nm*
sergeant	sargento *nm*

offices

admiralty	almirantazgo *nm*
captaincy	capitanía *nf*
colonelcy, colonelship	coronelato *nm*
generalship	generalato *nm*
lieutenantship	lugartenencia *nf*
sergeancy	sargentía *nf*

type of service

career	carrera *nf*
compulsory	compulsorio *aj*
conscription	conscripción *nf*
enlistment	alistamiento *nm*
recruitment	reclutamiento *nm*
regular	regular *aj*
reserves	reservas *nfpl*
voluntary	voluntario *aj*

crimes

atrocity	atrocidad *nf*
desertion	deserción *nf*
mutiny	motín *nm*
rapine	rapiña *nf*
torture	tortura *nf*

uniform

bandoleer, bandolier	bandolera *nf*
decoration	condecoración *nf*
helmet	yelmo *nm*
insignia	insignias *nfpl*
kepi	quepis, kepis *nm*
khaki	caqui, kaki *nm*
medal	medalla *nf*
plume (helmet)	plumero *nm*
shako Ⓑ	chacó *nm*

protocol

attention!	¡atención! *intj*
countermarch	contramarcha *nf*
countersign	contraseña *nf*
halt!	¡alto! *vi*
review	revista *nf*
safe-conduct	salvoconducto *nm*

salute   saludo *nm*
salvo Ⓑ   salva *nf*

other terms

bivouac   vivaque *nm*
depredation   depredación *nf*
march   marcha *nf*
martial law   ley marcial *nf*
morale   moral *nf*
obedience   obediencia *aj*
ration   ración *nf*
regimentation   regimentación *nf*
rigors Ⓐ   rigores *nmpl*

TACTICS AND COMBAT

kinds of wars

biological   biológico *aj*
conventional   convencional *aj*
defensive   defensivo *aj*
guerrilla   guerrilla *nf*
mechanized   mecanizado *aj*
naval   naval *aj*
nonnuclear   no nuclear *aj*
nuclear   nuclear *aj*
offensive   ofensiva *nf*
psychological   (p)sicológico *aj*
terrorism   terrorismo *nm*
undeclared   no declarado *aj*

beginnings of wars

alert   alerta *aj, av, nf*
declaration   declaración *nf*
hostile encounter   encuentro,
    encuentronazo *nm*
insurrection   insurrección *nf*
invasion   invasión *nf*
mobilization   movilización *nf*
preparedness   estado de preparación
    nm, nf
rebellion   rebelión *nf*

during wars

battle   batalla *nf*
campaign   campaña *nf*
censorship   censura *nf*
deescalation   desescalada *nf*
escalation   escalada *nf*
flank   flanco *nm*
formation   formación *nf*
line   línea *nf*
maneuver Ⓐ   maniobra *nf*
mission   misión *nf*

mount (offensive)   montar *vt*
operation   operación *nf*
position   posición *nf*
reinforcements   refuerzos *nmpl*
replacement   reemplazo *nm*
salient   saliente *nm*
stratagem   estratagema *nf*
tactic   táctica *nf*

ends of wars

armistice   armisticio *nm*
capitulation   capitulación *nf*
captivity   cautiverio, cautividad
    nm, nf
cease-fire   cese del fuego *nm*
conquest   conquista *nf*
demilitarization   desmilitarización *nf*
demobilization   desmovilización *nf*
devastation   devastación *nf*
disarmament   desarme *nm*
fraternization   confraternización *nf*
pacification   pacificación *nf*
peace   paz *nf*
reparations   reparaciones *nfpl*
subjugation   subyugación *nf*
surrender   rendición *nf*
triumph   triunfo *nm*
victory   victoria *nf*

offensive actions

advance   avance *nm*
ambush   emboscada *nf*
assault   asalto *nm*
attack   ataque *nm*
blockade   bloqueo *nm*
bombing,   bombardeo *nm*
    bombardment
capture   captura *nf*
counterattack   contraataque *nm*
embargo Ⓑ   embargo *nm*
imprison   aprisionar *vt*
incursion   incursión *nf*
infiltration   infiltración *nf*
interception   interceptación *nf*
occupation   ocupación *nf*
penetration   penetración *nf*
pillage   pillaje *nm*
sabotage   sabotaje *nm*
sacking   saqueo *nm*

defensive actions

barricade   barricada *nf*
camouflage   camuflaje *nm*

counteroffensive	contraofensiva *nf*
evacuation	evacuación *nf*
retirement	retirada *nf*
retreat	retreta *nf*
submersion	sumersión *nf*

descriptive words

bellicose	belicoso *aj*
combative	combativo *aj*
conquering (hero)	conquistador *aj*
ferocious	feroz *aj*
impregnable	impregnable *aj*
indefensible	indefendible *aj*
invincible	invencible *aj*
invulnerable	invulnerable *aj*
paramilitary	paramilitar *aj*
triumphant	triunfante *aj*
valiant	valiente *aj*
victorious	victorioso *aj*

other terms

booty	botín *nm*
combat fatigue	fatiga de combate *nf*
contraband	contrabando *nm*
expeditionary	expedicionario *aj*
antimilitarist	antimilitarista *aj*

WEAPONS AND EQUIPMENT

general terms

ammunition	munición *nf*
armaments *npl*	armamento *nm*
arms	armas *nfpl*
arsenal	arsenal *nm*
munitions	municiones *nfpl*

types of weapons

amphibious	anfibio *aj*
antiaircraft	antiaéreo *aj*
antiballistic	antibalístico *aj*
antimissile	antiproyectil *aj*
antipersonnel	antipersonal *nm*
antisubmarine	antisubmarino *aj*
artillery	artillería *nf*
atomic	atómico *aj*
bacteriological	bacteriológico *aj*
ballistic	balístico *aj*
chemical	químico *aj*
gas	gas *nm*
strategic	estratégico *aj*
tactical	táctico *aj*

vessels, vehicles, aircraft

bomber	bombardero *nm*
convoy	convoy *nm*
corvette	corbeta *nf*
cruiser	crucero *nm*
destroyer	destructor *nm*
frigate	fragata *nf*
galley	galera *nf*
helicopter	helicóptero *nm*
interceptor	interceptor, interceptador *nm*
minelayer	minador *nm*
minesweeper	dragaminas *nm*
reconnaissance	reconocimiento *nm*
submarine	submarino *aj, nm*
tank	tanque *nm*
torpedo boat	torpedero *nm*
transport	transporte *nm*
troop carrier	transporte de tropas *nm, nfpl*
troop tren	tren militar *nm*

hand weapons

automatic weapon	arma automática *nf(el)*
bayonet	bayoneta *nf*

other weapons

bomb	bomba *nf*
cannon	cañón *nm*
cruise missile	misil de crucero *nm*
mine	mina *nf*

other equipment

baggage	bagaje *nm*
bunker	búnker *nm*
impedimenta	impedimenta *nf*
launcher (missile)	lanzamisiles *nm*
launcher (rocket)	lanzacohetes *nm*
mask (gas)	máscara *nf*
materiel, matériel	material *nm*
paraphernalia	parafernalia *nf*

HISTORICAL TERMS

archery	tiro de arco *nm*
armor Ⓐ	armadura *nf*
brassard	brazal *nm*
catapult	catapulta *nf*
cavalier	caballero *nm*
cavalry	caballería *nm*
centurion	centurión *nm*
cohort	cohorte *nf*
corsair	corsario *nm*

cors(e)let	coselete *nm*
dragoon	dragón *nm*
duel	duelo *nm*
galleon	galeón *nm*
gauntlet	guantelete *nm*
gladiator	gladiador *nm*
halberd	alabarda *nf*
harquebus	arcabuz *nm*
hussar	húsar *nm*
janissary	jenízaro *nm*
kamikaze	kamikaze *nm*
laurels	laureles *nmpl*
mace	maza *nf*
mail	malla *nf*
musket	mosquete *nm*
musketeer	mosquetero *nm*
musketry	mosquetería *nf*
panoply	panoplia *nf*
petard	petardo *nm*
phalanx Ⓑ	falange *nm*
pretorian, praetorian	pretoriano *aj, nm*
samurai Ⓑ	samurai *nm*

PERSONS

adjutant	ayudante *nmf*
adversary	adversario, -a *nmf*
aggressor	agresor(a) *nmf*
aide	ayudante *nmf*
allies	aliados *nmpl*
archenemy, arch-enemy	archienemigo *nm*
archer	arquero, -a *nmf*
artilleryman	artillero, -a *nmf*
assailant	asaltante *nmf*
attacker	atacador *nm*
belligerent	parte beligerante *nf*
bombardier	bombardero *nm*
cadet	cadete *nmf*
cannoneer	cañonero *nm*
captive	cautivo, -a *aj, nmf*
captor	captor(a) *nmf*
cavalryman Ⓑ	soldado de caballería *nm, nf*
chief	jefe *nmf*
civilian	civil *aj, nmf*
coastguard	guardacostas *nmf*
collaborator	colaboracionista *nmf*
combatant	combatiente *nmf*
commandant, commander	comandante *nmf*
commando Ⓑ	comando *nm*
conqueror	conquistador(a) *nmf*
conscript	conscripto *nm*
counterspy	contraespía *nmf*

cryptographer	criptógrafo, -a *nmf*
defender	defensor(a) *nmf*
deserter	desertor *nm*
duelist	duelista *nmf*
engineer	ingeniero, -a *nmf*
evacuee	evacuado, -a *nmf*
gendarme	gendarme *nm*
grenadier	granadero *nm*
guard	guardia *nmf*
guerrilla (person)	guerrillero *nm*
hero Ⓑ	héroe *nm*
infantryman	infante *nm*
infiltrator	infiltrado, -a *nmf*
insurgent	insurgente *aj, nmf*
invader	invasor(a) *nmf*
lancer	lancero *nm*
legionnaire	legionario *nm*
liberator	liberador, libertador *nm*
marine	marino *nm*
mercenary	mercenario, -a *nmf*
militant	militante *aj, nmf*
militarist	militarista *nmf*
militiaman Ⓑ	miliciano *nm*
mutineer	amotinado, -a *nmf*
nonbelligerant	no beligerante *aj, nmf*
officer	oficial *nmf*
orderly	ordenanza *nmf*
pacifist	pacifista *nmf*
partisan	partisano, -a *nmf*
personnel	personal *nm*
pillager	pillador *nm*
prisoner	prisionero, -a *nmf*
propagandist	propagandista *nmf*
rearguard	retaguardia *nf*
rebel	rebelde *nmf*
recruit	recluta *nmf*
refugee	refugiado, -a *nmf*
relief	relevo *nm*
renegade	renegado, -a *aj, nmf*
reservist	reservista *nmf*
saboteur	saboteador(a) *nmf*
sapper	zapador *nm*
sentinel	centinela *nm*
sentry	centinela *nm*
soldier	soldado *nmf*
spy	espía *nmf*
strategist	estratega *nmf*
tactician	táctico *nm*
terrorist	terrorista *aj, nmf*
veteran	veterano, -a *nmf*
subjugate	subyugar, sojuzgar *vt*

(*See also statesmen and generals* under
ANCIENT CIVILIZATIONS; *CAUSES OF DEATH
BY KILLING* under **DEATH**; **WEAPONS**)

POLITICS AND GOVERNMENT

GENERAL TERMS

administration	administración *nf*
autonomy	autonomía *nf*
ballot	balota *nf*
capital (city)	capital *nf*
capitol (building)	capitolio *nm*
charter	carta *nf*
constitution	constitución *nf*
diplomacy	diplomacia *nf*
election	elección *nf*
emigration	emigración *nf*
geopolitics	geopolítica *nf*
government	gobierno *nm*
immigration	inmigración *nf*
independence	independencia *nf*
movement	movimiento *nm*
official	oficial *aj*
party	partido *nm*
patriotism	patriotismo *nm*
peace	paz *nf*
political science *nsg*	ciencias políticas *nfpl*
politics	política *nf*
power	poder *nm*
regime	régimen *nm*
reign	reinado *nm*
status	estado *nm*
system	sistema *nm*
veto B	veto *nm*
vote	voto *nm*

ORGANIZATION

form of government

anarchy	anarquía *nf*
coalition	coalición *nf*
constitutional	constitucional *aj*
democracy	democracia *nf*
dictatorship	dictadura *nf*
matriarchy	matriarcado *nm*
monarchy	monarquía *nf*
patriarchy	patriarcado *nm*
republic	república *nf*

scope of governmnent

de facto	de facto *aj, av*
domestic	doméstico *aj*
federal	federal *aj*

global	global *aj*
international	internacional *aj*
interregnum B	interregno *nm*
local	local *aj*
national	nacional *aj*
provincial	provinciano *aj*
provisional	provisional *aj*
state	estatal *aj*

ruling group

aristocracy	aristocracia *nf*
autarchy	autarquía *nf*
autocracy	autocracia *nf*
bureaucracy	burocracia *nf*
dynasty	dinastía *nf*
gerontocracy	gerontocracia *nf*
gynecocracy	ginecocracia *nf*
meritocracy	meritocracia *nf*
ochlocracy	oclocracia *nf*
oligarchy	oligarquía *nf*
plutocracy	plutocracia *nf*
technocracy	tecnocracia *nf*
theocracy	teocracia *nf*

entities

colony	colonia *nf*
confederacy	confederación *nf*
confederation	confederación *nf*
county	condado *nm*
dependency	dependencia *nf*
dominion	dominio *nm*
duchy	ducado *aj*
emirate	emirato *nm*
empire	imperio *nm*
federation	federación *nf*
khanate	kanato *nm*
mandate	mandato *nm*
nation	nación *nf*
prefecture	prefectura *nf*
principality	principado *nm*
protectorate	protectorado *nm*
province	provincia *nf*
regency	regencia *nf*
reservation (Indian)	reserva *nf*
state	estado *nm*
territory	territorio *nm*

FUNCTIONING

rights and freedoms

civil rights	derechos civiles *nmpl*
equality	igualdad *nf*
justice	justicia *nf*

liberty	libertad *nf*
press	prensa *nf*
protection	protección *nf*
religion	religión *nf*

government responsibilities

censure	censura *nf*
census	censo *nm*
civil defense Ⓐ	defensa civil *nf*
intelligence	inteligencia *nf*
legislation	legislación *nf*
national security	seguridad nacional *nf*
police	policía *nf*
public health	salud pública *nf*
regulation	regulación *nf*

legislative bodies

assembly	asamblea *nf*
Soviet (obs)	soviet *nm*
commissariat	comisaría *nf*
congress	Congreso *nm*
diet	dieta *nf*
junta	junta *nf*
legislature	legislatura *nf*
parliament	parlamento *nm*
presidium, praesidium Ⓑ	presidio *nm*
senate	senado *nm*

official announcements

declaration	declaración *nf*
edict	edicto *nm*
manifesto Ⓑ	manifiesto *nm*
memorandum	memorándum *nm*
proclamation	proclama, proclamación *nf*
propaganda	propaganda *nf*
resolution	resolución *nf*
ultimatum Ⓑ	ultimátum *nm*

international relations

accord	acuerdo *nm*
alignment	alineamiento *nm*
alliance	alianza *nf*
annexation	anexión *nf*
bilateral	bilateral *aj*
breach	brecha *nf*
cede	ceder *vt*
compact	pacto *nm*
concordat	concordato *nm*
consulate	consulado *nm*
containment	contención *nf*
credentials	credenciales *nfpl*
embargo Ⓑ	embargo *nm*

embassy	embajada *nf*
extraterritoriality	extraterritorialidad *nf*
foreign aid	ayuda externa *nf*
mission	misión *nf*
multilateral	multilateral *aj*
multinational	multinacional *aj*
negotiation	negociación *nf*
neutrality	neutralidad *nf*
pact	pacto *nm*
passport	pasaporte *nm*
protocol	protocolo *nm*
ratification	ratificación *nf*
reciprocity	reciprocidad *nf*
recognition	reconocimiento *nm*
SALT *nsg*	SALT *npl*
treaty	tratado *nm*
unification	unificación *nf*
unilateral	unilateral *aj*
visa	visa *nf*

immigration and emigration

Americanization	americanización *nf*
asylum	asilo *nm*
exile	exilio *nm*
expatriation	expatriación *nf*
nationality	nacionalidad *nf*
naturalization	naturalización *nf*
repatriation	repatriación *nf*

influences on government

activism	activismo *nm*
consensus	consenso *nm*
ideology	ideología *nf*
initiative	iniciativa *nf*
lobby	lobby *nm*
plebiscite	plebiscito *nm*
pressure group	grupo de presión *nm, nf*
public opinion	opinión pública *nf*
referendum Ⓑ	referéndum *nm*

opposition to government

agitation	agitación *nf*
assassination	asesinato *nm*
civil disobedience	desobediencia civil *nf*
defection	defección *nf*
dissension	disensión *nf*
dissidence	disidencia *nf*
disturbances	disturbios *nmpl*
espionage	espionaje *nm*
insurrection	insurrección *nf*
pamphlet (political)	panfleto *nm*
protest	protesta *nf*

purge	purga *nf*
rebellion	rebelión *nf*
resistance	resistencia *nf*
revolution	revolución *nf*
sabotage	sabotaje *nm*

ceremonies and events

coronation	coronación *nf*
crowning	coronamiento *nm*
inauguration	inauguración *nf*

symbols

swastika	esvástica *nf*
crown	corona *nf*
emblem	emblema *nm*
heraldry	heráldica *nf*
national anthem	himno nacional *nm*
seal	sello *nm*
standard (flag)	estandarte *nm*
throne	trono *nm*

pejorative descriptions

authoritarian	autoritario *aj*
bureaucratic	burocrático *aj*
chauvinistic	chovinista *aj*
corrupt	corrupto *aj*
despotic	despótico *aj*
dictatorial	dictatorial *aj*
extremist	extremista *aj*
inefficient	ineficiente *aj*
jingoistic	jingoísta *aj*
oppressive	opresivo *aj*
radical	radical *aj*
repressive	represivo *aj*
tyrannical	tiránico *aj*

other terms

bicameral	bicameral *aj*
bipartisan	bipartidista *aj*
constituent (assembly)	constituyente *aj*
discretionary (powers)	discrecional *aj*
presentation	presentación *nf*
session	sesión *nf*
unicameral	unicameral *aj*

MOVEMENTS AND PHILOSOPHIES

absolutism	absolutismo *nm*
anarchism	anarquismo *nm*
capitalism	capitalismo *nm*
centrism	centrismo *nm*
coexistence	coexistencia *nf*
collectivism	colectivismo *nm*
communism	comunismo *nm*
conservatism	conservadurismo, conservatismo *nm*
expansionism	expansionismo *nm*
extremism	extremismo *nm*
federalism	federalismo *nm*
feminism	feminismo *nm*
imperialism	imperialismo *nm*
internationalism	internacionalismo *nm*
isolationism	aislacionismo *nm*
liberalism	liberalismo *nm*
Marxism	marxismo *nm*
materialism	materialismo *nm*
mercantilism	mercantilismo *nm*
militarism	militarismo *nm*
nationalism	nacionalismo *nm*
nihilism	nihilismo *nm*
nonintervention	no intervención *nf*
nonproliferation	no proliferación *nf*
nonviolence	no violencia *nf*
obstructionism	obstruccionismo *nm*
pacifism	pacifismo *nm*
paternalism	paternalismo *nm*
pluralism	pluralismo *nm*
populism	populismo *nm*
privatization	privatización *nf*
protectionism	proteccionismo *nm*
radicalism	radicalismo *nm*
regionalism	regionalismo *nm*
revanchism	revanchismo *nf*
revisionism	revisionismo *nm*
separatism	separatismo *nm*
socialism	socialismo *nm*
suffrage	sufragio *nm*
totalitarianism	totalitarismo *nm*
Zionism	sionismo *nm*

U.S. POLITICS

constitution

amendment	enmienda *nf*
article	artículo *nm*
preamble	preámbulo *nm*

branches of government

executive	ejecutivo *aj*
judicial	judicial *aj*
legislative	legislativo *aj*

cabinet departments

agriculture	agricultura *nf*
commerce	comercio *nm*
defense Ⓐ	defensa *nf*
education	educación *nf*

interior	interior *nm*
treasury	tesorería *nf*

other government agencies

CIA	CIA *nf*
FBI	FBI *nm*
Medicare	Medicare *nm*
Social Security	Seguro Social *nm*

election terms

acceptance (speech)	aceptación *nf*
Americanism	americanismo *nm*
arena	arena *nf*
campaign	campaña *nf*
contribution	contribución *nf*
convention	convención *nf*
count (of votes)	recuento *nm*
Democratic Party	Partido Democrático *nm*
electoral college	colegio electoral *nm*
eligible	eligible *aj*
meeting	mitin *nm*
nomination	nominación *nf*
opposition	oposición *nf*
platform	plataforma *nf*
politicking	politiqueo *nm*
primary	elección primaria *nf*
recount	recuento *nm*
Republican Party	Partido Republicano *nm*
residency	residencia *nf*
strategy	estrategia *nf*
voting	votación *nf*

other terms

historical record	historial *nm*
representation	representación *nf*
statehood	condición de estado *nf, nm*

BRITISH AND EUROPEAN POLITICS

abdication	abdicación *nf*
accession	accesión *nf*
House of Commons	Cámara de los Comunes *nf*
House of Lords	Cámara de los Lores *nf*
royal family	familia real *nf*

UNITED NATIONS TERMS

aggression	agresión *nf*
atomic energy	energía atómica *nf*
colonialism	colonialismo *nm*
crisis B	crisis C *nf*

disarmament	desarme *nm*
displacement (refugees)	desplazamiento *nm*
emergent, emerging (nation)	emergente *aj*
General Assembly	Asamblea General *nf*
hegemony	hegemonía *nf*
humanitarian aid	ayuda humanitaria *nm*
intervention	intervención *nf*
militancy	militancia *nf*
neocolonialism	neocolonialismo *nm*
neutrality	neutralidad *nf*
nonaligned	no alineado *aj*
nonproliferation	no proliferación *nf*
pacifism	pacifismo *nm*
partition	partición *nf*
peacekeeping	mantenimiento de la paz *nm, nf*
peacetime	época de paz *nf*
proliferation	proliferación *nf*
propaganda	propaganda *nf*
sanctions	sanciones *nfpl*
Secretariat	Secretaría *nf*
security	seguridad *nf*
Security Council	Consejo de Seguridad *nm, nf*
self-determination	autodeterminación *nf*
simultaneous interpretation	interpretación simultánea *nf*
superpower	superpotencia *nf*
supremacy	supremacia *nf*
UNESCO	UNESCO *nf*
UNICEF	UNICEF *nm or nf*
volunteer forces	fuerzas voluntarias *nfpl*
World Bank	Banco Mundial *nm*

HISTORICAL TERMS

United States

abolition	abolición *nf*
antebellum	antes de la Guerra Civil
antislavery	antiesclavista *aj*
colonial	colonial *aj*
confederacy	confederación *nf*
emancipation	emancipación *nf*
prohibition	prohibición *nf*
reconstruction	reconstrucción *nf*
segregation	segregación *nf*
slavery	esclavitud *nf*

Soviet Union

Bolshevism	bolchevismo *nm*
destalinization	desestalinización *nf*
glasnost	glasnost *nm*

gulag	gulag *nm*
KGB	KGB *nf*
Leninism	leninismo *nm*
Politburo	Politburó *nm*
Soviet	soviético *aj*
Stalinism	stalinismo *nm*

former empires

Austria-Hungary	Austria-Hungría
Byzantine	bizantino *aj*
Ottoman	otomano *aj*
Roman	romano *aj*

other historical terms

apartheid	apartheid *nm*
crusade	cruzada *nf*
Falangism	falangismo *nm*
fascism	fascismo *nm*
feudalism	feudalismo *nm*
Gestapo	Gestapo *nf*
guillotine	guillotina *nf*
Hapsburg	hapsburgo, Habsburgo *aj, nm*
Jacobean	jacobino *aj*
League of Nations	Sociedad de Naciones *nf*
Machiavelli	Maquiavelo
Maoism	maoísmo *nm*
Nazism, Naziism	nazismo *nm*
palatinate	palatinado *nm*
peonage	condición de peón *nf, nm*
Restoration	Restauración *nf*
tribune	tribuno *nm*
triumvirate	triunvirato *nm*
Tudor	tudor, Tudor *aj, nm*
Versailles	Versalles *nf*

PERSONS

groups

bloc	bloque *nm*
cabinet	gabinete *nm*
cell (party)	célula *nf*
commission	comisión *nf*
committee	comité *nm*
council (advisory)	consejo *nm*
delegation	delegación *nf*
electorate	electorado *nm*
faction	facción *nf*
judiciary	judicatura *nf*
leadership	liderazgo, liderato *nm*

legation	legación *nf*
majority	mayoría *nf*
minority	minoría *nf*
nobility	nobleza *nf*
royalty	realeza *nf*

historical

abolitionist	abolicionista *nmf*
Bolshevik	bolchevique *nmf*
Bolshevist	bolchevista *aj*
colonialist	colonialista *aj, nmf*
commissar	comisario *nmf*
confederate	confederado, -a *aj, nmf*
czarist	zarista *aj, nmf*
Falangist	falangista *nmf*
Leninist	leninista *aj, nmf*
Menshevik	menchevique *nm*
Nazi	nazi *aj, nmf*
peon	peón *nm*
revisionist	revisionista *aj, nmf*
segregationist	segregacionista *nmf*
slave	esclavo, -a *nmf*
Stalinist	estalinista *aj, nmf*
suffragist	sufragista *nmf*
Trotskyite	trotskista *aj, nmf*

other persons

activist	activista *nmf*
agitator	agitador(a) *nmf*
ally	aliado, -a *nmf*
ambassador	embajador(a) *nmf*
amnestied person	amnistiado, -a *nmf*
anarchist	anarquista *nmf*
anticommunist, anti-Communist	anticomunista *aj, nmf*
aristocrat	aristócrata *nmf*
assassin	asesino, -a *nmf*
assemblyman Ⓑ	asambleísta *nmf*
assemblywoman Ⓑ	asambleísta *nmf*
autocrat	autócrata *nmf*
bureaucrat	burócrata *nmf*
candidate	candidato, -a *nmf*
capitalist	capitalista *nmf*
centrist	centrista *nmf*
chancellor	canciller *nm*
chauvinist	chovinista *aj, nmf*
colonist	colono, -a *nmf*
colonizer	colonizador(a) *nmf*
communist, Communist	comunista *aj, nmf*
compatriot	compatriota *nmf*
congressman Ⓑ	congresista *nm*
congresswoman Ⓑ	congresista *nf*

conscientious objector	objetor(a) de conciencia *nmf, nf*	monarch	monarca *nm*
conservative	conservador(a) *aj, nmf*	monarchist	monarquista *nmf*
		nationalist	nacionalista *nmf*
consort	consorte *nmf*	negotiator	negociador(a) *nmf*
consul	cónsul *nm*	neo-Nazi	neonazi *aj, nmf*
councilman Ⓑ	concejal *nm*	nonresident	no residente *aj, nmf*
councilwoman Ⓑ	concejala *nf*	observer	observador(a) *nmf*
counterspy	contraespía *nmf*	obstructionist	obstruccionista *nmf*
delegate	delegado, -a *nf*	oligarch	oligarca *nm*
demagog(ue)	demagogo *nm*	pacifist	pacifista *nmf*
Democrat	demócrata *nmf*	pamphleteer	panfletista *nmf*
despot	déspota *nm*	parliamentarian	parlamentario, -a *nmf*
dignitary	dignatario, -a *nmf*	party member	partidista *nmf*
diplomat	diplomático *nmf*	patriot	patriota *nmf*
displaced person	desplazado, -a *nmf*	plenipotentiary	plenipotentiario *aj, nm*
dissenter, dissident	disidente *nmf*	plutocrat	plutócrata *nmf*
egalitarian	igualitario, -a *aj, nmf*	political schemer	politiquero, -a *nmf*
elector	elector(a) *nmf*	political scientist	politólogo, -a *nmf*
emancipator	emancipador(a) *nmf*	politician	político, -a *nmf*
emigre	emigrado *nm*	populist	populista *aj, nmf*
emigree	emigrada *nf*	potentate	potentado *nm*
emissary	emisario, -a *nmf*	president	presidente *nmf*
emperor	emperador *nm*	president-elect	presidente electo *nm*
empress	emperatriz *nf*	pretender	pretendiente *nmf*
envoy	enviado, -a *nmf*	prime minister (man)	primer ministro *nm*
exile	exil(i)ado, -a *nmf*	prime minister (woman)	primera ministra *nf*
expatriate	expatriado, -a *aj, nmf*	progressive	progresista *aj, nmf*
extremist	extremista *nmf*	proletarian	proletario, -a *aj, nmf*
fascist	fascista *aj, nmf*	propagandist	propagandista *nmf*
federalist	federalista *aj, nmf*	protectionist	proteccionista *aj, nmf*
feminist	feminista *aj, nmf*	provocateur	agente provocador *nmf*
functionary	funcionario, -a *nmf*	radical	radical *nmf*
governor	gobernador(a) *nmf*	reactionary	reaccionario, -a *aj, nmf*
immigrant	inmigrante *aj, nmf*		
imperialist	imperialista *aj, nmf*	rebel	rebelde *nmf*
insurgent	insurgente *aj, nmf*	refugee	refugiado, -a *nmf*
integrationist	integracionista *nmf*	repatriate	repatriado, -a *nmf*
interventionist	intervencionista *nmf*	representative	representante *nmf*
isolationist	aislacionista *aj, nmf*	Republican	republicano, -a *nmf*
jingo, jingoist	jingoísta *nmf*	revanchist	revanchista *aj, nmf*
laborite	laborista *nmf*	revolutionary	revolucionario, -a *aj, nmf*
leader	líder *nm*		
legislator	legislador(a) *nmf*	royalist	realista *aj, nmf*
liberal	liberal *aj, nmf*	saboteur	saboteador(a) *nmf*
libertarian	libertario, -a *nmf*	secretary	secretario, -a *nmf*
martyr	mártir *nmf*	secretary-general	secretario, -a general *nmf*
Marxist	marxista *aj, nmf*		
matriarch	matriarca *nf*	senator	senador(a) *nmf*
member	miembro *nmf*	separatist	separatista *aj, nmf*
militarist	militarista *nmf*	socialist	socialista *aj, nmf*
minister	ministro, -a *nmf*	sovereign	soberano, -a *aj, nmf*
moderate	moderado, -a *aj, nmf*	Sovietologist	sovietólogo, -a *nmf*

spy	espía *nmf*	undersecretary	subsecretario, -a *nmf*
statesman/ stateswoman Ⓑ	estadista *nmf*	vice-president	vicepresidente *nmf*
subversive	subversivo, -a *aj, nmf*	voter	votante *nmf*
sympathizer	simpatizante *nmf*	Zionist	sionista *aj, nmf*
technocrat	tecnócrata *nmf*		
traitor	traidor(a) *nmf*		
treasurer	tesorero, -a *nmf*		
tyrant	tirano, -a *nmf*		
ultraconservative	ultraconservador(a) *aj, nmf*		

(*See also* FAMOUS NAMES under **ANCIENT CIVILIZATIONS**; *political and military* under **LAW**; *procedures* under **ORGANIZATIONS AND MEETINGS**; *OBSOLETE NAMES* under **PLACE NAMES II: POLITICAL**; **TITLES**)

Buying and Selling

ECONOMICS

GENERAL TERMS

balance of trade	balanza de comercio *nf*
Benelux	Benelux *nm*
by-product	subproducto *nm*
capital	capital *nm*
class	clase *nf*
collective	colectivo *nm*
collective bargaining	negociación colectiva *nf*
commerce	comercio *nm*
Common Market	Mercado Común *nm*
consumption	consumo *nm*
distribution	distribución *nf*
economy	economía *nf*
ECU, ecu	ECU, ecu *nm*
Federal Reserve Board	Junta de la Reserva Federal
GATT	GATT *nm*
index Ⓑ	índice *nm*
industry	industria *nf*
infrastructure	infraestructura *nf*
intervention	intervención *nf*
labor	laboral *aj*
market	mercado *nm*
mass production	producción en serie *nf*
medium of exchange	medio de pago *nm*
modeling Ⓐ	modelización *nf*
NAFTA	NAFTA *nm*
national (debt)	nacional *aj*
nationalization	nacionalización *nf*
OPEC	OPEC, OPEP *nf*
petrodollar	petrodólar *nm*
product	producto *nm*
production	producción *nf*
property	propiedad *nf*
protective tariff	tarifa proteccionista *nf*
quota	cuota *nf*
sanction	sanción *nf*
service	servicio *nm*
socioeconomic	socioeconómico *aj*
standard of living	estándar de vida *nm, nf*
tariff	tarifa *nf*

SPECIALIZATIONS

consumerism	consumismo *nm*
econometrics	econometría *nf*
macroeconomics	macroeconomía *nf*
microeconomics	microeconomía *nf*

ASPECTS OF ECONOMICS

classes

aristocracy	aristocracia *nf*
bourgeoisie	burguesía *nf*
intelligentsia	inteligentsia *nf*
lumpenproletariat	lumpenproletariado *nm*
proletariat	proletariado *nm*

systems and theories

autarchy	autarquía *nf*
capitalism	capitalismo *nm*
communism	comunismo *nm*
expansionism	expansionismo *nm*
fascism	fascismo *nm*
feudalism	feudalismo *nm*
industrialism	industrialismo *nm*
mercantilism	mercantilismo *nm*
monetarism	monetarismo *nm*
protectionism	proteccionismo *nm*
slavery	esclavitud *nf*
socialism	socialismo *nm*
syndicalism	sindicalismo *nm*
vassalage	vasallaje *nm*

kinds of economies

centralized	centralizado *aj*
controlled	controlado *aj*
free market	de libre mercado *aj*
industrialized	industrializado *aj*
international	internacional *aj*
invisible	invisible *aj*
planned	planificada *aj*
stable	estable *aj*

economic conditions

boom	boom *nm*
deflation	deflación *nf*
depression	depresión *nf*
employment	empleo *nm*
inflation	inflación *nf*
poverty	pobreza *nf*
productivity	productividad *nf*
recession	recesión *nf*
scarcity	escasez *nf*
stagflation	estagflación *nf*

stagnation	estancamiento *nm*
unemployment	desempleo *nm*

PERSONS

bourgeois	burgués, -esa *aj, nmf*
capitalist	capitalista *nmf*
consumer	consumidor(a) *nmf*
economist	economista *nmf*
industrialist	industrial *nmf*
Keynesian	keynesiano, -a *aj, nmf*
Marxist	marxista *aj, nmf*
producer	productor(a) *nmf*
proletarian	proletario, -a *aj, nmf*
protectionist	proteccionista *aj, nmf*

(*See also* **BUSINESS**; **MONEY AND FINANCE**)

BUSINESS

GENERAL TERMS

audit	auditoría *nf*
boycott	boicot, boicoteo *nm*
cancellation	cancelación *nf*
capital	capital *nm*
cargo Ⓑ	carga, cargamento *nf, nm*
commerce	comercio *nm*
competition	competencia *nf*
cost	costo, coste *nm*
credit	crédito *nm*
cycle	ciclo *nm*
demand	demanda *nf*
employment	empleo *nm*
expansion	expansión *nf*
financing	financiamiento, financiación *nm, nf*
fixed (price, interest)	fijo *aj*
freightage (cost)	flete *nm*
gain	ganancia *nf*
inventory	inventario *nm*
market, marketplace	mercado *nm*
moratorium Ⓑ	moratoria *nf*
net (profit)	neto *aj*
operate	operar *vti*
price	precio *nm*
price-fixing	fijación de precios *nf, nmpl*
product	producto *nm*
prohibitive (cost)	prohibitivo *aj*
quality	calidad *nf*
receipt	recibo *nm*
regulations *npl*	reglamento *nm*
representation	representación *nf*

residual (profit)	residual *aj*
service	servicio *nm*
unit	unidad *nf*
value	valor *nm*

KINDS OF BUSINESSES

ownership and organization

cartel	cártel *nm*
company	compañía *nf*
conglomerate	conglomerado *nm*
consortium Ⓑ	consorcio *nm*
cooperative	cooperativa *nf*
corporation	corporación *nf*
firm	firma *nf*
franchise	franquicia *nf*
monopoly	monopolio *nm*
multinational	multinacional *aj, nf*
mutual *nsgnsg*	seguros mutuos *nmpl*
subsidiary	subsidiario *aj, nm*

type of product or service

accounting	contabilidad *nf*
agriculture	agricultura *nf*
banking	banca *nf*
construction	construcción *nf*
consulting	consultoría *nf*
contracting	contratación *nf*
exporting	exportación *nf*
fabrication	fabricación *nf*
importing	importación *nf*
manufacturing	manufactura *nf*
marketing	mercadeo *nm*
mining	minería *nf*
publications	publicaciones *nfpl*
transportation	tra(n)sportación *nf*

RETAIL MARKETING

places

antique shop	anticuario *nm*
bank	banco *nm*
bazaar, bazar	bazar *nm*
boutique	boutique *nf*
concession	concesión *nf*
department store	tienda por departamentos *nf, nmpl*
emporium Ⓑ	emporio *nm*
establishment	establecimiento *nm*
hotel	hotel *nm*
kiosk	kiosco, quiosco *nm*

motel	motel *nm*
perfumery	perfumería *nf*
pharmacy	farmacia *nf*
restaurant	restaurante *nm*
souk	zoco *nm*
supermarket	supermercado *nm*

advertising

announcement	anuncio *nm*
campaign	campaña *nf*
catalog(ue)	catálogo *nm*
circular	circular *nf*
commercial	anuncio comercial *nm*
economical	económico *aj*
exposition	exposición *nf*
logo	logo, logotipo *nm*
promotion	promoción *nf*
slogan	slogan, eslogan *nm*

selling

assortment	surtido *nm*
commission	comisión *nf*
consignment	consignación *nf*
container	contenedor *nm*
discount	descuento *nm*
merchandise *nsg*	mercancias *nfpl*
offer	oferta *nf*
option	opción *nf*
package	paquete *nm*
packaging	empaque *nm*
prospectus	prospecto *nm*
quotation	cotización *nf*
receipt	recibo *nm*
transaction	transacción *nf*

LEGAL TERMS

ad valorem	ad valorem *av*
contraband	contrabando *nm*
contract	contrato *nm*
contractual	contractual *aj*
embargo Ⓑ	embargo *nm*
guarantee	garantía *nf*
obligation	obligación *nf*
patent	patente *nf*
title	título *nm*

OFFICE EQUIPMENT

calendar	calendario *nm*
clip	clip *nm*
computer	computadora *nf*
copier	fotocopiadora *nf*
duplicator	duplicador *aj*
fax	fax *nm*
numbering machine	numeradora *nf*
paper	papel *nm*
photocopier	fotocopiadora *nf*
portfolio	portafolio *nm*
telephone	teléfono *nm*

PERSONS

buyers

clientele	clientela *nf*
consumer	consumidor(a) *nmf*

sellers

coffee merchant	cafetero, -a *nmf*
concessionaire	concesionario *nm*
fruit merchant	frutero, -a *nmf*
lottery ticket seller	lotero, -a *nmf*
merchant	mercante, mercader, merchante *nmf*
proprietor	propietario, -a *nmf*
trafficker	traficante *nmf*
vendor	vendedor(a) *nmf*

other business people

auditor	auditor(a) *nmf*
competitor	competidor(a) *nmf*
consignee	consignatorio, -a *nmf*
consignor	cosignador(a) *nmf*
contractor	contratista *nmf*
directors (board of)	directiva *nf*
executive	ejecutivo *nm*
exporter	exportador(a) *nmf*
fabricator	fabricante *nmf*
importer	importador(a) *nmf*
personnel	personal *nm*
subcontractor	subcontratista *nmf*
supervisor	supervisor(a) *nmf*
consultant	consultor(a) *nmf*
demonstrator	demostrador(a) *nmf*
director	director(a) *nmf*
employee, employe	empleado, -a *nmf*
inspector	inspector(a) *nmf*
producer	productor(a) *nmf*
promoter	promotor(a) *nmf*
rival	rival *aj, nmf*
secretary	secretario, -a *nmf*

(*See also* **ECONOMICS**; **MONEY AND FINANCE**)

MONEY AND FINANCE

GENERAL TERMS

banking	banca *nf*
credit card	tarjeta de crédito *nf*
currency	moneda corriente *nf*
devaluation	devaluación, desvalorización *nf*
finance	finanza *nf*
fiscal	fiscal *aj*
guaranty	garantía *nf*
interest	interés *nm*
monetary	monetario *aj*
par	par *nf*
payment	pago *nm*
per capita	per cápita *av*
per cent	por ciento *av*
realization	realización *nf*
valuables	objetos de valor *nmpl, nm*

FINANCIAL CONDITION

having/making money

accumulate	acumular(se) *vt(r)*
amass	amasar *vt*
compensation	compensación *nf*
fortune	fortuna *nf*
honorarium Ⓑ	honorarios *nmpl*
lucrative	lucrativo *aj*
luxury	lujo *nm*
pension	pensión *nf*
recompense	recompensa *nf*
reimbursement	reembolso *nm*
remuneration	remuneración *nf*
riches	riquezas *nfpl*
salary	salario *nm*
solvency	solvencia *nf*
stipend	estipendio *nm*
subsidy	subsidio *nm*
subvention	subvención *nf*

not having/losing money

bankruptcy	bancarrota *nf*
debt	deuda *nf*
deficit	déficit *nm*
dissipation	disipación *nf*
impoverishment	empobrecimiento *nm*
incur (expense)	incurrir *vt*
indebtedness	adeudo *nm*
insolvency	insolvencia *nf*
parsimony	parsimonia *nf*
pauperism	pauperismo *nm*

penury	penuria *nf*
poor	pobre *aj*
poverty	pobreza *nf*
reversal	revés *nm*
ruin	ruina *nf*

ASPECTS OF MONEY AND FINANCE

banking

account	cuenta *nf*
balance	balance *nm*
bank	banco *nm*
blank (check)	en blanco
CD	CD *nm*
certified (check)	certificado *aj*
check Ⓐ	cheque *nm*
checkbook Ⓐ	chequera *nf*
credit	crédito *nm*
debit	debe, débito *nm*
deposit	depósito *nm*
endorsement	endoso *nm*
floating	flotante *aj*
percentage	porcentaje *nm*
personal (check)	personal *aj*
PIN	PIN *nm*
promissory (note)	promisorio *aj*
redeem	redimir *vt*
refinancing	refinanciamiento *nm*
self-financing	autofinanciamiento *nm*
transaction	transacción *nf*
transfer, transference	tra(n)sferencia *nf*

stock market

appreciation	apreciación *nf*
arbitrage, arbitration	arbitraje *nm*
bond	bono *nm*
calculated (risk)	calculado *aj*
commission	comisión *nf*
convertible	convertible *aj*
correction	corrección *nf*
coupon	cupón *nm*
dilution (of assets)	dilución *nf*
discount rate	tasa de descuento *nf, nm*
dividend	dividendo *nm*
fund	fondo *nm*
futures	futuros *nmpl*
gain	ganancia *nf*
liquid (assets)	líquido *aj*
list	lista *nf*
margin	margen *nm*
negotiable	negociable *aj*
nominal (value)	nominal *aj*

nonnegotiable	no negociable *aj*
obligation	obligación *nf*
offering	ofrenda *nf*
option	opción *nf*
parity	paridad *nf*
preferred	preferente *aj*
price	precio *nm*
principal	principal *nm*
pro rata	prorrata *av*
quotation	cotización *nf*
speculation	especulación *nf*
value	valor *nm*

insurance

– types of insurance –

accident	accidente *nm*
collision	colisión *nf*
hospitalization	hospitalización *nf*
medical	médico *aj*
postal	postal *aj*
property	propiedad *nf*

– other insurance terms –

actuarial	actuarial *aj*
annuity	anualidad *nf*
claim	reclamación *nf*
coverage	cobertura *nf*
damage	daño *nm*
expectancy (life)	expectativa *nf*
indemnity (compensation)	indemnización *nf*
indemnity (exemption)	indemnidad *nf*
lapse	lapso *nm*
mutual	mutuo *aj*
policy	póliza *nf*
premium	primo *nm*
risk	riesgo *nm*

taxes

amortization	amortización *nf*
audit	auditoría *nf*
charity	caridad *nf*
collect	colectar *vt*
deduction	deducción *nf*
depreciation	depreciación *nf*
exclusion	exclusión *nf*
exemption	exención *nf*
intangible	intangible *aj*

other terms

acceptance	aceptación *nf*
cancel (a debt)	cancelar *vt*
charge	cargo *nm*
consolidation (debts)	consolidación *nf*

disposable income *nsg*	ingresos disponibles *nmpl*
gratis	gratis *av*
order (to pay)	orden *nf*
pecuniary	pecuniario *aj*
remit	remitir *vt*
surcharge	sobrecarga *nf*
tribute (obs)	tributo *nm*

MONETARY UNITS

current

balboa	balboa *nm*
bolivar	bolívar *nm*
boliviano	boliviano *nm*
cent	centavo *nm*
centesimo	centésimo *nm*
centime	céntimo *nm*
colon Ⓑ	colón *nm*
cordoba	córdoba *nm*
cruzeiro	cruzeiro *nm*
dinar	dinar *nm*
dollar	dólar *nm*
drachma	dracma *nm*
escudo	escudo *nm*
florin	florín *nm*
forint	forint *nm*
franc	franco *nm*
guarani	guaraní *nm*
guilder	gulden *nm*
kopeck	copec *nm*
krona Ⓑ	corona *nf*
krone Ⓑ	corona *nf*
krugerrand	krugerrand *nm*
lempira	lempira *nm*
leu Ⓑ	leu *nm*
lev Ⓑ	lev *nm*
lira	lira *nf*
mark	marco *nm*
penny Ⓑ	penique *nm*
peseta	peseta *nf*
peso	peso *nm*
pfennig	pfennig *nm*
piaster, piastre	piastra *nf*
quetzal	quetzal *nm*
rand Ⓑ	rand *nm*
rial	rial *nm*
riyal	riyal *nm*
ruble Ⓐ	rublo *nm*
rupee	rupia *nf*
schilling (Austrian)	chelín *nm*
shekel	shekel, siclo *nm*
shilling (British)	chelín *nm*

119

sol	sol *nm*	actuary	actuario *nm*
sterling	esterlina *nf*	adjuster	ajustador(a) *nmf*
yen	yen *nm*	analyst	analista *nmf*
yuan	yuan *nm*	auditor	auditor(a) *nmf*
zloty Ⓑ	zloty *nm*	banker	banquero *nmf*
		beneficiary	beneficiario, -a *nmf*

historical and obsolete

crown	corona *nf*	billionaire	billonario, -a *nmf*
denarius	denario *nm*	cashier	cajero, -a *nmf*
doubloon	doblón *nm*	cosignatory	cosignatario, -a *nmf*
ducat	ducado *nm*		
guinea	guinea *nf*	creditor	acreedor(a) *nmf*
napoleon	napoleón *nm*	debtor	deudor(a) *nmf*
real	real *nm*	depositor	depositante *nmf*
sequin	cequí *nm*	endorser	endosador(a), endosante *nmf*
talent	talento *nm*	financier	financiero, -a *nmf*

other terms

bill	billete *nm*	guarantor	garante *nmf*
billfold	billetera *nf*	indigent	indigente *aj, nmf*
circulation	circulación *nf*	magnate	magnate *nmf*
Eurodollar	eurodólar *nm*	millionaire	millonario, -a *nmf*
inscription	inscripción *nf*	multimillionaire	multimillonario, -a *nmf*
legend (on coin)	leyenda *nf*	numismatist	numismatista *nmf*
piece	pieza *nf*		
reverse (of coin)	reverso *nm*	speculator	especulador(a) *nmf*
stable (currency)	estable *aj*		
		statistician	estadístico, -a *nmf*
		treasurer	tesorero, -a *nmf*
		usurer	usurero, -a *nmf*

PERSONS

accountant	contable, contador(a) *nmf*

(*See also* **BUSINESS**; *financial* under **LAW**)

Transportation

AVIATION AND SPACE TRAVEL

GENERAL TERMS

aerospace	espacio *nm*
air	aire *nm*
airline	aerolínea *nf*
aviation	aviación *nf*
instrument	instrumento *nm*
pressurized (cabin)	a presión *nf*
satellite	satélite *nm*
solo	volar solo *vi*
space	espacio *nm*
spaceship	nave espacial *nf*

FIELDS OF SPECIALIZATION

aerobatics	acrobacia *nf*
aerodynamics	aerodinámica *nf*
aeromedicine	aeromedicina *nf*
aeronautics	aeronáutica *nf*
altimetry	altimetría *nf*
astronautics	astronáutica *nf*
astronomy	astronomía *nf*
avionics	aviónica *nf*
bioastronautics	bioastronáutica *nf*
cosmogony	cosmogonía *nf*
cosmography	cosmografía *nf*
cosmology	cosmología *nf*
exobiology	biología espacial *nf*
navigation	navegación *nf*
telemetry	telemetría *nf*

ASPECTS OF AIR TRAVEL

places

aerodrome	aeródromo *nm*
airport	aeropuerto *nm*
hangar	hangar *nm*
heliport	helipuerto *nm*
terminal	terminal *nm*
tower	torre *nf*

types of aircraft

aerostat	aeróstato *nm*
air taxi	aerotaxi *nm*
airliner	aeronave *nf*
airplane	aeroplano *nm*
aquaplane	acuaplano *nm*
balloon	balón *nm*
biplane	biplano *nm*
bomber	bombardero *nm*
dirigible	dirigible *nm*
helicopter	helicóptero *nm*
monoplane	monoplano *nm*
ornithopter	ornitóptero *nm*
transport	transporte *nm*
turbojet	turborreactor *nm*
turboprop	turbopropulsor *nm*
zeppelin	zepelín *nm*

parts and equipment

aileron	alerón *nm*
astrodome	astródomo *nm*
autogyro	autogiro *nm*
board	bordo *nm*
cabin	cabina *nf*
chart	carta *nf*
compass	compás *nm*
ejector	eyector *nm*
float	flotador *nm*
fuselage	fuselaje *nm*
gyrostabilizer	giroestabilizador *nm*
interceptor	interceptor *nm*
manifest	manifiesto *nm*
marker	marcador *nm*
mask	máscara *nf*
oxygen	oxígeno *nm*
panel	panel *nm*
retractable (wheels)	retractable *aj*
rotor	rotor *nm*
stabilizer	estabilizador *nm*

instruments

altimeter	altímetro *nm*
controls	controles *nmpl*
gyrocompass	girocompás *nm*
gyropilot	giropiloto *nm*
gyroscope	giroscopio *nm*
indicator	indicador *nm*
radio	radio *nm*
tachometer	tacómetro *nm*
telemeter	telemetro *nm*
transmitter	transmisor *nm*

flying and navigation

airway	aerovía *nf*
altitude	altura *nf*

ascent	ascenso *nm*
descent	descenso *nm*
deviation	desviación *nf*
direction	dirección *nf*
horizon	horizonte *nm*
piloting	pilotaje *nm*
taxi	taxear *vi*
traffic	tráfico *nm*
turbulence	turbulencia *nf*
velocity	velocidad *nf*

communications systems

loran	lorán *nm*
radar	radar *nm*
shoran	shoran *nm*

TERMS IN SPACE TRAVEL

parts and equipment

capsule	cápsula *nf*
module	módulo *nm*
propellant	propelente *nm*
retrorocket	retrocohete *nm*
umbilical	cordón umbilical *nm*

other terms

destruct	destrucción deliberada *nf*
ejection	eyección *nf*
escape	escape *nm*
exploration	exploración *nf*
extraterrestrial	extraterrestre *aj*
launch	lancha *nf*
mission	misión *nf*
NASA	NASA *nf*
orbit	órbita *nf*
propulsion	propulsión *nf*
sonic	sónico *aj*
space probe	sonda espacial *nf*
space-walk	pasear por el espacio *vi*
station	estación *nf*
stratospheric	estratosférico *aj*
supersonic	supersónico *aj*
zero gravity	gravedad nula *nf*

PERSONS

ace	as *nmf*
astronaut	astronauta *nmf*
aviator	aviador(a) *nmf*
captain	capitán, -ana *nmf*
copilot	copiloto *nmf*
cosmonaut	cosmonauta *nmf*
engineer	ingeniero *nmf*

navigator	navegante *nmf*
passenger	pasajero, -a *nmf*
pilot	piloto *nmf*
radar operator	radarista *nmf*

(*See also* **METEOROLOGY**)

BOATS AND SHIPS

GENERAL TERMS

aboard	a bordo *av*
boat	bote *nm*
navigation	navegación *nf*
port	puerto *nm*
sailboat	bote de vela *nm, nf*
tonnage	tonelaje *nm*

WATER VESSELS

sailboats

brigantine	bergantín *nm*
caravel	carabela *nf*
catamaran	catamarán *nm*
clipper	clíper *nm*
junk	junco *nm*
ketch	queche *nm*
trimaran	trimarán *nm*
yawl	yola *nf*

military ships

convoy	convoy *nm*
corsair	corsario *nm*
corvette	corbeta *nf*
cruiser	crucero *nm*
destroyer	destructor *nm*
frigate	fragata *nf*
galleon	galeón *nm*
minelayer	minador *nm*
minesweeper	dragaminas *nm*
squadron	escuadra *nf*
submarine	submarino *nm*
torpedo boat	torpedero *nm*

other craft

aquaplane	acuaplano *nm*
barge	barcaza *nf*
bathyscaph(e)	batiscafo *nm*
bathysphere	batisfera *nf*
canoe	canoa *nf*
cargo boat	carguero *nm*
cutter	cúter *nm*
derelict	derrelicto *nm*
gondola	góndola *nf*

hydrofoil	hidrofoil *nm*
hydroplane	hidroplano *nm*
kayak	kayac *nm*
launch	lancha *nf*
motorboat	motora *nf*
pirogue	piragua *nf*
rowboat	bote de remos *nm,* *nmpl*
sampan	sampán *nm*
skiff	esquife *nm*
tanker	tanquista *nf*
yacht	yate *nm*

groups of ships

armada	armada *nf*
fleet	flota *nf*
flotilla	flotilla *nf*

parts and sections

board	bordo *nm*
cabin	cabina *nf*
galley	galera *nf*
keel	quilla *nf*
lateen	latina *aj*
mast	mástil *nm*
poop deck	castilla de popa *nf*
porthole	portilla *nf*
prow	proa *nf*
stabilizer	estabilizador *nm*
superstructure	superestructura *nf*

NAVIGATION

kinds of navigation

celestial navigation	navegación astronómica *nf*
loran	lorán *nm*
radar	radar *nm*
radio navigation	radionavegación *nf*
sonar	sónar *nm*

tools and equipment

anchor	ancla, áncora *nf*
bowline	bolina *nf*
buoy	boya *nf*
chart	carta *nf*
compass	compás *nm*
dredger	draga *nf*
float	flotador *nm*
gyrocompass	girocompás *nm*
gyropilot	giropiloto *nm*
gyroscope	giroscopio *nm*
gyrostabilizer	giroestabilizador *nm*

hydrophone	hidrófono *nm*
line	línea *nf*
marker	marcador *nm*
monitor	monitor *nm*
periscope	periscopio *nm*
pontoon	pontón *nm*
sextant	sextante *nm*
tachometer	tacómetro *nm*

plotting

deviation	desviación *nf*
distance	distancia *nf*
point	punto *nm*
position	posición *nf*
route	ruta *nf*
sounding	sondeo *nm*
time	tiempo *nm*
wind	viento *nm*

measurements

knot	nudo *nm*
league	legua *nf*
octant	octante *nm*
quadrant	cuadrante *nm*

waterways

canal	canal *nm*
channel	canal *nm*
coast, seacoast	costa *nf*
lake	lago *nm*
ocean	océano *nm*
river	río *nm*

starting and ending

anchorage (action)	anclaje *nm*
anchorage (place)	ancladero *nm*
arrival	arribo *nm*
disembarcation (cargo)	desembarque *nm*
embarcation	embarcación, embarco *nf, nm*
launching	lanzamiento *nm*

other terms

afloat	a flote *av*
ahoy	ahó *intj*
careen	carena, carenadura *nf*
circumnavigation	circunnavegación *nf*
crosscurrent	contracorriente *nf*
displacement	desplazamiento *nm*
flotation	flotación *nf*
radio beacon	radiofaro *nm*
salvage	salvamento *nm*
submersion	sumersión *nf*

undercurrent	corriente submarina *nf*
unnavigable	innavegable *aj*
waterline	línea de flotación *nf*
windward	barlovento *aj, av*

MARITIME TRADE TERMS

cabotage	cabotaje *nm*
cargo Ⓑ	carga, cargamento *nf, nm*
embargo Ⓑ	embargo *nm*
freightage (cost)	flete *nm*
manifest	manifiesto *nm*
merchant marine	marina mercante *nf*
quarantine	cuarentena *nf*

PERSONS

aquanaut	acuanauta *nmf*
captain	capitán, -ana *nmf*
chief	jefe *nmf*
commodore	comodoro *nm*
gondolier	gondolero *nm*
launcher	lanzador(a) *nmf*
marine	marino, -a *nmf*
mariner	marinero, marino *nm*
navigator	navegante *nmf*
officer	oficial *nmf*
pilot	piloto *nmf*
pirate	pirata *nmf*
stevedore	estibador *nm*

(*See also* **crimes on the high seas** under **LAW**; *directional winds* under **METEOROLOGY**; *water sports* under **SPORTS**)

LAND TRANSPORTATION

GENERAL TERMS

beast of burden	bestia de carga *nf*
motor vehicle	vehículo automotor *nm*
traffic	tráfico *nm*
transportation	tra(n)sportación *nf*
vehicle	vehículo *nm*

MEANS OF TRANSPORTATION

motor-driven vehicles

ambulance	ambulancia *nf*
automobile	automóvil *nm*
bus Ⓑ	autobús, bus *nm*
car	carro *nm*
elevated railroad	ferrocarril elevado *nm*
funicular	funicular *nm*
limousine	limusina *nf*
metro	metro *nm*
monorail	monorriel *nm*
motorcycle	moto, motocicleta *nf*
omnibus	ómnibus *nm*
taxi, taxicab	taxi, taxímetro *nm*
trailer	trailer *nm*
train	tren *nm*
tramway	tranvía *nf*
trolley	trole *nm*
trolleybus	trolebús *nm*

human-driven vehicles

bicycle	bicicleta *nf*
cart	carreta *nf*
litter (obs)	litera *nf*
scooter	escúter *nm*
ski	esquí Ⓒ *nm*
toboggan	tobogán *nm*
tricycle	triciclo *nm*
unicycle	monociclo *nm*
velocipede	velocípedo *nm*

animal-driven vehicles

caravan	caravana *nf*
carriage	carruaje *nm*
phaeton (obs)	faetón *nm*
troika	troica *nf*

mechanical devices

carrousel (baggage)	carrusel *nm*
elevator	elevador *nm*
escalator	escalera *nf*
skilift	telesquí *nm*

animals

ass	asno, -a *nmf*
buffalo Ⓑ	búfalo *nm*
camel	camello *nm*
elephant	elefante *nm*
llama	llama *nf*
mule	mulo, -a *nmf*
yak	yac *nm*

RELATED TERMS

artery	arteria *nf*
freight	flete *nm*
pedal	pedalear *vi*
rail	riel *nm*
ramp	rampa *nf*

semaphore	semáforo *nm*	coolie	culí *nmf*
tandem	tándem *nm*	motorcyclist	motociclista *nmf*
tender	ténder *nm*	muleteer	mulero *nm*
tunnel	túnel *nm*	passenger	pasajero, -a *nmf*
		skier	esquiador(a) *nmf*
		taxi driver	taxista *nmf*

PERSONS

chauffeur	chófer *nm*
coachman	cochero *nm*

(*See also* **AUTOMOBILES**; *streets and traffic* under **THE CITY**; **TRAVEL AND TOURISM**)

Living Things Great and Small

PLANTS

GENERAL TERMS

agriculture	agricultura *nf*
androgyny	androginia *nf*
coloration Ⓐ	coloración *nf*
conservation, conservancy	conservación *nf*
cultivation	cultivo *nm*
deforestation	desforestación *nf*
flora Ⓑ	flora *nf*
florescence	florescencia *nf*
forestation	forestación *nf*
garden	jardín *nm*
gardening	jardinería *nf*
habitat	habitat *nm*
nature	naturaleza *nf*
plant	plantar *vt*
reforestation	reforestación *nf*
vegetation	vegetación *nf*
verdure	verdor, verdura *nm, nf*

MAJOR FIELDS OF SPECIALIZATION

agronomy	agronomía *nf*
botany	botánica *nf*
dendochronology	dendocronologia *nf*
dendrology	dendrologia *nf*
ecology	ecología *nf*
floriculture	floricultura *nf*
forestry	ingenería forestal *nf*
horticulture	horticultura *nf*
hydroponics	hidroponía, hidroponia *nf*
lichenology	liquenología *nf*
phytogeography	fitogeografía *nf*
phytopathology	fitopatología *nf*
pomology	pomología *nf*
silviculture	silvicultura *nf*

PLANT CLASSIFICATIONS

angiosperm	angiosperma *nf*
annual	planta anual *nf*
aquatic	acuático, acuátil *aj*
biennial	planta bienal *aj, nf*
bryophyte	briofita *nf*
carnivorous	carnívoro, carnicero *aj*
chaparral	chaparral *nm*

chlorophyte	clorofita *nf*
composite	compuesto *aj, nm*
conifer	conífera *nf*
coniferous	conífero *aj*
cryptogam	criptógama *nf*
cycad	cicadácea *nf*
datura	datura *nf*
deciduous (tree)	deciduo *aj*
epiphyte	epífita *nf*
exotic	exótico *aj*
flowering	floreciente *aj*
foliate	foliado *aj*
fungus Ⓑ	fungo *nm*
gramineous	gramíneo *aj*
gymnosperm	gimnosperma *nf*
herb	hierba *nf*
hermaphrodite	hermafrodita *aj, nmf*
hybrid	híbrido *aj, nm*
insectivore	insectívoro *nm*
legume	legumbre *nf*
lichen	líquen *nm*
lycopod	licopodio *nm*
moss	musgo *nm*
perennial	planta perenne *nf*
phytoplankton	fitoplancton *nm*
pteridophyte	pteridófita *nf*
spermatophyte	espermatófita *nf*
spermatozoid	espermatozoide *nm*
succulent	suculento *nm*
thalophyte	talofita *nf*
vascular	vascular *aj*
xerophyte	xerofita *nf*

NAMES OF PLANTS

trees and shrubs

acacia	acacia *nf*
acanthus	acanto *nm*
ailanthus	ailanto *nm*
almond tree	almendro *nm*
anil	añil *nm*
azalea	azalea *nf*
balsa	balsa *nf*
balsam	abeto balsámico *nm*
banana	banano *nm*
banyan	baniano *nm*
baobab	baobab *nm*
bougainvillea	buganvilla *nf*

box, boxwood	boj *nm*
cacao	cacao *nm*
calabash	calabacero *nm*
camellia	camelia *nf*
camphor	alcanforero, alcanfor *nm*
catalpa	catalpa *nf*
cedar	cedro *nm*
ceiba	ceiba *nf*
cherry	cerezo *nm*
cinchona	chinchona *nf*
citron	cidro *nm*
clove	clavero *nm*
coca	coca *nf*
coconut palm	cocotero *nm*
coffee tree	cafeto *nm*
cola, kola	cola *nf*
cork oak	alcornoque *nm*
croton	crotón *nm*
cypress	ciprés *nm*
date palm	datilera *nf*
ebony	ébano *nm*
elm	olmo *nm*
eucalyptus	eucalipto *nm*
fig	higuera *nf*
forsythia	forsitia *nf*
fruit tree	frutal *nm*
ginkgo B	gingco *nm*
guava	guayabo *nm*
guayule	guayule *nm*
gum	goma *nf*
jacaranda	jacarandá *nm*
jasmine	jazmín *nm*
jojoba	jojoba *nf*
juniper	junípero *nm*
kalmia	kalmia *nf*
kamala	kamala *nm*
kapok	capoquero *nm*
kumquat	kuncuat *nm*
laburnum	laburno *nm*
laurel	laurel, lauro *nm*
lemon	limonero *nm*
lilac	lila *nf*
lime	limero *nm*
magnolia	magnolia *nf*
mango B	mango *nm*
manzanita	manzanita *nf*
mesquite	mezquita *nf*
mimosa	mimosa *nf*
myrtle	mirto *nm*
ocotillo	ocotillo *nm*
olive	olivo *nm*
orange	naranjo *nm*

palm	palma, palmera *nf*
palmetto	palmito *nm*
papaya	papayo *nm*
pear	peral *nm*
pecan	pacana *nf*
pine	pino *nm*
pineapple	piña *nf*
pistachio	pistacho *nm*
poinciana	poinciana *nf*
pomegranate	granado *nm*
quassia	cuasia *nf*
rhododendron	rododendro *nm*
rosebush	rosal *nm*
sago	sagú *nm*
sandalwood	sándalo *nm*
sapodilla	zapotillo *nm*
sassafras	sasafrás *nm*
sequoia	secoya *nf*
spiraea	espirea *nf*
sumac(h)	zumaque *nm*
sycamore	sicomoro, sicómoro *nm*
tamarind	tamarindo *nm*
tamarisk	tamarisco *nm*
teak	teca *nf*
tragacanth	tragacanto *nm*
tulip tree	tulipanero, tulipero *nm*
upas	upas *nm*
viburnum	viburno *nm*
yucca	yuca *nf*

house and garden plants

abutilon	abutilón *nm*
ageratum	agérato *nm*
amaryllis	amarilis *nf*
anemone	anémona *nf*
aspidistra	aspidistra *nf*
aster	áster *nm*
balsam	balsamina *nf*
begonia	begonia *nf*
belladonna	belladona *nf*
bromeliad	bromelia, bromeliacea *nf*
caladium	caladio *nm*
cattleya	catleya *nf*
chrysanthemum	crisantemo *nm*
colchicum	cólquico *nm*
coleus	coleo *nm*
crocus	croco *nm*
cyclamen	ciclamen, ciclamino *nm*
dahlia	dalia *nf*
delphinium	delfinio *nm*
dracaena	drago *nm*
formal	formal *aj*

freesia	fresia *nf*
fuchsia	fucsia *nf*
gardenia	gardenia *nf*
geranium	geranio *nm*
gladiolus B	gladiolo *nm*
gloxinia	gloxínea *nf*
heliotrope	heliotropo *nm*
hibiscus B	hibisco *nm*
hyacinth	jacinto *nm*
informal	informal *aj*
jonquil	junquillo *nm*
lily	lirio *nm*
lobelia B	lobelia *nf*
lotus	loto *nm*
lupine	lupino *aj*
marguerite	margarita *nf*
narcissus B	narciso *nm*
nicotiana	nicotiana *nf*
orchid	orquídea *nf*
ornamental	ornamental *aj*
passionflower	pasionaria *nf*
pelargonium	pelargonio *nm*
peony	peonía *nf*
petunia	petunia *nf*
philodendron	filodendro *nm*
phlox B	flox *nm*
pimpernel	pimpinela *nf*
pyrethrum	piretro *nm*
rose	rosa *nf*
salvia	salvia *nf*
saxifrage	saxífraga, saxifragia *nf*
snapdragon	boca de dragón *nf*
spathe	espata *nf*
tuberose	tuberosa *nf*
tulip	tulipán *nm*
verbena	verbena *nf*
violet	violeta *nf*
zinnia	cinnia *nf*

wild flowers

aconite (plant)	acónito *nm*
amaranth	amaranto *nm*
cinquefoil	quinquefolio *nm*
clematis	clemátide *nf*
edelweiss	edelweiss *nm*
gentian	genciana *nf*
hepatica	hepática *nf*
locoweed	loco *nm*
scabious	escabiosa *nf*
solanum	solanácea *nf*

herbs

calendula	caléndula *nf*

cineraria	cineraria *nf*
coriander	coriandro *nm*
cumin	comino *nm*
fritillary	fritilaria *nf*
ginseng	ginsén, ginseng *nm*
hellebore	heléboro, eléboro *nm*
lavender	lavanda *nf*
marjoram	mejorana *nf*
mint	menta *nf*
quinoa	quinua *nf*
saffron	azafrán *nm*
tarragon	estragón *nm*
vanilla	vainilla *nf*

aquatic plants

alga B	alga *nf(el)*
diatom	diatomea *nf*
hydrophyte	hidrófita *nf*
kelp	kelp *nm*
papyrus	papiro *nm*
sargasso	sargazo *nm*

succulents

agave	agave *nf*
aloe	áloe, aloe *nm*
cactus B	cactus C, cacto *nm*
euphorbia	euforbio *nm*
opuntia	opuncia *nf*

grasses

bamboo	bambú C *nm*
brome	bromo *nm*
sorghum	sorgo *nm*

other plants

bignonia	bignonia *nf*
bonsai	bonsai *nm*
bryony	brionia *nf*
campanula	campánula *nf*
jalap	jalapa *nf*
liana	liana *nf*
mandrake	mandrágora *nf*
morel	morilla *nf*
myrrh	mirra *nf*
penicillium B	penicilium *nm*
ramie	ramio *nm*
rattan	rota *nf*
sphagnum	musgo esfagnáceo *nm*
spikenard	espicanardo, espicanardi *nm*
truffle	trufa *nf*
nectar	néctar *nm*

PLANT ANATOMY

adventitious	adventicio *aj*
anther	antera *nf*
apterous	áptero *aj*
bulb	bulbo *nm*
callus	callo *nm*
calyx B	cáliz *nm*
carpel	carpelo *nm*
cell	célula *nf*
cellulose	celulosa *nf*
chlorophyl A	clorofila *nf*
chloroplast	cloroplast(i)o *nm*
cilia	cilios *nmpl*
cirrus	cirro *nm*
cone	cono *nm*
corolla	corola *nf*
corona B	corona *nf*
cortex B	corteza *nf*
corymb	corimbo *nm*
cotyledon	cotiledón *nm*
cuticle	cutícula *nf*
cyme	cima *nf*
dendrite	dendrita *nf*
dicotyledon	dicotiledón *nm*
drupe	drupa *nf*
endosperm	endoesperma *nm*
epidermis	epidermis *nf*
filament	filamento *nm*
flower	flor *nf*
foliage	follaje *nm*
frond	fronda *nf*
fruit	fruto *nm*
gland	glándula *nf*
grain	grano *nm*
hypodermis	hipodermis *nf*
inflorescence	inflorescencia *nf*
isomerism	isomerismo *nm*
isomerous	isómero *aj*
labiate	labiado *aj, nm*
labium B	labio *nm*
lamina	lámina *nf*
latex (rubber)	látex *nm*
lemma	lema *nm*
lenticel	lenticela *nf*
lignin	lignina *nf*
lobe	lóbulo *nm*
lobed	lobulado *aj*
medulla B	médula *nf*
moniliform	moniliforme *aj*
monocotyledon	monocotiledón *nm*
node	nodo *nm*
ovary	ovario *nm*
ovate	aovado *aj*

panicle	panícula *nf*
papilla	papila *nf*
parenchyma	paréquima *nm*
pericycle	periciclo *nm*
petal	pétalo *nm*
petiole	pecíolo, peciolo *nm*
phloem	floema *nm*
pinnate	pinada *nf*
pistil	pistilo *nm*
pore	poro *nm*
procumbent	procumbente *aj*
pulp	pulpa *nf*
raceme	racimo *nm*
rachis	raquis *nm*
radicle	radícula *nf*
rhizome	rizoma *nf*
sac	saco *nm*
samara	sámara *nf*
sepal	sépalo *nm*
serrate(d) (leaf)	serrado *aj*
sinuous	sinuoso *aj*
spadix B	espádice *nm*
spike	espiga *nf*
spine	espina *nf*
spore	espora *nf*
stamen	estambre *nm*
stele	estela *nf*
stigma B	estigma *nm*
stipule	estípula *nf*
stoma B	estoma *nf*
style	estilo *nm*
theca B	teca *nf*
trefoil	trifolio *nm*
trifoliate	trifoliado *aj*
trilobate(d), trilobed	trilobulado *aj*
trunk	tronco *nm*
tuber	tubérculo *nm*
tubercle	tubérculo *nm*
umbel	umbela *nf*
vein	vena *nf*
ventral	ventral *aj*
xylem	xilema *nf*

GROWING OF PLANTS

groups of plants

arboretum	arboreto *nm*
bed of violets	violar *nm*
herbarium B	herbario *nm*
olive grove	olivar *nm*
palm grove	palmar *nm*
pine grove	pinar *nm*
ricefield	arrozal *nm*

rose garden | roselada *nf*
terrarium B | terrario *nm*
tomato patch/field | tomatal *nm*
vineyard | viña, viñedo *nf, nm*

stages and processes

auximone | auximón *nm*
cambium | cambium *nm*
defoliation | defoliación *nf*
dormant (period) | durmiente *aj*
flowering (period) | floración *nf*
foliation | foliación *nf*
fructification | fructificación *nf*
geotropism | geotropismo *nm*
germination | germinación *nf*
heliotropism | heliotropismo *nm*
osmosis | osmosis *nf*
photoperiodism | fotoperiodicidad *nf*
photosynthesis | fotosíntesis *nf*
phototaxis | fototaxis *nf*
phototropism | fototropismo *nm*
pollen | polen *nm*
reproduction | reproducción *nf*
transpiration | tra(n)spiración *nf*

reproduction

dichogamy | dicogamia *nf*
fertilization | fertilización *nf*
ovule | óvulo *nm*
pine kernel/nut | piñón *nm*
pollination | polinización *nf*
sporophyte | esporófito *nm*
tetrad | tétrade *nm*
transplantion | tra(n)splante *nm*
zoospore | zoospora *nf*
zygospore | cigospora, zigospora *nf*

pests and diseases

aphid | áfido *nm*
parasite | parásito *nm*
phylloxera | filoxera *nf*

growth and pest control

defoliant | defoliante *nm*
espalier | espaldera *nf*
fertilizer | fertilizante *nm*
herbicide | herbicida *nm*
insecticide | insecticida *nm*
stake | estaca *nf*

plant display

florist shop | floristería *nf*
flower vase | florero *nm*
jardiniere | jardinera *nf*

PERSONS

botanist | botanista, botánico, -a *nmf*
conservationist | conservacionista *nmf*
herbalist | herbalario *nm*
horticulturist | horticultor(a) *nmf*
naturalist | naturalista *nmf*
naturist | naturista *nmf*
rice grower | arrocero *nm*
florist | florista *nmf*
forester | guarda forestal *nmf*
palm farmer | palmero, -a *nmf*
pomologist | pomólogo, -a *nmf*

(*See also major food crops* under **AGRICULTURE**; *natural fibers* under *ASPECTS OF TEXTILES*; *vegetables*; *fruits*; *nuts*; *sauces, spices, syrups* under **FOOD AND NUTRITION**)

ANIMALS

GENERAL TERMS

animal | animal *aj, nm*
beast | bestia *nf*
brute | bruto *aj, nm*
creature | criatura *nf*
fauna B | fauna *nf*

SPECIALIZATIONS

anatomy | anatomía *nf*
apiculture | apicultura *nf*
aquaculture | acuacultura *nf*
aviculture | avicultura *nf*
biochemistry | bioquímica *nf*
ecology | ecología *nf*
embryology | embriología *nf*
entomology | entomología *nf*
ethology | etología *nf*
helminthology | helmintología *nf*
herpetology | herpetología *nf*
histology | histología *nf*
ichthyology | ictiología *nf*
morphology | morfología *nf*
neurobiology | neurobiología *nf*
ophiology | ofiología *nf*
ornithology | ornitología *nf*
physiology | fisiología *nf*
sericulture | sericultura *nf*
taxidermy | taxidermia *nf*
zoogeography | zoogeografía *nf*
zoography | zoografía *nf*
zoology | zoología *nf*

CLASSIFICATIONS

acephalous	acéfalo *aj*
amphibious, amphibian	anfibio *aj, nm*
anthropoid	antropoide *aj, nm*
arthropod	artrópodo *nm*
avian	ave *nf(el)*
biped	bípedo *nm*
bivalve	bivalvo *nm*
bovine	bovino *nm*
canine	canino *aj, nm*
carnivore	carnívoro, -a *nmf*
cephalopod	cefalópodo *nm*
cetacean	cetáceo *aj, nm*
chordate	cordado *nm*
constrictor	constrictor *nm*
crustacean	crustáceo *nm*
ctenophore	ctenóforo *nm*
cyclostome	ciclóstoma *nm*
decapod	decápodo *nm*
domesticated	domesticado *aj*
echinoderm	equiodermo *nm*
edentate	edentado *aj, nm*
equine	equino *aj, nm*
exotic	exótico *aj*
feline	felino *aj, nm*
feral	feral *aj*
gallinaceous	gallináceo *aj*
herbivore	herbívoro, -a *nmf*
hermaphrodite	hermafrodita *aj, nmf*
hibernating	hibernante *aj*
hybrid	híbrido *aj, nm*
hymenopteran	himenóptero *aj, nm*
insect	insecto *nm*
insectivore	insectívoro *nm*
invertebrate	invertebrado *aj, nm*
lepidoptera	lepidópteros *nmpl*
lupine	lupino *aj*
mammalian	mamífero *nm*
marsupial	marsupial *aj, nm*
migratory	migratorio *aj*
mollusk	molusco *nm*
omnivore	omnívoro, -a *nmf*
ophidian	ofidio *aj, nm*
oviparous	ovíparo *aj*
pachyderm	paquidermo *nm*
parasite	parásito *nm*
piscatorial	piscatorio *aj*
porcine	porcino *aj*
predator	predador *nm*
primate	primate *nm*
prosimian	prosimio *aj, nm*
protozoan, protozoon Ⓑ	protozoo, protozoario *nm*
quadruped	cuadrúpedo *nm*
reptile	reptil *nm*
rodent	roedor *nm*
rorqual	rorcual *nm*
ruminant	rumiante *aj, nm*
satyr, satyrid	sátiro *nm*
saurian	saurio *aj, nm*
simian	simio, -a *nmf*
tetrapod	tetrápode *nm*
ungulate	ungulado *nm*
univalve	univalvo *aj, nm*
venomous	venenoso *aj*
vertebrate	vertebrado *aj, nm*
viviparous	vivíparo *aj*
zooid	zooide *nm*
zoophyte	zoófito *nm*

MAMMALS

primates

baboon	babuino *nm*
chimpanzee	chimpancé *nm*
gibbon	gibón *nm*
glutton	glotón *nm*
gorilla	gorila *nf*
human	humano, -a *nmf*
lemur	lémur *nm*
macaque	macaco, -a *nmf*
mandrill	mandril *nm*
orangutan	orangután *nm*
tarsier	tarsero *nm*
titi	tití *nm*

felines

angora	angora *nm*
cat	gato *nm*
cheetah	chita *nf*
civet	civeta *nf*
jaguar	jaguar *nm*
kitty	gatito, -a *nmf*
leopard	leopardo *nm*
lion	león *nm*
lioness	leona *nf*
lynx Ⓑ	lince *nm*
ocelot	ocelote *nm*
panther	pantera *nf*
puma	puma *nf*
tiger	tigre *nm*
tigress	tigresa *nf*
wildcat	gato montés *nm*

canines

arab horse	caballo árabe *nm*
basset hound	basset *nm*
beagle	beagle *nm*
boxer (dog)	bóxer *nm*
bull terrier	bulterrier *nm*
bulldog	buldog *nm*
chihuahua	chihuahua *nmf*
cocker spaniel	cocker C *nmf*
collie	collie *nmf*
coyote	coyote *nm*
dalmatian	dálmata *nm*
dingo B	dingo *nm*
griffon	grifón *nm*
jackal	chacal *nm*
labrador	labrador *nm*
malamute	malamut *nm*
mastiff	mastín *nm*
Pekinese, Pekingese	pequinés, -esa *nmf*
spaniel	spaniel *nm*
terrier	terrier *nm*

equines

ass	asno, -a *nmf*
burro	burro, -a *nmf*
mule	mulo, -a *nmf*
mustang	mustang, mustango *nm*
onager	onagro *nm*
pinto	pinto *nm*
zebra B	cebra *nf*

marsupials

kangaroo B	canguro *nm*
koala	koala *nm*
opossum	oposum *nm*
wallaby	wallabi *nm*
wombat	uombat *nm*

ruminants

alpaca	alpaca *nf*
antelope B	antílope *nm*
bison B	bisonte *nm*
buffalo B	búfalo *nm*
camel	camello *nm*
carabao	carabao *nm*
caribou B	caribú C *nm*
cheviot	cheviot *nm*
dromedary	dromedario *nm*
elk	alce *nm*
gaur	gaur *nm*
gazelle	gacela *nf*
giraffe B	jirafa *nf*
gnu	ñu *nm*
guanaco B	guanaco *nm*
ibex B	íbice *nm*
impala	impala *nf*
karakul	karakul *nm*
kudu B	kudu *nm*
llama	llama *nf*
merino	merino *nm*
okapi	okapí *nm*
peccary	pecarí *nm*
vicuna, vicuña	vicuña *nf*
wapiti	wapití *nm*
yak	yac, yak *nm*
zebu B	cebú C *nm*

rodents

agouti, agouty	agutí *nm*
chinchilla	chinchilla *nf*
gerbil	gerbo *nm*
hamster	hámster *nm*
jerboa	jerbo *nm*
lemming	lemming *nm*
marmot	marmota *nf*
mongoose B	mangosta *nf*
nutria	nutria *nf*
paca	paca *nf*
porcupine	puercoespín *nm*
rat	rata *nf*

pachyderms

elephant	elefante *nm*
hippopotamus B	hipopótamo *nm*
rhinoceros	rinoceronte *nm*

cetaceans

beluga	beluga *nf*
cachalot	cachalote *nm*
dolphin	delfín *nm*
dugong	dugongo *nm*
manatee	manatí C *nm*
narwhal, narwal	narval *nm*

other mammals

armadillo	armadillo *nm*
babirusa, babiroussa, babirussa	babirusa *nf*
echidna	equidna *nf*
ermine	armiño *nm*
hyena	hiena *nf*
leveret	lebrato *nm*
marten B	marta *nf*
panda	panda *nmf*
pangolin	pangolín *nm*
tapir	tapir *nm*

BIRDS

flying birds

bulbul	bulbul *nm*
canary	canario *nm*
cardinal	cardenal *nm*
cockatoo	cacatúa *nf*
condor	cóndor *nm*
cuckoo	cuco *nm*
eagle	águila *nf*
falcon	halcón *nm*
gyrfalcon, gerfalcon	gerifalco, gerifalte *nm*
kea	kea *nf*
marabou	marabú *nm*
myna(h)	mainato *nm*
oriole	oriopéndula *nf*
parakeet	periquito *nm*
partridge Ⓑ	perdiz *nf*
phalarope	falaropo, falárope *nm*
pheasant	faisán *nm*
pigeon	pichón *nm*
tanager	tanagra *nf*
toucan	tucán *nm*
tragopan	tragopón *nm*
trogon	trogón *nm*
vireo	vireo *nm*
vulture	buitre *nm*

flightless and aquatic birds

albatross Ⓑ	albatros *nm*
avocet	avoceta *nf*
cassowary	casuario *nm*
cormorant	cormorán *nm*
eider	eider *nm*
emu	emú *nm*
flamingo Ⓑ	flamenco *nm*
goose	ganso, -a *nmf*
guan	guan *nm*
ibis Ⓑ	ibis *nm*
kiwi	kiwi *nm*
merganser	mergánsar, mergo *nm*
pelican	pelicano *nm*
penguin	pingüino *nm*
petrel	petrel *nm*
pullet	pollo, -a *nmf*

INSECTS AND WORMS

acarid	acárido *nm*
acarus	ácaro *nm*
annelid	anélido *aj*
anopheles	anofeles *nm*
aphid	áfido *nm*
arachnid	arácnido *nm*
centipede	ciempiés *nm*
cockroach	cucaracha *nf*
hemiptera	hemíptero *nm*
kermes	quermes, kermes *nm*
mantis Ⓑ	mantis *nf*
millipede	milpiés *nm*
mosquito Ⓑ	mosquito *nm*
phylloxera	filoxera *nf*
planarian	planario *nm*
scarab	escarabajo *nm*
tarantula	tarántula *nf*
termite	termita *nf*
thysanopteran	tisanópter *aj, nm*
trichina Ⓑ	triquina *nf*
trichoptera	tricóptero *nm*
tsetse	tse-tsé *nf*
wasp	avispa *nf*

FISH AND MARINE LIFE

fish

albacore	albacora *nf*
anchovy	ancho(v)a *nf*
angelfish	angelote *nm*
barracuda Ⓑ	barracuda *nf*
bonito Ⓑ	bonito *nm*
bream	brema *nf*
carp Ⓑ	carpa *nf*
goby Ⓑ	gobio *nm*
grenadier	granadero *nm*
halibut	halibut *nm*
herring	arenque *nm*
lamprey	lamprea *nf*
manta ray	manta *nf*
moray	morena *nf*
perch Ⓑ	perca *nf*
piranha	piraña *nf*
pompano	pámpano *nm*
ray	raya *nf*
remora	rémora *nf*
salmon Ⓑ	salmón *nm*
sardine	sardina *nf*
sturgeon	esturión *nm*
tarpon	tarpón *nm*
trout Ⓑ	trucha *nf*
tuna	atún *nm*
turbot	turbo *nm*

marine animals

abalone	abalone *nm*
ameba, amoeba Ⓑ	ameba, amiba *nf*

amphioxus	anfioxo *nm*
anemone	anémone *nf*
argonaut	argonauta *nm*
bryozoan	briozoario *nm*
chiton	quitón *nm*
conch	concha *nf*
conger	congrio *nm*
coral	coral *nm*
cowrie, cowry	cauri *nm*
gastropod	gasterópodo *nm*
hermit crab	ermitaño *nm*
hydra Ⓑ	hidra *nf*
hydroid	hidroideo *nm*
medusa	medusa *nf*
nautilus Ⓑ	nautilo *nm*
oyster	ostra *nf*
paramecium Ⓑ	paramecio *nm*
polyp	pólipo *nm*
scorpion	escorpión *nm*
sepia	sepia *nf*
sponge	esponja *nf*
triton	tritón *nm*
trypanosome	tripanosoma *nm*
vorticella	vorticela *nf*

REPTILES

snakes

anaconda	anaconda *nf*
asp	áspid(e) *nm*
boa	boa *nf*
cobra	cobra *nf*
coral	coral *nm*
moccasin	mocasín *nm*
python	pitón *nm*
serpent	serpiente, sierpe (poetic) *nf*
viper	víbora *nf*

other reptiles

alligator	aligátor *nm*
axolotl	ajolote *nm*
caiman, cayman	caimán *nm*
chameleon	camaleón *nm*
crocodile	cocodrilo *nm*
gecko Ⓑ	geco *nm*
iguana	iguana *nf*
salamander	salamandra *nf*
skink	esquinco, estinco *nm*
tortoise	tortuga *nf*
tuatara	tuatara, tuatera *nf*
turtle	tortuga *nf*

OTHER ANIMALS

extinct animals

archaeopteryx	arqueópterix *nm*
behemoth	behemot *nm*
brontosaurus Ⓑ	brontosaurio *nm*
coelacanth	celacanto *nm*
dinosaur	dinosaurio *nm*
dodo Ⓑ	dodo *nm*
glyptodont	gliptodonte *nm*
mammoth	mamut *nm*
mastodon	mastodonte *nm*
nummulite	numulite *nm*
pterodactyl	pterodáctilo *nm*
pterosaur	pterosaurio *nm*
stegosaurus	estegosauro *nm*
triceratops	tricerátopo *nm*
trilobite	trilobita *nm*
tyrannosaur	tiranosauro *nm*

animals in myth and folklore

centaur	centauro *nm*
Cerberus	Cerbero
chimera	quimera *nf*
Cyclops	cíclope *nm*
dragon	dragón *nm*
dryad	dríada, dríade *nf*
faun	fauno *nm*
griffin	grifo *nm*
halcyon	alción *nm*
Harpy	arpía *nf*
Hydra	hidra *nf*
leviathan	leviatán *nm*
Medusa	Medusa
Minotaur	Minotauro
monster	monstruo *nm*
ogre	ogro *nm*
Pegasus	Pegaso
Phoenix	Fénix *nm*
roc	rocho, ruc *nm*
sphinx	esfinge *nf*
unicorn	unicornio *nm*
yeti Ⓑ	yeti *nm*

TERMS RELATED TO ANIMALS

specialized animal anatomy

alveolus	alvéolo *nm*
antenna Ⓑ	antena *nf*
apterous	áptero *aj*
beak	pico *nm*
branchia Ⓑ	branquia *nf*
carapace	caparazón *nm*

caudal	caudal *aj*
cilia	cilios *nmpl*
cirrus	cirro *nm*
covert	cobertera *nf*
endoskeleton	endoesqueleto *nm*
exoskeleton	dermatoesqueleto *nm*
hypodermis	hipodermis *nf*
labium B	labio *nm*
lamina	lamina *nf*
mantle	manto *nm*
marsupium	bolsa de marsupial *nf,* *nm*
moniliform	moniliforme *aj*
patella	patela *nf*
pectoral	pectoral *aj, nm*
pellicle	película *nf*
petiole	pecíolo, peciolo *nm*
plumage	plumaje *nm*
plume	pluma *nf*
prehensile	prensil *aj*
proboscis B	probóscide *nf*
protractil	protractil *aj*
rachis	raquis *nm*
reticulum	retículo *nm*
retractile (claws)	retractíl *aj*
simple (eye)	simple *aj*
speculum	espéculo *nm*
tarsus	tarso *nm*
teat	teta *nf*
tentacle	tentáculo *nm*
thorax B	tórax *nm*
tympanum B	tímpano *nm*
versatile	versatil *aj*
xiphoid	xifoideo *aj*

reproduction

castration	castración *nf*
copulation	cópula, copulación *nf*
estrus	estro *nm*
incubate (eggs)	incubar *vt*
lactation	lactancia *nf*
multiparous	multípara *aj*
neuter	neutro *aj*
pregnant	preñado *aj*
spermaceti	espermaceti *nm*
zoospore	zoospora *nf*

dogs and horses

amble	ambladura *nf*
bridle	brida *nf*
cavalry	caballería *nf*
cinch	cincha *nf*
collar (for a dog)	collar *nm*
collar (for a horse)	collera *nf*
equestrian	ecuestre *aj*
gallop	galope *nm*
harness	arnés *nm*
jockey	jockey, yoquei C *nmf*
lasso B	lazo *nm*
mascot	mascota *nf*
mount	montar *vt*
palfrey (obs)	palfrén *nm*
pedigree	pedigrí *nm*
quirt	cuarta *nf*
rein	rienda *nf*
roan	ruano *aj, nm*
trot	trote *nm*
trotter	trotón *nm*
yoke	yugo *nm*

insects

chrysalis B	crisálida *nf*
formic (acid)	fórmico *aj*
fumigation	fumigación *nf*
imago B	imago *nm*
infestation	infestación *nf*
larva B	larva *nf*
nymph	ninfa *nf*
parathion	paratión *nm*
pupa B	pupa *nf*
segment	segmento *nm*

places

apiary	apiario *nm*
aquarium B	acuario *nm*
aviary	averío *nm*
habitat	hábitat, habitación *nm,* *nf*
pasture	pastura, pasto *nf, nm*
perch	percha *nf*
serpentarium	serpentario *nm*
stable	establo *nm*
vivarium	vivero *nm*
zoo	zoo *nm*

sounds

baa	be *nm*
bow-wow	guau-guau *nm*
cluck, clucking	cloqueo *nm*
cock-a-doodle-doo	quiquiriquí *nm*
croak	croar *nm*
cuckoo call	cucú *nm*
meow	miau *nm*
moo	mu *nm*
quack	cua, cuac *nm*

events

rodeo	rodeo *nm*
safari	safari *nm*
stampede	estampida *nf*

other terms

bioluminescence	bioluminiscencia *nf*
dissection	disección *nf*
territoriality	territorialidad *nf*
trap	trampa *nf*
vivisection	vivisección *nf*
zooplankton	zooplancton *nm*
zootomy	zootomía *nf*

PERSONS

apiculturist	apicultor(a) *nmf*
entomologist	entomólogo, -a *nmf*
herpetologist	herpetolólogo, -a *nmf*
jockey, yoquei	jockey Ⓒ *nmf*
muleteer	mulero *nm*
ornithologist	ornitólogo *nmf*
taxidermist	taxidermista *nmf*
trapper	trampero, -a *nmf*
veterinarian	veterinario, -a *nmf*
vivisectionist	viviseccionista *nmf*
zoologist	zoólogo, -a *nmf*

(*See also* **care of animals** under **AGRICULTURE;** **meat and poultry** and *seafood* under **FOOD AND NUTRITION**)

BIOLOGY

GENERAL TERMS

bioactive	bioactivo *aj*
biodegradable	biodegradable *aj*
biodiversity	biodiversidad *nf*
biology	biología *nf*
biomass	biomasa *nf*
biorhythm	biorritmo *nm*
biosphere	biosfera *nf*
biotype	biotipo *nm*
cell	célula *nf*
characteristic	característica *nf*
colony	colonia *nf*
creature	criatura *nf*
culture	cultivo *nm*
ecosystem	ecosistema *nm*
generic	genérico *aj*
germ	germen *nm*
habitat	habitat *nm*
instinct	instinto *nm*

intelligent	inteligente *aj*
microorganism	microorganismo *nm*
molecule	molécula *nf*
nature	naturaleza *nf*
ontogeny	ontogenia, ontogénesis *nf*
organism	organismo *nm*
phylogeny	filogenia *nf*
protoplasm	protoplasma *nm*
soma	soma *nm*
specimen	espécimen Ⓒ *nm*
stimulus Ⓑ	estímulo *nm*
tissue	tejido *nm*
viable	viable *aj*

BRANCHES OF BIOLOGY

major fields

bacteriology	bacteriología *nf*
biophysics	biofísica *nf*
biotechnology	biotecnología *nf*
botany	botánica *nf*
cryobiology	criobiología *nf*
cytology	citología *nf*
ecology	ecología *nf*
embryology	embriología *nf*
entomology	entomología *nf*
ethology	etología *nf*
evolution	evolución *nf*
exobiology	biología espacial *nf*
genetics	genética *nf*
histology	histología *nf*
ichthyology	ictiología *nf*
immunology	inmunología *nf*
limnology	limnología *nf*
marine biology	biología marina *nf*
medicine	medicina *nf*
microbiology	microbiología *nf*
molecular (biology)	molecular *aj*
morphology	morfología *nf*
neurobiology	neurobiología *nf*
ornithology	ornitología *nf*
paleontology	paleontología *nf*
physiology	fisiología *nf*
sociobiology	sociobiología *nf*
systematics	sistemática *nf*
taxonomy	taxonomía *nf*
virology	virología *nf*
zoology	zoología *nf*

related fields

anatomy	anatomía *nf*
bioacoustics	bioacústica *nf*

bioastronautics	bioastronáutica *nf*
biochemistry	bioquímica *nf*
bioclimatology	bioclimatología *nf*
bioecology	bioecología *nf*
bioelectronics	bioelectrónica *nf*
bioengineering	bioingeniería *nf*
biogeography	biogeografía *nf*
biomechanics	biomecánica *nf*
biomedicine	biomedicina *nf*
biometrics	biometría *nf*
biometry	biometría *nf*
bionics	biónica *nf*
bioscopy	biscopía *nf*
chromatography	cromatografía *nf*
cytogenetics	citogenética *nf*
electrophoresis	electroforesia *nf*
eugenics	eugenesia *nf*
mycology	micología *nf*
oology	oología *nf*
parasitology	parasitología *nf*
phenology	fenología *nf*
psychobiology	(p)sicobiología *nf*
somatology	somatalogía *nf*
zymology	cimología *nf*

ASPECTS OF BIOLOGY

theories

biogenesis	biogénesis *nf*
Darwinism	darvinismo *nm*
Lamarckism	lamarquismo *nm*
Malthusianism	maltusismo *nm*
natural selection	selección natual *nf*
spontaneous generation	generación espontánea *nf*
vitalism	vitalismo *nm*

classifications

class	clase *nf*
division	división *nf*
family	familia *nf*
genus Ⓑ	género *nm*
order	orden *nm*
phylum Ⓑ	filum, filo *nm*
species Ⓑ	especie *nf*
subclass	subclase *nf*
subspecies	subespecie *nf*
variety	variedad *nf*

major biotypes

ecotype	ecotipo *nm*
genotype	genotipo *nm*
monotype	monotipo *nm*
phenotype	fenotipo *nm*

characteristics of life

adaptation	adaptación *nf*
differentiation	diferenciación *nf*
irritability	irritabilidad *nf*
movement	movimiento *nm*
nutrition	nutrición *nf*
reproduction	reproducción *nf*

life form types

aerobe	aerobio *nm*
anaerobe	anaerobio *nm*
animal	animal *aj, nm*
bacterium	bacteria *nf*
fossil	fósil *aj, nm*
hermaphrodite	hermafrodita *aj*
heterosexual	heterosexual *aj*
human	humano *aj*
microbe	microbio *nm*
monad	mónada *nf*
monomorphic, monomorphous	monomorfo *aj*
multicellular	multicelular *aj*
oviparous	ovíparo *aj*
photobiotic	fotobiótico *aj*
plant	planta *nf*
polymorph	polimorfo *nm*
protist	protisto *nm*
saprophyte	saprófito *nm*
subhuman	infrahumano *aj*
unicellular, single-celled	unicelular *aj*
unisexual	unisexual *aj*
vector	vector *nm*
vegetable	vegetal *aj*
virus	virus *nm*

biological processes

acclimatization	aclimatización *nf*
anabolism	anabolismo *nm*
autogenesis	autogénesis *nf*
biolysis	biolisis *nf*
bisexual	bisexual *aj*
catabolism	catabolismo *nm*
chemotaxis	quimotaxis *nf*
cytolysis	citólisis *nf*
degeneration	degeneración *nf*
fertilization	fertilización *nf*
gamogenesis	gamogénesis *nf*
gemmation	gemación *nf*
germination	germinación *nf*
gestation	gestación *nf*
heredity	herencia *nf*
hibernation	hibernación *nf*

hydrotropism — hidrotropismo *nm*
involution — involución *nf*
metabolism — metabolismo *nm*
metagenesis — metagénesis *nf*
metamorphosis B — metamorfosis C *nf*
mimesis — mimetismo *nm*
mimicry — mimetismo *nm*
modification — modificación *nf*
motility — motilidad *nf*
mutation — mutación *nf*
neogenesis — neogénesis *nf*
oogenesis — oogénesis *nf*
orthogenesis — ortogénesis *nf*
ossification — osificación *nf*
ovulation — ovulación *nf*
parthenogenesis — partenogénesis *nf*
photokinesis — fotocinesis *nf*
photoperiodism — fotoperiodicidad *nf*
photosynthesis — fotosíntesis *nf*
regeneration — regeneración *nf*
respiration — respiración *nf*
reversion — reversión *nf*
selection — selección *nf*
symbiosis B — simbiosis C *nf*
synthesis B — síntesis C *nf*
taxis — taxia, taxismo *nf, nm*
tropism — tropismo *nm*
variation — variación *nf*
xenogenesis — xenogénesis, xenogenia *nf*

reproduction

asexual — asexual *aj*
fecundity — fecundidad *nf*
fertility — fertilidad *nf*
fission — fisión *nf*
gonad — gónada *nf*
impregnate — empreñar *vt*
infecundity — infecundidad *nf*
myosis — miosis *nf*
procreation — procreación *nf*
prolific — prolífico *aj*
propagation — propagación *nf*
self-fertilization — autofertilización *nf*
sex — sexo *nm*
sexuality — sexualidad *nf*
sperm — esperma *nf*

other terms

biosensor — biosensor *nm*
coloration (protective) A — coloración defensiva *nf*
cycle — ciclo *nm*

dichromatic — dicromático *aj*
distinctive — distintivo *aj*
homolog(ue) — elemento homólogo *nm*
homomorphism — homomorfismo *nm*
isomorphism — isomorfismo *nm*
latency — latencia *nf*
macrobiotic — macrobiótico *aj*
mutualism — mutualismo *nm*
photoreceptor — fotorreceptor *nm*
pigmentation — pigmentación *nf*
trinomial name — nombre trinomial *nm*

TERMS IN EMBRYOLOGY

ectoderm — ectodermo *nm*
embryo — embrión *nm*
endoderm — endodermo *nm*
gamete — gameto *nm*
gametogenesis — gametogénesis *nf*
gastrula B — gástrula *nf*
gemma — gema *nf*
mesoderm — mesodermo *nm*
oocyte — oocito, ovocito *nm*
organizer — organizador *nm*
ovum B — óvulo *nm*
primitive — primitivo *aj*
rudiment — rudimento *nm*
segmentation — segmentación *nf*
spermatozoon — espermatozoo *nm*
vestige, vestigium — vestigio *nm*
zygote — zigoto, cigoto *nm*

TERMS IN GENETICS

adenosine — adenosina *nf*
albino — albino, -a *aj, nmf*
allele — alelo *nm*
atavism — atavismo *nm*
autosome — autosoma *nf*
bivalent — bivalente *aj*
chromosome — cromosoma *nm*
clone — clon *nm*
code — código *nm*
complementary (genes) — complementario *aj*
defective — defectivo *aj*
DNA — DNA *nm*
dominant (gene) — dominante *aj*
dyad — díade *nf*
gene — gen, gene *nm*
genetic engineering — ingeniería genética *nf*
genome — génoma *nf*
inherited — heredero *aj*
locus B — locus *nm*

maternal	materno *aj*
mutant	mutante *nm*
paternal	paterno *aj*
recessive (gene)	recesivo *aj*
ribonucleic	ribonucleico *aj*
synapsis Ⓑ	sinapsis Ⓒ *nf*
tetrad	tétrade *nm*

TERMS IN CYTOLOGY

cellule	celulilla *nf*
cytoplasm	citoplasma *nm*
ectoplasm	ectoplasma *nm*
endoplasm	endoplasma *nm*
flagellum	flagelo *nm*
nucleus Ⓑ	núcleo *nm*
basal	basal *aj*
biogenic	biogénico *aj*
cytogenesis	citogénesis *nf*
cytotoxin	citotoxina *nf*
excrescence	excrescencia *nf*
hypertrophy	hipertrofia *nf*
lacuna Ⓑ	laguna *nf*
macrophage	macrófago *nm*
meiosis	meiosis, meyosis *nf*
membrane	membrana *nf*
mitosis	mitosis *nf*
monocyte	monocito *nm*
organelle	organela *nf*
phagocyte	fagocito *nm*
ribosome	ribosoma *nm*
squamose, squamous	escamoso *aj*
vacuole	vacuola *nf*

TERMS IN ECOLOGY

biome	bioma *nm*
decomposition	descomposición *nf*
disequilibrium	desequilibrio *nm*
equilibrium	equilibrio *nm*
niche	nicho *nm*

phytoplankton	fitoplancton *nm*
plankton	plancton *nm*
zooplankton	zooplancton *nm*

TERMS IN BIOCHEMISTRY

acid	ácido *nm*
antiserum Ⓑ	antisuero *nm*
bioassay	bioensayo *nm*
biocatalyst	biocatalizador *nm*
biosynthesis	biosíntesis *nf*
carbohydrate	carbohidrato *nm*
coenzyme	coenzima *nf*
enzyme	enzima *nf*
hormone	hormona *nf*
hydrolysis	hidrólisis *nf*
lipid(e)	lípido *nm*
pectin	pectina *nf*
peptide	péptido *nm*
protein	proteína *nf*
putrefaction	putrefacción *nf*
vitamin	vitamina *nf*

PERSONS

bacteriologist	bacteriólogo, -a *nmf*
biochemist	bioquímico, -a *nmf*
biologist	biólogo, -a *nmf*
biophysicist	biofísico, -a *nmf*
ecologist	ecólogo, -a *nmf*
embryologist	embriólogo, -a *nmf*
geneticist	genetista, geneticista *nmf*
microbiologist	microbiólogo, -a *nmf*
mycologist	micólogo, -a *nmf*
paleontologist	paleontólogo, -a *nmf*

(*See also* **ANIMALS**; *NUTRITION* under **FOOD AND NUTRITION**; **PLANTS**; *BIOCHEMICALS* under **THE HUMAN BODY**)

Medical Matters

THE HUMAN BODY

GENERAL TERMS

absorption	absorción *nf*
anatomy	anatomía *nf*
apparatus Ⓑ	aparato *nm*
articulation	articulación *nf*
birthmark	marca de nacimiento *nf*
circadian (rhythm)	circadiano *aj*
corporeal	corpóreo *aj*
corpus Ⓑ	cuerpo *nm*
figure	figura *nf*
flaccidity	flaccidez *nf*
orifice	orificio *nm*
physiological	fisiológico *aj*
physique	físico *aj*
region	región *nf*
reproduction	reproducción *nf*
stature	estatura *nf*
synergy	sinergia *nf*
temperature	temperatura *nf*
tone	tono *nm*
vital (organs)	vital *aj*

STRUCTURE

systems

circulatory	circulatorio *aj*
digestive	digestivo *aj*
endocrine	endocrino *aj*
genitourinary	genitourinario *aj*
lymphatic	linfático *aj*
nervous	nervioso *aj*
parasympathetic	parasimpático *aj*
reproductive	reproductivo *aj*
respiratory	respiratorio *aj*
skeletal	esquelético *aj*

components

adnexa	anexos *nmpl*
appendage	apéndice *nm*
canal	canal *nm*
cartilage	cartílago *nm*
cavity	cavidad *nf*
cord	cordel *nm*
duct	conducto *nm*
fluid	fluido *nm*
gland	glándula *nf*

humor (obs) Ⓐ	humor *nm*
membrane	membrana *nf*
musculature	musculatura *nf*
nerve	nervio *nm*
node	nodo *nm*
nodule	nódulo *nm*
organ	órgano *nm*
passage	pasaje *nm*
sac	saco *nm*
tissue	tejido *nm*
tube	tubo *nm*

major sections

abdomen	abdomen *nm*
bust	busto *nm*
extremities	extremidades *nfpl*
torso	torso *nm*
trunk	tronco *nm*

regions

anal	anal *aj*
cardiopulmonary	cardiopulmonar *aj*
caudal	caudal *aj*
cephalic	cefálico *aj*
cerebrospinal	cerebroespinal *aj*
costal	costal *aj*
dental	dental *aj*
erogenous	erógeno *aj*
facial	facial *aj*
gastrointestinal	gastrointestinal *aj*
gingival	gingival *aj*
gutteral	guteral *aj*
intercostal	intercostal *aj*
intestinal	intestino *aj*
limbic	límbico *aj*
lumbar	lumbar *aj*
pancreatic	pancreático *aj*
pelvic	pélvico *aj*
postnasal	pos(t)nasal *aj*
pubic	púbico *aj*
pulmonary	pulmonar *aj*
rectal	rectal *aj*
renal	renal *aj*
sacroiliac	región sacroilíaca *aj*
sigmoidal	sigmoide, sigmoideo *aj*
spinal	espinal *aj*
suprarenal	suprarrenal *aj*
ulnar	ulnar *aj*

urogenital	urogenital *aj*
ventral	ventral *aj*

relative locations

anterior	anterior *aj*
dorsal	dorsal *aj*
external	externo *aj*
internal	interno *aj*
posterior	posterior *aj*

other terms

intramuscular	intramuscular *aj*
intravenous	intravenoso *aj*
subcutaneous	subcutáneo *aj*
submaxillary	submaxilar *aj*

NAMES OF BODY PARTS

cavities

abdominal	abdominal *aj*
oral	oral *aj*

bones and joints

carpal	carpiano *aj*
clavicle	clavícula *nf*
coccyx Ⓑ	cóccix *nm*
endoskeleton	endoesqueleto *nm*
ethmoid	etmoides *aj, nm*
femur Ⓑ	fémur *nm*
fibula Ⓑ	fíbula *nf*
humerus Ⓑ	húmero *nm*
ilium Ⓑ	ilion *nm*
ischium	isquión *nm*
malleolus Ⓑ	maleólo *nm*
mandible	mandíbula *nf*
maxilla	hueso maxilar *nm*
occiput	occipucio *nm*
parietal	parietal *aj*
pelvis Ⓑ	pelvis Ⓒ *nf*
phalange	falange *nf*
phalanx Ⓑ	falange *nm*
pubis	pubis *nm*
radius Ⓑ	radio *nm*
sacrum Ⓑ	sacro *nm*
scapula Ⓑ	escápula *nf*
skeleton	esqueleto *nm*
sphenoid	esfenoides *nm*
spine	espina, espinazo *nf, nm*
sternum Ⓑ	esternón *nm*
tarsus	tarso *nm*
thorax Ⓑ	tórax *nm*
tibia Ⓑ	tibia *nf*
trapezium	trapecio *nm*

trapezoid	trapezoide *nm*
ulna	ulna *nf*
vertebra Ⓑ	vértebra *nf*
zygoma	cigoma, zigoma *nm*

muscles

abductor	abductor *nm*
adductor	aductor *nm*
biceps Ⓑ	bíceps Ⓒ *nm*
constrictor	constrictor *nm*
deltoid *nsg*	deltoides *nmpl*
erector	erector *nm*
extensor	extensor *nm*
flexor	flexor *nm*
frontal	frontal *aj*
gluteus	glúteo *nm*
involuntary	involuntario *aj*
masseter	masetero *nm*
occipital	occipital *aj*
pectoral	pectoral *aj, nm*
quadriceps	cuadriceps *nm*
retractor	retractor *nm*
sphincter	esfinter *nm*
suspensory	suspensorio *aj*
temporal	temporal *aj*
trapezium, trapezius	trapecio *nm*
triceps Ⓑ	tríceps *nm*
zygomatic	cigomatico, zigomatico *aj*

glands

adrenal	suprarrenal *aj*
adrenocortical	adrenocortical *aj*
endocrine	endocrino *aj*
exocrine	exocino *aj*
hypothalamus	hipotálamo *nm*
lachrymal, lacrimal	lacrimal *aj*
lymph	linfa *nf*
mammary	mamario *aj*
pancreas	páncreas *nm*
parathyroid	paratiroides *nf*
parotid	parótida *nf*
pineal	pineal *aj*
pituitary	pituitario *aj*
sebaceous	sebáceo *aj*
thymus	timo *nm*
thyroid	tiroides *nf*
thyroxine	tiroxina *nf*

blood and blood vessels

aorta Ⓑ	aorta *nf*
artery	arteria *nf*
brachial	braquial *aj*

capillary	vaso capilar *nm*
carotid	carótida *aj, nf*
coronary	coronario *aj*
corpuscle	corpúsculo *nm*
erythrocyte	eritrocito *nm*
femoral	femoral *aj*
gamma globulin	gammaglobulina *nf*
globule	glóbulo *nm*
hematic Ⓐ	hemático *aj*
hemoglobin Ⓐ	hemoglobina *nf*
jugular	yugular *aj*
leukocyte Ⓐ	leucocito *nm*
monocyte	monocito *nm*
phagocyte	fagocito *nm*
plasma	plasma *nm*
plexus Ⓑ	plexo *nm*
portal	porta *aj*
Rh-factor	factor Rh *nm*
serum Ⓑ	suero *nm*
thromboplastin	tomboplastina *nf*
vein	vena *nf*

tissues

adenoids	adenoides *nmpl*
adipose	adiposo *aj*
collagen	colágena *nf*
connective	conectivo *aj*
dentin(e)	dentina *nf*
epithelium Ⓑ	epitelio *nm*
erectile	eréctil *aj*
ligament	ligamento *nm*
lymphocyte	linfocito *nm*
membranous	membranoso *aj*
muscle	músculo *nm*
parenchyma	paréquima *nm*
periosteum Ⓑ	periostio *nm*
tendon	tendón *nm*
uvula Ⓑ	úvula *nf*

eye

aqueous	acuoso *aj*
cilia	cilios *nmpl*
cone	cono *nm*
cornea	córnea *nf*
globe	globo *nm*
iris	iris *nm*
ocular	ocular *aj*
pupil	pupila *nf*
retina Ⓑ	retina *nf*
sclera	esclerótica *nf*
vitreous	vítreo *aj*

ear

ampulla Ⓑ	ampolla *nf*
cochlea	cóclea *nf*
Eustachian tube	tubo de Eustaquio *nm*
helix Ⓑ	hélice *nf*
labyrinth	laberinto *nm*
lobule	lobulillo *nm*
mastoid	mastoides *nf*
ossicle	osículo *nm*
petrous	petrosal, petroso *aj*
semicircular	semicircular *aj*
tympanum Ⓑ	tímpano *nm*
vestibule	vestíbulo *nm*

digestive tract

alimentary	alimenticio *aj*
appendix Ⓑ	apéndice *nm*
colon Ⓑ	colon *nm*
diverticulum	divertículo *nm*
duodenum Ⓑ	duodeno *nm*
epiglottis Ⓑ	epiglotis *nf*
esophagus Ⓑ	esófago *nm*
ileum Ⓑ	íleon *nm*
intestine	intestino *nm*
jejunum Ⓑ	yeyuno *nm*
peptic	péptico *aj*
rectum Ⓑ	recto *nm*
salivary	salival *aj*
stomach	estómago *nm*
viscera	vísceras *nfpl*

organs of reproduction

cervix Ⓑ	cerviz *nf*
clitoris	clítoris *nm*
Fallopian	de Falopio
fibroid	fibroide *nm*
genitalia, genitals	genitales *nmpl*
glans Ⓑ	glande *nm*
labia	labios *nmpl*
labium Ⓑ	labio *nm*
ovary	ovario *nm*
oviduct	oviducto *nm*
ovule	óvulo *nm*
ovum Ⓑ	óvulo *nm*
penis Ⓑ	pene *nm*
phallus Ⓑ	falo *nm*
placenta Ⓑ	placenta *nf*
prepuce	prepucio *nm*
prostate	próstata *nf*
pudenda	partes pudendas *nfpl*
scrotum Ⓑ	escroto *nm*
testes	testes *nmpl*
testicle	testículo *nm*

testis Ⓑ	teste *nm*
tubule	túbulo *nm*
umbilicus Ⓑ	ombligo *nm*
uterus Ⓑ	útero *nm*
vagina	vagina *nf*
vesicle	vesícula *nf*
vulva Ⓑ	vulva *nf*

head and brain

Adam's apple	nuez de Adán *nf*
aquiline (nose)	aguileño, aquilino *aj*
buccal	bucal *aj*
cornu Ⓑ	cornu *nm*
corpus callosum	cuerpo calloso *nm*
cortex Ⓑ	corteza *nf*
cranium Ⓑ	cráneo *nm*
encephalon	encéfalo *nm*
fissure	fisura *nf*
follicle	folículo *nm*
fontanel, fontanelle	fontanela *nf*
glottis Ⓑ	glotis Ⓒ *nf*
hemisphere	hemisferio *nm*
lineaments	lineamientos *nmpl*
lobe	lóbulo *nm*
medulla Ⓑ	médula *nf*
meninges	meninges *nm*
mustache, moustache	mostacho *nm*
palate	paladar *nm*
pallium	palio *nm*
peduncle	pedúnculo *nm*
pericranium	pericráneo *nm*
sinus Ⓑ	seno *nm*
thalamus Ⓑ	tálamo *nm*
vocal chords	cuerdas vocales *nfpl*

skin

areola Ⓑ	aréola, areola *nf*
callus	callo *nm*
cutis	cutis *nm*
derm, derma, dermis	dermis *nf*
dermis	dermis *nf*
epidermis	epidermis *nf*
frenum Ⓑ	frenillo *nm*
papilla	papila *nf*
pigment	pigmento *nm*
pore	poro *nm*

lung

alveolus	alvéolo *nm*
bronchia	bronquios *nmpl*
bronchiole	bronquíolo *nm*
diaphragm	diafragma *nm*
larynx Ⓑ	laringe *nf*

nasal	nasal *aj*
pharynx Ⓑ	faringe *nf*
trachea Ⓑ	tráquea *nf*

nerves

autonomic	antónomo *aj*
axon	axón *nm*
center Ⓐ	centro *nm*
cerebellum Ⓑ	cerebelo *nm*
cerebrum Ⓑ	cerebro *nm*
chiasma Ⓑ	quiasma *nm*
dendrite	dendrita *nf*
ganglion Ⓑ	ganglio *nm*
neuron	neurona *nf*
neurotransmitter	neurotransmisor *nm*
nucleus Ⓑ	núcleo *nm*
olfactory	olfatorio *aj*
optic	óptico *aj*
radial	radial *aj*
receptor	receptor *nm*
reflex	reflejo *nm*
sciatic	ciático *aj*
solar plexus	plexo solar *nm*
synapse	sinapsis *nf*

arms and legs

Achilles' tendon	tendón de aquiles *nm*
arch	arco *nm*
axilla	axila *nf*
carpus Ⓑ	carpo *nm*
cuticle	cutícula *nf*
index finger Ⓑ	dedo índice *nm*
meniscus Ⓑ	menisco *nm*
metacarpal	metacarpo *nm*
metatarsus Ⓑ	metatarso *nm*
palm	palma *nf*

heart

atrium	atrio *nm*
auricle	aurícula *nf*
cardiac	cardíaco *aj*
endocardium	endocardio *nm*
myocardium	miocardio *nm*
pericardium Ⓑ	pericardio *nm*
septum	septo, septum *nm*
valve	válvula *nf*
ventricle	ventrículo *nm*

teeth and jaw

bicuspid	bicúspide *aj, nm*
canine	canino *aj, nm*
cementum	cemento *nm*
cingulum	cíngulo *nm*
crown	corona *nf*

cusp	cúspide *nf*
cusp, cuspid	cúspide *nf*
dentine	dentina *nf*
enamel	esmalte *nm*
incisor	incisivo *nm*
molar	molar *nm*
periodontal	periodontal *aj*
premolar	premolar *nm*
pulp	pulpa *nf*

membranes

hymen	himen *nm*
mucous	mocoso *aj*
peritoneum Ⓑ	peritoneo *nm*
pleura Ⓑ	pleura *nf*
velum	velo *nm*

excretory organs

anus Ⓑ	ano *nm*
ureter	uréter *nm*
urethra Ⓑ	uretra *nf*

other terms

dissymmetrical	disimétrico *aj*
isthmus Ⓑ	istmo *nm*
lacuna Ⓑ	laguna *nf*
lumen Ⓑ	lumen *nm*
promonotory	promonotorio *nm*
radicle	radícula *nf*
reticulum	retículo *nm*
transverse	tra(n)sverso *aj*
tricuspid	tricúspide *aj, nf*
vascular	vascular *aj*
vasomotor	vasomotor *aj*
vermiform (appendix)	vermiforme *aj*

PHYSIOLOGY

physical body types

ectomorph	ectomorfo *nm*
endomorph	endomorfo *nm*
mesomorph	mesomorfo *nm*

functions and operations

accomodation	acomodación *nf*
adaptation	adaptación *nf*
ambidextrous	ambidextro *aj*
assimilation	asimilación *nf*
audition	audición *nf*
circulation	circulación *nf*
climacteric	climaterio *nm*
compensation	compensación *nf*
conduction	conducción *nf*

defecation	defecación *nf*
deflection	deflexión *nf*
digestion	digestión *nf*
ejaculation	eyaculación *nf*
elimination	eliminación *nf*
erection	erección *nf*
eructation	eructación, eructo *nf, nm*
evacuation	evacuación *nf*
excitation	excitación *nf*
excitement	excitación *nf*
excretion	excreción *nf*
exhalation	exhalación *nf*
expiration	espiración *nf*
extension	extensión *nf*
fertilization	fertilización *nf*
flection	flexión *nf*
gargling *nsg*	gárgaras, gargarismos *nfpl, nmpl*
gestation	gestación *nf*
ingestion	ingerión *nf*
inhalation	inhalación *nf*
inspiration	inspiración *nf*
involution	involución *nf*
lactation	lactancia *nf*
mastication	masticación *nf*
menopause	menopausia *nf*
menstruation	menstruación *nf*
metabolism	metabolismo *nm*
ovulation	ovulación *nf*
regurgitation	regurgitación *nf*
relaxation	relajación *nf*
respiration	respiración *nf*
salivation	salivación *nf*
secretion	secreción *nf*
senses	sentidos *nmpl*
stimulation	estimulación *nf*
vasoconstriction	vasoconstricción *nf*
vasodilation	vasodilatación *nf*
vision	visión, vista *nf*

movements and body positions

abduction	abducción *nf*
adduction	aducción *nf*
afferent	aferente *aj*
efferent	eferente *aj*
erect	erecto *aj*
gesticulation	gesticulación *nf*
inclination	inclinación *nf*
profile	perfil *nm*
prone	prono *aj*
prostrate	postrar *vt*

recline	reclinarse *vr*
supine	supino *aj*

secretions and body products

bile	bilis *nf*
bilirubin	bilirrubina *nf*
cerumen	cerumen *nm*
chyle	quilo *nm*
chyme	quimo *nm*
dopamine	dopamina *nf*
excrement	excremento *nm*
excreta	excrementos *nmpl*
feces Ⓐ	heces *nfpl*
juice	jugo *nm*
mucus	moco, mucosidad *nm, nf*
phlegm	flema *nf*
saliva	saliva *nf*
sebum	sebo *nm*
semen	semen *nm*
sperm	esperma *nf*
sputum Ⓑ	esputo *nm*
urine	orina *nf*

elements and minerals

calcium	calcio *nm*
carbon	carbono *nm*
carotene	caroteno *nm*
chlorine	cloro *nm*
pee, peepee	pipí *nm*

other terms

appetite	apetito *nm*
corpulence	corpulencia *nf*
diastole	diástole *nf*
electrotonus	electrotono *nm*
endomorphic	endomórfico *aj*
focus Ⓑ	foco *nm*
homeostasis	homeóstasis *nf*
impulse	impulso *nm*
kinesthesia	cinestesia, quin-, kine- *nf*
kinesthetic	cinestético *aj*
lymph	linfa *nf*
metabolic	metabólico *aj*
monocyte	monocito *nm*
motoneuron	motoneurona *nf*
motor	motor *aj*
period	período *nm*
peristalsis	peristalsis *nf*
photokinesis	fotocinesis *nf*
photokinetic	fotocinético *aj*
photopia	fotopía *nf*

phototonus	fototonía *nf*
posture	postura *nf*
potent	potente *aj*
pressure	presión *nf*
pulsation	pulsación *nf*
pulse	pulso *nm*
seminal (fluid)	seminal *aj*
sensory	sensorial, sensorio *aj*
stertorous	estertoroso *aj*
stimulant	estimulante *nm*
sympathetic	simpático *aj*
synergism, synergy	sinergia *nf*
systaltic	sistáltico *aj*
systemic	sistémico *aj*
systole	sístole *nm*
systolic	sistólico *aj*
tactile	táctil *aj*
tampon	tampón *nm*
tonicity	tonicidad *nf*
transmitter	tra(n)smisor *nm*
vomit	vómito *nm*

BIOCHEMICALS

classification

acid	ácido *nm*
carbohydrate	carbohidrato *nm*
enzyme	enzima *nf*
hormone	hormona *nf*
lipid(e)	lípido *nm*
peptide	péptido *nm*
protein	proteína *nf*
vitamin	vitamina *nf*

acids

algin	algina *nf*
amino acid	aminoácido *nm*
deoxyribonucleic	desoxirribonucleico *aj*
lactic	láctico *aj*
nucleic	nucleico *aj*
prostaglandin	prostaglandina *nf*
ribonucleic	ribonucleico *aj*

hormones

adrenaline	adrenalina *nf*
androgen	andrógeno *nm*
corticosteroid	corticosteroide *nm*
corticosterone	corticosterona *nf*
cortisone	cortisona *nf*
epinephrine	epinefrina *nf*
estrogen	estrógeno *nm*
gastrin	gastrina *nf*
insulin	insulina *nf*

oxytocin	oxitocina *nf*
progesterone	progesterona *nf*
prolactin	prolactina *nf*
relaxin	relaxina *nf*
serotonin	serotonina *nf*
steroid	esteroide *nm*
testosterone	testosterona *nf*
thyroxine	tiroxina *nf*

enzymes

cholinesterase	colinesterasa *nf*
diastase	diastasa *nf*
esterase	esterasa *nf*
lactase	lactasa *nf*
lipase	lipasa *nf*
maltase	maltasa *nf*
papain	papaína *nf*
pepsin	pepsina *nf*
protease	proteasa *nf*
ptyalin	tialina *nf*
renin, rennin	renina *nf*
thrombin	trombina, tombasa *nf*
trypsin	tripsina *nf*
zymase	cimasa, zimasa *nf*

peptides

endorphin	endorfina *nf*
interleukin	interleukin *nm*

proteins

albumen	albumen *nm*
albumin	albúmina *nf*
casein	caseína *nf*
collagen	colágena *nf*
fibrin	fibrina *nf*
fibrinogen	fibrinógeno *aj*
gelatin(e)	gelatina *nf*
globulin	globulina *nf*
interferon	interferona *nf*
keratin	queratina *nf*
zein	ceína, zeína *nf*

vitamins

biotin	biotina *nf*
niacin	niacina *nf*
pantothenic	pantoténico *aj*
retinol	retinol *nm*
riboflavin	riboflavina *nf*
thiamin(e)	tiamina *nf*

sugars

dextrose	dextrosa *nf*
fructose	fructosa *nf*
glucose	glucosa *nf*

glycogen	glicógeno *nm*
lactose	lactosa *nf*
maltose	maltosa *nf*

lipids

cholesterol	colesterol *nm*
triglyceride	triglicérido *nm*
antiserum Ⓑ	antisuero *nm*
bioassay	bioensayo *nm*
biocatalyst	biocatalizador *nm*
pectin	pectina *nf*

other substances

agglutinin	aglutinina *nf*
antioxidant	antioxidante *nm*
creatine	creatina *nf*
dopamine	dopamina *nf*
heparin	heparina *nf*
histamine	histamina *nf*
melanin	melanina *nf*
urea	urea *nf*
xanthine	xantina *nf*

(*See also* **BIOLOGY**; *organic compounds* under **CHEMISTRY**; *NUTRITION* under **FOOD AND NUTRITION**; **DRUGS**)

MEDICAL PRACTICE

GENERAL TERMS

antibody	anticuerpo *nm*
antisepsis	antisepsia *nf*
antiseptic	antiséptico *aj, nm*
autopsy	autopsia *nf*
bank (blood, bone, eye)	banco *nm*
biofeedback	biorreacción *nf*
biomedical	biomédico *aj*
caduceus	caduceo *nm*
case	caso *nm*
coma	coma *nm*
complication	complicación *nf*
consultation	consulta, consultación *nf*
contamination	contaminación *nf*
cure	cura *nf*
decontamination	descontaminación *nf*
diagnosis (act) Ⓑ	diagnósis *nf*
diagnosis (conclusion) Ⓑ	diagnóstico *nm*
dose	dosis Ⓒ *nf*
Hippocratic	hipocrático *aj*
internship	internado *nm*

license Ⓐ	licencia *nf*
medical	médico *aj*
medicine	medicina *nf*
operation	operación *nf*
panacea	panacea *nf*
patient	paciente *nmf*
physical	físico *aj*
placebo Ⓑ	placebo *nm*
prevention	prevención *nf*
prognosis Ⓑ	pronóstico *nm*
reciprocity	reciprocidad *nf*
remedy	remedio *nm*
residency	residencia *nf*
socialized medicine	medicina estatal *nf*
specialty	especialidad *nf*
symptom	síntoma *nm*
symptomatology	sintomatología *nf*
syndrome	síndrome *nm*
therapy	terapia *nf*
treatment	tratamiento *nm*

BRANCHES OF MEDICINE

major fields

aeromedicine	aeromedicina *nf*
allergy	alergia *nf*
cardiology	cardiología *nf*
dermatology	dermatología *nf*
endocrinology	endocrinología *nf*
epidemiology	epidemiología *nf*
family (medicine)	familiar *aj*
gastroenterology	gastroenterología *nf*
geriatrics	geriatría *nf*
gynecology Ⓐ	ginecología *nf*
hematology Ⓐ	hemotología *nf*
internal (medicine)	interno *aj*
laryngology	laringología *nf*
neonatology	neonatología *nf*
nephrology	nefralogía *nf*
neurology	neurología *nf*
nuclear (medicine)	nuclear *aj*
obstetrics	obstetricia *nf*
occupational (medicine)	ocupacional *aj*
oncology	oncología *nf*
ophthalmology	oftalmología *nf*
orthopedics Ⓐ	ortopedia *nf*
otolaryngology	otolaringología *nf*
otorhinolaryngology	otorrinolaringología *nf*
pathology	patología *nf*
pediatrics Ⓐ	pediatría *nf*
physiatrics, physiatry	fisiatría *nf*
proctology	proctología *nf*

psychiatry	(p)siquiatría *nf*
rheumatology	reumatología *nf*
sports medicine	medicina deportiva *nf*
surgery	cirugía *nf*
therapeutics	terapéutica *nf*
urology	urología *nf*
veterinary medicine	veterinaria *nf*

subspecialties

anesthesiology Ⓐ	anestesiología *nf*
bacteriology	bacteriología *nf*
etiology	etiología *nf*
forensic medicine	medicina forense *nf*
immunology	inmunología *nf*
neuropathology	neuropatalogía *nf*
odontology	odontología *nf*
osteopathy	osteopatía *nf*
pharmacology	farmacología *nf*
podiatry	podiatría *nf*
prosthetics	protética *nf*
radiology	radiología *nf*
therapeutics	terapéutica *nf*
topology	topología *nf*
toxicology	toxicología *nf*
virology	virología *nf*

related fields

anatomy	anatomía *nf*
audiology	audiología *nf*
biochemistry	bioquímica *nf*
biomedicine	biomedicina *nf*
chiropody	quiropedia *nf*
dietetics	dietética *nf*
histology	histología *nf*
hygienics	higiene *nf*
immunochemistry	inmunoquímica *nf*
immunogenetics	inmunogenética *nf*
macrobiotics	macrobiótica *nf*
microbiology	microbiología *nf*
optometry	optometría *nf*
osteology	osteología *nf*
physiology	fisiología *nf*
psychopharmacology	(p)sicofarmacología *nf*
public health	salud pública *nf*
radiography	radiografía *nf*
roentgenology	roentgenología *nf*
serology	serología *nf*

DIAGNOSIS

general symptoms

adiposity	adiposidad *nf*
analgesia	analgesia *nf*

colic	cólico *nm*	urgency	urgencia *nf*
congestion	congestión *nf*	vomiting	el vomitar *nm*
consciousness	conciencia *nf*		
constriction	constricción *nf*		
convulsion	convulsión *nf*		
crepitation	crepitación *nf*		
debility	debilidad *nf*		
dehydration	deshidratación *nf*		

diagnostic fields

angiography	angiografía *nf*
arteriography	arteriografía *nf*
audiometry	audiometría *nf*
bronchoscopy	broncoscopia *nf*
cardiography	cardiografía *nf*
celioscopy	celioscopia *nf*
cystoscopy	ciscoscopia *nf*
dosimetry	dosimetría *nf*
endoscopy	endoscopia *nf*
fluoroscopy	fluoroscopia *nf*
gastroscopy	gastroscopia *nf*
laparoscopy	laparoscopia *nf*
mammography	mamografía *nf*
pyelography	pielografía *nf*
radioscopy	radioscopia *nf*
retinoscopy	retinoscopia *nf*
sigmoidoscopy	sigmoidoscopia *nf*
tomography	tomografía *nf*

devices

arthroscope	artroscopio *nm*
audiometer	audiómetro *nm*
bronchoscope	broncoscopio *nm*
cystoscope	ciscoscopio *nm*
dosimeter	dosímetro *nm*
electrocardiograph	electrocardiógrafo *nm*
electroencephalograph	electroencefalógrafo *nm*
endoscope	endoscopio *nm*
fluoroscope	fluoroscopio *nm*
gastroscope	gastroscopio *nm*
kymograph	quimógrafo *nm*
laparoscope	laparoscopio *nm*
laryngoscope	laringoscopio *nm*
manometer	manómetro *nm*
microscope	microscopio *nm*
otoscope	otoscopio *nm*
radiograph	radiografía *nf*
retinoscope	retinoscopio *nm*
scanner	escanógrafo *nm*
sigmoidoscope	sigmoidoscopio *nm*
speculum B	espéculo *nm*
spirograph	espirógrafo *nm*
spirometer	espirómetro *nm*
stethoscope	estetoscopio *nm*
X ray	rayo X *nm*

charts and pictures

angiogram	angioscopio *nm*
arteriogram	arteriograma *nm*

The following is the first (left) column:

delirium B	delirio *nm*
diarrhea A	diarrea *nf*
distension, distention	distensión *nf*
dyspepsia	dispepsia *nf*
edema A	edema *nm*
expectoration	expectoración *nf*
exudation	exudación *nf*
fatigue	fatiga *nf*
fever	fiebre *nf*
fibrillation	fibrilación *nf*
flatulence	flatulencia *nf*
hemorrhage A	hemorragia *nf*
hypothermia	hipotermia *nf*
icterus (jaundice)	ictericia *nf*
indigestion	indigestión *nf*
inflammation	inflamación *nf*
irritation	irritación *nf*
lassitude	lasitud *nf*
lethargy	letargo, aletargamiento *nm*
lumbago	lumbago *nm*
nausea	náusea *nf*
neuralgia	neuralgia *nf*
pallor	palidez *nf*
palpitation	palpitación *nf*
paroxysm	paroxismo *nm*
phlegm	flema *nf*
pulse	pulso *nm*
purulence	purulencia *nf*
pus	pus *nm*
pustulation	pustulación *nf*
retention (of fluids)	retención *nf*
shock	choque *nm*
somnolence	somnolencia *nf*
spasm	espasmo *nm*
stress	estrés *nm*
stricture	estrictura *nf*
stupor	estupor *nm*
syncope	síncope *nm*
tic	tic *nm*
tumefaction	tumefacción *nf*
tumescence	tumescencia *nf*
turgescence	turgencia *nf*
ulceration	ulceración *nf*

audiogram	audiograma *nm*
echocardiogram	ecocardiograma *nm*
electrocardiogram	electrocardiograma *nm*
electroencephalogram	electroencefalograma *nm*
mammogram	mamograma *nm*
pyelogram	pielograma *nm*
tomogram	tomograma *nm*

techniques and procedures

amniocentesis	amniocentesis *nf*
auscultation	auscultación *nf*
biopsy	biopsia *nf*
dissection	disección *nf*
evaluation	evaluación *nf*
examination	examen *nm*
history	historia *nf*
observation	observación *nf*
palpation	palpación *nf*
percussion	percusión *nf*
sperm count	cuenta espermática *nf*
tuberculin test	prueba tuberculina *nf*
ultrasound	ultrasonido *nm*
urinalysis	urinálisis *nf*

other diagnostic terms

anomaly	anomalía *nf*
astatic	astático *aj*
asymptomatic	asintomático *aj*
atonic	atónico *aj*
autogenous	autógeno *aj*
autoimmune, auto-immune	autoinmuno *aj*
benign	benigno *aj*
conscious	consciente *aj*
degeneration	degeneración *nf*
facies B	facies *nf*
flux	flujo *nm*
infected	infecto *aj*
inoperable	inoperable *aj*
irreversible	irreversible *aj*
mimesis	mimética *nf*
normal	normal *aj*
predisposition	predisposición *nf*
reversible	reversible *aj*
Rhesus (factor)	rhesus *aj*
sign	señal *nf*
state	estado *nm*
unconscious	inconsciente *aj*
vital (signs, function)	vital *aj*

TREATMENT

prevention

checkup	chequeo *nm*
chlorination	clorinación *nf*
defenses A	defensas *nfpl*
douche	ducha *nf*
exercise	ejercicio *nm*
fluoridation	fluorización *nf*
fumigation	fumigación *nf*
holistic	holístico *aj*
hygiene	higiene *nf*
immunity	inmunidad *nf*
immunization	inmunización *nf*
inoculation	inoculación *nf*
nutrition	nutrición *nf*
precaution	precaución *nf*
prophylaxis	profilaxis *nf*
purge	purga *nf*
quarantine	cuarentena *nf*
relaxation	relajación *nf*
sanitation	saneamiento *nm*
vaccination	vacunación *nf*
vaccine	vacuna *nf*

medications

antibiotic	antibiótico *nm*
bactericide	bactericida *nm*
cure-all	curalotodo *nm*
fungicide	fungicida *nm*
lithium	litio *nm*
microbicide	microbicida *nf*
sedation	sedación *nf*
suppository	supositorio *nm*
unguent	ungüento *nm*

other treatments

acupuncture	acupuntura *nf*
aeration	aeración *nf*
alleviation	alivio *nm*
allopathy	alopatía *nf*
aromatherapy	aromaterapia *nf*
artificial respiration	respiración artificial *nf*
balneotherapy	balneoterapia *nf*
biotherapy	bioterapia *nf*
catharsis B	catarsis *nf*
chelation	quelación *nf*
chemotherapy	quimioterapia *nf*
compress	compresa *nf*
compression (to stop bleeding)	compresión *nf*
curettage	curetaje *nm*
decompression	descompresión *nf*

defibrillation	defibrilación *nf*
desensitization	desensibilización *nf*
detoxification	desintoxicación *nf*
dialysis ▣	diálisis *nf*
diathermy	diatermia *nf*
diet	dieta *nf*
drugs	drogas *nfpl*
electrotherapy	electroterapia *nf*
enema	enema *nf*
fomentation	fomento *nm*
galvanism	galvanismo *nm*
gamma ray	rayo gamma *nf*
gene therapy	terapia génica *nf*
homeopathy	homeopatía *nf*
hospitalization	hospitalización *nf*
hydrotherapy	hidroterapia *nf*
hyperbaric (chamber)	hiperbárico *aj*
hypnotherapy	hipnoterapia *nf*
immunotherapy	inmunoterapia *nf*
infrared (radiation)	infrarrojo *aj*
infusion	infusión *nf*
inhalation	inhalación *nf*
injection	inyección *nf*
intensive (care)	intensivo *aj*
irrigation	irrigación *nf*
isolation	aislamiento *nm*
lavage	lavado *nm*
localization	localización *nf*
manipulation	manipulación, manipuleo *nf, nm*
massage	masaje *nm*
mecanotherapy	mecanoterapia *nf*
medication (medicine)	medicamento *nm*
medication (treatment)	medicación *nf*
oxygen	oxígeno *nm*
pacemaker	marcapasos *nm*
perfusion	perfusión *nf*
phlebotomy	flebotomía *nf*
phototherapy	fototerapia *nf*
physiotherapy	fisioterapia *nf*
puncture	punción *nf*
radiotherapy	radioterapia *nf*
regimen	régimen *nm*
resuscitation	resucitación *nf*
stimulation	estimulación *nf*
surgery	cirugía *nf*
traction	tracción *nf*

healing terms

agglutination	aglutinación *nf*
cicatrix (scar) ▣	cicatriz ▣ *nf*

coagulation	coagulación *nf*
coagulum ▣	coágulo *nm*
coalescence	coalescencia *nf*
convalescence	convalecencia *nf*
crisis ▣	crisis ▣ *nf*
critical	crítico *aj*
recovery (consciousness)	recobro *nm*
recuperation	recuperación *nf*
rehabilitation	rehabilitación *nf*

SELECTED SPECIALIZED FIELDS

allergy

allergen	alérgeno *nm*
histamine	histamina *nf*
hypersensitive	hipersensible *aj*
pollinosis	polinosis *nf*
reaction	reacción *nf*
rhinitis	rinitis *nf*

gynecology and obstetrics

abortion	aborto *nm*
amenorrhea, amenorrhoea	amenorrea *nf*
amniotic	amniótico *aj*
Caesarean section	cesárea *nf*
canal (birth)	canal (parto) *nm*
cervicitis	cervicitis *nf*
climacteric	climaterio *nm*
colostrum	calostro *nm*
conception	concepción *nf*
condom	condón *nm*
confinement	confinamiento *nm*
contraception	contracepción *nf*
contraceptive	contraceptivo, anticonceptivo *aj, nm*
contraction	contracción *nf*
decidua	decidua *nf*
diaphragm	diafragma *nm*
dilatation	dilatación *nf*
ectopia	ectopia *nf*
endometriosis	endometriosis *nf*
episiotomy	episiotomía *nf*
estrogen	estrógeno *nm*
fertility	fertilidad *nf*
fetal, foetal	fetal *aj*
fetus ▣ ▣	feto *nm*
fibroid	fibroide *nm*
gravida	mujer grávida *nf*
impregnate	empreñar *vt*
in vitro (fertilization)	en vitro *aj*

induce (labor)	inducir *vt*
infertility	infertilidad *nf*
insemination	inseminación *nf*
intrauterine	intrauterino *aj*
lochia	loquios *nmpl*
maternity	maternidad *nf*
menopause	menopausia *nf*
menorrhagia	menorragia *nf*
multipara	multípara *nf*
multiple (births)	múltiple *aj*
neonatal	neonatal *aj*
oxytocin	oxitocina *nf*
parturition	parto *nm*
pessary	pesario *nm*
pica	pica *nf*
placenta Ⓑ	placenta *nf*
postnatal	postnatal *aj*
postpartum	de posparto
potency	potencia *nf*
premature	prematuro *aj*
presentation	presentación *nf*
progesterone	progesterona *nf*
puerperal	puerperal *aj*
sterility	esterilidad *nf*
sterilization	esterilización *nf*
toxemia Ⓐ	toxemia *nf*
tubal	tubárico *aj*
umbilical	umbilical *aj*
vaginitis	vaginitis *nf*
virility	virilidad *nf*

oncology

carcinogenic	cancerígeno *aj*
carcinoma Ⓑ	carcinoma *nm*
lymphoma Ⓑ	linfoma *nf*
malignancy	malignidad *nf*
metastasis	metástasis *nf*
neoplasm	neoplasma, neoplasia *nm, nf*
remission	remisión *nf*
sarcoma Ⓑ	sarcoma *nm*

ophthalmology

achromatopsia	acromatopsia *nf*
amblyopia	ambliopía *nf*
ametropia	ametropía *nf*
astigmatism	astigmatismo *nm*
bifocal	bifocal *aj*
bifocals	lentes bifocales *nmpl* or *nfpl*
binocular	binocular *aj*
blepharoptosis	blefaroptosis *nf*
cataract	catarata *nf*

conjunctivitis	conjunctivitis *nf*
daltonism (color-blindness)	daltonismo *nm*
diopter Ⓐ	dioptría *nf*
diplopia	diplopia *nf*
emmetropia	emetropía *nf*
exophthalmos, exophthalmus	exoftalmía *nf*
focal	focal *aj*
focus Ⓑ	foco *nm*
glaucoma	glaucoma *nm*
hyperopia	hipermetropía *nf*
iritis	iritis *nf*
keratitis	queratitis *nf*
leukoma, leucoma	leucoma *nm*
myopia	miopía *nf*
nebula Ⓑ	nébula *nf*
nyctalopia	nictalopía *nf*
nystagmus	nistagmo *nm*
ophthalmia	oftalmia *nf*
ophthalmic	oftálmico *aj*
ophthalmoscope	oftalmoscopio *nm*
photophobia	fotofobia *nf*
presbyopia	presbiopía *nf*
retinitis	retinitis *nf*
retinopathy	retinopatía *nf*
scleritis	escleritis *nf*
scotoma Ⓑ	escotoma *nm*
strabismus	estrabismo *nm*
trachoma	tracoma *nm*
trifocal	trifocal *aj*
uveitis	uveítis *nf*

psychiatry

Alzheimer's Disease	enfermedad de Alzheimer *nf*
amnesia	amnesia *nf*
autism	autismo *nm*
catalepsy	catalepsia *nf*
catatonia	catatonía *nf*
delirium Ⓑ	delirio *nm*
dementia	demencia *nf*
echolalia	ecolalia *nf*
electroshock	electrochoque *nm*
hyperactivity	hiperactividad *nf*
hypnotherapy	hipnoterapia *nf*
hysteria	histeria, histerismo *nf, nm*
idiocy	idiotez *nf*
infantilism	infantilismo *nm*
mania	manía *nf*
manic-depressive	maniacodepresivo, -a *aj, nmf*

narcoanalysis	narcoanálisis *nf*
narcosynthesis	narcosíntesis *nf*
paranoia	paranoia *nf*
psychosis B	(p)sicosis C *nf*
psychotic	(p)sicótico *aj*
schizophrenia	esquizofrenia *nf*
senility	senilidad/senilismo *nm*
trance	trance *nm*

TERMS IN SURGERY

general terms

anesthesia A	anestesia *nf*
asepsis	asepsia *nf*
aseptic	aséptico *aj*
cauterization	cauterización *nf*
donor	donador(a), donante *nmf*
effusion	efusión *nf*
enterostomy	enterostomía *nf*
excision	excisión *nf*
exploration	exploración *nf*
group (blood)	grupo *nm*
hemostasis A	hemostasis *nf*
implant	implante *nm*
incision	incisión *nf*
intravenous	intravenoso *aj*
ligation	ligación *nf*
oxygenation	oxigenación *nf*
postoperative	posoperatorio *aj*
premedication	medicación previa *nf*
procedure	procedimiento *nm*
prosthesis B	prótesis *nf*
resection	resección *nf*
scarify	escarificar *vt*
section	sección *nf*
sequela B	secuela *nf*
taxis	taxis *nf*
transfusion	tra(n)sfusión *nf*

types of surgery

ambulatory	ambulatorio *aj*
cosmetic	cosmético *aj, nm*
electrosurgery	electrocirugía *nf*
emergency	emergencia *nf*
explorative, exploratory	exploratorio *aj*
invasive	invasor *aj*
microsurgery	microcirugía *nf*
neurosurgery	neurocirujía *nf*
orthopedic A	ortopédico *aj*
plastic surgery	cirugía plástica *nf*
reconstructive	reconstructivo *aj*

| rectal | rectal *aj* |
| thoracic | torácico *aj* |

types of anesthesia

caudal	caudal *aj*
conduction	conducción *nf*
cryoanesthesia A	crioanestesia *nf*
epidural	epidural *aj*
general	general *aj*
hypnosis B	hipnosis *nf*
hypothermia	hipotermia *nf*
local	local *aj*
peridural	peridural *aj*
spinal	espinal *aj*

surgical procedures

adenectomy	adenectomía *nf*
amputation	amputación *nf*
angioplasty	angioplastía *nf*
appendectomy	apendectomía *nf*
arthrocentesis	artrocentesis *nf*
arthroplasty	artroplastia *nf*
arthroscopy	artroscopia *nf*
bypass	bypass *nm*
castration	castración *nf*
cholecystectomy	colecistectomía *nf*
circumcision	circuncisión *nf*
colostomy	colostomía *nf*
craniotomy	craniotomía *nf*
cryosurgery	criocirugía *nf*
cystectomy	ciscectomía *nf*
gastrectomy	gastrectomía *nf*
hysterectomy	histerectomía *nf*
implantation	implantación *nf*
laparotomy	laparotomía *nf*
liposuction	liposucción *nf*
lobectomy	lobectomía *nf*
lobotomy	lobotomía *nf*
mammoplasty	mamoplastia *nf*
mastectomy	mastectomía *nf*
nephrectomy	nefrectomía *nf*
nephrotomy	nefrotomía *nf*
oophorectomy	ooforectomia *nf*
ovariectomy	ovariectomía *nf*
pneumonectomy	neumonectomía *nf*
psychosurgery	(p)sicocirugía *nf*
rhinoplasty	rinoplastia *nf*
sterilization	esterilización *nf*
sterilize	esterilizar *vt*
tonsillectomy	tonsilectomía *nf*
tracheotomy	traqueotomía *nf*
transplant	trasplante *nm*
vasectomy	vasectomía *nf*

TOOLS AND EQUIPMENT

adhesive (tape)	adhesivo *aj, nm*
ambulance	ambulancia *nf*
aspirator	aspirador *nm*
atomizer	atomizador *nm*
autoclave	autoclave *nf*
bandage	venda, vendaje *nf, nm*
cannula	cánula *nf*
catgut	catgut *nm*
catheter	catéter *nm*
cautery	cauterio *nm*
curet, curette	cureta *nf*
depressor	depresor *nm*
dilator	dilator *nm*
disinfectant	desinfectante *nm*
ether	éter *nm*
forceps B	fórceps C *nm*
gauze	gasa *nf*
hemostat A	hemóstato *nm*
hypodermic	inyección hipodérmica *nf*
incubator	incubadora *nf*
instruments	instrumental *nmsg*
laser	láser *nm*
mask	mascarilla *nf*
microtome	micrótomo *nm*
monitor (device)	monitor *nm*
pipette	pipeta *nf*
respirator	respirador *nm*
resuscitator	resucitator *nm*
retractor	retractor *nm*
scalpel	escalpelo *nm*
sphygmomanometer	esfigmomanómetro *nm*
sponge	esponja *nf*
sterilizer	esterilizador *nm*
suture	sutura *nf*
syringe	jeringa *nf*
thermometer	termómetro *nm*
tourniquet	torniquete *nm*
trephine	trefina *nf*
xyster	xister *nm*

MEDICAL FACILITIES

asylum	asilo *nm*
clinic	clínica *nf*
dispensary	dispensario *nm*
hospice	hospicio *nm*
hospital	hospital *nm*
infirmary	enfermería *nf*
laboratory	laboratorio *nm*
leprosarium	leprosería *nf*
pharmacy	farmacia *nf*

polyclinic	policlínica, policlínico *nf, nm*
sanatorium, sanitarium B	sanatorio *nm*
solarium B	solana, solario *nf, nm*

PERSONS

health professionals

abortionist	abortista *nmf*
allergist	alergista *nmf*
allopath	alópata *nmf*
ambulance driver	ambulanciero, -a *nmf*
anesthesiologist A	anestesiólogo, -a *nmf*
anesthetist A	anestetista *nmf*
audiologist	audiólogo, -a *nmf*
cardiologist	cardiólogo *nmf*
chiropodist	quiropodista *nmf*
chiropractor	quiropráctico, -a *nmf*
clinician	clínico, -a *nmf*
consultant	consultor(a) *nmf*
dermatologist	dermatólogo *nmf*
dietician	dietista *nmf*
diplomate	diplomada, -a *nmf*
doctor	doctor(a) *nmf*
druggist	droguero, droguista *nmf*
embryologist	embriólogo, -a *nmf*
endocrinologist	endocrinólogo, -a *nmf*
epidemiologist	epidemiólogo, -a *nmf*
gastroenterologist	gastroenterologista *nmf*
geriatrician	geriatra *nmf*
gynecologist A	ginecólogo, -a *nmf*
hematologist A	hematólogo, -a *nmf*
histologist	histólogo, -a *nmf*
homeopath	homeópata *nmf*
hygienist	higienista *nmf*
hypnotist	hipnotizador(a), hipnotista *nmf*
immunologist	inmunólogo, -a *nmf*
intern	interno, -a *nmf*
internist	internista *nmf*
kinesologist	cinesiólogo, -a, kines-, quine- *nmf*
neurologist	neurólogo *nmf*
neurosurgeon	neurocirujano, -a *nmf*
obstetrician	obstetra *nmf*
oculist	oculista *nmf*
odontologist	odontólogo, -a *nmf*
oncologist	oncologista *nmf*
ophthalmologist	opftalmólogo *nmf*
optician	óptico, -a *nmf*
optometrist	optometrista *nmf*

orthopedist Ⓐ	ortopedista *nmf*
osteopath	osteópata *nmf*
otolaringologist	otolaringólogo, -a *nmf*
paramedic	auxiliar médico/médica *nmf*
pathologist	patólogo, -a *nmf*
pediatrician	pediatra *nmf*
pharmacist	farmacéutico, -a *nmf*
pharmacologist	farmacólogo, -a *nmf*
physiologist	fisiólogo, -a *nmf*
physiotherapist	fisioterapeuta *nmf*
podiatrist	podólogo, -a *nmf*
proctologist	proctólogo *nm*
psychiatrist	(p)siquiatra *nmf*
radiologist	radiólogo, -a *nmf*
specialist	especialista *nmf*
surgeon	cirujano, -a *nmf*
technician	técnico, -a *nmf*
therapist	terapeuta *nmf*
toxicologist	toxicólogo, -a *nmf*
urologist	urólogo, -a *nmf*
veterinarian	veterinario, -a *nmf*
virologist	virólogo, -a *nmf*

patients

addict	adicto, -a *nmf*
alcoholic	alcohólico, -a *nmf*
amnesiac, amnesic	amnésico, -a *aj, nmf*
amputee	amputado, -a *nmf*
anorexic	anoréxico, -a *nmf*
aphasic	afásico, -a *aj, nmf*
asthmatic	asmático, -a *aj, nmf*
convalescent	convaleciente *aj, nmf*
cretin	cretino, -a *nmf*
diabetic	diabético, -a *aj, nmf*
drug addict	drogadicto, -a *nmf*
epileptic	epiléptico, -a *aj, nmf*
hemophiliac Ⓐ	hemofílico, -a *nmf*
hypochondriac	hipocondríaco, -a *nmf*
hypothyroid	hipotiroide, hipotiroideo, -a *nmf*
idiot	idiota *nmf*
insomniac	insomne *nmf*
invalid	inválido, -a *nmf*
leper	leproso, -a *nmf*
mute	mudo, -a *nmf*
outpatient	paciente externo *nmf*
paraplegic	parapléjico, -a *nmf*
quadriplegic	cuadripléjico, -a *aj, nmf*
recipient (transplant)	receptor *nmf*
schizophrenic	esquizofrénico, -a *aj, nmf*

somnambulist	somnambulista *nmf*
spastic	espástico, -a *aj, nmf*

HISTORICAL TERMS

affection (= disease)	afección *nf*
consumption (= tuberculosis)	consunción *nf*
lancet (= scalpel)	lanceta *nf*
ligature (= suture)	ligadura *nf*
mesmerism (= hypnotism)	mesmerismo *nm*
mongolism (= Down's syndrome)	mo(n)golismo *nm*
phthisis (= tuberculosis)	tisis *nf*
St. Vitus' dance (= chorea)	baile de San Vito *nm*
trepanation (= drilling)	trepanación *nf*

(*See also* **physicians** under **ANCIENT CIVILIZATIONS**; *TERMS IN . . .* under **BIOLOGY**)

PHYSICAL DISORDERS

GENERAL TERMS

abnormality	anormalidad *nf*
affliction	aflicción *nf*
defect	defecto *nm*
incubation	incubación *nf*
indisposition	indisposición *nf*
infection	infección *nf*
latency	latencia *nf*
malady	mal *nm*
malaise	malestar *nm*
pathogenesis Ⓑ	patogénesis *nf*
stasis	estasis *nf*
transmit (disease)	transmitir *vt*
virulence	virulencia *nf*

TYPES OF ILLNESS

etiology

bacterial	bacteriano *aj*
cardiovascular	cardiovascular *aj*
circulatory	circulatorio *aj*
communicable (disease)	comunicable *aj*
congenital	congénito *aj*
contagious	contagioso *aj*
coronary	coronario *aj*
debilitating	debilitante *aj*

degenerative	degenerativo *aj*
dietary	dietético *aj*
functional	funcional *aj*
fungal	fungal, fungino *aj*
genetic	genético *aj*
geriatric	geriátrico *aj*
hereditary	hereditario *aj*
hormonal	hormonal *aj*
immunogenic	inmunógeno, inmunizador *aj*
immunological	inmunológico *aj*
infectious	infeccioso *aj*
inflammatory	inflamatorio *aj*
malignant	maligno *aj*
mental	mental *aj*
metabolic	metabólico *aj*
nervous	nervioso *aj*
nutritional	nutritivo *aj*
occupational	ocupacional *aj*
oncological	oncológico *aj*
organic	orgánico *aj*
parasitic	parasitario *aj*
pediatric Ⓐ	pediátrico *aj*
pernicious	pernicioso *aj*
psychogenic	(p)sicógeno *aj*
psychosomatic	(p)sicosomático *aj*
respiratory	respiratorio *aj*
systemic	sistémico *aj*
venereal	venéreo *aj*
verminous	verminoso *aj*
viral	virulento *aj*

other terms

acute	agudo *aj*
catastrophic	catastrófico *aj*
chronic	crónico *aj*
curable	curable *aj*
endemic	endémico *aj*
epidemic	epidémico, epidemial *aj*
grave	grave *aj*
incurable	incurable *aj*
pandemic	pandémico *aj*
rabid	rabioso *aj*
terminal	terminal *aj*
treatable	tratable *aj*
untreatable	no tratable *aj*

CAUSES OF ILLNESS

infectious diseases

bacillus Ⓑ	bacilo *nm*
bacteria	bacterias *nfpl*
bacteriophage	bacteriófago *nm*
coccus Ⓑ	coco *nm*
fungus Ⓑ	hongo *nm*
germ	germen *nm*
gonococcus Ⓑ	gonococo *nm*
microorganism	microorganismo *nm*
pathogen	microbio patógeno *nm*
protozoan, protozoon Ⓑ	protozoario *nm*
retrovirus Ⓑ	retrovirus *nm*
rickettsia	ricketsia *nf*
spirochete	espiroqueta *nf*
staphylococcus	estafilococo *nm*
streptococcus Ⓑ	estreptococo *nm*
virus	virus *nm*

other causes

accident	accidente *nm*
avulsion	avulsión *nf*
carcinogen	agente cancerígeno *nm*
chemical	químico *nm*
collapse	colapso *nm*
decrepitude	decrepitud *nf*
dysfunction	disfunción *nf*
embolus Ⓑ	émbolo *nm*
exacerbation	exacerbación *nf*
heredity	herencia *nf*
hypersensitivity	hipersensibilidad *nf*
immunodeficiency	inmunodeficiencia *nf*
insufficiency	insuficiencia *nf*
irritant	agente irritante *nm*
malnutrition	desnutrición *nf*
obesity	obesidad *nf*
oncogene	oncogén *nm*
parasite	parásito *nm*
radiation	radiación *nf*
recrudescence	recrudecimiento *nm*
toxin	toxina *nf*
trauma Ⓑ	trauma *nm*
tubercle	tubérculo *nm*
venom	veneno *nm*
vitamin deficiency	déficit vitamínico *nm*

means of transmission

air	aire *nm*
animals	animales *nmpl*
contact	contacto *nm*
contagion	contagio *nm*
contaminant	contaminador, contaminante *nm*

NAMES OF DISORDERS

infection, contagious diseases

abscess	absceso *nm*
anthrax	ántrax *nm*
athlete's foot	pie de atleta *nm*
bubonic plague	peste bubónica *nf*
cholera	cólera *nm*
croup	crup *nm*
dengue	dengue *nm*
diphtheria	difteria *nf*
dysentery	disentería *nf*
elephantiasis	elefantiasis *nf*
erysipelas	erisipela *nf*
grippe	gripe *nf*
herpes	herpes *nm*
HIV	virus VIH, virus del sida *nm*
impetigo	impétigo *nm*
influenza, flu	influenza *nf*
leprosy	lepra *nf*
lupus	lupus *nm*
malaria	malaria *nf*
mononucleosis	mononucleosis *nf*
paratyphoid fever	fiebre paratifoidea *nf*
pneumonia	neumonía *nf*
psoriasis	psoriasis *nf*
rabies	rabia *nf*
rheumatism	reumatismo *nm*
rubella, rubeola	rubéola *nf*
scabies	escabies *nf*
scarlet fever	escarlatina *nf*
scrofula	escrófula *nf*
tetanus	tétano(s) *nm*
trichinosis	triquinosis *nf*
tuberculosis	tuberculosis *nf*
tularemia	tularemia *nf*
typhoid fever	fiebre tifoidea *nf*
typhus	tifus, tifo *nm*
undulant fever	fiebre ondulante *nf*

inflammatory

adenitis	adenitis *nf*
appendicitis	apendicitis *nf*
arthritis	artritis *nf*
bronchitis	bronquitis *nf*
bursitis	bursitis *nf*
cellulitis	celulitis *nf*
colitis	colitis *nf*
cystitis	cistitis *nf*
dermatitis	dermatitis *nf*
diverticulitis	diverticulitis *nf*
encephalitis	encefalitis *nf*
encephalomyelitis	encefalomielitis *nf*
endocarditis	endocarditis *nf*
enteritis	enteritis *nf*
gastritis	gastritis *nf*
gastroenteritis	gastroenteritis *nf*
hepatitis	hepatitis *nf*
laryngitis	laringitis *nf*
mastitis	mastitis *nf*
mastoiditis	mastoiditis *nf*
meningitis	meningitis *nf*
myelitis	mielitis *nf*
myocarditis	miocarditis *nf*
nephritis	nefritis *nf*
neuritis	neuritis *nf*
osteoarthritis	osteoartritis *nf*
osteomyelitis	osteomielitis *nf*
pericarditis	pericarditis *nf*
peritonitis	peritonitis *nf*
pharyngitis	faringitis *nf*
phlebitis	flebitis *nf*
polio, poliomyelitis	poliomielitis *nf*
prostatitis	prostatitis *nf*
sinusitis	sinusitis *nf*
stomatitis	estomatitis *nf*
tendonitis	tendonitis *nf*

metabolic

catabolism	catabolismo *nm*
diabetes	diabetes *nf*
gout	gota *nf*
obesity	obesidad *nf*
polydipsia	polidipsia *nf*
polyphagia	polifagia *nf*
porphyria	porfiria *nf*
steatorrhea	esteatorrea *nf*
xanthoma Ⓑ	xantoma *nm*

digestive

anorexia	anorexia *nf*
bulimia	bulimia *nf*
dysphagia	disfagia *nf*
halitosis	halitosis *nf*
hemorrhoids Ⓐ	hemorroides *nfpl*
reflux	reflujo *nm*

heart

angina	angina *nf*
arrhythmia	arritmia *nf*
attack	ataque *nm*
bradycardia	bradicardia *nf*
cardiomegaly	cardiomegalia *nf*
rheumatic fever	fiebre reumática *nf*
tachycardia	taquicardia *nf*
thrombosis Ⓑ	trombosis *nf*

skin

acne	acné *nm*
albinism	albinismo *nm*
callus	callo *nm*
contusion	contusión *nf*
cyst	quiste *nm*
eczema	eczema *nm*
eruption	erupción *nf*
erythema	eritema *nf*
excoriation	excoriación *nf*
laceration	laceración *nf*
lesion	lesión *nf*
papilloma	papiloma *nm*
pemphigus	pénfigo *nm*
tinea	tiña *nf*
ulcer	úlcera *nf*
uticaria	uticaria *nf*

blood

anemia Ⓐ	anemia *nf*
angioma Ⓑ	angioma *nm*
anoxemia, anoxia Ⓐ	anoxemia, anoxia *nf*
atheroma	ateroma *nm*
bacteremia	bacteremia *nf*
cyanosis	cianosis *nf*
embolism	embolia *nf*
hematuria Ⓐ	hematuria *nf*
hemolysis Ⓐ	hemolisis *nf*
hemophilia Ⓐ	hemofilia *nf*
hemoptysis Ⓐ	hemoptisis *nf*
hypertension	hipertensión *nf*
hypoglycemia	hipoglicemia *nf*
ischemia, ischaemia	isquemia *nf*
leukemia	leucemia *nf*
purpura	purpura *nf*
thrombus Ⓑ	trombo *nm*

muscles

ataxia	ataxia *nf*
clonus	clonus, clono *nm*
dystrophy	distrofia *nf*
myasthenia	myastenia *nf*
trismus	trismo *nm*

brain

cephalalgia	cefalalgia, cefalea *nf*
cerebral palsy	parálisis cerebral *nf*
concussion	concusión *nf*
epilepsy	epilepsia *nf*
glioma Ⓑ	glioma *nm*
hydrocephalus, hydrocephaly	hidrocefalia *nf*
hydrophobia	hidrofobia *nf*

poisoning

atropism	atropismo *nm*
autointoxication	autointoxicación *nf*
barbiturism	barbiturismo *nm*
botulism	botulismo *nm*
caffeinism	cafeinismo *nm*
intoxication	intoxicación *nf*
phosphorism	fosforismo *nm*
ptomaine	tomaína *nf*
salmonella	salmonela *nf*
septicemia Ⓐ	septicemia *nf*

language disorders

agraphia	agrafia *nf*
alalia	alalia *nf*
alexia	alexia *nf*
aphasia	afasia *nf*
aphonia	afonía *nf*
cataphasia	catafasia *nf*
coprolalia	coprolalia *nf*
dyslexia	dislexia *nf*
echolalia	ecolalia *nf*
muteness	mudez *nf*

sleep disorders

apnea Ⓐ	apnea *nf*
insomnia	insomnio *nm*
narcolepsy	narcolepsia *nf*
somnambulism	somnambulismo *nm*

other illnesses

acidosis	acidosis *nf*
acromegaly	acromegalia *nf*
addiction	adicción *nf*
adenopathy	adenopatía *nf*
alcoholism	alcoholismo *nm*
alkalosis	alcalosis *nf*
Alzheimer's disease	enfermedad de Alzheimer *nf*
anaphylaxis	anafilaxis *nf*
aneurysm, aneurism	aneurisma *nm*
anhydrosis	anhidrosis *nf*
ankylosis	anquilosis *nf*
anosmia	anosmia *nf*
aplasia	aplasia *nf*
apoplexy	apoplejía *nf*
arteriosclerosis	arteriosclerosis *nf*
arthralgia	artralgia *nf*
asbestosis	asbestosis *nf*
asphyxia, asphyxiation	asfixia *nf*
asthenia	astenia *nf*
asthma	asma *nf(el)*
atherosclerosis	aterosclerosis *nf*

atrophy	atrofia *nf*
avitaminosis	avitaminosis *nf*
beriberi	beriberi *nm*
bilharzia	bilharziosis *nf*
brucellosis	brucelosis *nf*
bubo B	bubón, buba *nm, nf*
cachexia	caquexia *nf*
calcification	calcificación *nf*
calculus	cálculo *nm*
canalization	canalización *nf*
cancer	cáncer *nm*
carbuncle	carbunclo *nm*
catarrh	catarro *nm*
chancre	chancro *nm*
chancroid	chancroide *nm*
chlamydia	clamidia *nf*
chondroma	condroma *nm*
chorea	corea *nf*
cirrhosis	cirrosis *nf*
claudication	claudicación *nf*
combat fatigue	fatiga de combate *nf*
coryza	coriza *nf*
crapulence	crápula *nf*
cretinism	cretinismo *nm*
cystic fibrosis	fibrosis cística *nf*
cystocele	ciscocele *nf*
decalcification	descalcificación *nf*
deformity	deformidad *nf*
delirium tremens B	delírium tremens *nm*
disfigurement	desfiguración *nf*
dislocation	dislocación *nf*
dismemberment	desmembramiento *nm*
diuresis	diuresis *nf*
drug addiction	drogadicción *nf*
dyspnea, dyspnoea	disnea *nf*
dysuria	disuria *nf*
emphysema	enfisema *nm*
enuresis	enuresis *nf*
epistaxis	epistaxis *nf*
epithelioma	epitelioma *nm*
eructation	eructación, eructo *nf, nm*
fibrosis	fibrosis *nf*
fistula	fístula *nf*
fracture	fractura *nf*
furuncle (boil)	furúnculo *nm*
gangrene	gangrena *nf*
giantism, gigantism	gigantismo *nm*
glycosuria	glicosuria, glucosuria *nf*
gonorrhea	gonorrea *nf*
hematoma A B	hematoma *nm*
hemiplegia (stroke)	hemiplejía *nf*
hernia B	hernia *nf*
herpes	herpes *nm*
hirsutism	hirsutismo *nm*
hydrops, hydropsy	hidropesía *nf*
hyperacidity	hiperacidez *nf*
hypercholesterolemia	hipercolesterolemia *nf*
hyperglycemia	hiperglicemia *nf*
hyperplasia	hiperplasia *nf*
hyperthermia	hipertermia *nf*
hyperthyroidism	hipertiroidismo *nm*
hypertrophy	hipertrofia *nf*
hyperventilation	hiperventilación *nf*
hypotension	hipotensión *nf*
hypothyroidism	hipotiroidismo *nm*
hypoxia	hipoxia *nf*
inanition	inanición *nf*
incontinence	incontinencia *nf*
infarct, infarction	infarto *nm*
keloid	queloide *nm*
kyphosis	cifosis *nf*
Legionnaires' disease	enfermedad del legionario *nf*
lipoma B	lipoma *nm*
lordosis	lordosis *nf*
macrocephaly	macrocefalia *nf*
melanism	melanismo, melanosis *nm, nf*
melanoma B	melanoma *nm*
microcephaly	microcefalía *nf*
migraine	migraña *nf*
myxedema, myxoedema	mixedema *nm*
narcosis	narcosis *nf*
narcotism	narcotismo *nm*
necrosis (gangrene)	necrosis *nf*
nephralgia	nefralgia *nf*
nephrolith (kidney stone)	nefrólito *nm*
neurasthenia	neurastenia *nf*
neuroma	neuroma *nm*
neuropathy	neuropatía *nf*
obstruction	obstrucción *nf*
occlusion	oclusión *nf*
osteoporosis	osteoporosis *nf*
otalgia	otalgia *nf*
palsy	perlesía *nf*
paralysis	parálisis *nf*
paresis	paresis, paresia *nf*
pellagra	pelagra *nf*
perforation	perforación *nf*
plethora	plétora *nf*
pleurisy	pleuresía *nf*
pneumoconiosis	neumoconiosis *nf*
pneumothorax	neumotórax *nm*

polyp	pólipo *nm*
polyuria	poliuria *nf*
presbycusis	presbicusis *nf*
progeria	progeria *nf*
prolapse	prolapso *nm*
prostatism	prostatismo *nm*
prostration	postración *nf*
psittacosis	psitacosis *nf*
ptosis	ptosis *nf*
pustule	pústula *nf*
pyuria	piuria *nf*
quadriplegia	cuadriplejía *nf*
radiation sickness	radiotoxemia *nf*
richets	raquitismo *nm*
rupture	ruptura *nf*
scald, scalding	escaldadura *nf*
schistosomiasis	esquistosomiasis *nf*
sciatica	ciática *nf*
scleroma	escleroma *nm*
sclerosis	esclerosis *nf*
scoliosis	escoliosis *nf*
seborrhea, seborrhoea	seborrea *nf*
silicosis	silicosis *nf*
spina bifida	espina bífida *nf*
syphilis	sífilis *nf*
tetany	tetania *nf*
tinnitus	tinnitus *nm*
torticolis (stiff neck)	tortícolis *nm*
trench foot	pie de trinchera *nm*
tumor Ⓐ	tumor *nm*
uremia	uremia *nf*
varicose veins	varices, várices *nfpl*
vertigo Ⓑ	vértigo *nm*

(*See also* SELECTED SPECIALIZED FIELDS under **MEDICAL PRACTICE**; *MENTAL AND EMOTIONAL DISORDERS* under **PSYCHOLOGY**; *MEDICAL ASPECTS* under **SEXUALITY**)

DENTISTRY

GENERAL TERMS

alignment	alineación *nf*
appearance	apariencia *nf*
consultation	consulta, consultación *nf*
cosmetic	cosmético *aj*
dental	dental *aj*
dentifrice	dentífrico *nm*
dentition	dentición *nf*
deposit	depósito *nm*
diagnosis	diagnóstico *nm*
emergency	emergencia *nf*

evaluation	evaluación *nf*
examination	examen *nm*
hygiene	higiene *nf*
impression	impresión *nf*
irreversible	irreversible *aj*
mastication	masticación *nf*
maxillary	maxilar *aj*
occlusion	oclusión *nf*
oral	oral *aj*
partial	parcial *aj*
polish	pulir *vt*
preventive	preventivo *aj*
procedure	procedimiento *nm*
prognosis Ⓑ	pronóstico *nm*
reduce	reducir *vt*
reversible	reversible *aj*
space	espacio *nm*
temporary	temporal *aj*
toothpaste	pasta dentífrica *nf*
topical	tópico *aj*

BRANCHES OF DENTISTRY

endodontics	endodoncia *nf*
oral and maxillofacial surgery	cirugía oral y maxilofacial *nf*
oral pathology	patología oral *nf*
orthodontics	ortodoncia *nf*
pedodontics	pedodoncia *nf*
periodontics	periodoncia *nf*
prosthodontics	prostodontia *nf*

KINDS OF TEETH

artificial	artificial *aj*
deciduous	deciduo *aj*
denture	dentadura *nf*
implant	implante *nm*
permanent	permanente *aj*
premolar	premolar *aj, nm*
primary	primario *aj*
prosthesis Ⓑ	prótesis *nf*

CONDITIONS AND DISORDERS

abscess	absceso *nm*
caries Ⓑ	caries Ⓒ *nf*
gingivitis	gingivitis *nf*
periodontitis	periodontitis *nf*
mobility	movilidad *nf*
plaque	placa *nf*
pyorrhea (obs) Ⓐ	piorrea *nf*
resorption	resorción *nf*

PROCEDURES

extraction	extracción *nf*
fluoridation	fluorización *nf*
frenectomy	frenectomía *nf*
implantation	implantación *nf*
prophylaxis	profilaxis *nf*
restoration	restauración *nf*
sedation	sedación *nf*

TREATMENT EQUIPMENT

tools

curette	cureta *nf*
explorer	explorador *nm*
forceps Ⓑ	forceps Ⓒ *nm*
mask	mascarilla *nf*
radiograph	radiografía *nf*
scalpel	escalpelo *nm*
syringe	jeringa *nf*

materials

amalgam	amalgama *nf*
anesthetic Ⓐ	anestético *aj, nm*
composite	compuesto *nm*
fluoride	fluoruro *nm*
gutta-percha	gutapercha *nf*
porcelain	porcelana *nf*

PERSONS

dentist	dentista *nmf*
endodontist	endodontista *nmf*
hygienist	higienista *nmf*
orthodontist	ortodontista *nmf*
patient	paciente *nmf*
pedodontist	pedodontista *nmf*
periodontist	periodontista *nmf*
surgeon	cirujano, -a *nmf*
oral pathologist	patólogo, -a oral *nmf*
prosthodontist	prostodontista *nmf*

(*See also* teeth and jaw under **THE HUMAN BODY**; *anesthetics* under **DRUGS**; *TERMS IN SURGERY* under **MEDICAL PRACTICE**)

PSYCHOLOGY

GENERAL TERMS

alter ego	álter ego *nm*
analysis Ⓑ	análisis Ⓒ *nm*
antisocial	antisocial *aj*
complex	complejo *nm*
conduct	conducta *nf*

conflict	conflicto *nm*
consciousness	conciencia *nf*
defense mechanism	mecanismo de defensa *nm*
deviance	desviación *nf*
dysfunction	disfunción *nf*
emotion	emoción *nf*
experience	experiencia *nf*
extroversion	extroversión *nf*
impulse	impulso *nm*
influence	influencia *nf*
integration	integración *nf*
introversion	introversión *nf*
latent	latente *aj*
mental	mental *aj*
mentality	mentalidad *nf*
mind	mente *nf*
neurosis Ⓑ	neurosis Ⓒ *nf*
normalcy, normality	normalidad *nf*
operant	operario *nm*
pathological	patológico *aj*
pattern	patrón *nm*
phobia	fobia *nf*
posthypnotic	posthipnótica *aj*
psyche	(p)siquis, (p)sique *nf*
psychic	(p)sícico *aj*
psychogenic	(p)sicógeno *aj*
psychomotor	(p)sicomotor *aj*
psychoneurosis Ⓑ	(p)siconeurosis Ⓒ *nf*
reason	razón *nf*
retentive (memory)	retentivo *aj*
state	estado *nm*
stimulus Ⓑ	estímulo *nm*
stress	estrés *nm*
telepathy	telepatía *nf*
temperament	temperamento *nm*
trauma Ⓑ	trauma *nm*

FIELDS OF SPECIALIZATION

branches

abnormal	anormal *aj*
analytic(al)	analítico *aj*
clinical	clínico *aj*
comparative	comparativo *aj*
educational	educativo *aj*
experimental	experimental *aj*
industrial	industrial *aj*
motivational	motivación *nf*
perception	percepción *nf*
physiological	fisiológico *aj*
social	social *aj*

schools of psychology

behaviorism Ⓐ	behaviorismo *nm*
cognitive	cognitivo *aj*
eclecticism	eclecticismo *nm*
Gestalt	gestaltismo
humanistic	humanístico *aj*
imagery *nsg*	imágenes *nfpl*
normal	normal *aj*
structuralism	estructuralismo *nm*

related fields

mnemonics	mnemotécnica, nemónica *nf*
paranormal, the	paranormal, lo *aj*
parapsychology	parasicología *nf*
psychoanalysis	(p)sicoanálisis *nm*
psychobiology	(p)sicobiología *nf*
psychology	(p)sicología *nf*
psychometrics	(p)sicometría *nf*
psychopathology	(p)sicopatología *nf*
psychopharmacology	(p)sicofarmacología *nf*
psychotherapy	(p)sicoterapia *nf*
sexology	sexología *nf*

THOUGHT PROCESSES

attention	atención *nf*
cognition	cognición *nf*
comprehension	comprensión *nf*
concentration	concentración *nf*
conception	concepción *nf*
conjecture	conjetura *nf*
consideration	consideración *nf*
empathy	empatía *nf*
expectation	expectativa *nf*
habit	hábito *nm*
identity	identidad *nf*
imagination (inventiveness)	imaginativa *nf*
imagination (mind power)	imaginación *nf*
introspection	introspección *nf*
intuition	intuición *nf*
judgment, judgement	juicio *nm*
meditation	meditación *nf*
memory	memoria *nf*
reasoning	razonamiento *nm*
recognition	reconocimiento *nm*
reflection Ⓐ	reflexión *nf*
sensation	sensación *nf*

PSYCHOLOGICAL MECHANISMS

alienation	alienación *nf*

association	asociación *nf*
compensation	compensación *nf*
conversion	conversión *nf*
depersonalization	despersonalización *nf*
displacement	desplazamiento *nm*
dissociation	disociación *nf*
escapism	escapismo *nm*
fixation	fijación *nf*
identification	identificación *nf*
inhibition	inhibición *nf*
obsession	obsesión *nf*
projection	proyección *nf*
rationalization	racionalización *nf*
regression	regresión *nf*
reinforcement	refuerzo *nm*
repression	represión *nf*
sublimation	sublimación *nf*

MENTAL AND EMOTIONAL DISORDERS

phobias

acrophobia	acrofobia *nf*
aerophobia	aerofobia *nf*
agoraphobia	agorafobia *nf*
androphobia	andofobia *nf*
arachnophobia	aracnofobia *nf*
claustrophobia	claustrofobia *nf*
conscience	conciencia *nf*
homophobia	homofobia *nf*
hydrophobia	hidrofobia *nf*
monophobia	monofobia *nf*
necrophobia	necrofobia *nf*
ophidophobia	ofidofobia *nf*
photophobia	fotofobia *nf*
thanatophobia	tanatofobia *nf*
xenophobia	xenofobia *nf*
zoophobia	zoofobia *nf*

manias

bibliomania	bibliomanía *nf*
dipsomania	dipsomanía *nf*
erotomania	erotomanía *nf*
kleptomania	cleptomanía *nf*
megalomania	megalomanía *nf*
monomania	monomanía *nf*
nymphomania	ninfomanía *nf*
pyromania	piromanía *nf*

complexes

castration	castración *nf*
inferiority	inferioridad *nf*
oedipal	edípico *aj*
Oedipus	edípico *aj*

persecution	persecución *nf*
superiority	superioridad *nf*

other conditions

aggression	agresión *nf*
agnosia	agnosia *nf*
ambivalence	ambivalencia *nf*
amnesia	amnesia *nf*
anxiety	ansiedad *nf*
catharsis ⒝	catarsis *nf*
cathexis	catexis *nf*
compulsion	compulsión *nf*
confabulation	confabulación *nf*
confusion	confusión *nf*
cyclothymia	ciclotimia *nf*
dependance, dependence	dependencia *nf*
depression	depresión *nf*
egocentricity	egocentrismo *nm*
euphoria	euforia *nf*
exhibitionism	exhibicionismo *nm*
expansiveness	expansibilidad *nf*
fantasy	fantasía *nf*
hallucination	alucinación *nf*
hypochondria	hipocondria *nf*
hysterics	ataque histérico *nm*
imbecility (obs)	imbecilidad *nf*
incoherence	incoherencia *nf*
melancholy	melancolía *nf*
misogamy	misogamia *nf*
misogyny	misoginia *nf*
narcissism	narcisismo *nm*
necrophilia	necrofilia *nf*
negativism	negativismo *nm*
nerves	nervios *nmpl*
panic	pánico *nm*
regression	regresión *nf*

forms of psychotherapy

autosuggestion	autosugestión *nf*
aversion	aversión *nf*
conditioning	condicionamiento *nm*
desensitization	desensibilización *nf*
Gestalt	gestáltico *aj*
group therapy	terapia grupal *aj*
hypnotism	hipnotismo *nm*
modification	modificación *nf*
persuasion	persuasión *nf*
psychodrama	(p)sicodrama *nm*
suggestion	sugestión *nf*
transactional (analysis)	de transacción

TERMS IN PSYCHOANALYSIS

abreaction	abreacción *nf*
anaclisis	anaclisis *nf*
block	bloqueo *nm*
ego	ego *nm*
Freudian	freudiano *aj*
id	id *nm*
imago	imago *nm*
instinct	instinto *nm*
Jungian	jungiano *aj*
libido	libido, líbido *nm*
neurotic	neurótico *aj*
psychoanalyze	(p)sicoanalizar *vt*
repressed	reprimido *aj*
role, rôle	rol *nm*
subconscious	subconsciente *aj, nm*
superego	superego *nm*
transfer, transference	tra(n)sferencia *nf*
unconscious	inconsciente *aj, nm*

PSYCHOMETRIC TESTS

apperception	apercepción *nf*
intelligence	inteligencia *nf*
personality	personalidad *nf*
projective	proyectivo *aj*

PERSONS

analyst	analista *nmf*
behaviorist ⒜	behaviorista *aj, nmf*
bibliomaniac	bibliómano, -a *nmf*
cataleptic	cataléptico, -a *aj, nmf*
counselor	consejero, -a *nmf*
deviant	persona de conducta desviada
dipsomaniac	dipsómano, -a *nmf*
extrovert	extrovertido, -a *nmf*
hallucinator	alucinador, -a *nmf*
homophobe	homófobo, -a *nmf*
hypnotist	hipnotizador(a), hipnotista *nmf*
imbecile (obs)	imbécil *nmf*
informant	informante *nmf*
introvert	introvertido, -a *nmf*
invert	invertido, -a *nmf*
kleptomaniac	cleptómano, -a *nmf*
lunatic	lunático, -a *aj, nmf*
maniac	maníaco, -a *nmf*
megalomaniac	megalómano, -a *nmf*
misogamist	misogamo, -a *nmf*
misogynist	misógino *nm*
narcissist	narcisista *nmf*

nymphomaniac	ninfómana, ninfomaníaca *nf*
paranoid, paranoiac	paranoide, paranoico, -a *aj, nmf*
psychoanalyst	(p)sicoanalista *nmf*
psychologist	(p)sicólogo, -a *nmf*
psychopath	(p)sicópata *nmf*
pyromaniac	pirómano *nm*
schizoid	esquizoide *aj, nmf*
schizophrenic	esquizofrénico, -a *aj, nmf*
xenophile	xenófilo, -a *nmf*
xenophobe	xenófobo, -a *nmf*

(*See also* TESTS AND EXAMINATIONS under **EDUCATION; FEELINGS AND EMOTIONS; ROLES AND RELATIONSHIPS**)

SEXUALITY

GENERAL TERMS

attraction	atracción *nf*
carnal	carnal *aj*
castration	castración *nf*
chastity	castidad *nf*
circumcision	circuncisión *nf*
consensual	consensual *aj*
desire	deseo *nm*
emasculation	emasculación *nf*
femininity	femineidad, feminidad *nf*
fidelity	fidelidad *nf*
gender	género *nm*
genitalia, genitals	genitales *nmpl*
identity	identidad *nf*
inclination	inclinación *nf*
intimacy	intimidad *nf*
libido	libido, líbido *nm*
masculinity	masculinidad *nf*
orientation	orientación *nf*
pair	pareja *nf*
proclivity	proclividad *nf*
puberty	pubertad *nf*
sensuality, sensuousness	sensualidad *nf*
sex	sexo *nm*
sex act	acto sexual *nm*
sex appeal	sex-appeal *nm*
sexology	sexología *nf*
sexuality	sexualidad *nf*
violate	violar *vt*
virginity	virginidad *nf*

SEXUAL PRACTICES

sexual orientation

bisexuality	bisexualidad *nf*
heterosexuality	heterosexualidad *nf*
homosexuality	homosexualidad *nf*
lesbianism	lesbianismo *nm*
transsexuality	transexualidad, transexualismo *nf, nm*

aids to sex

aphrodisiac	afrodisíaco *nm*
coquetry	coquetería *nf*
fetish	fetiche *nm*
flagellation	flagelación *nf*
flirting, flirtation	flirteo *nm*
philter Ⓐ (obs)	filtro *nm*
pornography	pornografía *nf*
potion	poción *nf*
romance	romance *nm*
seduction	seducción *nf*
striptease	striptease *nm*

kinds of physical contact

anal	anal *aj*
autoeroticism	autoerotismo *nm*
caress	caricia *nf*
coitus	coito *nm*
copulation	cópula, copulación *nf*
cunnilingus	cunilinguo *nm*
embrace	abrazo *nm*
fellatio	felacio *nm*
masturbation	masturbación *nf*
oral	oral *aj*
osculation	ósculo *nm*
penetration	penetración *nf*
stimulation	estimulación *nf*
touch	toque *nm*

physiological aspects

ecstasy	éxtasis *nm*
ejaculation	eyaculación *nf*
erection	erección *nf*
excitement	excitación *nf*
orgasm	orgasmo *nm*
passion	pasión *nf*
position	posición *nf*

places

bordello	burdel *nm*
harem	harén *nm*
sex shop	sex-shop *nm or nf*

abnormal practices

bestiality	bestialidad *nf*
necrophilia	necrofilia *nf*
onanism	onanismo *nm*
pederasty	pederastía *nf*
pedophilia Ⓐ	pedofilia *nf*
perversion	perversión *nf*
sadism	sadismo *nm*
sadomasochism	sadomasoquismo *nm*
sodomy	sodomía *nf*
voyeurism	voyeurismo *nm*

other terms

adultery	adulterio *nm*
concubinage (obs)	concubinato *nm*
fornication	fornicación *nf*
incest	incesto *nm*
orgy	orgía *nf*
promiscuity	promiscuidad *nf*
prostitution	prostitución *nf*

MEDICAL ASPECTS

sexual dysfunction

anaphrodisia	anafrodisia *nf*
concupiscence	concupiscencia *nf*
effeminacy	afeminación *nf*
eroticism	erotismo *nm*
frigidity	frigidez *nf*
impotence	impotencia *nf*
misogyny	misoginia *nf*
nymphomania	ninfomanía *nf*
premature ejaculation	eyaculación precoz *nf*
satyriasis	satiriasis *nf*
virilism	virilismo *nm*

venereal diseases

chancroid	chancroide *nm*
chlamydia	clamidia *nf*
gonorrhea	gonorrea *nf*
herpes	herpes *nm*
syphilis	sífilis *nf*

DESCRIPTIVE TERMS

describing women

chaste	casto *aj*
coquettish	coqueta *aj*
curvaceous	curvilíneo *aj*
feminine	femenino *aj*
frigid	frígido *aj*
lesbian	lesbiano, lésbico *aj*
nubile	núbil *aj*

seductive	seductor *aj*
virgin(al)	virginal *aj*
voluptuous	voluptuoso *aj*

describing men

Don Juan	donjuán *nm*
effeminate	afeminado *aj*
impotent	impotente *aj*
macho	macho, machista *aj*
virile	viril *aj*

other descriptions

amatory	amatorio *aj*
attractive	atractivo, atrayente *aj*
enamored Ⓐ	enamorado *aj*
erogenous	erógeno *aj*
erotic	erótico *aj*
faithful	fiel *aj*
lascivious	lascivo *aj*
libidinous	libidinoso *aj*
licentious	licencioso *aj*
mixed	mixto *aj*
obscene	obsceno *aj*
oversexed	hipersexuado *aj*
passionate	apasionado *aj*
promiscuous	promiscuo *aj*
sadistic	sádico *aj*
salacious	salaz *aj*
sated	saciado *aj*
sensuous	sensual *aj*
sexy	sexy *aj*
suggestive	sugestivo *aj*
unfaithful	infiel *aj*

PERSONS

ancient love gods

Aphrodite	Afrodita *nf*
Cupid	Cupido *nm*
Eros	Eros *nm*
Venus	Venus *nf*

real persons

adulterer	adúltero, -a *nmf*
adulteress	adúltera *nf*
bisexual	bisexual *nmf*
chaperon(e)	chaperón, -ona *nmf*
concubine	concubina *nf*
coquette	coqueta *nf*
courtesan (obs)	cortesana *nf*
emasculator	emasculador(a) *nmf*
eunuch (obs)	eunuco *nm*
flagellator	flagelador(a) *nmf*

fornicator	fornicador(a) *nmf*
gigolo	gigoló, gígolo *nm*
heterosexual	heterosexual *nmf*
homophobe	homófobo, -a *nmf*
homosexual	homosexual *nmf*
lesbian	lesbiana *nf*
libertine	libertino, -a *nmf*
misogynist	misógino *nm*
nymphomaniac	ninfómana, ninfomaníaca *aj, nf*
pederast	pederasta *nm*
pedophile Ⓐ	pedofilo, -a *nmf*
pervert	pervertido, -a *nmf*
prostitute	prostituta *nf*
romantic	romántico, -a *nmf*
sadist	sádico, -a *nmf*
seducer	seductor(a) *nmf*
seductress	seductora *nf*
sensualist	sensualista *nmf*
sexist	sexista *nmf*
sexologist	sexólogo, -a *nmf*
sodomite	sodomita *nmf*
transsexual	transexual *nmf*
transvestite	transvestido, -a *nmf*
virgin	virgen *nmf*
voluptuary	voluptuoso, -a *nmf*
voyeur	voyeur *nmf*

(*See also* **sexual aspects** under **FAMILY**)

DRUGS

GENERAL TERMS

abuse	abuso *nm*
adulterant	sustancia adulterante *nf*
antidote	antídoto *nm*
contraindication	contraindicación *nf*
drug addiction	drogadicción *nf*
drugstore	droguería *nf*
effect	efecto *nm*
formulary	formulario *nm*
generic	genérico *aj*
incompatibility	incompatibilidad *nf*
intolerance	intolerancia *nf*
medicine	medicina *nf*
mixture	mixtura *nf*
overdose	sobredosis Ⓒ *nf*
patent medicine	medicamento patentado *nm*
pharmaceutical	farmacéutico *aj, nm*
pharmacist	farmacéutico, -a *nmf*
pharmacologist	farmacólogo, -a *nmf*
pharmacology	farmacología *nf*

pharmacopeia Ⓐ	farmacopea *nf*
pharmacy	farmacia *nf*
potent	potente *aj*
preparation	preparación, preparado *nf, nm*
psychopharmacology	(p)sicofarmacología *nf*
reaction	reacción *nf*
sensitivity	sensibilidad *nf*
specific	específico *nm*
substance	sustancia *nf*
synergy	sinergia *nf*
synthetic	sintético *aj*
tolerance	tolerancia *nf*
toxicity	toxicidad *nf*

CLASSES OF DRUGS

analgesic	analgésico *aj, nm*
anaphrodisiac	anafrodisíaco *aj, nm*
anesthetic Ⓐ	anestético *aj, nm*
antacid	antiácido *aj, nm*
anthelmintic	antihelmíntico *aj, nm*
antibacterial	antibacteriano, antibactérico *aj*
antibiotic	antibiótico *aj, nm*
anticoagulant	anticoagulante *aj, nm*
anticonvulsant	anticonvulsivante *aj, nm*
antihistamine	antihistamínico *nm*
antimalarial	antipalúdico *aj*
antipyretic	antipirético *aj, nm*
antiseptic	antiséptico *aj, nm*
antiserum Ⓑ	antisuero *nm*
antispasmodic	antiespasmódico *aj, nm*
antitoxin	antitoxina *nf*
antitussive	antitusígeno *aj*
antiviral	antiviral *aj*
aphrodisiac	afrodisíaco *aj, nm*
astringent	astringente *aj, nm*
bactericide	bactericida *nm*
bronchodilator	broncodilatador *nm*
calefacient	remedio calefaciente *nm*
cardiovascular	cardiovascular *aj*
carminative	carminativo *aj, nm*
contraceptive	contraceptivo, anticonceptivo *aj, nm*
counterirritant	contrairritante *nm*
decongestant	descongestivo *nm*
disinfectant	desinfectante *nm*
diuretic	diurético *nm*
emetic	emético *aj, nm*

expectorant	expectorante *nm*
gargle	gargarismo *nm*
germicide	germicida *nf*
hormones	hormonas *nfpl*
immunosuppresives	inmunosupresivos *nmpl*
laxative	laxante *aj, nm*
medicinal	medicinal *aj*
narcotic	narcótico *aj, nm*
purgative	purgante, purgativo *aj, nm*
relaxant	relajante *nm*
salts	sales *nfpl*
soporific	soporífero *nm*
spermicide	espermicida, espermaticida *nm*
steroid	esteroide *nm*
stimulant	estimulante *nm*
vaccine	vacuna *nf*
vermicide	vermicida *nm*
vitamins	vitaminas *nfpl*

COMMON MEDICINAL DRUGS

antibiotics

ampicillin	ampicilina *nf*
aureomycin	aureomicina *nf*
bacitracin	bacitracina *nf*
calomel	calomelanos, calomel *nm*
cyclosporine	ciclosporina *nf*
erythromycin	eritromicina *nf*
gramicidin	gramicidina *nf*
iodine	yodo *nm*
mercurochrome	mercurocromo *nm*
penicillin	penicilina *nf*
streptomycin	estreptomicina *nf*
sulfa	sulfa *nf*
sulfonamide	sulfonamida *nf*
Terramycin	terramicina *nf*
tetracycline	tetraciclina *nf*

cardiovascular drugs

antiarrhythmic	antiarrítmico *aj*
antihypertensive	antihiperténsico *aj*
beta (blocker)	beta *nf*
cardiotonic	cardiotónico *aj*
digitalis	digital *nf*
reserpine	reserpina *nf*
vasoconstrictor	vasoconstrictor *nm*
vasodilator	vasodilatador *nm*

analgesics

acetaminophen	acetaminofen *nm*

anodyne	anodino *aj, nm*
aspirin	aspirina *nf*
camphorated oil	aceite alcanforado *nm*
codeine	codeína *nf*
ibuprofen	ibuprofen *nm*
liniment	linimento *nm*
menthol	mentol *nm*
morphine	morfina *nf*
opiate	opiata *nf*
paregoric	elixir paregórico *nm*

anesthetics

benzocaine	benzocaíne *nf*
chloroform	cloroformo *nm*
ether	éter *nm*
nitrous oxide	óxido nitroso *nm*
Novocain (= procaine)	novocaína *nf*
procaine	procaína *nf*

stimulants

adrenalin(e)	adrenalina *nf*
analeptic	analéptico *aj, nm*
benzedrine (= amphetamine)	bencedrina *nf*
caffein(e)	cafeína *nf*
camphor	alcanfor *nm*
cocain(e)	cocaína *nf*
elixir	elíxir *nm*
ephedrine	efedrina *nf*
epinephrine	epinefrina *nf*
nicotine	nicotina *nf*
tonic	tónico *nm*

antianxiety drugs

antidepressant	antidepresivo *aj, nm*
antipsychotic	antipsicótico *aj*
barbiturate	barbitúrico *nm*
bromide	bromuro *nm*
calmative	calmante *aj, nm*
laudanum	láudano *nm*
sedative	sedante, sedativo *aj, nm*
tranquilizer	tranquilizante *nm*

poisons

arsenic	arsénico *nm*
curare	curare *nm*
nux vomica	nuez vómica *nf*
strychnine	estricnina *nf*

other common drugs

aloe	áloe, aloe *nm*
antigen	antígeno *nm*

arnica	árnica *nf*
atropine (= belladonna)	atropina *nf*
balm	bálsamo *nm*
balsam	bálsamo *nm*
belladonna (= atropine)	belladona *nf*
calamine (lotion)	calamina *nf*
coagulant	coagulante *nm*
colchicine	colquicina *nf*
cortisone	cortisona *nf*
creosote	creosota *nf*
depressant	depresivo *nm*
digestive	digestivo *nm*
Dramamine	dramamina *nf*
heparin	heparina *nf*
hypnotic	hipnótico *aj, nm*
immunosuppressant	inmunosupresor *nm*
insulin	insulina *nf*
interferon	interferón *nm*
ipecac, ipecacuanha	ipecacuana *nf*
L-dopa	L-dopa *nf*
laetrile	laetril *nm*
magnesia	magnesia *nf*
nitroglycerin(e)	nitroglicerina *nf*
petrolatum	petrolato *nm*
quinine	quinina *nf*
serum B	suero *nm*
suppressant	supresor *aj, nm*
taxol	taxol *nm*
thalidomide	talidomida *nf*
toxoid	toxoide *nm*
Vaseline	vaselina *nf*
vermifuge	vermífugo *aj, nm*

FORMS AND ADMINISTRATION

ampule, ampoule	ampolla, ampolleta *nf*
capsule	cápsula *nf*
cream	crema *nf*
gas	gas *nm*
gel	gel *nm*
inhalant	inhalante *aj, nm*
inhaler	inhalador *nm*
injection	inyección *nf*
liquid	líquido *aj, nm*
lotion	loción *nf*
oral	oral *aj*
pastille	pastilla *nf*
patch	parche *nm*
pill	píldora *nf*
tablet	tableta *nf*

TERMS IN DRUG ABUSE

types of drugs

amphetamine	anfetamina *nf*
depressant	depresivo *nm*
hallucinogen	alucinógeno *nm*
inhalant	inhalante *nm*
narcotic	narcótico *nm*
opiate	opiata *nf*
stimulant	estimulante *nm*

commonly abused drugs

alcohol	alcohol *nm*
barbital	barbital *nm*
cannabis	cannabis *nm*
cocaine	cocaína *nf*
crack	crack *nm*
hashish	hachís *nm*
heroin	heroína *nf*
LSD	droga LSD, ácido lisérgico
marijuana, marihuana	mariguana *nf*
mescaline	mescalina *nf*
opium	opio *nm*
PCP	droga PCP *nf*
peyote, peyotl	peyote *nm*
psilocybin	silocibina *nf*
tobacco	tabaco *nm*

possible effects

agitation	agitación *nf*
coma	coma *nm*
confusion	confusión *nf*
convulsion	convulsión *nf*
disorientation	desorientación *nf*
euphoria	euforia *nf*
excitement	excitación *nf*
hallucination	alucinación *nf*
incoherence	incoherencia *nf*
insomnia	insomnio *nm*
panic	pánico *nm*
psychosis B	(p)sicosis C *nf*
vomiting	el vomitar *nm*

persons

cocaine addict	cocainómano, -a *nmf*
drug addict	drogadicto, -a *nmf*
fixer	fijador *nm*
junkie	yonqui *nmf*
trafficker	traficante *nmf*

other terms

addictive	que forma hábito
cigar	cigarro *nm*

cigarette	cigarrillo *nm*
cocaine addiction	cocainomanía *nf*
dependance, dependence	dependencia *nf*
illegal	ilegal *aj*
methadone	metadona *nf*
pipe	pipa *nf*
psychedelia	(p)sicodelia *nf*
sniff (of glue)	esnife, esnifada *nm, nf*
trip	trip *nm*

TOOLS AND MEASUREMENTS

dosage	dosificación *nf*
dosimeter	dosímetro *nm*
dram	dracma *nf*
milligram Ⓐ	miligramo *nm*
scruple	escrúpulo *nm*
tincture	tintura *nf*

(*See also* substances under **COSMETICS AND GROOMING**)

DEATH

GENERAL TERMS

cause	causa *nf*
comfort	confortar *vt*
condolence	condolencia *nf*
console	consolar *vt*
defunct	difunto *aj*
dismember	desmembrar *vt*
expectancy (life)	expectativa *nf*
extinction	extinción *nf*
fatal	fatal *aj*
inter	enterrar *vt*
lethal	letal *aj*
macabre	macabro *aj*
moribund	moribundo *aj*
perish	perecer *vi*
posthumous	póstumo *aj*

CAUSES OF DEATH BY KILLING

individual killing

asphyxiation	asfixia *nf*
assassination	asesinato *nm*
decapitation	decapitación *nf*
electrocution	electrocución *nf*
euthanasia	eutanasia *nf*
execution	ejecución *nf*
fratricide (act)	fratricidio *nm*
harakiri, hara-kiri	haraquiri *nm*

homicide (act)	homicidio *nm*
infanticide (act)	infanticidio *nm*
lynching	linchamiento *nm*
matricide (act)	matricidio *nm*
parricide (act)	parricidio *nm*
regicide (act)	regicidio *nm*
scalp	escalpar *vt*
strangulation	estrangulación *nf*
suffocation	sofocación, sofoco *nf*
suicide (act)	suicidio *nm*

mass killing

atrocity	atrocidad *nf*
bombing	bombardeo *nm*
cannibalism	canibalismo *nm*
cataclysm	cataclismo *nm*
catastrophe	catástrofe *nf*
conflagration	conflagración *nf*
disaster	desastre *nm*
epidemic	epidemia *nf*
gas	gasear *vt*
genocide	genocidio *nm*
holocaust	holocausto *nm*
massacre	masacre *nf*
pestilence	pestilencia *nf*
pogrom	pogromo *nm*

instruments

dagger	daga *nf*
garrote, garotte	garrote *nm*
guillotine	guillotina *nf*
pistol	pistola *nf*
rifle	rifle *nm*

poisons

arsenic	arsénico *nm*
phosgene	fosgeno *nm*
strychnine	estricnina *nf*
venom	veneno *nm*

ASPECTS OF DYING

medical aspects

cadaver	cadáver *nm*
decease	deceso *nm*
embalming	embalsamamiento *nm*
expiration	expiración *nf*
morbidity	morbosidad *nf*
mortality	mortalidad *nf*
survival	supervivencia *nf*

legal aspects

administrator	administrador(a) *nmf*
autopsy	autopsia *nf*

certificate	certificado *nm*
disposition	disposición *nf*
executor	ejecutor(a) *nmf*
exhumation	exhumación *nf*
forensic	forense *aj*
heir/heiress	heredero, -a *nmf*
inheritance	herencia *nf*
inquest	encuesta *nf*
interment	entierro *nm*
intestate	intestado *aj*
legacy	legado *nm*
nuncupative (will)	nuncupativo *aj*
perpetuity	perpetuidad *nf*
testate	testado *aj*
testator	testador(a) *nmf*

religious aspects

cortege, cortège	cortejo *nm*
cremation	cremación *nf*
eschatology	escatología *nf*
eternity	eternidad *nf*
funeral	funeral *nm*
immortality	inmortalidad *nf*
metempsychosis	metempsicosis *nf*
preservation	preservación *nf*
reincarnation	reencarnación *nf*
reliquary	relicario *nm*
resurrection	resurrección *nf*

places

cemetery	cementerio *nm*
crematorium, crematory	crematorio *nm*
crypt	cripta *nf*
funeral home	funeraria *nf*
hospice	hospicio *nm*
hospital	hospital *nm*
mausoleum	mausoleo *nm*
pyre	pira *nf*
sepulcher Ⓐ	sepulcro *nm*
sepulture	sepultura *nf*
tomb	tumba *nf*

historical terms

catacombs	catacumbas *nfpl*
catafalque	catafalco *nm*
cenotaph	cenotafio *nm*
hecatomb	hecatombe *nf*
mastaba	mastaba *nf*
mummy	momia *nf*
necropolis	necrópolis *nf*
ossuary	osario *nm*
pantheon	panteón *nm*

art, music, and language

elegy	elegía *nf*
epitaph	epitafio *nm*
mask	máscara *nf*
memorial	memorial *nm*
necrology	necrología *nf*
obituary	obituario *nm*
oration (funeral)	oración *nf*
requiem	réquiem *nm*
sarcophagus Ⓑ	sarcófago *nm*
stela, stele Ⓑ	estela *nf*

other terms

carrion	carroña *nf*
necromancy	nigromancía *nf*
necrophagia	necrofagia *nf*
necrophilia	necrofilia *nf*
necrophobia	necrofobia *nf*

PERSONS

killers

assassin	asesino, -a *nmf*
cannibal	caníbal *nmf*
exterminator	exterminador(a) *nmf*
fratricide	fratricida *nmf*
homicide	homicida *nmf*
infanticide	infanticida *nmf*
matricide	matricida *nmf*
parricide	parricida *nmf*
regicide	regicida *nmf*
strangler	estrangulador(a) *nmf*
suicide	suicida *nmf*

other persons

consoler	consolador(a) *nmf*
embalmer	embalsamador(a) *nmf*
mortal	mortal *aj, nmf*
organ donor	donante de órgano *nmf*
spiritualist	espiritista *nmf*
survivor	sobreviviente *nmf*
widow	viuda *nf*
widower	viudo *nm*

(*See also* **pesticides** under **AGRICULTURE**; *violent* under **LAW**; *birth and death* under **RELIGION**)

AGE AND AGING

GENERAL TERMS

celebrate (birthday)	celebrar *vt*
gerontocracy	gerontocracia *nf*

life expectancy *nsg*   expectativas de vida *nfpl*
long-lived   longevo *aj*
maturation   maduración *nf*
Medicare   Medicare *nm*
rejuvenation   rejuvenecimiento *nm*
retirement   retiro *nm*
Social Security   Seguro Social *nm*

FIELDS OF SPECIALIZATION

childhood

pediatrics Ⓐ   pediatría *nf*
pedodontics   pedodoncia *nf*
pedology   pedología *nf*

old age

geriatrics   geriatría *nf*
gerontology   gerontología *nf*

ASPECTS OF AGING

stages of life

adolescence   adolescencia *nf*
adulthood   edad adulta *nf*
climacteric   climaterio *nm*
infancy   infancia *nf*
maturity   madurez *nf*
menopause   menopausia *nf*
preadolescence   preadolescencia *nf*
prepubescence   prepubescencia *nf*
puberty   pubertad *nf*
pubescence   pubescencia *nf*
senescence   senectud *nf*

age determination

chronological   cronológico *aj*

emotional   emocional *aj*
mental   mental *aj*
physical   físico *aj*
psychological   (p)sicológico *aj*

legal categories

adult   adulto, -a *aj, nmf*
juvenile   juvenil *aj, nmf*
majority   mayoría *nf*
minor   menor *aj, nmf*
minority   minoría *nf*

geriatic disorders

Alzheimer's disease   enfermedad de Alzheimer *nf*
presbycusis   presbicusis *nf*
presbyopia   presbiopía *nf*
puerilism   puerilismo *nm*
senility   senilidad, senilismo *nm*

PERSONS

adolescent   adolescente *aj, nmf*
babe, baby   bebé *nmf*
centenarian   centenario, -a *aj, nmf*
geriatrician   geriatra *nmf*
gerontologist   gerontologo, -a *nmf*
nonagenarian   nonagenario, -a *nmf*
octogenarian   octogenario, -a *nmf*
pederast   pederasta *nm*
pediatrician   pediatra *nmf*
septuagenarian   septuagenario, -a *aj, nmf*
sexagenarian   sexagenario, -a *aj, nmf*

(*See also lineage terms* under **FAMILY**)

Understanding Our Universe

SCIENCE AND THE SCIENCES

GENERAL TERMS

cosmos	cosmos *nm*
energy	energía *nf*
evolution	evolución *nf*
fundamental	fundamento *nm*
matter	materia *nf*
nature	naturaleza *nf*
order	orden *nm*
origin	origen *nm*
relativity	relatividad *nf*
science	ciencia *nf*
state	estado *nm*
system	sistema *nm*
taxonomy	taxonomía *nf*
technology	tecnología *nf*
type	tipo *nm*
universe	universo *nm*

MAJOR SCIENTIFIC FIELDS

basic divisions

applied	aplicado *aj*
pure	puro *aj*

abstract sciences

logic	lógica *nf*
mathematics *nsg*	matemáticas *nfpl*
metaphysics	metafísica *nf*

physical sciences

astronomy	astronomía *nf*
chemistry	química *nf*
geography	geografía *nf*
geology	geología *nf*
meteorology	meteorología *nf*
physics	física *nf*

biological sciences

anatomy	anatomía *nf*
biochemistry	bioquímica *nf*
biology	biología *nf*
botany	botánica *nf*
medicine	medicina *nf*
paleontology	paleontología *nf*
physiology	fisiología *nf*
psychology	(p)sicología *nf*
zoology	zoología *nf*

social sciences

anthropology	antropología *nf*
economics	economía *nf*
history	historia *nf*
linguistics	lingüística *nf*
political science *nsg*	ciencias políticas *nfpl*
sociology	sociología *nf*

technical sciences

biotechnology	biotecnología *nf*
chronometry	cronometría *nf*
microscopy	microscopia, microscopía *nf*
radiology	radiología *nf*
robotics	robótica *nf*
systematics	sistemática *nf*

TERMS IN SCIENTIFIC RESEARCH

analysis Ⓑ	análisis Ⓒ *nm*
chaos	caos *nm*
classification	clasificación *nf*
collection	colección *nf*
conclusion	conclusión *nf*
control	control *nm*
data *nsg* or *npl*	datos *nmpl*
definition	definición *nf*
diagram	diagrama *nm*
discovery	descubrimiento *nm*
dissemination	diseminación *nf*
evidence	evidencia *nf*
experiment	experimento *nm*
formula Ⓑ	fórmula *nf*
generalization	generalización *nf*
hypothesis Ⓑ	hipótesis Ⓒ *nf*
interpretation	interpretación *nf*
investigation	investigación *nf*
laboratory	laboratorio *nm*
mass	masa *nf*
method	método *nm*
methodology	metodología *nf*
model	modelo *nm*
notation	notación *nf*
observation	observación *nf*
principle	principio *nm*
prove	probar *vt*
quantification	cuantificación *nf*
repetition	repetición *nf*
result	resultado *nm*

solution	solución *nf*
supposition	suposición *nf*
theory	teoría *nf*
time	tiempo *nm*
validation	validación *nf*
verification	verificación *nf*

PERSONS

discoverer	descubridor(a) *nmf*
evolutionist	evolucionista *nmf*
genius	genio *nm*
inventor	inventor(a) *nmf*
scientist	científico, -a *nmf*
theoretician	teórico, -a *nmf*

(*See also* TERMS IN LOGIC under **PHILOSOPHY**)

MATHEMATICS

GENERAL TERMS

algorithm	algoritmo *nm*
analysis Ⓑ	análisis Ⓒ *nm*
axiom	axioma *nm*
chaos	caos *nm*
characteristic	característica *nf*
computation (general)	computación *nf*
decrement	decremento *nm*
determinant	determinante *nm*
discontinuity	discontinidad *nf*
domain	dominio *nm*
duality	dualidad *nf*
element	elemento *nm*
equality	igualdad *nf*
equation	ecuación *nf*
example	ejemplo *nm*
expression	expresión *nf*
extract	extraer *vt*
function	función *nf*
gradient	gradiente *nm*
group	grupo *nm*
harmonic	armónico *aj*
homomorphism	homomorfismo *nm*
increment	incremento *nm*
inequality	desigualdad *nf*
infinity	infinidad *nf*
intersection	intersección *nf*
invariant	invariante *nf*
isomorphism	isomorfismo *nm*
lemma	lema *nm*
logarithm	logaritmo *nm*
magnitude	magnitud *nf*
mathematician	matemático, -a *nmf*
mathematics *nsg*	matemáticas *nfpl*

matrix Ⓑ	matriz *nf*
modulus Ⓑ	módulo *nm*
multiple	múltiplo *nm*
notation	notación *nf*
number, numeral	número *nm*
numerical	numérico *aj*
operation	operación *nf*
operator	operador *nm*
order	orden *nm*
parameter	parámetro *nm*
part	parte *nf*
percent	por ciento *nm*
period	período *nm*
point	punto *nm*
problem	problema *nm*
progression	progresión *nf*
proof	prueba *nf*
proportion	proporción *nf*
proposition	proposición *nf*
quantity	cantidad *nf*
residual	variancia residual *nf*
result	resultado *nm*
scalar	escalar *aj*
sign	signo *nm*
solution	solución *nf*
space	espacio *nm*
subgroup	subgrupo *nm*
symbol	símbolo *nm*
tensor	tensor *nm*
theorem	teorema *nm*
three-dimensional	tridimensional *aj*
two-dimensional	bidimensional *aj*
union	unión *nf*
unit	unidad *nf*
unity	unidad *nf*
variation	variación *nf*
vector	vector *nm*
postulate	postulado *nm*

BRANCHES

pure mathematics

algebra	álgebra *nf*
arithmetic	aritmética *nf*
calculus Ⓑ	cálculo *nm*
geometry	geometría *nf*
logic	lógica *nf*
probability	probabilidad *nf*
topology	topología *nf*
trigonometry	trigonometría *nf*

applied mathematics

accounting	contabilidad *nf*

econometrics	econometría *nf*
statistics	estadística *nf*

BASIC CONCEPTS

systems

binary	binario *aj*
decimal	decimal *aj, nm*
duodecimal	duodecimal *aj*
hexadecimal	hexadecimal *aj, nm*
infinitesimal	infinitesimal *aj*
metric	métrico *aj*
scale	escala *nf*
sexagesimal	sexagesimal *aj*
ternary	ternario *aj*

numerals

Arabic	arábigo *aj*
cipher	cifra *nf*
digit	dígito *nm*
reciprocal	número recíproco *nm*
Roman	romano *aj*

types of numbers

abstract	abstracto *aj*
base	base *nf*
cardinal	cardinal *aj*
complex	complejo *aj, nm*
constant	constante *aj, nf*
discrete	discreto *aj*
dual	dual *aj*
finite	finito *aj*
fraction	fracción *nf*
imaginary	imaginario *aj*
index 🅑	índice *nm*
infinite	infinito *aj, nm*
integer	número entero
irrational (number)	irracional *aj*
minimum 🅑	mínimo *nm*
mixed	mixto *aj*
natural	natural *aj*
negative	negativo *aj*
ordinal	ordinal *aj*
positive	positivo *aj, nm*
prime	primo *aj*
rational	rational *nf*
real	real *aj*
variable	variable *aj, nf*

fractions

cancellation	cancelación *nf*
common	común *aj*

denominator	denominador *nm*
equivalent	equivalente *aj, nm*
improper	impropio *aj*
mantissa	mantisa *nf*
numerator	numerador *nm*
proper	propio *aj*
term	término *nm*
value	valor *nm*

multiples

double	doble *aj, nmf*
duple	duplo *aj*
octuple	óctuplo *aj*
quadruple	cuádruplo *nm*
quintuple	quíntuplo *aj, nm*
sextuple	séxtuplo *aj, nm*
triple	triple *aj*

other quantities

billion	billón *nm*
dozen	docena *nf*
million	millón *nm*
null	nulo *aj*
octillion	octillón *nm*
zero 🅑	cero *nm*

groupings

dichotomy	dicotomía *nf*
quadruplet	cuádruplo *nm*
trichotomy	tricotomía *nf*

operations and processes

addition	adición *nf*
calculation	cálculo *nm*
computation (specific)	cómputo *nm*
conversion	conversión *nf*
division	división *nf*
duplication	duplicación *nf*
estimation	estimación *nf*
factorization	división en factores
induction	inducción *nf*
inversion	inversión *nf*
involution	involución *nf*
multiplication	multiplicación *nf*
permutation	permutación *nf*
reduction	reducción *nf*
subtraction	su(b)stracción *nf*
transposition	tra(n)sposición *nf*

ordinal numbers

billionth	billonésimo *aj, nm*
centesimal	centésimo *aj, nm*

millionth	millonésimo *aj, nm*
sixth	sexto *aj, nm*

TERMS IN ALGEBRA

abscissa Ⓑ	abscisa *nf*
binomial	binomio *aj, nm*
coefficient	coeficiente *nm*
coordinate	coordenada *nf*
exponent	exponente *nm*
formula Ⓑ	fórmula *nf*
monomial	monomio *nm*
ordinate	ordenada *nf*
polynomial	polinomio *nm*
transcendental	tra(n)scendental *aj*
trinomial	trinomio *nm*

TERMS IN ARITHMETIC

cube	cubo *nm*
difference	diferencia *nf*
divide	dividir *vt*
dividend	dividendo *nm*
divisible	divisible *aj*
divisor	divisor *nm*
factor	factor *nm*
indivisible	indivisible *aj*
minuend	minuendo *nm*
minus	menos *nm*
multiplicand	multiplicando *nm*
multiplier	multiplicador *nm*
product	producto *nm*
quotient	cociente *nm*
rest (remainder)	resto *nm*
subtotal	subtotal *nm*
subtrahend	substraendo, sustraendo *nm*
sum	suma *nf*
total	total *aj, nm*

TERMS IN CALCULUS

convergence	convergencia *nf*
deduct	deducir *vt*
derivative	derivada *nf*
differential	diferencial *nf*
differentiation	diferenciación *nf*
divergence	divergencia *nf*
infinitesimal	infinitésimo *nm*
integral	integral *nf*
integration	integración *nf*
limit	límite *nm*
sequence	secuencia *nf*
series Ⓑ	serie *nf*

TERMS IN GEOMETRY

branches

analytic	analítico *aj*
Cartesian	cartesiano *aj*
elliptic	elíptico *aj*
Euclidean	euclidiano *aj*
hyperbolic	hiperbólico *aj*
non-Euclidean	no euclidiano
plane	plano *aj, nm*
projective	proyectivo *aj*
solid	sólido *aj, nm*
transformational	tra(n)sformacional *aj*

general terms

area	área *nf(el)*
directrix Ⓑ	directriz *nf*
generate	generar *vt*
volume	volumen *nm*
quadrilateral	cuadrilátero *aj, nm*
compass	compás *nm*
complement	complemento *nm*
congruence	congruencia *nf*
curvature	curvatura *nf*
diagram	diagrama *nm*
dimension	dimensión *nf*
envelope	envolvente *nf*
equidistant	equidistante *aj*
figure	figura *nf*
focus Ⓑ	foco *nm*
generatrix Ⓑ	generatriz *nf*
hypothesis Ⓑ	hipótesis Ⓒ *nf*
incidence	incidencia *nf*
median	mediana *nf*
minute	minuto *nm*
multidimensional	multidimensional *aj*
pi	pi *nf*
rectification	rectificación *nf*
similarity	similitud *nf*
supplement	suplemento *nm*
symmetry	simetría *nf*
trace	traza *nf*

geometric figures

– plane –

circle	círculo *nm*
cycloid	cicloide *nf*
decagon	decágono *nm*
ellipse	elipse *nf*
ellipsoid	elipsoide *nm*
epicycle	epiciclo *nm*
epicycloid	epicicloide *nf*
heptagon	heptágono *nm*

hexagon	hexágono *nm*	parallel	paralelo *aj, nm*
hyperbola B	hipérbola *nf*	perimeter	perímetro *nm*
hypocycloid	hipocicloide *nf*	quadrant	cuadrante *nm*
octagon	octágono *nm*	radius B	radio *nm*
oval	óvalo *nm*	secant	secante *nf*
parabola	parábola *nf*	section	sección *nf*
pentagon	pentágono *nm*	sector	sector *nm*
polygon	polígono *nm*	segment	segmento *nm*
quadrate	cuadrado *nm*	sextant	sextante *nm*
semicircle	semicírculo *nm*	tangent	tangente *aj, nf*
spiral	espiral *nf*	transversal	transversal *nf*
triangle	triángulo *nm*	trisection	trisección *nf*
trihedral	triedro *nm*	vertex B	vértice *nm*

— solid (regular polyhedra) —

dodecahedron B	dodecaedro *nm*
icosahedron B	icosaedro *nm*
octahedron B	octaedro *nm*
pentahedron B	pentaedro *nm*
tetrahedron B	tetraedro *nm*

kinds of angles

adjacent	adyacente *aj*
alternate	alterno *aj*
acute	agudo *aj*
complementary	complementario *aj*
exterior	exterior *aj*
interior	interior *aj*
obtuse	obtuso *aj*
opposite	opuesto *aj*
supplementary	suplementario *aj*
vertical	vertical *aj, nf*

— other 3-dimensional figures —

cone	cono *nm*
conic	sección cónica *nf*
cylinder	cilindro *nm*
helix B	hélice *nf*
hyperboloid	hiperboloide *nf*
parallepiped	paralelepípedo *nm*
polyhedron B	poliedro *nm*
prism	prisma *nm*
pyramid	pirámide *nf*
sphere	esfera *nf*
spheroid	esferoide *nm*

kinds of triangles

equilateral	equilateral *aj*
isosceles	isósceles *aj*
right	recto *aj*
scalene	escaleno *aj*

kinds of quadrilaterals

parallelogram	paralelogramo *nm*
quadrangle	cuadrángulo *nm*
rectangle	rectángulo *nm*
rhombus	rombo *nm*
trapezoid	trapecio *nm*
radian	radián *nm*

— parts of figures —

altitude	altura *nf*
angle	ángulo *nm*
apex B	ápice *nm*
apothem	apotema *nf*
arc	arco *nm*
axis	eje(*nm*)
bisection	bisección *nf*
bisector	bisector, bisectriz *nm, nf*
center A	centro *nm*
chord	cuerda *nf*
circumference	circunferencia *nf*
curve	curva *nf*
diameter	diámetro *nm*
evolute	evoluta *nf*
hypotenuse	hipotenusa *nf*
involute	involuta *nf*
line	línea *nf*
node	nodo *nm*
octant	octante *nm*

description

circumscribed	circunscrito *aj*
contiguous	contiguo *aj*
geometric(al)	geométrico *aj*
Pythagorean (theorem)	pitagórico *aj*
angular	angular *aj*
circular	circular *aj*
collinear	colineal *aj*
concentric	concéntrico *aj*
congruent	congruente *aj*
coplanar	coplanario *aj*
curved	curvo *aj*
curvilinear	curvilíneo *aj*

cylindrical	cilíndrico *aj*
diagonal	diagonal *aj, nf*
eccentric	excéntrico *aj*
helical	helicoida *aj*
hexagonal	hexagonal *aj*
horizontal	horizontal *aj, nf*
linear	lineal *aj*
normal	normal *aj*
oblique	oblicuo *aj*
oblong	oblongo *aj, nm*
octagonal	octagonal *aj*
oval	oval, ovalado *aj*
parabolic	parabólico *aj*
perpendicular	perpendicular *aj, nf*
quadrangular	cuadrangular *aj*
rectangular	rectangular *aj*
rectilinear	rectilinear *aj*
regular	regular *aj*
rhombic	rombal, rómbico *aj*
semicircular	semicircular *aj*
similar	similar *aj*
symmetrical	simétrico *aj*
tangential	tangencial *aj*
tetrahedral	tetraédrico *aj*
transverse	tra(n)sverso *aj*
triangular	triangular *aj*
trilateral	trilateral *aj*
unidirectional	unidireccional *aj*

TERMS IN STATISTICS

correlation	correlación *nf*
covariance	covariancia *nf*
dependent	dependiente *aj*
deviation	desviación *nf*
extrapolation	extrapolación *nf*
frequency	frecuencia *nf*
independent	independiente *aj*
interpolation	interpolación *nf*
margin of error	margen de error *nm*
median (number)	mediano *aj*
percentile	percentil *nm*
population	población *nf*
quartile	cuartil *nm*
regression	regresión *nf*
variance	variancia *nf*

TERMS IN TRIGONOMETRY

cosecant	cosecante *nf*
cosine	coseno *nm*
cotangent	cotangente *nf*
sine	seno *nm*
spherical	esférico *aj*

TOOLS

abacus Ⓑ	ábaco *nm*
calculator	calculadora *nf*
computer	computadora *nf*
counter	contador *nm*
graph	gráfica *nf*
table	tabla *nf*

(*See also* **scientists** under **ANCIENT CIVILIZATIONS**)

PHYSICS

GENERAL TERMS

activity	actividad *nf*
atmosphere	atmósfera *nf*
component	componente *aj, nm*
cosmos	cosmos *nm*
crystal	cristal *nm*
dimension	dimensión *nf*
electric	eléctrico *aj*
element	elemento *nm*
energy	energía *nf*
ether (obs)	éter *nm*
flux	flujo *nm*
formula Ⓑ	fórmula *nf*
gas	gas *nm*
gravity	gravedad *nf*
impact	impacto *nm*
ion	ion *nm*
liquid	líquido *aj, nm*
magnetic	magnético *aj*
mass	masa *nf*
matter	materia *nf*
metal	metal *nm*
molecule	molécula *nf*
motion	moción *nf*
number	número *nm*
pressure	presión *nf*
property	propiedad *nf*
reaction	reacción *nf*
relativity	relatividad *nf*
saturation	saturación *nf*
semiconductor	semiconductor *nm*
solid	sólido *nm*
sound	son, sonido *nm*
space	espacio *nm*
space-time	espacio-tiempo *nm*
stability	estabilidad *nf*
structure	estructura *nf*
temperature	temperatura *nf*
time	tiempo *nm*
transformation	tra(n)sformación *nf*
universe	universo *nm*

BRANCHES OF PHYSICS

major fields

acoustics	acústica *nf*
atomic	atómico *aj*
biophysics	biofísica *nf*
cryogenics	criogenia *nf*
electromagnetism	electromagnetismo *nm*
geophysics	geofísica *nf*
mathematical	matemático *aj*
mechanics	mecánica *nf*
molecular (physics)	molecular *aj*
nuclear (physics)	nuclear *aj*
optics	óptica *nf*
particle	partícula *nf*
plasma	plasma *nm*
quantum (physics)	cuántico *aj*
solid-state	estado sólido *nm*
thermodynamics	termodinámica *nf*

subfields

astronomy	astronomía *nf*
astrophysics	astrofísica *nf*
cosmology	cosmología *nf*
crystallography	cristalografía *nf*
electricity	electricidad *nf*
electrodynamics	electrodinámica *nf*
electrokinetics	electrocinética *nf*
electronics	electrónica *nf*
energetics	energética *nf*
hydrodynamics	hidrodinámica *nf*
hydrostatics	hidrostática *nf*
kinematics	cinemática *nf*
kinetics	cinética *nf*
micrography	micrografía *nf*
micrometry	micrometría *nf*
microscopy	microscopia, microscopía *nf*
pneumatics	neumática *nf*
radiography	radiografía *nf*
spectroscopy	espectroscopia *nf*
thermography	termografía *nf*

TERMS IN MECHANICS

subfields

aerodynamics	aerodinámica *nf*
ballistics	balística *nf*
dynamics	dinámica *nf*
fluid (mechanics)	fluido *aj, nm*
hydraulics	hidráulica *nf*
statics	estática *nf*

other terms

absolute	absoluto *aj*
acceleration	aceleración *nf*
adhesion	adhesión *nf*
angular	angular *aj*
capillarity	capilaridad *nf*
centrifugal	centrífugo *aj*
centripetal	centrípeto *aj*
circumvolution	circunvolución *nf*
coherence	coherencia *nf*
cohesion	cohesión *nf*
cohesive	cohesivo *aj*
collision	colisión *nf*
convection	convección *nf*
deceleration	deceleración *nf*
decompression	descompresión *nf*
efficiency	eficiencia *nf*
effort	esfuerzo *nm*
equilibrium	equilibrio *nm*
force	fuerza *nf*
friction	fricción *nf*
fulcrum Ⓑ	fulcro *nm*
gradient	gradiente *nm*
gravitation	gravitación *nf*
impact	impacto *nm*
impetus	ímpetu *nm*
impulse	impulso *nm*
inclination	inclinación *nf*
inclined (plane)	inclinado *aj*
inelastic	inelástico *aj*
kinematic	cinemático *aj*
kinetic	cinético *aj*
laminar	laminar *aj*
metacenter	metacentro *nm*
modulus Ⓑ	módulo *nm*
moment	momento *nm*
momentum	momento *nm*
Newtonian	newtoniano, neutoniano *aj*
osmosis	osmosis *nf*
pendulum	péndulo *nm*
percussion	percusión *nf*
pneumatic	neumático *aj*
position	posición *nf*
potential	potencial *nm*
precession	precesión *nf*
projectile	proyectil *nm*
rotation	rotación *nf*
torsion	torsión *nf*
trajectory	trayectoria *nf*
vacuum	vacío *nm*
velocity	velocidad *nf*
volume	volumen *nm*

TERMS IN THERMODYNAMICS

convection	convección *nf*
cryostat	criostato *nm*
enthalpy	entalpia *nf*
entropy	entropía *nf*
evaporation	evaporación *nf*
isotherm	isoterma *nf*
isothermal	isotermo, isotérmico *aj*
precipitation	precipitación *nf*
solution	solución *nf*
thermodynamic	termodinámico *aj*
vaporization Ⓐ	vaporización *nf*
vapor Ⓐ	vapor *nm*

TERMS IN WAVE PHYSICS

acoustics

acoustic(al)	acústico *aj*
echo Ⓑ	eco *nm*
harmonics	armonía *nfsg*
hypersonic	hipersónico *aj*
infrasonic	infrasónico *aj*
infrasound	infrasonido *nm*
rarefaction	rarefacción *nf*
repercussion	repercusión *nf*
reverberation	reverberación *nf*
sonic	sónico *aj*
subsonic	subsónico *aj*
supersonic	supersónico *aj*
ultrasonic	ultrasónico *aj*
ultrasonics	ultraacústica *nf*

optics

aberrant	aberrante *aj*
aberration	aberración *nf*
achromatic	acromático *aj*
achromatism	acromatismo *nm*
birefringence	birrefringencia *nf*
concave	cóncavo *aj*
concave-convex	cóncavo-convexo *aj*
concavity	concavidad *nf*
convergent	convergente *aj*
convex	convexo *aj*
convexity	convexidad *nf*
diffraction	difracción *nf*
diffusion	difusión *nf*
dispersion	dispersión *nf*
distortion	distorsión *nf*
divergent	divergente *aj*
fluorescence	fluorescencia *nf*
fluorescent	fluorescente *aj*
focal	focal *aj*
focus Ⓑ	foco *nm*

image	imagen *nf*
incidence	incidencia *nf*
infrared	infrarrojo *aj*
laser	láser *nm*
lens Ⓑ	lente *nm or nf*
luminance	luminancia *nf*
luminescence	luminescencia *nf*
luminescent	luminescente *aj*
magnification	magnificación *nf*
magnify	magnificar *vt*
meniscus Ⓑ	menisco *nm*
opacity	opacidad *nf*
optical	óptico *aj*
parallax	paralaje *nf*
photon	fotón *nm*
polarization	polarización *nf*
prism	prisma *nm*
prismatic	prismático *aj*
radiant	radiante *aj*
ray	rayo *nm*
reflectance	reflectancia *nf*
reflectivity	poder de reflexión *nm*
reflector	reflector *nm*
refracted	refracto *aj*
refraction	refracción *nf*
refractor	refractor *nm*
reticle	retícula *nf*
spectral	espectral *aj*
spectrogram	espectrograma *nm*
spectroscopic	espectroscópico *aj*
spectrum Ⓑ	espectro *nm*
stereoscope	estereoscopio *nm*
stereoscopic	estereoscópico *aj*
ultraviolet	ultravioleta *aj*
undulatory	ondulatorio, undulatorio *aj*
virtual	virtual *aj*

terms in common

absorption	absorción *nf*
amplitude	amplitud *nf*
frequency	frecuencia *nf*
intensity	intensidad *nf*
interference	interferencia *nf*
phase	fase *nf*
reflection	reflejo *nm*
transmittance	tra(n)smitencia *nf*
vibration	vibración *nf*

TERMS IN ELECTROMAGNETISM

antenna Ⓑ	antena *nf*
astatic	astático *aj*
attraction	atracción *nf*

capacitance	capacitancia *nf*	antiproton	antiprotón *nm*
charge	carga *nf*	atom	átomo *nm*
conductive	conductivo *aj*	beta	beta *nf*
conductivity	conductibilidad *nf*	betatron	betatrón *nf*
conductor	conductor *nm*	bombardment	bombardeo *nm*
diamagnetic	diamagnético *aj*	capture	captura *nf*
dielectric	dieléctrico *aj*	cosmic	cósmico *aj*
dipole	dipolo *nm*	critical	crítico *aj*
domain	dominio *nm*	decay	desintegración *nm*
electroacoustics	electroacústica *nf*	decontamination	descontaminación *nf*
electrodynamic	electrodinámico *aj*	deuteron	deuterón *nm*
electrokinetics	electrocinética *nf*	disintegration	desintegración *nf*
electromagnetic	electromagnético *aj*	electrode	electrodo *nm*
electromotive	electromotriz *aj*	electron volt	electronvoltio *nm*
electrophysiology	electrofisiología *nf*	emission	emisión *nf*
electropositive	electropositivo *aj*	enriched	enriquecido *aj*
electrostatic	electrostático *aj*	enrichment	enriquecimiento *nm*
electrostatics	electrostática *nf*	excite	excitar *aj*
ferromagnetic	ferromagnético *aj*	fission	fisión *nf*
Hertzian	herziano *aj*	fissionable	fisible *aj*
inductance	inductancia *nf*	fusion	fusión *nf*
induction	inducción *nf*	irradiation	irradiación *nf*
inductor	inductor *nm*	isomer	isómero *nm*
insulation	aislamiento *nm*	isomeric	isómero *aj*
insulator	aislador, aislante *nm*	isomerism	isomería *nf*
magnetism	magnetismo *nm*	isotope	isótopo *nm*
magnetization	magnetización *nf*	moderator	moderator *nm*
medium Ⓑ	medio *nm*	neutron	neutrón *nm*
negative	negativo *aj*	nucleon	nucleón *nm*
neutral	neutro *aj*	nucleus Ⓑ	núcleo *nm*
oscillating	oscilador, oscilante *aj*	parity	paridad *nf*
paramagnetic	paramagnético *aj*	photodisintegration	fotodesintegración *nf*
permeability	permeabilidad *nf*	photoelectron	fotoelectrón *nm*
piezoelectricity	piezoelectricidad *nf*	pile	pila *nf*
pole	polo *nm*	proton	protón *nm*
positive	positivo *aj, nm*	quantum Ⓑ	cuanto, quántum *nm*
potential	potencial *nm*	radiance	radiancia *nf*
quadrupole	cuadrípolo *nm*	radiation	radiación *nf*
reluctance	reluctancia *nf*	radioactive	radiactivo, radioactivo *aj*
repulsion	repulsión *nf*	radioactivity	radi(o)actividad *nf*
resistance	resistencia *nf*	radioelement	radioelemento *nm*
resistivity	resistividad *nf*	radioisotope	radioisótopo *nm*
resistor	resistor *nm*	ray	rayo *nm*
superconductivity	superconductividad *nf*	ray	rayo *nm*
susceptibility	susceptibilidad *nf*	reactor	reactor *nm*
unipolar	unipolar *aj*	roentgen	roentgen *nm*
oscillation	oscilación *nf*	scintillation	centelleo *nm*
		subatomic	subatómico *aj*
		synchroton	sincrotrón *nm*

TERMS IN NUCLEAR PHYSICS

activation	activación *nf*	thermal	térmico *aj*
alpha	alfa *nf(el)*	thermonuclear	termonuclear *aj*
antiparticle	antipartícula *nf*	tracer	trazador *nm*

transmutation	tra(n)smutación *nf*
transuranic	tra(n)suránico *aj*
tritium	tritio *nm*
triton	tritón *nm*
unstable	inestable *aj*
explosion	explosión *nf*

TERMS IN PARTICLE PHYSICS

accelerator	acelerador *nm*
antimatter	antimateria *nf*
antineutrino	antineutrino *nm*
antineutron	antineutrón *nm*
electron	electrón *nm*
elementary	elemental *aj*
gamma	gamma *nf*
lepton	leptón *nm*
meson	mesón *nm*
monopole	monopolo *nm*
muon	muón *nm*
neutrino	neutrino *nm*
omega	omega *nf*
pion	pión *nm*
positron	positón, positrón *nm*
psi	psi *nf*
quark	quark *nm*
upsilon	ípsilon *nf*

TERMS IN SOLID-STATE PHYSICS

density	densidad *nf*
displacement	desplazamiento *nm*
ductility	ductilidad *nf*
elasticity	elasticidad *nf*
expansion	expansión *nf*
extension	extensión *nf*
flexibility	flexibilidad *nf*
inertia	inercia *nf*
malleability	maleabilidad *nf*
porosity	porosidad *nf*
specific gravity	peso específico *nm*
tenacity	tenacidad *nf*
viscosity	viscosidad *nf*

TOOLS AND EQUIPMENT

alidade	alidada *nf*
barometer	barómetro *nm*
bolometer	bolómetro *nm*
calorimeter	calorímetro *nm*
centrifuge	centrífuga, centrifugadora *nf*
counter	contador *nm*
cyclotron	ciclotrón *nm*

dynamometer	dinamómetro *nm*
electrometer	electrómetro *nm*
electroscope	electroscopio *nm*
galvanometer	galvanómetro *nm*
heliograph	heliógrafo *nm*
hydrometer	hidrómetro *nm*
hygrometer	higrómetro *nm*
interferometer	interferómetro *nm*
magnetometer	magnetómetro *nm*
manometer	manómetro *nm*
microscope	microscopio *nm*
oscillator	oscilador *nm*
oscillograph	oscilógrafo *nm*
oscilloscope	osciloscopio *nm*
photometer	fotómetro *nm*
piezometer	piezómetro *nm*
pyrometer	pirómetro *nm*
radiometer	radiómetro *nm*
spectrograph	espectrógrafo *nm*
spectrometer	espectrómetro *nm*
spectroscope	espectroscopio *nm*
thermograph	termógrafo *nm*
thermometer	termómetro *nm*
transducer	transductor *nm*
ultramicroscope	ultramicroscopio *nm*
detector	detector *nm*
diffuser	difusor *nm*
filter	filtro *nm*
liquefier	aparato de licuefacción *nm*
pulley	polea *nf*
siphon	sifón *nm*
spectrophotometer	espectrofotómetro *nm*
voltameter	voltámetro *nm*

MEASUREMENTS

subfields

calorimetry	calorimetría *nf*
photometry	fotometría *nf*
piezometry	piezometría *nf*
pyrometry	pirometría *nf*

units of measurement

angstrom	angstrom *nm*
bar	bar *nm*
candela	candela *nf*
Celsius	Celsio *nm*
centimeter Ⓐ	centímetro *nm*
coulomb	culombio *nm*
curie (unit)	curie *nm*
decibel	decibel *nm*
dyne	dina *nf*

electron-volt — electrón-voltio *nm*
erg (obs) — ergio *nm*
fermi — fermi *nm*
gauss — gauss *nm*
hertz Ⓑ — hertz, hertzio, hercio *nm*
joule — julio *nm*
kelvin — kelvin *nm*
kilocalorie — kilocaloría *nf*
kilohertz — kilohercio *nm*
  (abbr: kHz) Ⓑ
kilojoule — kilojulio *nm*
kilorad — kilorad *nm*
kiloton — kilotón *nm*
lumen Ⓑ — lumen *nm*
lux Ⓑ — lux *nm*
megacycle (obs) — megaciclo *nm*
megahertz — megahertzio *nm*
  (abbr: mHz)
megaton — megatón *nm*
megawatt — megavatio *nm*
meter Ⓐ — metro *nm*
micromillimeter (obs) — micromilímetro *nm*
millimeter Ⓐ — milímetro *nm*
nanometer Ⓐ — nanometro *nm*
newton — newtón, neutonio *nm*
phon — fon, fonio *nm*
phot — fot, fotio *nm*
poise — poise *nm*
rad — rad *nm*
watt — vatio *nm*
wattage — vataje *nm*
physicist — físico, -a *nmf*
distort — distorsionar *vt*

(*See also* MEASURING TOOLS under **MEASUREMENTS**)

CHEMISTRY

GENERAL TERMS

activity — actividad *nf*
anode — ánodo *nm*
catalyst — catalizador *nm*
cathode — cátodo *nm*
chemical — químico *aj, nm*
chemist — químico, -a *nmf*
composition — composición *nf*
equation — ecuación *nf*
equilibrium — equilibrio *nm*
formula Ⓑ — fórmula *nf*
fraction — fracción *nf*
group — grupo *nm*

homology — homología *nf*
isobar — isobara *nf*
mass — masa *nf*
mole — mol *nm*
number — número *nm*
orbit — órbita *nf*
periodic table — tabla periódica *nf*
product — producto *nm*
property — propiedad *nf*
qualitative — cualitativo *aj*
quantitative — cuantitativo *aj*
reaction — reacción *nf*
series Ⓑ — serie *nf*
state — estado *nm*
substance — sustancia *nf*
substrate — substrato *nm*
symbol — símbolo *nm*
valence — valencia *nf*

BRANCHES

major fields

analytical — analítico *aj*
inorganic — inorgánico *aj*
organic — orgánico *aj*
physical — físico *aj*
polymer — polímero *nm*
synthetic — sintético *aj*

interdisciplinary fields

biochemistry — bioquímica *nf*
electrochemistry — electroquímica *nf*
geochemistry — geoquímica *nf*
photochemistry — fotoquímica *nf*
radiochemistry — radioquímica *nf*
thermochemistry — termoquímica *nf*

other specializations

metallurgy — metalurgia *nf*
microchemistry — microquímica *nf*
stereochemistry — estereoquimica *nf*
zymology — cimología *nf*
zymurgy — cimurgia, zimurgia *nf*

BASIC CONCEPTS

components

atom — átomo *nm*
compound — compuesto *nm*
electron — electrón *nm*
element — elemento *nm*
ion — ion *nm*
molecule — molécula *nf*

neutron	neutrón *nm*
nucleus B	núcleo *nm*
proton	protón *nm*

composition

dyad	díada *nf*
monad	mónada *nf*
radiocarbon	radiocarbono *nm*
tetrad	tétrade *nm*

forms of matter

allotrope	forma alotrópica *nf*
crystal	cristal *nm*
crystaloid	cristaloide *nm*
gas	gas *nm*
gel	gel *nm*
liquid	líquido *nm*
phase	fase *nf*
solid	sólido *nm*

kinds of substances

additive	aditivo *aj, nm*
aerosol	aerosol *nm*
agent	agente *nm*
amphoteric	anfótero *aj*
antioxidant	antioxidante *nm*
concentrate	concentrado *nm*
cryogen	criógeno *nm*
derivative	derivado *nm*
enzyme	enzima *nf*
extract	extracto *nm*
ferment	fermento *nm*
flowers	flor *nf*
halogen	halógeno *nm*
inductor	inductor *nm*
inhibitor	inhibidor *nm*
isotope	isótopo *nm*
metal	metal *nm*
neutralizer	neutralizador *nm*
oxidant	oxidante *nm*
precipitate	precipitado *nm*
reactant	agente reactor
residue	residuo *nm*
resin	resina *nf*
saturant	substancia saturativa
solute	soluto *nm*

properties

acidity	acidez *nf*
alkalinity	alcalinidad *nf*
atomicity	atomicidad *nf*
basicity	basicidad *nf*
isomerism	isomería *nf*
isomorphism	isomorfismo *nm*

phosphorescence	fosforescencia *nf*
polymerism	polimerismo *nm*
polymorphism	polimorfismo *nm*
salinity	salinidad *nf*
solubility	solubilidad *nf*
volatility	volatilidad *nf*

other terms

equimolecular	equimolecular *aj*
exothermic	exotérmico *aj*
ferrous	ferroso *aj*
inert	inerte *aj*
linear	lineal *aj*
miscible	miscible *aj*
nascent	naciente *aj*
orthorhombic	otorrómbico *aj*
radioactive	radiactivo, radioactivo *aj*
reversible (reaction)	reversible *aj*
stability	estabilidad *nf*

CHEMICAL ELEMENTS

series

actinide	actínido *aj*
lanthanide	lantánido *aj*

gases

argon (Ar)	argón *nm*
chlorine (Cl)	cloro *nm*
fluorine (F)	flúoro *nm*
helium (He)	helio *nm*
hydrogen (H)	hidrógeno *nm*
krypton (Kr)	criptón *nm*
neon (Ne)	neón *nm*
nitrogen (N)	nitrógeno *nm*
oxygen (O)	oxígeno *nm*
radon (Rn)	radón *nm*
xenon (Xe)	xenón *nm*

radioactive metals

actinium (Ac)	actinio *nm*
astatine (At)	astatinio *nm*
berkelium (Bk)	berkelio *nm*
californium (Cf)	californio *nm*
curium (Cm)	curio *nm*
einsteinium (Es)	einstenio *nm*
fermium (Fm)	fermio *nm*
francium (Fr)	francio *nm*
lawrencium (Lr)	laurencio *nm*
nobelium (No)	nobelio *nm*
plutonium (Pu)	plutonio *nm*
polonium (Po)	polonio *nm*

promethium (Pm)	prometrio, prometeo, promecio *nm*
protactinium (Pa)	protactinio *nm*
radium (Ra)	radio *nm*
technetium (Tc)	tecnecio *nm*
thorium (Th)	torio *nm*
uranium (U)	uranio *nm*

rare-earth metals

americium (Am)	americio *nm*
cerium (Ce)	cerio *nm*
dysprosium (Dy)	disprosio *nm*
erbium (Er)	erbio *nm*
europium (Eu)	europio *nm*
gadolinium (Gd)	gadolinio *nm*
holmium (Ho)	holmio *nm*
lanthanum (La)	lantano *nm*
neodymium (Nd)	neodimio *nm*
praseodymium (Pr)	praseodimio *nm*
samarium (Sm)	samario *nm*
scandium (Sc)	escandio *nm*
terbium (Tb)	terbio *nm*
thulium (Tm)	tulio *nm*
ytterbium (Yb)	iterbio *nm*
yttrium (Y)	itrio *nm*

other metals

aluminum (Al) A	aluminio *nm*
antimony (Sb)	antimonio *nm*
arsenic (As)	arsénico *nm*
barium (Ba)	bario *nm*
bismuth (Bi)	bismuto *nm*
cadmium (Cd)	cadmio *nm*
calcium (Ca)	calcio *nm*
cesium (Cs) A	cesio *nm*
chromium (Cr)	cromo *nm*
cobalt (Co)	cobalto *nm*
copper (Cu)	cobre *nm*
gallium (Ga)	galio *nm*
germanium (Ge)	germanio *nm*
hafnium (Hf)	hafnio *nm*
indium (In)	indio *nm*
iridium (Ir)	iridio *nm*
lithium (Li)	litio *nm*
lutetium (Lu)	lutecio *nm*
magnesium (Mg)	magnesio *nm*
manganese (Mn)	manganeso *nm*
mendelevium (Md)	mendelevio *nm*
mercury (Hg)	mercurio *nm*
molybdenum (Mo)	molibdeno *nm*
neptunium (Np)	neptunio *nm*
nickel (Ni)	níquel *nm*
niobium (Nb)	niobio *nm*

osmium (Os)	osmio *nm*
palladium (Pd)	paladio *nm*
platinum (Pt)	platino *nm*
potassium (K)	potasio *nm*
rhenium (Re)	renio *nm*
rhodium (Rh)	rodio *nm*
rubidium (Rb)	rubidio *nm*
ruthenium (Ru)	rutenio *nm*
sodium (Na)	sodio *nm*
strontium (Sr)	estroncio *nm*
tantalum (Ta)	tantalio *nm*
thallium (Tl)	talio *nm*
titanium (Ti)	titanio *nm*
tungsten (W)	tungsteno *nm*
vanadium (V)	vanadio *nm*
zinc (Zn)	zinc, cinc *nm*
zirconium (Zr)	circonio, zirconio *nm*

other elements

beryllium (Be)	berilio *nm*
boron (B)	boro *nm*
bromine (Br)	bromo *nm*
carbon (C)	carbono *nm*
deuterium (D)	deuterio *nm*
hahnium (Ha)	hahnio *nm*
iodine (I)	yodo *nm*
magnesia (Mg)	magnesia *nf*
phosphorus (P)	fósforo *nm*
rutherfordium (Rf)	ruterfordio *nm*
selenium (Se)	selenio *nm*
silicon (Si)	silicio *nm*
sulfur (S) A	azufre *nm*
tellurium (Te)	telurio *nm*

CHEMICAL COMPOUNDS

types of compounds and mixtures

acid	ácido *nm*
aldehyde	aldehido *nm*
alloy	aleación *nf*
antifreeze	anticongelante *nm*
aromatic	aromático *aj*
base	base *nf*
binary	binario *aj*
carbide	carburo *nm*
carbohydrate	carbohidrato *nm*
carbonate	carbonato *nm*
chloride	cloruro *nm*
colloid	coloide *nm*
deodorizer	desodorante *nm*
electrolyte	electrólito *nm*
emulsion	emulsión *nf*
essence	esencia *nf*

ester	éster *nm*
hydrate	hidrato *nm*
hydrocarbon	hidrocarburo *nm*
hydroxide	hidróxido *nm*
ketone	quetona, cetona *nf*
monomer	monómero *nm*
nitrate	nitrato *nm*
nitrite	nitrito *nm*
oxide	óxido *nm*
petrochemical	petroquímico *nm*
phosphate	fosfato *nm*
ptomaine	(p)tomaína *nf*
radical	radical *nm*
salt	sal *nf*
soda	soda, sosa *nf*
solution	solución *nf*
solvent	solvente *nm*
sulfate Ⓐ	sulfato *nm*
sulfide Ⓐ	sulfuro *nm*
suspension	suspensión *nf*
tincture	tintura *nf*

inorganic compounds

anhydride	anhidrido *nm*
bichloride of mercury	bicloruro de mercurio *nm*
blue vitriol	vitriolo azul *nm*
borazon	borazón *nm*
ferrous sulfate Ⓐ	sulfato ferroso *nm*
hydrogen peroxide	peróxido de hidrógeno *nm*
mercuric oxide	óxido mercúrico *nm*
potash	potasa *nf*
silver nitrate	nitrato de plata *nm*
sulfur dioxide	dióxido de azufre *nm*
vitriol	vitriolo *nm*

organic compounds

acetaldehyde	acetaldehido *nm*
acetone	acetona *nf*
alcohol	alcohol *nm*
aliphatic	alifático *aj*
amide	amida *nf*
amine	amina *nf*
aniline	anilina *nf*
benzene	benceno *nm*
benzine	bencina *nf*
bicarbonate of soda	bicarbonato de sodio/sosa *nm*
butane	butano *nm*
calcium carbide	carburo de calcio *nm*
calcium carbonate	carbonato de calcio *nm*
camphor	alcanfor *nm*

chloral hydrate	hidrato de cloral *nm*
chlorofluorocarbon	clorofluorocarbono *nm*
chloroform	cloroformo *nm*
collodion	colodión *nm*
cream of tartar	cremor tártaro *nm*
creosol	creosol *nm*
cyclic, cyclical	cíclico *aj*
dextrose	dextrosa *nf*
dioxin	dióxina *nf*
diphenyl	difenilo *nm*
enol	enol *nm*
ethanol	etanol *nm*
ether	éter *nm*
ethyl	etilo *nm*
ethylene	etileno *nm*
fluorocarbon	fluorocarburo *nm*
formalin	formalina *nf*
furfural	furfural, furfuro *nm*
glucose	glucosa *nf*
glycogen	glicógeno *nm*
glycol	glicol *nm*
indamine	indamina *nf*
indigo Ⓑ	índigo *nm*
isomer	isómero *nm*
ligroin	ligroína *nf*
maltose	maltosa *nf*
menthol	mentol *nm*
methanol	metanol *nm*
methyl	metilo *nm*
naphthalene	naftalina *nf*
naphthol	naftol *nm*
nicotine	nicotina *nf*
nitrocellulose	nitrocelulosa *nf*
octane	octano *nm*
olein	oleína *nf*
paraffin	parafina *nf*
parathion	paratión *nm*
pentane	pentano *nm*
phenol	fenol *nm*
phenolphthalein	fenolftaleína *nf*
phosgene	fosgeno *nm*
phosphine	fosfina *nf*
propane	propano *nm*
resorcinol, resorcin	resorcinol, resorcina *nm, nf*
rotenone	rotenona *nf*
saccharide	sacárido *nm*
saccharin(e)	sacarina *nf*
sal ammoniac	sal amoníaco *nm*
stearin	estearina *nf*
sterol	esterol *nm*
tannin	tanino *nm*
toluene	tolueno *nm*

urea	urea *nf*
urethane	uretano *nm*
vanillin	vainillina *nf*
vitamins	vitaminas *nfpl*
xylene	xileno *nm*

acids

acetic	acético *aj*
acetylsalicylic	acetilosalicílico *aj*
amino acid	aminoácido *nm*
ascorbic	ascórbico *aj*
boric	bórico *aj*
carbolic	carbólico *aj*
chloric	clórico *aj*
citric	cítrico *aj*
formic	fórmico *aj*
gallic	gálico *aj*
hydrochloric	clorhídrico *aj*
hydrocyanic	hidrociánico *aj*
hydrofluoric	fluorhídrico *aj*
hypochlorous	hipocloroso *aj*
lactic	láctico *aj*
lysergic	lisérgico *aj*
muriatic	muriático *aj*
nicotinic	nicotínico *aj*
nitric	nítrico *aj*
nucleic	nucleico *aj*
oxalic	oxálico *aj*
pantothenic	pantoténico *aj*
pectic	péctico *aj*
phosphoric	fosfórico *aj*
picric	pícrico *aj*
prussic	prúsico *aj*
salicylic	salicílico *aj*
sorbic	sórbico *aj*
stearic	esteárico *aj*
sulfuric Ⓐ	sulfúrico *aj*
tannic	tánico *aj*
tartaric	tartaro *aj*
uric	úrico *aj*
xanthic	xántico *aj*

bases

alkali Ⓑ	álcali *nm*
alkaloid	alcaloide *nm*
caustic	cáustico *aj, nm*
hydrazine	hidrazina *nf*
lye	lejía *nf*

salts

alum	alumbre *nm*
benzoate	benzoato *nm*
bicarbonate	bicarbonato *nm*

bisulfate	bisulfato *nm*
borax	bórax *nm*
bromide	bromuro *nm*
chlorate	clorato *nm*
citrate	citrato *nm*
cyanide	cianuro *nm*
cyclamate	ciclamato *nm*
dichloride	bicloruro *nm*
disulfide	disulfuro *nm*
fluoride	fluoruro *nm*
fulminate	fulminato *nm*
glutamate	glutamato *nm*
glyceride	glicérido *nm*
hydride	hidruro *nm*
hydrochloride	clorhidrato *nm*
iodide	yoduro *nm*
lactate	lactato *nm*
manganate	manganato *nm*
methylate	metilato *nm*
nitrous	nitroso *aj*
permanganate	permanganato *nm*
salicylate	salicilato *nm*
silicate	silicato *nm*
stearate	estearato *nm*
sulfite Ⓐ	sulfito *nm*
sulfonamide Ⓐ	sulfonamida *nf*
sulfurous Ⓐ	sulfuroso *aj*
superphosphate	superfosfato *nm*
tartrate	tartrato *nm*
tetrachloride	tetracloruro *nm*
trichloride	tricloruro *nm*
triphosphate	trifosfato *nm*
trisulfide	trisulfuro *nm*
urate	urato *nm*
xanthate	xantato *nm*

gases

acetylene	acetilénico *aj*
ammonia	amoníaco *nm*
carbon dioxide	bióxido de carbono *nm*
carbon monoxide	monóxido de carbono *nm*
cyanogen	cianógeno *nm*
ethane	etano *nm*
formaldehyde	formaldehido *nm*
methane	metano *nm*
oxyacetylene	oxiacetilénico *aj*
ozone	ozono *nm*

alkaloids

atropine	atropina *nf*
caffein(e)	cafeína *nf*
cocain(e)	cocaína *nf*

mescaline	mescalina *nf*
morphine	morfina *nf*
quinine	quinina *nf*
strychnine	estricnina *nf*

saccharides

fructose	fructosa *nf*
monosaccharide	monosacárido *nm*
polysaccharide	polisacárido *nm*

oxides

alumina	alúmina *nf*
calamine	calamina *nf*
dioxide	dióxido *nm*
ferric	férrico *aj*
monoxide	monóxido *nm*
peroxide	peróxido *nm*
trioxide	trióxido *nm*

radicals

acetyl	acetilo *nm*
alkyl	alquilo *nm*
ammonium	amonio *nm*
amyl	amilo *nm*
anion	anión *nm*
cation	catión *nm*
phenyl	fenilo *nm*
propyl	propilo *nm*

synthetics

acetate	acetato *nm*
acrylic	acrílico *aj*
cellophane Ⓐ	celofán *nm*
celluloid	celuloide *nm*
Formica	formica *nf*
linoleum	linóleo *nm*
Lucite	lucita *nf*
melamine	melamina *nf*
neoprene	neopreno *nm*
nylon	nilón *nm*
olefin	olefina *nf*
polyester	poliester *nm*
polyethylene	polietileno *nm*
polyurethane	poliuretano *nm*
polyvinyl	polivinilo *nm*
rayon	rayón *nm*
silicone	silicón, silicona *nm, nf*
styrene	estireno *nm*
vinyl	vinilo *nm*

commercial products

Benzedrine	bencedrina *nf*
Carborundum	carborundo *nm*
Dacron	dacrón *nm*
Freon	freón *nm*
Malathion	Malatión *nm*
Orlon	orlón *nm*
Phenobarbital	fenobarbital *nm*
Plexiglas	plexiglas *nm*
Saran	sarán *nm*
Teflon	teflón *nm*

PROCESSES, REACTIONS, TESTS

absorption	absorción *nf*
activation	activación *nf*
adsorption	adsorción *nf*
aeration	aeración *nf*
alkalinization	alcalinización *nf*
amalgamation	amalgamación *nf*
analysis Ⓑ	análisis Ⓒ *nm*
assay	ensaye *nm*
calcination	calcinación *nf*
carbonation, carbonization	carbonización *nf*
catalysis	catálisis *nf*
chlorination	clorinación *nf*
chromatography	cromatografía *nf*
combination	combinación *nf*
combustion	combustión *nf*
contamination	contaminación *nf*
corrosion	corrosión *nf*
cracking	craqueo *nm*
crystallization	cristalización *nf*
decomposition	descomposición *nf*
deflagration	deflagración *nf*
degradation	degradación *nf*
dehydration	deshidratación *nf*
dehydrogenation	deshidrogenación *nf*
denaturation	desnaturalización *nf*
deoxidization	desoxidación *nf*
digestion	digestión *nf*
dissociation	disociación *nf*
dissolution	disolución *nf*
distillation	destilación *nf*
efflorescence	eflorescencia *nf*
electroanalysis	electroanálisis *nf*
electrodialysis	electrodiálisis *nf*
electrolysis	electrólisis *nf*
electrophoresis	electroforesia *nf*
electrosynthesis	electrosíntesis *nf*
emanation	emanación *nf*
emulsification	emulsificación *nf*
fermentation	fermentación *nf*
filtration	filtración *nf*
fixation	fijación *nf*
flotation	flotación *nf*

fluoridation	fluorización *nf*
fractionation	fraccionamiento *nm*
fulmination	fulminación *nf*
fumigation	fumigación *nf*
galvanization	galvanización *nf*
gasification	gasificación *nf*
gelation	gelificación *nf*
homogenization	homogeneización *nf*
hydration	hidratación *nf*
hydrogenation	hidrogenación *nf*
hydrolysis	hidrólisis *nf*
inversion	inversión *nf*
ionization	ionización *nf*
liberation	liberación *nf*
microanalysis	microanálisis *nf*
neutralization	neutralización *nf*
nitrification	nitrificación *nf*
occlusion	oclusión *nf*
oxidation	oxidación *nf*
oxygenation	oxigenación *nf*
pasteurization	past(e)urización *nf*
photolysis	fotólisis *nf*
polymerization	polimerización *nf*
precipitation	precipitación *nf*
pyrolysis	pirólisis *nf*
rectification	rectificación *nf*
reduction	reducción *nf*
regelation	regelación *nf*
replacement	reemplazo *nm*
saponification	saponificación *nf*
separation	separación *nf*
sublimation	sublimación *nf*
synthesis B	síntesis C *nf*
transmutation	tra(s)mutación *nf*
vitrification	vitrificación *nf*
volatilization	volatilización *nf*
vulcanization	vulcanización *nf*

TOOLS AND EQUIPMENT

apparatus B	aparato *nm*
aspirator	aspirador *nm*
atomizer	atomizador *nm*
balance	balanza *nf*
buret, burette	bureta *nf*
centrifuge	centrífuga, centrifugadora *nf*
indicator	indicador *nm*
pipet, pipette	pipeta *nf*
receiver	recipiente *nm*
reductor	reductor *nm*
retort	retorta *nf*
test tube	tubo de ensayo *nm*

HISTORICAL TERMS

alchemist	alquimista *nmf*
alchemy	alquimia *nf*
choler	cólera *nf*
elixir	elíxir *nm*
phlogiston	flogisto *nm*
sylph	sílfide *nf*
wolfram (= tungsten)	volframio *nm*

USES AND PRODUCTS

distillate	destilado *nm*
agriculture	agricultura *nf*
alloys	aleaciones *nfpl*
batteries	baterías *nfpl*
beverage	bebida *nf*
construction	construcción *nf*
cosmetics	cosméticos *nmpl*
defoliant	defoliante *nm*
detergents	detergentes *nmpl*
drugs	drogas *nfpl*
electronics	electrónica *nf*
explosives	explosivos *nmpl*
fertilizers	fertilizantes *nmpl*
fibers A	fibras *nfpl*
fumigant	substancia fumigatoria
fungicide	fungicida *nm*
herbicide	herbicida *nm*
insecticide	insecticida *nm*
medicines	medicinas *nfpl*
naphtha	nafta *nf*
paint	pintura *nf*
paper	papel *nm*
plastics	plásticos *nmpl*
synthetics	sintéticos *nmpl*

(*See also* **alloys and metalic substances** under **METALLURGY**; *BIOCHEMICALS* under **THE HUMAN BODY**)

ASTRONOMY

GENERAL TERMS

astronomy	astronomía *nf*
cosmos	cosmos *nm*
cycle	ciclo *nm*
distance	distancia *nf*
ether (obs)	éter *nm*
firmament (poetic)	firmamento *nm*
gravitation	gravitación *nf*
macrocosm	macrocosmo *nm*
microcosm	microcosmo *nm*
movement	movimiento *nm*

observatory	observatorio *nm*
period	período *nm*
planetarium	planetario *nm*
solar system	sistema solar *nm*
space	espacio *nm*
sphere	esfera *nf*
telescope	telescopio *nm*
universe	universo *nm*
zodiac	zodíaco *nm*

SPECIALIZATIONS

astrobiology	astrobiología *nf*
astrophysics	astrofísica *nf*
cosmogony	cosmogonía *nf*
cosmography	cosmografía *nf*
cosmology	cosmología *nf*
exobiology	biología espacial *nf*
radio astronomy	radioastronomía *nf*
telemetry	telemetría *nf*

DESCRIPTION AND CLASSIFICATION

heavenly bodies

asteroid	asteroide *nm*
comet	cometa *nm*
constellation	constelación *nf*
galaxy	galaxia *nf*
luminary	luminar *nm*
meteor	metéoro, meteoro *nm*
meteoroid, meteorite	meteorito *nm*
nebula ⓑ	nebulosa *nf*
orb	orbe *nm*
planet	planeta *nm*
pulsar	púlsar *nm*
quasar	cuásar *nm*
satellite	satélite *nm*

types of stars

binary	binario *aj*
double	doble *aj*
fixed	fijo *aj*
giant	gigantesco *aj*
magnitude	magnitud *nf*
neutron	neutrón *nm*
nova ⓑ	nova *nf*
supernova	supernova *nf*
variable	variable *aj*
meridian	meridiano *nm*

movement, distance, position

aberration	aberración *nf*
aphelion	afelio *nm*
apogee	apogeo *nm*
apsides	ápsides *nmpl*
ascent (sun, moon)	ascenso *nm*
conjunction	conjunción *nf*
declination	declinación *nf*
eclipse	eclipse *nm*
ecliptic	eclíptica *nf*
epicycle	epiciclo *nm*
magnetosphere	magnetoesfera *nf*
nadir	nadir *nm*
node	nodo *nm*
nutation	nutación *nf*
occultation	ocultación *nf*
octant	octante *nm*
opposition	oposición *nf*
orbit	órbita *nf*
parallax	paralaje *nf*
perigee	perigeo *nm*
perihelion	perihelio *nm*
perturbation	perturbación *nf*
precession	precesión *nf*
quadrature	cuadratura *nf*
retrograde	retrógrado *aj*
revolution	revolución *nf*
solstice	solsticio *nm*
transit	tránsito *nm*
tropic	trópico *nm*
variation	variación *nf*
zenith	cénit *nm*

visual phenomena

aura	aura *nf(el)*
aureole	aureola *nf*
aurora	aurora *nf*
corona ⓑ	corona *nf*
halo ⓑ	halo *nm*
penumbra ⓑ	penumbra *nf*
phase	fase *nf*

other terms

annular	anular *aj*
astral	astral *aj*
celestial	celeste *aj*
intergalactic	intergaláctico *aj*
interplanetary	interplanetario *aj*
interstellar	interestelar *aj*
luminosity	luminosidad *nf*
lunar	lunar *aj*
lunisolar	lunisolar *aj*
photosphere	fotosfera *nf*
Ptolemaic	tolemaico *aj*
stellar	estelar *aj*

NAMES

planets

Jupiter	Júpiter *nm*
Mars	Marte *nm*
Mercury	Mercurio *nm*
Neptune	Neptuno *nm*
Pluto	Plutón *nm*
Saturn	Saturno *nm*
Uranus	Urano *nm*
Venus	Venus *nf*

stars

Arcturus	Arturo *nm*
Betelgeuse	Betelgeuse *nm*
Canopus	Canopo *nm*
Polaris	estrella polar *nf*
Pollux	Pólux *nm*
Regulus	Régulus *nm*
Sirius	Sirio *nm*
Vega	Vega *nf*

constellations

Alpha	Alfa *nf*
Andromeda	Andrómeda *nf*
Aquarius	Acuario *nm*
Aries	Aries *nm*
Cancer	Cáncer *nm*
Canis Major	Can Mayor *nm*
Canis Minor	Can Menor *nm*
Capricorn	Capricornio *nm*
Cassiopeia	Casiopea *nf*
Centaurus	Centauro *nm*
Cygnus	Cisne *nm*
Dragon, Draco	Dragón *nm*
Gemini	Géminis *nmpl*
Hercules	Hércules *nm*
Leo	Leo *nm*
Libra	Libra *nf*
Lion	León, Leo *nm*
Lyra	Lira *nf*
Orion	Orión *nm*
Pegasus	Pegaso *nm*
Perseus	Perseo *nm*
Phoenix	ave fénix *nm*
Pisces	Piscis *nm*
Pleiades	Pléyades *nmpl*
Sagittarius	Sagitario *nm*
Scorpius	Escorpión *nm*
Southern Cross	Cruz del Sur *nf*
Taurus	Tauro *nm*
Virgo	Virgo *nm*

asteroids and satellites

Ceres	Ceres *nf*
Eros	Eros *nm*
Ganymede	Ganimedes *nm*
Hyperion	Hiperión *nm*
Io	Io *nf*
Phobos	Fobos *nm*
Phoebe	Febe *nf*
Rhea	Rea *nf*
Titan	Titán *nm*
Triton	Tritón *nm*

TOOLS AND MEASUREMENTS

types of telescopes

optical	óptico *aj*
radiotelescope	radiotelescopio *nm*
reflecting	reflector *aj*
refracting	refractor *aj*

other terms

alidade	alidada *nf*
astrolabe	astrolabio *nm*
azimuth	acimut, azimut *nm*
ephemeris Ⓑ	efemérides *nf*
epoch	época *nf*
parsec	parsec *nm*
spectrometer	espectrómetro *nm*
spectroscope	espectroscopio *nm*
spectrum Ⓑ	espectro *nm*

PERSONS

astronomer	astrónomo, -a *nmf*
astrophysicist	astrofísico, -a *nmf*
Copernicus	Copérnico *nm*
cosmographer	cosmógrafo, -a *nmf*
cosmologist	cosmólogo, -a *nmf*
Galileo	Galileo *nm*

(*See also* **scientists** under **ANCIENT CIVILIZATIONS**; *TERMS IN SPACE TRAVEL* under **AVIATION AND SPACE TRAVEL**)

GEOLOGY

GENERAL TERMS

deposit	depósito *nm*
eon	eón *nm*
epoch	época *nf*
era	era *nf*
fault	falta *nf*
formation	formación *nf*

fossil	fósil *aj, nm*
geology	geología *nf*
gneiss	gneis *nm*
period	período *nm*
rock	roca *nf*
schist	esquisto *nm*
sediment	sedimento *nm*
stratum Ⓑ	estrato *nm*
substratum Ⓑ	sustrato *nm*
superstratum Ⓑ	superestrato *nm*
volcano Ⓑ	volcán *nm*

SPECIALIZATIONS

geochemistry	geoquímica *nf*
geochronology	geocronología *nf*
geochronometry	geocronometría *nf*
geodesy	geodesia *nf*
geodynamics	geodinámica *nf*
geognosy	geognosia *nf*
geomorphology	geomorfología *nf*
geophysics	geofísica *nf*
glaciology	glaciología *nf*
paleontology	paleontología *nf*
petrography	petrografía *nf*
petrology	petrología *nf*
physiography	fisiografía *nf*
radiogeology	radiogeología *nf*
seismology	sismología *nf*
speleology	espeleología *nf*
tectonics	tectónica *nf*
topography	topografía *nf*
volcanology, vulcanology	vulcanología *nf*

HISTORICAL DIVISIONS

eras

Archeozoic	arqueozoico *aj*
Azoic	azoico *aj*
Cenozoic	cenozoico *aj*
Mesozoic	mesozoico *aj*
Neolithic	neolítico *aj*
Paleolithic	paleolítico *aj*
Paleozoic	paleozoico *aj*
Precambrian	precámbrico *aj*

periods

Cambrian	cámbrico, cambriano *aj*
Carboniferous	carbonífero *aj*
Cretaceous	cretáceo *aj*
Devonian	devoniano, devónico *aj*
Jurassic	jurásico *aj*

Laurentian	larentino *aj*
Ordovician	ordovícico, ordovicence *aj*
Permian	pérmico *aj*
Quaternary	cuaternario *aj*
Silurian	siluriano, silúrico *aj*
Tertiary	terciario *aj*
Triassic	triásico *aj*

epochs

Miocene	mioceno *aj*
Pleistocene	pleistoceno *aj*
Pliocene	plioceno *aj*
Recent	reciente *aj*
Proterozoic	proterozoico *aj*

DESCRIPTION

geological formations

abyss	abismo *nm*
anticline	anticlinal *nm*
batholith	batolito *nm*
canyon	cañón *nm*
cave	cueva *nf*
cirque	circo *nm*
cleavage	clivaje *nm*
defile	desfiladero *nm*
dike	dique *nm*
escarpment	escarpa, escarpadura *nf*
fissure	fisura *nf*
fulgurite	fulturita *nf*
geode	geoda *nf*
geyser	géiser, géyser *nm*
glacier	glaciar *nm*
lamina Ⓑ	lámina *nf*
mantle	manto *nm*
mountain	montaña *nf*
nodule	nódulo *nm*
stalactite	estalactita *nf*
stalagmite	estalagmita *nf*
syncline	sinclinical *nm*
valley	valle *nm*

deposits

accretion	acrecencia *nf*
aggregate	agregado *nm*
alluvium Ⓑ	aluvión *nm*
loess	loes *nm*
moraine	morrena, morena *nf*

other descriptive terms

basic (rock)	básico *aj*
conglomerate	conglomerado *aj*

erratic	errático *aj*
facies B	facies *nf*
geomorphic	geomórfico *aj*
geothermal	geotérmico *aj*
igneous	ígneo *aj*
metamorphic	metamórfico *aj*
orthorhombic	otorrómbico *aj*
petrified	petrificado *aj*
petrous	pétreo *aj*
primary	primario *aj*
primitive	primario *aj*
rocky	rocoso *aj*
salic	sálico *aj*
saliferous	salífero *aj*
saturated	saturado *aj*
sedimentary	sedimentario *aj*
seismic	sísmico *aj*
stratified	estratificado *aj*
tectonic	tectónico *aj*
volcanic	volcánico *aj*

EARTHQUAKES AND VOLCANOES

crater	cráter *nm*
epicenter	epicentro *nm*
eruption	erupción *nf*
fumarole	fumarola *nf*
hypocenter	hipocentro *nm*
lava	lava *nf*
magma B	magma *nm*
Richter scale	escala Richter *nf*
seismograph	sismógrafo *nm*
seismometer	sismómetro *nm*
tremor	temblor *nm*

GEOLOGICAL PROCESSES

abrasion	abrasión *nf*
agglomeration	aglomeración *nf*
crystallization	cristalización *nf*
deformation	deformación *nf*
disintegration	desintegración *nf*
displacement	desplazamiento *nm*
erosion	erosión *nf*
fossilization	fosilización *nf*
glaciation	glaciación *nf*
intrusion	intrusión *nf*
lamination	laminación *nf*
metamorphism	metamorfismo *nm*
mineralization	mineralización *nf*
sedimentation	sedimentación *nf*
stratification	estratificación *nf*
volcanism	volcanismo, vulcanismo *nm*

PERSONS

geologist	geólogo, -a *nmf*
geophysicist	geofísico, -a *nmf*
paleontologist A	paleontólogo, -a *nmf*
speleologist	espeleólogo, -a *nmf*
volcanologist, vulcanologist	vulcanólogo, -a *nmf*

(*See also* ROCKS AND MINERALS under **MINERALS AND MINING**)

METEOROLOGY
GENERAL TERMS

air	aire *nm*
climate	clima *nm*
clime (poetic)	clima *nm*
direction	dirección *nf*
elements	elementos *nmpl*
equinox	equinoccio *nm*
front	frente *nm*
pattern	patrón *nm*
prediction	predicción *nf*
prognostication	pronóstico *nm*
solstice	solsticio *nm*
zone	zona *nf*

FIELDS OF SPECIALIZATION

aerology	aerología *nf*
bioclimatology	bioclimatología *nf*
climatology	climatología *nf*
meteorology	meteorología *nf*
phenology	fenología *nf*

FACTORS DETERMINING WEATHER

altitude	altitud *nf*
aridity	aridez *nf*
condensation	condensación *nf*
current (ocean)	corriente *nf*
evaporation	evaporación *nf*
humidity	humedad *nf*
movement	movimiento *nm*
occluded front	oclusión *nf*
precipitation	precipitación *nf*
pressure	presión *nf*
temperature	temperatura *nf*
turbulence	turbulencia *nf*
wind	viento *nm*

ASPECTS OF METEOROLOGY

climates

Arctic	ártico *aj*
continental	continental *aj*
maritime	marítimo *aj*
Mediterranean	mediterráneo *aj*
temperate	templado *aj*
tropical	tropical *aj*

air zones

aerosphere	aerosfera *nf*
atmosphere	atmósfera *nf*
hydrosphere	hidrosfera *nf*
ionosphere	ionosfera *nf*
mesosphere	mesosfera *nf*
ozonosphere	ozonosfera *nf*
stratosphere	estratosfera, estratósfera *nf*
thermosphere	termosfera *nf*
troposphere	troposfera *nf*

cloud types

cirrocumulus	cirrocúmulo *nm*
cirrostratus	cirrostrato *nm*
cirrus	cirro *nm*
cumulonimbus Ⓑ	cumulonimbo *nm*
cumulus Ⓑ	cúmulo *nm*
nimbostratus	nimboestrato *nm*
nimbus Ⓑ	nimbo *nm*
stratocumulus Ⓑ	estratocúmulo *nm*
stratus Ⓑ	estrato *nm*

storms

avalanche	avalancha *nf*
cyclone	ciclón *nm*
deluge	diluvio *nm*
hurricane	huracán *nm*
monsoon	monzón *nm*
tempest	tempestad *nf*
tornado Ⓑ	tornado *nm*
torrent	torrente *nm*
typhoon	tifón *nm*

directional winds

easterly	del este
northerly	del norte
southerly	del sur
westerly	del oeste

other winds

anticyclone	anticiclón *nm*
breeze	brisa *nf*
foehn	fohn *nm*
harmattan	harmatán *nm*
khamsin	kamsín *nm*
mistral	mistral *nm*
norther	nortada *nf*
simoom	simún *nm*
sirroco	siroco *nm*
trade winds	vientos alisios *nmpl*
vortex Ⓑ	vórtice *nm*
zephyr	céfiro *nm*

other weather terms

balmy	balsámico *aj*
brrr!	¡brrr! *intj*
calm	calma *nf*
clear (sky)	claro *aj*
clement	clemente *aj*
frigid	frígido *aj*
global	global *aj*
inclement	inclemente *aj*
inhospitable	inhóspito *aj*
inundation	inundación *nf*
invigorating	vigorizador *aj*
parhelion Ⓑ	parhelia, parhelio *nf, nm*
pluvial	pluvial *aj*
tempestuous	tempestuoso *aj*
torrid	tórrido *aj*
turbulent	turbulento *aj*
variable	variable *aj*
windy	ventoso

AIR QUALITY TERMS

alert	alerta *nf*
inversion	inversión *nf*
miasma	miasma *nm*
ozone	ozono *nm*
pollution	polución *nf*
smog	esmog *nm*

TOOLS, EQUIPMENT, MEASUREMENTS

anemometer	anemómetro *nm*
aneroid (barometer)	aneroide *aj*
barogram	barograma *nm*
barograph	barógrafo *nm*
barometer	barómetro *nm*
centigrade	centígrado *aj, nm*
Fahrenheit	Fahrenheit *aj, nm*
hygrometer	higrómetro *nm*
isobar	isobara *nf*
isogram	isograma *nm*
isotherm	isoterma *nf*
millibar	milibar *nm*

nephoscope	nefoscopio *nm*
psychrometer	psicrómetro *nm*
radiosonde	radiosonda *nf*
satellite	satélite *nm*
thermograph	termógrafo *nm*
thermometer	termómetro *nm*

PERSONS

climatologist	climatólogo, -a *nmf*
meteorologist	meteorólogo, -a *nmf*

(*See also* *flying and navigation* under **AVIATION AND SPACE TRAVEL**; **GEOGRAPHY**)

Putting Science to Work

TECHNOLOGY OVERVIEW

GENERAL TERMS

automation	automación, automatización *nf*
engineering	ingeniería *nf*
equipment	equipo *nm*
industry	industria *nf*
innovation	innovación *nf*
instrument	instrumento *nm*
invention	invento *nm*
machine	máquina *nf*
machinery	maquinaria *nf*
mechanism	mecanismo *nm*
motor	motor *nm*
patent	patente *nf*
progress	progreso *nm*
project	proyecto *nm*
prototype	prototipo *nm*
repair	reparación *nf*
technique	técnica *nf*
technology	tecnología *nf*

ASPECTS OF TECHNOLOGY

new technologies

bionics	biónica *nf*
biotechnology	biotecnología *nf*
desalinization	desalinización *nf*
electronics	electrónica *nf*
electrotechnology	electrotecnia *nf*
nanotechnology	nanotecnología *nf*
radiography	radiografía *nf*
robotics	robótica *nf*
telecommunications	telecomunicaciones *nfpl*

engineering fields

acoustic(al)	acústico *aj*
aeronautical	aeronáutico *aj*
aerospace	aeroespacial *aj*
agricultural	agrícola *aj*
architectural	arquitectónico *aj*
automotive	automotor, automotriz *aj*
biomedical	biomédico *aj*
chemical	químico *aj*
civil	civil *aj*
construction	construcción *nf*

electrical	eléctrico *aj*
electromechanical	electromecánico *aj*
genetics	genética *nf*
hydraulic	hidráulico *aj*
hydroelectric	hidroeléctrico *aj*
industrial	industrial *aj*
manual	manual *aj*
marine	marino *aj*
mechanical	mecánico *aj*
metallurgical	metalúrgico *aj*
military	militar *aj*
mining *aj*	minero, de minas *aj, nfpl*
nuclear	nuclear *aj*
petrochemical	petroquímico *aj*
sanitary	sanitario *aj*
structural	estructural *aj*
transit	de tránsito *nm*

important inventions

adding machine	máquina de sumar *nf*
air brake	freno de aire *nm*
air conditioning	aire acondicionado *nm*
Bunsen burner	mechero Bunsen *nm*
calculator	calculadora *nf*
calendar	calendario *nm*
cash register	caja registradora *nf*
cassette	cassete, casete *nm or nf*
catapult	catapulta *nf*
cellophane ▲	celofán *nm*
cellular telephone	teléfono celular *nm*
celluloid	celuloide *nm*
combination lock	cerradura de combinación *nf*
computer	computadora *nf*
cyclotron	ciclotrón *nm*
derrick	derrick *nm*
diesel	diesel *nm*
dynamite	dinamita *nf*
escalator	escalera mecánica *nf*
fluorescent light	luz fluorescente *nf*
generator	generador *nm*
gyroscope	giroscopio *nm*
hypodermic needle	aguja hipodérmica *nf*
incandescent light	luz incandescente *nf*
inclined plane	plana inclinada *nf*
internal-combustion engine	motor de combustión interna *nm, nf*
knitting machine	máquina de tejer *nf*

linotype	linotipia, linotipo *nf, nm*	machine tool	máquina herramienta *nf*
locomotive	locomotora *nf*	micrometer	micrómetro *nm*
microphone, mike	micrófono *nm*	pallet	paleta *nf*
microscope	microscopio *nm*	pantograph	pantógrafo *nm*
milking machine	máquina de ordeñar *nf*	pinion	piñón *nm*
		piston	pistón *nm*
nuclear reactor	reactor nuclear *nm*	pivot	pivote *nm*
pistol	pistola *nf*	pulverizer	pulerizador *nm*
poloroid camera	cámara poloroid *nf*	purifier	depurador *nm*
printing press	prensa, imprenta *nf*	rectifier	rectificador *nm*
pulley	polea *nf*	reducer	reductor *nm*
pump	bomba *nf*	regenerator	regenerador *nm*
radar	radar *nm*	register	registro *nm*
radio	radio *nm*	regulator	regulador *nm*
revolver	revólver *nm*	rotary	máquina rotativa *nf*
robot	robot *nm*	selector	selector *nm*
sewing machine	máquina de coser *nf*	servomechanism	servomecanismo *nm*
sonar	sónar *nm*	servomotor	servomotor *nm*
stethoscope	estetoscopio *nm*	sling	eslinga *nf*
telegraph	telégrafo *nm*	stamper	estampador *nm*
telephone	teléfono *nm*	stator	estator *nm*
television	televisión *nf*	tubing	tubería *nf*
thermometer	termómetro *nm*	turbine	turbina *nf*
thermostat	termostato *nm*	turbocompressor	turbocompresor *nm*
tractor	tractor *nm*	unit	unidad *nf*
transistor	transistor *nm*	universal (joint)	universal *aj*
vending machine	máquina expendedora *nf*	valve	válvula *nf*

washing machine	máquina de lavar *nf*		
X-ray machine	aparato de rayos X *nm*		
zipper	zíper *nm*		

TECHNICAL TERMS

other terms

alignment	alineación *nf*
articulation	articulación *nf*
assembly	ensamblaje *nm*
calibration	calibración *nf*
coaxial	coaxial *aj*
coupling	acoplamiento *nm*
dismantle	desmantelar *vt*
efficiency	eficiencia *nf*
expansion	expansión *nf*
fulcrum Ⓑ	fulcro *nm*
lubrication	lubricación *nf*
management (of a machine)	manejo *nm*
modular	modular *aj*
mounting	montaje *nm*
penetration	penetración *nf*
performance	performance *nf*
plumb	aplomado *aj*
precision	precisión *nf*
process	proceso *nm*
recycle	reciclar *vt*
refrigeration	refrigeración *nf*
resilience, resiliency	resilencia *nf*

tools, parts, equipment

automaton Ⓑ	autómata *nm*
calender	calandria *nf*
carburetor	carburador *nm*
compressor	compresor *nm*
condenser	condensador *nm*
connector	conectador *nm*
controller	controlador *nm*
differential	diferencial *nm*
duplex	dúplex *nm*
dynamometer	dinamómetro *nm*
eccentric	excéntrica *nf*
electrodynamometer	electrodinamómetro *nm*
equalizer	igualador *nm*
implement	implemento *nm*
joint	junta *nf*
lute	luten *nm*

solder, soldering	soldadura *nf*
suction	succión *nf*
synchronous (machine)	sincrónico *aj*
tolerance	tolerancia *nf*
torsion	torsión *nf*
traction	tracción *nf*
treatment	tratamiento *nm*
vibration	vibración *nf*

PERSONS

engineer	ingeniero, -a *nmf*
innovator	innovador(a) *nmf*
inventor	inventor(a) *nmf*
machinist	maquinista *nmf*
mechanic	mecánico, -a *nmf*
repairman	reparador(a) *nmf*
technician	técnico, -a *nmf*

(*See also* components under **AMATEUR RADIO**; *TERMS IN CONSTRUCTION* under **ARCHITECTURE**; *parts and equipment* under **AUTOMOBILES**; *commercial products* under **CHEMISTRY**; *TOOLS AND EQUIPMENT* under **MEDICAL PRACTICE**; *TOOLS AND EQUIPMENT* under **MOVIES**; **PERSONAL COMPUTERS**; *TOOLS AND EQUIPMENT* under **PHYSICS**; *TOOLS AND EQUIPMENT* under **TELEVISION AND VIDEO**)

AGRICULTURE

GENERAL TERMS

agrarian	agrario *aj*
agriculture	agricultura *nf*
animal	animal *nm*
conservation	conservación *nf*
cultivation	cultivo *nm*
electrification	electrificación *nf*
fertilizer	fertilizante *nm*
mechanization	mecanización *nf*
pesticide	pesticida *nm*
plant	planta *nf*
produce	producto *nm*
property	propiedad *nf*
rural	rural *aj*

SPECIALIZATIONS

agronomy	agronomía *nf*
hydroponics	hidroponía, hidroponia *nf*
pedology	pedología *nf*
pomology	pomología *nf*

ASPECTS OF FARMING

organization and ownership

collective farm	granja colectiva *nf*
cooperative	cooperativa *nf*
kibbutz Ⓑ	kibbutz *nm*
latifundium	latifundio *nm*
plantation	plantación *nf*
ranch	rancho *nm*

land units

acre	acre *nm*
hectare	hectárea *nf*
parcel	parcela *nf*
tract	tracto *nm*

farming method

diversified	diversificado *aj*
extensive	extensivo, extenso *aj*
intensive	intensivo *aj*

soils and soil conservation

alkaline	alcalino *aj*
arable	arable *aj*
compact	compacto *aj*
drainage	drenaje *nm*
erosion	erosión *nf*
fertile	fértil *aj*
gumbo	gumbo *nm*
humus	humus *nm*
irrigation	irrigación *nf*
loess	loes *nm*
rotation	rotación *nf*
subsoil	subsuelo *nm*
substratum Ⓑ	sustrato *nm*
terrace	terraza *nf*

types of farms

aquaculture	acuacultura *nf*
banana plantation	bananar *nm*
cherry orchard	cerezal *nm*
coca plantation	cocal *nm*
coconut plantation	cocotal *nm*
coffee plantation	cafetal *nm*
floriculture	floricultura *nf*
fruit growing	fruticultura *nf*
horticulture	horticultura *nf*
olive growing	olivicultura *nf*
oyster culture	ostricultura *nf*
silviculture	silvicultura *nf*
tobacco plantation	tabacal *nm*
viniculture	vinicultura *nf*

planting groups

olive grove	olivar *nm*
oyster bed	ostrero *nm*
rice field/paddy	arrozal *nm*
tomato patch	tomatal *nm*
tomato plant	tomatera *nf*
vineyard	viña, viñedo *nf, nm*

types of crops

fiber **A**	fibra *nf*
fruit	fruta *nf*
grain	grano *nm*
tobacco	tabaco *nm*
vegetable	vegetal *nm*

major food crops

alfalfa	alfalfa *nf*
cereal	cereal *nm*
cocoa	cacao *nm*
coffee	café *nm*
copra	copra *nf*
olive (fruit)	oliva *nf*
potato **B**	patata *nf*
raffia	rafia *nf*
rice	arroz *nm*
sesame	sésamo *nm*
sorghum	sorgo *nm*
soy, soybean	soja *nf*
sugar	azúcar *nm or nf*
tea	té *nm*

care of animals

corral	corral *nm*
forage	forraje *nm*
silage	ensilaje *nm*
stable	establo *nm*

pesticides

DDT	DDT *nm*
fumigant	substancia fumigatoria *nf*
fungicide	fungicida *nm*
herbicide	herbicida *nm*
insecticide	insecticida *nm*
Malathion	Malatión *nm*
parathion	paratión *nm*
pyrethrum	piretrina *nf*
rotenone	rotenona *nf*

fertilizers

chemical	químico *aj*
compost	compost *nm*
guano	guano *nm*

organic	orgánico *aj*
potash	potasa *nf*

other terms

clearing (in forest)	claro *nm*
hybrid	híbrido *aj, nm*
parasite	parásito *nm*
pasture	pastura, pasto *nf, nm*
transplant	trasplantar *vt*

TOOLS AND EQUIPMENT

elevator	elevador *nm*
granary	granero *nm*
incubator	incubadora *nf*
separator	separador *nm*
silo	silo *nm*
stake	estaca *nf*
tractor	tractor *nm*

PERSONS

absentee landlord	absentista, ausentista *nmf*
agronomist	agrónomo, -a *nmf*
coffee grower/ merchant	cafetero, -a, cafelero, -a *nmf*
cowboy	cowboy **C** *nm*
cultivator	cultivador(a) *nmf*
fruit farmer/grower	fruticultor(a) *nmf*
fumigator	fumigador *nm*
gardener	jardinero, -a *nmf*
gaucho	gaucho *nm*
horticulturist	horticultor(a) *nmf*
olive grower	olivarero, -a *nmf*
palm farmer	palmero, -a *nmf*
planter	plantador(a) *nmf*
rancher	ranchero, -a *nmf*
winegrower	vinicultor, -a *nmf*

(*See also* GROWING OF PLANTS under **PLANTS**)

COMMUNICATIONS

GENERAL TERMS

communication	comunicación *nf*
connection **A**	conexión *nf*
contact	contacto *nm*
electronic	electrónico *aj*
interactive	interactivo *aj*
interconnect	interconectar *vt*
message	mensaje *nm*
receive	recibir(se) *vt(r)*
satellite	satélite *nm*

SPECIALIZATIONS

communication theory	comunicología *nf*
information technology	informática *nf*
phototelegraphy	fototelegrafía *nf*
radiocommunication	radiocomunicación *nf*
radiotelegraphy	radiotelegrafía *nf*
radiotelephony	radiotelefonía *nf*
telecommunications	telecomunicaciones *nfpl*
telegraphy	telegrafía *nf*
telephony	telefonía *nf*

FORMS OF TELECOMUNICATION

aerogram Ⓐ	aerograma *nm*
cable	cable *nm*
cablegram	cablegrama *nm*
cellular telephone	teléfono celular *nm*
E-mail, electronic mail	correo electrónico *nm*
fax, facsimile	fax, facsímil *nm*
intercom, interphone	interfono *nm*
postcard	postal *nf*
radio	radio *nm*
radiogram	radiograma *nm*
radiophone	radiófono *nm*
radiotelephone	radioteléfono *nm*
teleconferencing *nsg*	teleconferencias *nfpl*
telegram	telegrama *nm*
telegraph	telégrafo *nm*
telephone	teléfono *nm*
teletype	teletipo *nm*
telex	telex *nm*
video	video *nm*
videoconference	videoconferencia *nf*
videophone	videófono *nm*

RELATED TERMS

mail

airmail	correo aéreo *nm*
certified	certificado *aj*
correspondence	correspondencia *nf*
express	expreso *aj*
franking	franqueo *nm*
paper	papel *nm*
registered	registrado *aj*
stamp	estampilla *nf*
zip code	código postal *nm*

telephone

answering service	servicio de mensajes *nm, nmpl*
busy signal	señal de ocupado *nf*
call blocking	bloqueo de llamadas *nm, nfpl*
dial tone	tono de marcar/discar *nm*
direct dial	discado directo *nm*
extension	extensión *nf*
line	línea *nf*
long-distance *aj*	de larga distancia *nf*
mobile	móvil, movible *aj*
number	número *nm*
person-to-person *av*	de persona a persona *nf*
prefix	prefijo *nm*
public	público *aj*
telephone directory	guía telefónica *nf*

other terms

beep	bip *nm*
diplex	diplex *aj*
intercept	interceptar *vt*
Internet	Internet *nm*
optical fiber Ⓐ	fibra óptica *nf*
simplex	simplex *aj*
teletext	teletex, teletexto *nm*
transmitter	transmisor *nm*

PERSONS

messenger	mensajero, -a *nmf*
radio operator	radiotelegrafista *nmf*
telegraph operator	telegrafista *nmf*
telephone operator	telefonista *nmf*

(*See also* **communication signals** under **LINGUISTIC SCIENCE**)

ELECTRICITY AND ELECTRONICS

GENERAL TERMS

atom	átomo *nm*
charge	carga *nf*
circuit	circuito *nm*
conduction	conducción *nf*
current	corriente *nf*
electrician	electricista *nmf*
electricity	electricidad *nf*
electron	electrón *nm*
electronics	electrónica *nf*
electrotechnology	electrotecnia *nf*
ion	ion *nm*

ASPECTS OF ELECTRICITY

types

alternating	alterno *aj*
direct	directo *aj*
static	estático *aj*
unidirectional (current)	unidireccional *aj*

sources

battery	batería *nf*
cell	célula *nf*
crystal	cristal *nm*
dynamo	dínamo *nm*
electrolyte	electrólito *nm*
galvanism	galvanismo *nm*
generator	generador *nm*
hydroelectricity	hidroelectricidad *nf*
piezoelectricity	piezoelectricidad *nf*
pile	pila *nf*
quartz	cuarzo *nm*
voltaic (cell)	voltaico *aj*

kinds of circuits

cycle	ciclo *nm*
integrated	integrado *aj*
parallel	paralelo *aj*
printed	impreso *aj*
series, serial B	en serie *nf*

conduction

anode	ánodo *nm*
arc	arco eléctrico *nm*
cathode	cátodo *nm*
conductor	conductor *nm*
connection A	conexión *nf*
contact	contacto *nm*
discharge	descarga *nf*
electrode	electrodo *nm*
electronegative	electronegativo *aj*
electropositive	electropositivo *aj*
flow	flujo *nm*
frequency	frecuencia *nf*
impulse	impulso *nm*
inductance	inductancia *nf*
insulator	aislador, aislante *nm*
negative	negativo *aj*
neutral	neutro *aj*
nonconductor	no conductor *nm*
photoconductivity	fotoconductibilidad *nf*
polarization	polarización *nf*
pole	polo *nm*
positive	positivo *aj*

potential	potencial *nm*
proton	protón *nm*
reactance	reactancia *nf*
reluctance	reluctancia *nf*
resistance	resistencia *nf*
terminal	terminal *nm*

effects

electrolysis	electrólisis *nf*
incandescence	incandescencia *nf*
magnetism	magnetismo *nm*
shock	choque *nm*
short circuit	cortocircuito *nm*

control

capacitance	capacitancia *nf*
circuit breaker	cortacircuitos C *nm*
condenser	condensador *nm*
fuse	fusible *nm*
impedance	impedancia *nf*
interrupter	interruptor *nm*
rheostat	reóstato *nm*
solenoid	solenoide *nm*
suppression	supresión *nf*
transformer	transformador *nm*

tools and parts

adapter	adaptador *nm*
alternator	alternador *nm*
armature	armadura *nf*
capacitor	capacitor *nm*
carbon	carbón *nm*
charger	cargador *nm*
commutator	conmutador *nm*
connector	conectador *nm*
converter	convertidor *nm*
cord	cordón *nm*
coupler	acoplador *nm*
dielectric	dieléctrico *aj, nm*
discharger	descargador *nm*
dynamotor	dinamotor *nm*
equalizer	igualador *nm*
exciter	excitador *nm*
extension (cord)	extensión *nf*
filament	filamento *nm*
inductor	inductor *nm*
inverter	inversor *nm*
line	línea *nf*
magneto	magneto *nm*
neutralizer	neutralizador *nm*
oscillator	oscilador *nm*
oscillograph	oscilógrafo *nm*
rectifier	rectificador *nm*

regulator	regulador *nm*
resistor	resistor *nm*
rotor	rotor *nm*
stator	estator *nm*
vibrator	vibrador *nm*

ASPECTS OF ELECTRONICS

specializations

avionics	aviónica *nf*
bioelectronics	bioelectrónica *nf*
microelectronics	microelectrónica *nf*
thermionics	termiónica *nf*

functioning

bias	bias *nm*
distortion	distorsión *nf*
echo ⓑ	eco *nm*
emission	emisión *nf*
gain	ganancia *nf*
microcircuit	microcircuito *nm*
photoelectron	fotoelectrón *nm*
photoemission	fotoemisión *nf*
response	respuesta *nf*
semiconductor	semiconductor *nm*
signal	señal *nf*
solid-state *aj*	de estado sólido *nm*

tools and parts

amplifier	amplificador *nm*
collector	colector *nmf*
diode	diodo *nm*
dynatron	dinatrón *nm*
dynode	dinodo *nm*
magnetron	magnetrón *nm*
maser	maser *nm*
monitor	monitor *nm*
pentode	pentodo, péntodo *nm*
photomultiplier	fotomultiplicador *nm*
sensor	sensor *nm*
servomechanism	servomecanismo *nm*
stroboscope	estroboscopio *nm*
suppressor	supresor *nm*
tetrode	tetrodo *nm*
transducer	transductor *nm*
transistor	transistor *nm*
triode	tríodo *nm*
tube	tubo *nm*
vacuum (tube)	vacío *nm*

useful applications

burglar alarm	alarma antirrobo *nf*
computer	computadora *nf*

diathermy	diatermia *nf*
electrocardiograph	electrocardiógrafo *nm*
electroencephalograph	electroencefalógrafo *nm*
fax	fax *nm*
fluorescent lamp	tubo fluorescente *nm*
Geiger counter	contador Geiger *nm*
iconoscope	iconoscopio *nm*
intercom	interfono *nm*
laser	láser *nm*
microscope	microscopio *nm*
microwave	microonda *nf*
missile	misil *nm*
multiplex	múltiplex *nm*
neon sign	letrero de neón *nm*
photocell, photoelectric cell	fotocélula *nf*
radar	radar *nm*
radio	radio *nm*
sonar	sónar *nm*
spectrograph	espectrógrafo *nm*
telephone	teléfono *nm*
telescope	telescopio *nm*
television	televisión *nf*
thermostat	termostato *nm*
ultrasound	ultrasonido *nm*

MEASUREMENTS

instruments

ammeter	amperímetro *nm*
electrometer	electrómetro *nm*
electroscope	electroscopio *nm*
galvanometer	galvanómetro *nm*
potentiometer	potenciómetro *nm*
voltammeter	voltamperímetro *nm*
voltmeter	voltímetro *nm*
wattmeter	vatímetro *nm*

units of measurement

amperage	amperaje *nm*
ampere	amperio *nm*
coulomb	culombio *nm*
farad	farad, faradio *nm*
gauss	gauss *nm*
joule	julio *nm*
kilohertz (abbr: kHz) ⓑ	kilohercio *nm*
kilovolt	kilovoltio *nm*
kilowatt	kilovatio *nm*
kilowatt-hour	kilovatio-hora *nf*
ohm	ohmio, ohm *nm*
volt	voltio *nm*
voltage	voltaje *nm*

watt	vatio *nm*
watt-hour	vatio-hora *nf*
wattage	vataje *nm*

(*See also* components under **AMATEUR RADIO**; *HARDWARE TERMS* under **PERSONAL COMPUTERS**; *TERMS IN ELECTROMAGNETISM* under **PHYSICS**)

FUELS

GENERAL TERMS

carburetor	carburador *nm*
gas pipeline	gasoducto *nm*
incendiary	incendiario *aj*
incinerator	incinerador *nm*
inflammable, flammable	inflamable *aj*
noxious	nocivo *aj*
octane number	octanaje *nm*
oxidizer	oxidante *nm*
particulate	de partículo
petrochemical	petroquímico *nm*
petrochemistry	petroquímica *nf*
petrology	petrología *nf*
pollution	polución *nf*
pump	bomba *nf*
refinery	refinería *nf*
stove	estufa *nf*

KINDS OF FUELS

general types

biogas	biogás *nm*
biomass	biomasa *nf*
chemical	químico *aj*
fossil	fósil *aj*
gas	gas *nm*
hydrocarbon	hidrocarburo *nm*
liquid	líquido *aj*
natural	natural *aj*
nuclear	nuclear *aj*
solid	sólido *aj*
synthetic	sintético *aj*

solid fuels

anthracite	antracita *nf*
bitumen	betún *nm*
briquet, briquette	briqueta *nf*
coke	coque, cok *nm*
crude, crude oil	crudo, petróleo crudo *nm*
lignite	lignito *nm*

liquid fuels

alcohol	alcohol *nm*
benzene	benceno *nm*
decane	decano *nm*
diesel	diesel *nm*
gasohol	gasohol *nm*
gasoline, gasolene	gasolina *nf*
hexane	hexano *nm*
kerosene, kerosine	queroseno *nm*
octane	octano *nm*
petroleum	petróleo *nm*
toluene	tolueno *nm*
xylene	xileno *nm*

gas fuels

acetylene	acetileno *nm*
butane	butano *nm*
carbon monoxide	monóxido de carbono *nm*
coal gas	gas de carbón *nm*
ethane	etano *nm*
ethylene	etileno *nm*
hydrazine	hidrazina *nf*
methane	metano *nm*
methanol	metanol *nm*
natural gas	gas natural *nm*
pentane	pentano *nm*
propane	propano *nm*
propylene	propileno *nm*

chemical fuels

aluminum 🇦	aluminio *nm*
beryllium	berilio *nm*
boron	boro *nm*
hydrogen	hidrógeno *nm*
lithium	litio *nm*
magnesium	magnesio *nm*
silicon	silicio *nm*
titanium	titanio *nm*

atomic fuels

plutonium	plutonio *nm*
thorium	torio *nm*
uranium	uranio *nm*

other forms

electricity	electricidad *nf*

PROCESSES

coking	coquificación *nf*
combustion	combustión *nf*
conversion	conversión *nf*

cracking	craqueo *nm*
explosion	explosión *nf*
fission	fisión *nf*
fuel injection	inyección *nf*
fusion	fusión *nf*
ignition	ignición *nf*
liquefaction	licuación *nf*
oxidation	oxidación *nf*
refining	refinación *nf*

(*See also* USES AND PRODUCTS under
CHEMISTRY)

METALLURGY

GENERAL TERMS

alloy	aleación *nf*
bar	barra *nf*
ingot	lingote *nm*
metal	metal *nm*

SPECIALIZATIONS

electrometallurgy	electrometalurgia *mf*
hydrometallurgy	hidrometalurgia *nf*
metallography	metalografía *nf*
metallurgy	metalurgia *nf*
metalwork	metalistería *nf*

ASPECTS OF METALLURGY

alloys and metallic substances

alumina	alúmina *nf*
amalgam	amalgama *nf*
bronze	bronce *nm*
cementite	cementita *nf*
chrome	cromo *nm*
cryolite	criolita *nf*
electrum	electro *nm*
ferrite	ferrita *nf*
ferromanganese	ferromanganeso *nm*
flux	flujo *nm*
matte	mata *nf*
metalloid	metaloide *nm*
pearlite	perlita *nf*
permalloy	permalloy *nm*
pewter	peltre *nm*
solder, soldering	soldadura *nf*

processes

amalgamation	amalgamación *nf*
anodize	anodizar *vt*
assay	ensaye *nm*

blanch	blanquear *vt*
bronzing	bronceadura *nf*
calcine	calcinar *vt*
carburize	carburar *vt*
cementation	cementación *nf*
corrosion	corrosión *nf*
cyanide process	cianuración *nf*
decarbonization	descarburación *nf*
electrolysis	electrólisis *nf*
extrusion	extrusión *nf*
flotation	flotación *nf*
forging	forjadura, forja *nf*
fusion	fusión *nf*
galvanize	galvanizar *vt*
precipitation	precipitación *nf*
refining	refinación *nf*
separation	separación *nf*
sinterization	sinterización *nf*
tempering	templadura *nf*

plating

chromium-plated	cromado *aj*
copper-plated	cobreado *aj*
nickel-plated	niquelado *aj*

metal characteristics

antimagnetic	antimagnético *aj*
contract	contraerse *vr*
ductility	ductilidad *nf*
expand	expandirse *vr*
fatigue	fatiga *nf*
ferruginous	ferruginoso *aj*
magnetic	magnético *aj*
malleable	maleable *aj*
patina	pátina *nf*

other terms

pure	puro *aj*
scoria	escoria *nf*
solidity	solidez *nf*
temper	temple *nm*

TOOLS AND EQUIPMENT

converter	convertidor *nm*
crucible	crisol *nm*
detector	detector *nm*
forge	forja *nf*
foundry	fundición *nf*
mold ▲	molde *nm*
retort	retorta *nf*
stamp	estampa *nf*
stamper	estampador *nm*
tank	tanque *nm*

PERSONS

alchemist (obs)	alquimista *nmf*
assayer	ensayista *nmf*
bronzesmith	broncista *nmf*
forger	forjador(a) *nmf*
founder	fundidor(a) *nmf*
metalworker	metalista *nmf*

(*See also CHEMICAL ELEMENTS* under
CHEMISTRY)

MINERALS AND MINING

GENERAL TERMS

crystal	cristal *nm*
deposit	depósito *nm*
igneous	ígneo *aj*
metamorphic	metamórfico *aj*
mine	mina *nf*
mineral	mineral *aj, nm*
mining	minería *nf*
natural resources	recursos naturales *nmpl*
sedimentary	sedimentario *aj*
vein	vena *nf*

SPECIALIZATIONS

geology	geología *nf*
minerology	mineralogía *nf*
petrochemistry	petroquímica *nf*
petrography	petrografía *nf*
petrology	petrología *nf*
crystallography	cristalografía *nf*

ASPECTS OF MINERALS

classification

metallic	metálico *aj*
nonmetallic	no metálico *aj*
specific gravity	peso específico *nm*

identification

color Ⓐ	color *nm*
luster Ⓐ	lustre *nm*
odor Ⓐ	olor *nm*
permeability	permeabilidad *nf*
porosity	porosidad *nf*
stria Ⓑ	estría *nf*
transparency	tra(n)sparencia *nf*

descriptive terms

acidic	ácido *aj*
amorphous	amorfo *aj*
carboniferous	carbonífero *aj*
crude	crudo *aj*
endomorphic	endomórfico *aj*
geode	geoda *nf*
homogeneous	homogéneo *aj*
isomorphic	isomorfo, isomórfico *aj*
nacreous	nacarado, nacarino *aj*
pearly	perlino *aj*
refractory	refractario *aj*
resinous	resinoso *aj*
salic	sálico *aj*

ROCKS AND MINERALS

igneous rocks

basalt	basalto *nm*
gabbro	gabro *nm*
granite	granito *nm*
obsidian	obsidiana *nf*
peridotite	peridotita *nf*
porphyry	pórfiro *nm*
pumice	pómez *nm*

metamorphic rocks

amphibolite	anfibolita *nf*
gneiss	gneis *nm*
marble	mármol *nm*
quartzite	cuarcita *nf*

sedimentary rocks

bituminous	betuminoso *aj*
cipolin	cipolino *nm*
travertine	travertino *nm*

ores

bauxite	bauxita *nf*
beryl	berilo *nm*
cinnabar	cinabrio *nm*
corundum	corindón *nm*
galena	galena *nf*
limonite	limonita *nf*
uraninite	uraninita *nf*
wolframite	volframita *nf*

gemstones

agate	ágata *nf*
amethyst	amatista *nf*
aquamarine	aguamarina *nf*
carbuncle	carbúnculo, carbunclo *nm*
carnelian	carniola, cornalina *nf*
chalcedony	calcedonia *nf*

diamond	diamante *nm*
diopside	diópsido *nm*
emerald	esmeralda *nf*
jade	jade *nm*
jasper	jaspe *nm*
lapis lazuli	lapislázuli *nm*
lazulite	lazulita *nf*
nacre	nácar *nm*
nephrite	nefrita *nf*
onyx	ónice, ónix, ónique *nm*
opal	ópalo *nm*
peridot	perdoto *nm*
sardonyx	sardónica, sardónice *nf*
topaz	topacio *nm*
tourmaline	turmalina *nf*
turquoise	turquesa *nf*
zircon	circón, zircón *nm*

other minerals

actinolite	actinolita *nf*
alabaster	alabastro *nm*
amazonite	amazonita *nf*
amphibole	anfíbol *nm*
anthracite	antracita *nf*
argentite	argentita *nf*
asbestos	asbesto *nm*
asphalt	asfalto *nm*
azurite	azurita *nf*
barite	barita *nf*
bitumen	betún *nm*
calcite	calcita *nf*
carnotite	carnotita *nf*
chalcanthite	cancantita *nf*
chalcocite	calcosita, calcosina *nf*
chalcopyrite	calcopirita *nf*
columbite	columbita *nf*
cyanite, kyanite	cianita *nf*
diaspore	diásporo *nm*
didymium	didimio *nm*
dolomite	dolomita *nf*
emery	esmeril *nm*
feldspar	feldespato *nm*
fluor	fluorita *nf*
fluorite	fluorita *nf*
gadolinite	gadolinita *nf*
glauconite	glauconita *nf*
graphite	grafito *nm*
halite	halita *nf*
hematite	hematita, hematites *nf*
hornblende	hornablenda, horoblenda *nf*

ilmenite	ilmenita *nf*
kaolin(e)	caolín *nm*
kaolinite	caolinita *nf*
lignite	lignito *nm*
magnetite	magnetita *nf*
malachite	malaquita *nf*
melanite	melanita *nf*
mica	mica *nf*
microcline	microclino *nm*
minium	minio *nm*
molybdenite	molibdenita *nf*
monazite	monacita *nf*
ocher △	ocre *nm*
olivine	olivino *nm*
orthoclase	ortoclasa *nf*
perlite	perlita *nf*
petroleum	petróleo *nm*
picrite	picrita *nf*
pitchblende	pechblenda, pecblenda *nf*
pyrite	pirita *nf*
pyroxene	piroxeno *nm*
quartz	cuarzo *nm*
rhodonite	rodonita *nf*
rutile	rutilo *nm*
serpentine	serpentina *nf*
siderite	siderita *nf*
silica	sílice *nf*
sillimanite	silimanita *nf*
sphalerite	esfalerita *nf*
spinel	espinela *nf*
stibnite	estibinita *nf*
talc	talco *nm*
talcum	talco *nm*
tektite	tectita *nf*
tephrite	tefrita *nf*
tripoli, tripolite	trípol, trípoli *nm*
trona	trona *nf*
vermiculite	vermiculita *nf*
wulfenite	wulfenita *nf*
zaffer, zaffre	safre, zafre *nm*
zeolite	ceolita, zeolita *nf*
zoisite	zoisita *nf*

TERMS IN MINING

tools and equipment

explosive	explosiva *nf*
extractor	extractor *nm*
lamp	lámpara *nf*
pick	pico *nm*
pickax △	piqueta *nf*
pump	bomba *nf*

| seismograph | sismógrafo *nm* |
| ventilator | ventilador *nm* |

other terms

bonanza	bonanza *nf*
exploit	explotar *vt*
extraction	extracción *nf*
flotation	flotación *nf*
gangue	ganga *nf*
mine entrance	bocamina *nf*
placer	placer *nm*
prospecting	prospección *nf*
station	estación *nf*
ventilation	ventilación *nf*

PERSONS

miner	minero *nm*
minerologist	mineralogista *nmf*
prospector	prospector(a) *nmf*
geophysicist	geofísico, -a *nmf*
mining engineer	ingeniero, -a de minas *nmf, nfpl*

(*See also* PROCESSES, REACTIONS, TESTS under **CHEMISTRY**; *TYPES OF GEMS* under **GEMS AND JEWELRY**; *DESCRIPTION* under **GEOLOGY**)

PRINTING

GENERAL TERMS

character	carácter *nm*
graphic	gráfico *nm*
impression	impresión *nf*
line	línea *nf*
paper	papel *nm*
print shop	imprenta *nf*
printing	imprenta *nf*
printing press	prensa, imprenta *nf*
symbol	símbolo *nm*
type	tipo *nm*

SPECIALIZATIONS

photocomposition	fotocomposición *nf*
photolithography	fotolitografía *nf*
phototypography	fototipografía *nf*
planography	planografía *nf*
serigraphy	serigrafía *nf*
thermography	termografía *nf*
typography	tipografía *nf*
zincography	cincografía *nf*

ASPECTS OF PRINTING

kinds of printing processes

collotype	colotipia *nf*
electrotyping	electrotipia *nf*
engraving	grabado *nm*
lithography	litografía *nf*
offset	offset *nm*
photoengraving	fotograbado *nm*
photogravure	fotograbado *nm*
phototype	fototipa *nf*
planographic	planográfico *aj*
relief	relieve *nm*
rotogravure	rotograbado *nm*
xerography	xerografía *nf*

kinds of printing presses

cylinder	cilindro *nm*
lithograph	litografía *nf*
platen	platina *nf*
rotary press	rotativa *nf*

characters and type sizes

asterisk	asterisco *nm*
elite, élite	élite *nf*
parenthesis B	paréntesis C *nm*
pica	pica *nf*
point	punto *nm*
Roman	romano *aj*
sign	signo *nm*
virgule	vírgula, virgulilla *nf*

bookprinting terms

colophon (obs)	colofón *nm*
erratum	errata *nf*
foliation	foliación *nf*
folio	folio *nm*
octavo	octavo *nm*
page	página *nf*
pagination	paginación *nf*
quarto	libro en cuarto *nm*
recto	recto *nm*
signature	signatura *nf*
verso	verso *nm*

other terms

deletion	dele *nm*
format	formato *nm*
galley, galley proof	galerada *nf*
imposition	imposición *nf*
interlinear	interlineal *aj*
italics *npl*	itálica *nf*
justification	justificación *nf*
movable type	tipo móvil *nm*

printed letter	letra de molde *nf, nm*
printer's error	error de imprenta *nm,* *nf*
printer's mark	pie de imprenta *nm, nf*
proof	prueba *nf*
proofreading	corrección de pruebas *nf, nfpl*
register	registro *nm*
spacing	espaciado *nm*
typeface	tipo de letra *nm, nf*

TOOLS, EQUIPMENT, MEASUREMENTS

case	caja *nf*
electrotype	electrotipo *nm*
font	fuente *nf*
galley	galera *nf*
linotype	linotipia, linotipo *nf, nm*
matrix Ⓑ	matriz *nf*
monotype	monotipia *nf*
quad	cuadratín *nm*
stereotype	estereotipo *nm*
teletype	teletipo *nm*
type gauge	tipómetro *nm*
typecase	caja de tipo *nf*

PERSONS

linotypist	linotipista *nmf*
lithographer	litógrafo, -a *nmf*
printer	impresor, -a *nmf*
proofreader	corrector(a) de pruebas *nmf, nfpl*
typographer	tipógrafo, -a *nmf*

(*See also* book preparation under **BOOKS AND LIBRARIES**)

TEXTILES

GENERAL TERMS

fiber Ⓐ	fibra *nf*
piece goods	géneros en piezas *nmpl, nfpl*
sericulture	sericultura *nf*
textile	textil *nm*
texture	textura *nf*
treatment	tratamiento *nm*

ASPECTS OF TEXTILES

types of fibers

animal	animal *aj*
artificial	artificial *aj*
natural	natural *aj*
optical	óptico *aj*
plant	planta *nf*
regenerated	regenerado *aj*
synthetic	sintético *aj*

natural fibers

abaca	abacá *nm*
alpaca	alpaca *nf*
angora	angora *nm*
asbestos	asbesto *nm*
drill	dril *nm*
henequen	henequén *nm*
jute	yute *nm*
kapok	kapoc *nm*
manila	manila *nf*
nutria	nutria *nf*
pita	pita *nf*
raffia	rafia *nf*
ramie	ramina *nf*
sisal	sisal *nm*

artificial fibers

acetate	acetato *nm*
acrylic	acrílico *aj*
cellulose	celulosa *nf*
fiberglass	vidrio fibroso *nm*
nylon	nilón *nm*
olefin	olefina *nf*
polyester	poliester *nm*

clothing fabrics

astrakhan	astracán *nm*
batiste	batista *nf*
brocade	brocado *nm*
calico Ⓑ	calicó *nm*
cambric	cambray *nm*
caracul, karakul	caracul, karakul *nm*
cashmere	cachemira *nf*
chiffon	chiffón *nm*
chintz	chintz, chinz *nm*
crepe	crepé, crespón *nm*
cretonne	cretona *nf*
crinoline	crinolina *nf*
Dacron	dacrón *nm*
damask	damasco *nm*
felt	fieltro *nm*
flannel	franela *nf*
flannelette	franela fina *nf*
fustian	fustán *nm*
gabardine	gabardina *nf*

gauze	gasa *nf*
georgette	georgette *nm*
gingham	guinga *nf*
jersey	jersey *nm*
khaki	caqui *nm*
lamé	lamé *nm*
linen	lino *nm*
madras	madrás *nm*
merino	merino *nm*
mohair	moer *nm*
moire, moiré	moaré *nm*
muslin	muselina *nf*
organdie, organdy	organdí *nm*
Orlon	orlón *nm*
percale	percal *nm*
poplin	popelina *nf*
rayon	rayón *nm*
sateen, satin	satín *nm*
satin	satén, satín *nm*
serge	sarga *nf*
taffeta	tafetán *nm*
tissue	tisú *nm*
toweling Ⓐ	tela de toalla *nf*
tricot	tricot *nm*
tulle	tul *nm*
veiling	tela para velos *nf, nmpl*
velour	velour *nm*
velveteen	velvetón *nm*
zibeline, zibelline	cebellina *nf*

treatments and techniques

batik	batik *nm*
calender	calandrar *vt*
carding	cardadura, cardado *nf, nm*
glacé	glaseado *aj*
impregnation	impregnación *nf*
mercerize	mercerizar *vt*
polymerization	polimerización *nf*
sanforized	sanforizado *aj*
temple	templén *nm*

other terms

absorbent	absorbente *aj, nm*
diaphanous	diáfano *aj*
elastic	elástico *aj, nm*
lustrous	lustroso *aj*
matte	mate *aj*
metallic	metálico *aj*
tartan	tartán *nm*

(*See also* SEWING TERMS under **CLOTHING**)

WEAPONS
GENERAL TERMS

ammunition	munición *nf*
destruction	destrucción *nf*
explosive	explosiva *nf*
kiloton (= kt)	kilotón *nm*
lethal	letal *aj*
megaton	megatón *nm*

NAMES OF WEAPONS
explosives

bomb	bomba *nf*
cartridge	cartucho *nm*
cordite	cordita *nf*
dynamite	dinamita *nf*
gelignite	gelignita *nf*
grenade	granada *nf*
lyddite	lidita *nf*
mine	mina *nf*
missile	misil *nm*
nitroglycerin(e)	nitroglicerina *nf*
TNT	TNT *nm*
trinitrotoluene (= TNT)	trinitrotolueno *nm*

crushing and piercing weapons

automatic (rifle)	atomática *nf*
ax Ⓐ	hacha *nf*
bayonet	bayoneta *nf*
boomerang	bumerang Ⓒ *nm*
cannon	cañón *nm*
carbine	carabina *nf*
catapult	catapulta *nf*
dagger	daga *nf*
dart	dardo *nm*
firearm	arma de fuego *nf(el), nm*
garrote Ⓐ	garrote *nm*
guillotine (obs)	guillotina *nf*
harpoon	arpón *nm*
hatchet	hacha *nf*
javelin	jabalina *nf*
lance	lanza *nf*
machete	machete *nm*
mortar	mortero *nm*
pistol	pistola *nf*
revolver	revólver *nm*
rifle	rifle *nm*
saber Ⓐ	sable *nm*
scimitar	cimitarra *nf*

torpedo Ⓑ   torpedo *nm*
trident (obs)   tridente *nm*

types of bombs

atomic   atómico *aj*
booby trap (bomb)   bomba trampa *nf*
demolition   demolición *nf*
fragmentation   fragmentación *nf*
hydrogen *aj*   de hidrógeno *nm*
incendiary   incendiario *aj*
napalm   napalm *nm*
neutron   de neutrones
time   de tiempo

types of missiles

ballistic   balístico *aj*
cruise *aj*   de crucero *nm*
ground-to-air   tierra-aire *aj*
guided missile   misil teledirigido *nm*

other weapons

bazooka   bazuca *nf*
defoliant   defoliante *nm*
projectile   proyectil *nm*
trap   trampa *nf*
vesicant   vesicante *nm*

OPERATION AND EFFECTS

activate   activar *vt*

ax blow   hachazo *nm*
bayonet pierce   bayonetazo *nm*
bomb explosion   bombazo *nm*
bottle hit/blow   botellazo *nm*
brandish   blandir *vt*
cannon shot   cañonazo *nm*
cannonade   cañoneo *nm*
charge   carga *nf*
deactivate   desactivar *vt*
detonation   detonación *nf*
explosion   explosión *nf*
implosion   implosión *nf*
lance thrust   lanzada *nf*
pistol shot   pistoletazo *nm*
trajectory   trayectoria *nf*

PARTS AND EQUIPMENT

bullet   bala *nf*
cannonball   bala de cañón *nf, nm*
cartridge case/belt   cartuchera *nf*
charger   cargador *nm*
detonator   detonador *nm*
ejector   eyector *nm*
extractor   extractor *nm*
fulminator   fulminador *nm*
fuse   fusible *nm*
pellet   pelotilla *nf*

(*See also* WEAPONS AND EQUIPMENT under **THE MILITARY ESTABLISHMENT**)

Quantification

MEASUREMENT

GENERAL TERMS

convert	convertir *vt*
dimension	dimensión *nf*
isometric	isométrico *aj*
measure	mensura *nf*
quantity	cantidad *nf*
standard	estándar *aj, nm*
system	sistema *nm*

ASPECTS OF MEASUREMENT

kinds of measures

approximate	aproximado *aj*
direct	directo *aj*
exact	exacto *aj*
indirect	indirecto *aj*
linear	linear, lineal *aj*
liquid	líquido *aj*

requirements

instrument	instrumento *nm*
scale	escala *nf*
unit	unidad *nf*

systems of measurement

analog(ue)	análogo *nm*
British	británico *aj*
decimal	decimal *nm*
metric	métrico *aj*

scales

Celsius	Celsio *nm*
centigrade	centígrado *aj, nm*
Fahrenheit	Fahrenheit *nm*
kelvin	kelvin *nm*

things measured

acreage	medida en acres *nf, nmpl*
area	área *nf(el)*
caliber Ⓐ	calibre *nm*
capacitance	capacitancia *nf*
capacity	capacidad *nf*
cylinder capacity	cilindrada *nf*
density	densidad *nf*
deviation	desviación *nf*
distance	distancia *nf*
electricity	electricidad *nf*
entropy	entropía *nf*
force	fuerza *nf*
frequency	frecuencia *nf*
gravity	gravedad *nf*
humidity	humedad *nf*
intensity	intensidad *nf*
magnitude	magnitud *nf*
mass	masa *nf*
pressure	presión *nf*
temperature	temperatura *nf*
time	tiempo *nm*
tonnage	tonelaje *nm*
velocity	velocidad *nf*
voltage	voltaje *nm*
volume	volumen *nm*

UNITS OF MEASUREMENT

length and distance

centimeter Ⓐ	centímetro *nm*
decameter, dekameter	decámetro *nm*
decimeter	decímetro *nm*
fermi	fermi *nm*
hectometer Ⓐ	hectómetro *nm*
kilometer Ⓐ	kilómetro *nm*
meter Ⓐ	metro *nm*
micromillimeter	micromilímetro *nm*
micron	micrón *nm*
mil	mil *nm*
mile	milla *nf*
millimeter Ⓐ	milímetro *nm*
nanometer Ⓐ	nanómetro *nm*
palm	palmo *nm*
vara	vara *nf*
yard	yarda *nf*

electricity

ampere	amperio *nm*
coulomb	culombio *nm*
farad	farad, faradio *nm*
gauss	gauss *nm*
kilovolt	kilovoltio *nm*
kilowatt	kilovatio *nm*
kilowatt-hour	kilovatio-hora *nf*
megawatt	megavatio *nm*

ohm	ohmio, ohm *nm*
volt	voltio *nm*
watt	vatio *nm*
watt-hour	vatio-hora *nf*

volume

barrel	barril *nm*
cartload	carretada *nf*
centiliter Ⓐ	centilitro *nm*
deciliter	decilitro *nm*
gallon	galón *nm*
hectoliter Ⓐ	hectolitro *nm*
kiloliter Ⓐ	kilolitro *nm*
liter Ⓐ	litro *nm*
magnum	magnum *nm*
milliliter	mililitro *nm*
minim	mínima *nf*
pint	pinta *nf*
quart	cuartilla *nf*
stere	estéreo *nm*
tierce (obs)	tercia *nf*
wagonload	vagón *nm*
cubic (inch/foot/yard)	cúbico *aj*

weight

centigram	centigramo *nm*
decigram	decigramo *nm*
dram	dracma *nf*
grain	grano *nm*
gram Ⓐ	gramo *nm*
hectogram Ⓐ	hectogramo *nm*
kilo	kilo *nm*
kilogram Ⓐ	kilogramo *nm*
milligram Ⓐ	miligramo *nm*
mole	mol *nm*
ounce	onza *nf*
quintal	quintal *nm*
scruple	escrúpulo *nm*
ton	tonelada *nf*
troy	troy *nm*

force

dyne	dina *nf*
erg	ergio *nm*
joule	julio *nm*
kilogram-meter	kilográmetro *nm*
kilojoule	kilojulio *nm*
kiloton	kilotón *nm*
megaton	megatón *nm*

other units

acre	acre *nm*
calorie	caloría *nf*

candela	candela *nf*
cord	cuerda *nf*
decibel	decibel *nm*
diopter, dioptre	dioptría *nf*
hectare	hectárea *nf*
hertz Ⓑ	hertz, hertzio, hercio *nm*
kilocalorie	kilocaloría *nf*
kilohertz Ⓑ	kilohercio *nm*
knot	nudo *nm*
league	legua *nf*
millibar	milibar *nm*

MEASURING TOOLS

altimeter	altímetro *nm*
anemometer	anemómetro *nm*
audiometer	audiómetro *nm*
balance	balanza *nf*
barometer	barómetro *nm*
buret, burette	bureta *nf*
calibrator	calibrador *nm*
calorimeter	calorímetro *nm*
chronometer	cronómetro *nm*
compass	compás *nm*
counterweight	contrapeso *nm*
dynamometer	dinamómetro *nm*
electrometer	electrómetro *nm*
electroscope	electroscopio *nm*
galvanometer	galvanómetro *nm*
gasometer	gasómetro *nm*
hydrometer	hidrómetro *nm*
hygrometer	higrómetro *nm*
inclinometer	inclinómetro *nm*
magnetometer	magnetómetro *nm*
micrometer	micrómetro *nm*
odometer	odómetro *nm*
pedometer	podómetro *nm*
photometer	fotómetro *nm*
potentiometer	potenciómetro *nm*
psychrometer	psicrómetro *nm*
radiocompass	radiocompás *nm*
rheostat	reóstato *nm*
seismometer	sismómetro *nm*
sextant	sextante *nm*
thermometer	termómetro *nm*
voltmeter	voltímetro *nm*
wattmeter	vatímetro *nm*

(*See also* **ASTRONOMY**; *TOOLS AND MEASUREMENTS* under **GEOGRAPHY**; *BASIC CONCEPTS* under **MATHEMATICS**; *MEASUREMENTS* under **PERSONAL COMPUTERS**; *MEASUREMENTS* under **PHYSICS**)

TIME

GENERAL TERMS

chronometry	cronometría *nf*
duration	duración *nf*
during	durante *prep*
event	evento *nm*
frequency	frecuencia *nf*
occasion	ocasión *nf*
occurrence	ocurrencia *nf*
recurrent	recurrente *aj*
spacing	espaciamiento *nm*
time	tiempo *nm*

ASPECTS OF TIME

kinds of time

biological	biológico *aj*
circadian	circadiano *aj*
free time	tiempo libre *nm*
geological	geológico *aj*
linguistic	lingüístico *aj*
lunar	lunar *aj*
real time	tiempo real *nm*
sidereal	sidéreo *aj*
solar	solar *aj*
time out	tiempo muerto *nm*
universal	universal *aj*

clocks

clepsydra	clepsidra *nf*
clock radio	radiodespertador *nm or nf*
cuckoo	cucú *nm*
digital	digital *aj*
quartz	cuarzo *nm*
ticktock	tictac *nm*

times of the day

antemeridian (AM)	antemeridiano *aj*
daytime	día *nm*
midday	mediodía *nm*
midnight	media noche *nf*
nocturnal	nocturno *aj*
postmeridian (PM)	postmeridiano *aj*

time zones in the U.S.

Central Standard Time	hora central *nf*
Eastern time	hora oficial del Este *nf, nm*
Pacific time	hora del Pacífico *nf, nm*

recurrent events

anniversary	aniversario *nm*
bicentenary, bicentennial	bicentenario *nm*
centenary, centennial	centenario *nm*
decennial	aniversario decenal *nm*
episode	episodio *nm*
equinox	equinoccio *nm*
quindecennial	quindenio *nm*
quinquennial	quinquenio *nm*
Sabbath	sábado *nm*
siesta	siesta *nf*
solstice	solsticio *nm*
tricentennial	tricentenario *nm*
vicissitude	vicisitud *nf*

recording and preserving

almanac	almanaque *nm*
chronicle	crónica *nf*
chronology	cronología *nf*
time capsule	cápsula del tiempo *nf, nm*

other time expressions

hourly (by the hour)	por horas *av*
nowadays *av*	hoy en día *nm*
time sharing	tiempo compartido *nm*
time warp	salto en el tiempo *nm*
time-saving *aj*	que ahorra tiempo *nm*

MONTHS OF THE YEAR

January	enero *nm*
February	febrero *nm*
March	marzo *nm*
April	abril *nm*
May	mayo *nm*
June	junio *nm*
July	julio *nm*
August	agosto *nm*
September	septiembre *nm*
October	octubre *nm*
December	diciembre *nm*
November	noviembre *nm*

EXACT TIME UNITS

nanosecond	nanosegundo *nm*
microsecond	microsegundo *nm*
millisecond	milisegundo *nm*
second	segundo *nm*
minute	minuto *nm*
quarter hour	cuarto de hora *nm, nf*
hour	hora *nf*

day	día *nm*
decade	década, decenio *nf, nm*
century	centuria *nf*
quadrennium	cuadrienio *nm*
decennium	decenio *nm*
millenium Ⓑ	milenio, milenario *nm*

INEXACT TIME UNITS

autumn	otoño *nm*
eon, aeon	eón *nm*
epoch	época *nf*
era	era *nf*
eternity	eternidad *nf*
future	futuro *nm*
instant	instante *nm*
interim	ínterin, interín *nm*
interval	intervalo *nm*
moment	momento *nm*
past	pasado *nm*
pause	pausa *nf*
period	período, periodo *nm*
present	presente *nm*

TOOLS AND EQUIPMENT

calendar	calendario *nm*
chronometer	cronómetro *nm*
chronoscope	cronoscopio *nm*
gnomon (obs)	gnomon *nm*
hour hand	horario *nm*
minute hand	minutero *nm*
pendulum	péndulo *nm*
pointer	puntero *nm*
second hand	segundero *nm*
synchronizer	sincronizador *nm*

TIME ASSOCIATIONS

duration

abrupt	abrupto *aj*
biennial	bienal *aj*
brief	breve *aj*
continual, continuous	continuo *aj*
durable	duradero *aj*
enduring	duradero *aj*
eternal	eterno *aj*
immemorial	inmemorial *aj*
interminable	interminable *aj*
long-lived	longevo *aj*
momentary	momentáneo *aj*
perennial	perenne *aj*
permanent	permanente *aj*
perpetual	perpetuo *aj*

prolonged	prolongado *aj*
provisional	provisional *aj*
temporal	temporal *aj*
temporary	temporario *aj*
tentative	tentativo *aj*
transient	transeúnte *aj*
transitory	transitorio *aj*

frequency

annual	anual *aj*
aperiodic	aperiódico *aj*
bicentenary, bicentennial	bicentenario *aj*
centenary, centennial	centenario *aj*
daily	diario *aj, av*
decennial	decenal *aj*
episodic	episódico *aj*
frequent	frecuente *aj*
hourly	horario *aj*
infrequent	infrecuente *aj*
intermittent	intermitente *aj*
periodic	periódico *aj*
quadrennial	cuadrienal *aj*
quindecennial	quindecenal *aj*
quinquennial	quinquenal *aj*
quotidian	cotidiano *aj*
rarely	raramente *av*
regular	regular *aj*
spasmodic	espasmódico *aj*
sporadic	esporádico *aj*
successive	sucesivo *aj*
tricentennial	tricentenario *aj*
triennial	trienal *aj*

speed

accelerated	acelerado *aj*
gradual	gradual *aj*
rapid	rápido *aj*

relational

antecedent	antecedente *aj*
anticipatory	anticipador *aj*
chronological	cronológico *aj*
consecutive	consecutivo *aj*
contemporary, contemporaneous	contemporáneo *aj*
current	corriente *aj*
final	final *aj*
initial	inicial *aj*
modern	moderno *aj*
obsolete	obsoleto *aj*
original	original *aj*
posterior	posterior *aj*

prehistoric	prehistórico *aj*
present-day *aj*	de hoy día *nm*
previous	previo *aj*
recent	reciente *aj*
remote	remoto *aj*
retroactive	retroactivo *aj*
subsequent	subsecuente *aj*

manner

abortive	abortivo *aj*
acyclic	acíclico *aj*
asynchronous	asíncrono *aj*
concurrent	concurrente *aj*
cyclic(al)	cíclico *aj*
dilatory	dilatorio *aj*
immediate	inmediato *aj*
imminent	inminente *aj*
inevitable	inevitable *aj*
inopportune	inoportuno *aj*
instantaneous	instantáneo *aj*
opportune	oportuno *aj*
predestined	predestinado *aj*
predetermined	predeterminado *aj*
premature	prematuro *aj*
prompt	pronto *aj*
punctual	puntual *aj*
simultaneous	simultáneo *aj*
synchronous	sincrónico *aj*
tardy	tardío *aj*
ultramodern	ultramoderno *aj*
urgent	urgente *aj*

seasons

autumnal	otoñal *aj*
hibernal	hibernal *aj*
vernal	vernal *aj*

other terms

anachronism	anacronismo *nm*
archetype	arquetipo *nm*
cease	cesar *vt*
celerity	celeridad *nf*
coincide	coincidir *vi*
commence	comenzar *vti*
concur	concurrir *vi*
date	datar *vt*
defer	diferir *vt*
intercalate	intercalar *vt*
interruption	interrupción *nf*
lapse	lapso *nm*
moratorium Ⓑ	moratoria *nf*
postpone	posponer *vt*
proximity	proximidad *nf*

retard	retardar *vt*
tempo Ⓑ	tempo *nm*

PERSONS

chronicler	cronista *nmf*
precursor	precursor(a) *nmf*
predecessor	predecesor(a) *nmf*
successor	sucesor(a) *nmf*

(*See also* **dates and keeping time** under **ANCIENT CIVILIZATIONS**)

SIZE AND DEGREE
GENERAL TERMS

criterion Ⓑ	criterio *nm*
distinction	distinción *nf*
equalization	igualación *nf*
gradation	gradación *nf*
norm	norma *nf*
scale	escala *nf*
standard	estándar *nm*

RATINGS OF THINGS
things rated

complexity	complejidad *nf*
deviation	desviación *nf*
extent	extensión *nf*
importance	importancia *nf*
intensity	intensidad *nf*
magnitude	magnitud *nf*
precision	precisión *nf*
quality	calidad *nf*
quantity	cantidad *nf*
rank	rango *nm*

average

acceptable	aceptable *aj*
adequate	adecuado *aj*
general	general *aj*
intermediate	intermedio *aj*
medial	medial *aj*
median, medium	mediano *aj*
mediocre	mediocre *aj*
moderate	moderado *aj*
natural	natural *aj*
normal	normal *aj*
ordinary	ordinario *aj*
passable	pasable *aj*
proportionate	proporcionado *aj*
reasonable	razonable *aj*

regular   regular *aj*
routine   rutinario *aj*
satisfactory   satisfactorio *aj*
standard   estándar *aj*
typical   típico *aj*
universal   universal *aj*
usual   usual *aj*

nonaverage

aberrant   aberrante *aj*
abnormal   anormal *aj*
acute   agudo *aj*
anomalous   anómalo *aj*
atypical   atípico *aj*
disparity   disparidad *nf*
disproportionate   desproporcionado *aj*
exaggerated   exagerado *aj*
exceptional   excepcional *aj*
extraordinary   extraordinario *aj*
immoderate   inmoderado *aj*
irregular   irregular *aj*
nonstandard   no estándar *aj*
uncommon   poco común *aj*
unique   único *aj*
unnatural   antinatural *aj*
unreasonable   desrazonable *aj*
unusual   inusual *aj*

above the norm

abundant   abundante *aj*
ample   amplio *aj*
appreciable   apreciable *aj*
astronomical   astronómico *aj*
augmented   aumentado *aj*
colossal   colosal *aj*
considerable   considerable *aj*
copious   copioso *aj*
crucial   crucial *aj*
definitive   definitivo *aj*
dominant, dominating   dominante *aj, nf*
elephantine   elefantino *aj*
enormous   enorme *aj*
excellent   excelente *aj*
excessive   excesivo *aj*
exhorbitant   exorbitante *aj*
extensive   extensivo, extenso *aj*
extravagant   extravagante *aj*
gigantic   gigante *aj*
grand   grande *aj*
herculean   hercúleo *aj*
ideal   ideal *aj*
immeasurable   inmensurable *aj*
immense   inmenso *aj*

innumerable   innumerable *aj*
intense   intenso *aj*
macroscopic   macroscópico *aj*
magnificent   magnífico *aj*
majestic   majestuoso *aj*
major   mayor *aj*
marvelous **A**   maravilloso *aj*
massive   masivo *aj*
maxi-   maxi- *pref*
maximal   máximo *aj*
meritorious   meritorio *aj*
monstruous   monstruoso *aj*
monumental   monumental *aj*
much   mucho *aj, av, pron*
necessary   necesario *aj*
optimal, optimum   óptimo *aj*
opulent   opulento *aj*
overestimated   sobreestimado *aj*
overvalued   sobrevalorado *aj*
palatial   palaciego *aj*
precious   precioso *aj*
precise   preciso *aj*
predominant   predominante *aj*
premier   primero *aj*
preponderant   preponderante *aj*
priceless   inapreciable *aj*
principal   principal *aj*
priority   prioridad *nf*
profound   profundo *aj*
profuse   profuso *aj*
prominent   prominente *aj*
regal   regio *aj*
remote   remoto *aj*
resplendent   resplandeciente *aj*
rich   rico *aj*
severe   severo *aj*
significant   significativo *aj*
spacious   espacioso *aj*
spectacular   espectacular *aj*
splendid   espléndido *aj*
stupendous   estupendo *aj*
substantial   su(b)stancial, su(b)stancioso *aj*

sufficient   suficiente *aj*
sumptuous   suntuoso *aj*
super-   super- *pref*
superb   soberbio *aj*
superfine   superfino, extrafino *aj*
superfluous   superfluo *aj*
superior   superior *aj*
superlative   superlativo *aj*
supersensitive   supersensible *aj*
terrific   terrífico *aj*

titanic	titánico *aj*	ultra-	ultra- *aj*
tremendous	tremendo *aj*	zero Ⓑ	cero *nm*
ubiquitous	ubicuo *aj*		
ultramodern	ultramoderno *aj*		
vast	vasto *aj*		
voluminous	voluminoso *aj*		

other terms

primary	primario *aj*
secondary	secundario *aj*
tertiary	terciario *aj*

below the norm

concise	conciso *aj*
deficient	deficiente *aj*
diminished	disminuido *aj*
imprecise	impreciso *aj*
inferior	inferior *aj*
infinitesimal	infinitesimal *aj*
insignificant	insignificante *aj*
insufficient	insuficiente *aj*
mere	mero *aj*
microscopic	microscópico *aj*
mini-	mini- *pref*
miniature *aj*	en miniatura *nf*
minimal	mínimo *aj*
minuscule	minúsculo *aj*
minute	minucioso *aj*
modest	modesto *aj*
poor	pobre *aj*
reduced	reducido *aj*
scarce	escaso *aj*
simplified	simplificado *aj*
subsidiary	subsidiario *aj*
substandard	no estándar *aj*
superficial	superficial *aj*
trivial	trivial *aj*
unimportant *aj*	sin importancia *nf*
unnecessary	innecesario *aj*
unsatisfactory	insatisfactorio *aj*

ends of the scale

absolute	absoluto *aj*
apex Ⓑ	ápice *nm*
basic	básico *aj*
complete	completo *aj*
consummate	consumado *aj*
culmination	culminación *nf*
epitome	epítome *nm*
essential	esencial *aj, nm*
extreme	extremado *aj*
fundamental	fundamental *aj*
maximum Ⓑ	máximo *nm*
minimum Ⓑ	mínimo *nm*
perfection	perfección *nf*
quintessence	quintaesencia *nf*
supreme	supremo *aj*
ultimate	último *aj*

(*See also* **overusers**, **underusers** under **USING LANGUAGE**)

COUNTING AND ARRANGEMENT

GENERAL TERMS

arrange	arreglar *vt*
classify	clasificar *vt*
copy	copia *nf*
count	contar(se) *vt(r)*
enumeration	enumeración *nf*
gradation	gradación *nf*
group	agrupar *vt*
grouping	modo de agrupar *nm, vt*
number	número *nm*
order	orden *nm*
organize	organizar *vt*
quantity	cantidad *nf*

ASPECTS OF ORGANIZATION

things to be organized

datum Ⓑ	dato *nm*
detail	detalle *nm*
entry	entrada *nf*
item	ítem Ⓒ *nm*
specific	específico *nm*
statistic	estadística *nf*

kinds of organization

diagram	diagrama *nm*
graph	gráfica *nf*
hierarchy	jerarquía *nf*
index Ⓑ	índice *nm*
list	lista *nf*
scheme	esquema *nm*
sequence	secuencia *nf*
series Ⓑ	serie *nf*
table	tabla *nf*

basic sorting orders

alphabetical	alfabético *aj*
ascending	ascendente *aj*

chronological	cronológico *aj*
descending	descendente *aj*
inverse	inverso *aj*
numerical	numérico *aj*

COUNTING TERMS

inexact quantities

approximate	aproximado *aj*
estimate	estimado *nm*
miscellany	miscelánea *nf*
multitude	multitud *nf*
myriad	miríada *nf*
plenitude	plenitud *nf*
plethora	plétora *nf*
various	vario *aj*

copies

duplicate	duplicado *aj, nm*
quadruplicate	cuadruplicado *aj, nm*
quintuplicate	quintuplicado *aj, nm*
triplicate	triplicado *aj, nm*

other terms

dozen	docena *nf*
gross	gruesa *nf*
numbering machine	numeradora *nf*
numerous	numeroso *aj*
sole	solo *aj*

GROUPING TERMS

things created

category	categoría *nf*

class	clase *nf*
combination	combinación *nf*
compilation	compilación, recopilación *nf*
entirety	entereza *nf*
entity	entidad *nf*
group	grupo *nm*
module	módulo *nm*
totality	totalidad *nf*
type	tipo *nm*
unit	unidad *nf*

boundaries

confines	confines *nmpl*
delimitation	delimitación *nf*
demarcation	demarcación *nf*
limit	límite *nm*
margin	margen *nm*
periphery	periferia *nf*

parts

certain (particular)	cierto *aj, pron*
compartment	compartimiento *nm*
component	componente *aj, nm*
constituent	constitutivo *aj, nm*
part	parte *nf*
portion	porción *nf*
respective	respectivo *aj*
section	sección *nf*
subdivision	subdivisión *nf*
subgroup	subgrupo *nm*

(*See also BASIC CONCEPTS* under **MATHEMATICS**; *performance groups* under **MUSIC**)

All About Language

LINGUISTIC SCIENCE

GENERAL TERMS

acquisition	adquisición *nf*
cognate	cognado *aj, nm*
communication	comunicación *nf*
dialect	dialecto *nm*
discourse	discurso *nm*
expression	expresión *nf*
formation	formación *nf*
grammar	gramática *nf*
grammatical rule	regla gramatical *nf*
language (general)	lenguaje *nm*
language (specific)	lengua *nf*
lexicon	léxico *nm*
linguistics	lingüística *nf*
metalanguage	metalenguaje *nm*
model	modelo *nm*
theory	teoría *nf*
vocabulary	vocabulario *nm*

BRANCHES OF LINGUISTICS

approaches

anthropological	antropólogico *aj*
applied	aplicado *aj*
comparative	comparativo *aj*
contrastive	contrastivo *aj*
diachronic	diacrónico *aj*
historical	histórico *aj*
mathematical	matemático *aj*
synchronic	sincrónico *aj*
theoretical	teorético, teórico *aj*

major fields

morphology	morfología *nf*
phonology	fonología *nf*
semantics	semántica *nf*
syntax	sintaxis *nf*

subfields

discourse analysis	análisis del discurso *nm*
metalinguistics	metalingüística *nf*
neurolinguistics	neurolingüística *nf*
sociolinguistics	sociolingüística *nf*

related specializations

cryptography	criptografía *nf*
dialectology	dialectología *nf*
epigraphy	epigrafía *nf*
etymology	etimología *nf*
glottochronology	glotocronología *nf*
graphology	grafología *nf*
lexicography	lexicografía *nf*
logography	logografía *nf*
metrics	métrica *nf*
paleography	paleografía *nf*
philology	filología *nf*
phonetics	fonética *nf*
phonics	fónica *nf*
semiology	semiología *mf*
semiotics	semiótica *nf*
stylistics	estilística *nf*

ASPECTS OF LINGUISTICS

grammatical models

descriptive	descriptivo *aj*
generative	generativo *aj*
normative	normativo *aj*
prescriptive	prescriptivo *aj*
stratificational	estratificacional *aj*
structural	estructural *aj*
traditional	tradicional *aj*
transformational	tra(n)sformacional *aj*

basic linguistic units

allomorph	alomorfo *nm*
allophone	alófono *nm*
grapheme	grafema *nm*
lexeme	lexema *nm*
morpheme	morfema *nm*
morphophoneme	morfofonema *nm*
phoneme	fonema *nm*

formative processes

abbreviation	abreviación *nf*
affixation	afijación *nf*
agglutination	aglutinación *nf*
analogy	analogía *nf*
calque	calco *nm*
collocation	colocación *nf*
concatenation	concatenación *nf*
derivation	derivación *nf*

distinctive feature	rasgo distintivo *nm*
gemination	geminación *nf*
inflection Ⓐ	inflexión *nf*
reduplication	reduplicación *nf*
syncretism	sincretismo *nm*
transformation	tra(n)sformación *nf*

language typology

agglutinating	aglutinante *aj*
analytical	analítico *aj*
click	clic Ⓒ *nm*
hybrid	híbrido *aj*
inflected	flexivo *aj*
primitive	primitivo *aj*
synthetic	sintético *aj*
tone	tonal *aj*

CHARACTERISTICS OF LANGUAGE

definition

acquired	adquirido *aj*
arbitrary	arbitrario *aj*
code	código *nm*
culture	cultura *nf*
human	humano *aj*
natural	natural *aj*
oral	oral *aj*
redundancy	redundancia *nf*
signal	señal *nf*
symbol	símbolo *nm*
system	sistema *nm*
universal	universal *aj*

communication signals

auditory	auditivo *aj*
Braille	Braille *nm*
gesture	gesto *nm*
nonverbal	no verbal *aj*
sign language	lenguaje de gestos *nm, nmpl*
tactile	táctil *aj*
verbal	verbal *aj*
visual	visual *aj*

PERSONS

linguists

cryptographer	criptógrafo, -a *nmf*
dialectician	dialectólogo, -a *nmf*
etymologist	etimólogo, -a *nmf*
grammarian	gramático, -a *nmf*
graphologist	grafólogo, -a *nmf*
lexicographer	lexicógrafo, -a *nmf*

linguist	lingüista *nmf*
neurolinguist	neurolingüista *nmf*
paleographer	paleógrafo, -a *nmf*
philologist	filólogo *nmf*
phonetician	fonetista *nmf*
sociolinguist	sociolingüista *nmf*

other persons

bilingual	bilingüe *aj, nmf*
informant	informante *nmf*
interpreter	intérprete *nmf*
monolingual	monolingüe *aj, nmf*
multilingual	multilingüe *aj, nmf*
polyglot	polígloto, -a *nmf*
purist	purista *nmf*
quadrilingual	cuatrilingüe *aj, nmf*
trilingual	trilingüe *aj, nmf*

(*See also* DICTIONARY INFORMATION under **DICTIONARIES**; *language disorders* under **PHYSICAL DISORDERS**; **PHONOLOGY**; **GRAMMAR**)

PHONOLOGY

GENERAL TERMS

accent	acento *nm*
articulation	articulación *nf*
homonym	homónimo *nm*
homophone	homófono *nm*
intonation	entonación *nf*
phonemics	fonémica *nf*
phonetics	fonética *nf*
phonology	fonología *nf*
pronunciation	pronunciación *nf*
sound	sonido *nm*
transcription	tra(n)scripción *nf*
variant	variante *nf*
vocal	vocal *aj*
voice	voz *nf*

SPECIALIZATIONS

branches of phonetics

acoustic(al)	acústico *aj*
articulatory	articulatorio *aj*
experimental	experimental *aj*
perceptual	perceptivo *aj*

other specializations

phonics	fónica *nf*
phonography	fonografía *nf*
prosody	prosodia *nf*

ASPECTS OF PHONOLOGY

units

allophone	alófono *nm*
consonant	consonante *nf*
morphophoneme	morfofonema *nm*
phone	fon *nm*
phoneme	fonema *nm*
syllable	sílaba *nf*
tone	tono *nm*
vowel	vocal *nf*

kinds of consonants

affricate	africada *nf*
alveolar	alveolar *aj, nf*
apical	apical *aj*
aspirate	aspirada *nf*
bilabial	bilabial *aj, nf*
dental	dental *aj, nf*
explosive	explosiva *aj, nf*
fricative	fricativa *nf*
geminate	geminado *aj*
glottal	glótico *aj*
gutteral	guteral *aj, nf*
interdental	interdental *aj, nf*
intervocalic	intervocálico *aj*
labial	labial *aj, nf*
labiodental	labiodental *aj, nf*
labiovelar	labiovelar *aj, nf*
lateral	lateral *aj, nf*
lingual	lingual *aj, nf*
liquid	líquida *aj, nf*
nasal	nasal *aj, nf*
occlusive	oclusiva *aj, nf*
oral	oral *aj*
palatal	palatal *aj, nf*
semiconsonant	semiconsonante *nf*
sibilant	sibilante *aj, nf*
spirant	espirante *aj, nf*
velar	velar *aj, nf*

kinds of vowels

accented	acentuado *aj*
diphthong	diptongo *nm*
labialized	labializado *aj*
nasalized	nasalizado *aj*
rounded	redondeado *aj*
triphthong	triptongo *nm*
unaccented	inacentuado *aj*

degrees of stress

atonic	atónico *aj*
primary	primario *aj*
secondary	secundario *aj*
tertiary	terciario *aj*

graphic accents

acute	agudo *aj*
breve	breve *nf*
circumflex	circunflejo *aj*
grave	grave *aj*

syllables

antepenultimate	antepenúltimo *aj*
monosyllable	monosílabo *nm*
penultimate	penúltimo *aj, nm*
polysyllable	polisílabo *nm*

phonetic processes

affrication	africación *nf*
alliteration	aliteración *nf*
assimilation	asimilación *nf*
consonance	consonancia *nf*
diphthongization	diptongación *nf*
dissimilation	disimilación, disímilo *nf, nm*
elision	elisión *nf*
epenthesis B	epéntesis C *nf*
gemination	geminación *nf*
metathesis B	metátesis C *nf*
nasalization	nasalización *nf*
reduplication	reduplicación *nf*
syncope	síncopa, síncope *nf, nm*
velarization	velarización *nf*
vowel harmony	harmonía vocálica *nf*

other terms

aphaeresis	aféresis *nf*
apocope	apócope *nf*
assonance	asonancia *nf*
cavity	cavidad *nf*
enunciation	enunciación *nf*
euphony	eufonía *nf*
hiatus B	hiato *nm*
implosion	implosión *nf*
monotone	monótono *aj*
onomatopoeia	onomatopeya *nf*
symbol	símbolo *nm*
timbre	timbre *nm*

(*See also* TERMS IN POETRY under **LITERATURE**)

GRAMMAR

GENERAL TERMS

class	clase *nf*
conjugation	conjugación *nf*
construction	construcción *nf*
declension	declinación *nf*
form	forma *nf*
formative	formativo *nm*
function	función *nf*
order	orden *nm*
paradigm	paradigma *nm*
part of speech	parte de la oración *nf*
syntax	sintaxis *nf*

ASPECTS OF GRAMMAR

grammatical categories

aspect	aspecto *nm*
case	caso *nm*
comparison	comparación *nf*
gender	género *nm*
number	número *nm*
person	persona *nf*

formatives

affix	afijo *nm*
base	base *nf*
clause	cláusula *nf*
enclitic	enclítico *nm*
inflection 🅰	inflexión *nf*
morpheme	morfema *nm*
particle	partícula *nf*
phrase	frase *nf*
prefix	prefijo *nm*
proclitic	proclítico *nm*
suffix	sufijo *nm*
termination	terminación *nf*
variant	variante *aj, nf*

parts of speech

adjective	adjetivo *nm*
adverb	adverbio *nm*
article	artículo *nm*
conjunction	conjunción *nf*
determiner	determinativo *nm*
interjection	interjección *nf*
noun	nombre *nm*
preposition	preposición *nf*
pronoun	pronombre *nm*
substantive	su(b)stantivo *nm*
verb	verbo *nm*

functions

adjunct	adjunto *nm*
antecedent	antecedente *nm*
complement	complemento *nm*
coordination	coordinación *nf*
intensifier	intensificador *nm*
modifier	modificador *nm*
negation	negación *nf*
object	objeto *nm*
qualifier	calificativo *nm*
quantifier	cuantificador *nm*
subordination	subordinación *nf*

NOUNS

number

dual	dual *aj*
plural	plural *aj, nm*
singular	singular *aj, nm*

gender

feminine	femenino *aj, nm*
masculine	masculino *aj, nm*
neuter	neutro *aj, nm*

classification

abstract	abstracto *aj*
animate	animado *aj*
collective	colectivo *aj*
common	común *aj*
compound	compuesto *nm*
concrete	concreto *aj*
countable	contable *aj*
epicene	epiceno *aj*
inanimate	inanimado *aj*
inseparable	inseparable *aj*
mass	masivo *aj*
proper	propio *aj*
separable	separable *aj*
uncountable	no contable *aj*

cases

ablative	ablativo *aj, nm*
accusative	acusativo *aj, nm*
concessive	concesivo *aj, nm*
dative	dativo *aj, nm*
genitive	genitivo *aj, nm*
instrumental	instrumental *aj, nm*
locative	locativo *aj, nm*
nominative	nominativo *aj, nm*
objective	objetivo *aj*
oblique	oblicuo *aj*
partitive	partitivo *aj*

possessive	posesivo *aj, nm*
vocative	vocativo *aj*

VERBS

general terms

copula **B**	cópula *nf*
direct object	complemento directo *aj*
indirect object	complemento indirecto *nm*
mood	modo *nm*
principal parts	partes principales *nfpl*
tense	tiempo *nm*
voice	voz *nf*

classification

auxiliary	auxiliar *aj, nm*
causative	causativo *aj, nm*
copulative	copulativo *aj*
defective	defectivo *aj*
gerund	gerundio *nm*
inchoative	incoativo *aj*
infinitive	infinitivo *nm*
interrogative	interrogativo *aj*
intransitive	intransitivo *aj*
irregular	irregular *aj*
modal	modal *aj*
participle	participio *nm*
phrasal verb	verbo con partícula *nm, nf*
pronominal	pronominal *aj*
reflexive	reflexivo *aj*
regular	regular *aj*
transitive	transitivo *aj*

principal parts

past participle	participio pasado *nm*
past tense	tiempo pasado *nm*
present participle	participio presente *nm*
simple form	forma simple *nf*

person

first person	primera persona *nf*
second person	segunda persona *nf*
third person	tercera persona *nf*

tense

future	futuro *aj, nm*
historical (present)	histórico *aj*
past	pasado *aj, nm*
perfect	perfecto *aj, nm*
pluperfect	plusquamperfecto *aj, nm*

present	presente *aj, nm*
preterit **A**	pretérito *aj, nm*

aspect and mood

active	activo *aj*
emphatic	enfático *aj*
frequentative	frecuentativo *aj, nm*
imperfect	imperfecto *aj, nm*
imperfective	imperfectivo *aj, nm*
indicative	indicativo *aj, nm*
passive	pasivo *aj*
perfective	perfectivo *aj, nm*
potential	potencial *aj, nm*
progressive	progresivo *aj, nm*
subjunctive	subjuntivo *aj, nm*

ADJECTIVES AND ADVERBS

kinds of adjectives

attributive	atributivo *aj*
augmentative	aumentativo *aj*
demonstrative	demostrativo *aj*
diminutive	diminutivo *aj*
possessive	posesivo *aj*
qualifying	calificativo *aj*

kinds of adverbs

conjunctive	conjuntivo *aj*
intensive	intensivo *aj*
interrogative	interrogativo *aj*

degrees of comparison

comparative	comparativo *aj*
positive	positivo *aj*
superlative	superlativo *aj*

OTHER PARTS OF SPEECH

pronouns

demonstrative	demostrativo *aj*
impersonal	impersonal *aj*
indefinite	indefinido *aj*
interrogative	interrogativo *aj*
personal	personal *aj*
reflexive	reflexivo *aj*
relative	relativo *aj*

articles

definite	definido *aj*
indefinite	indefinido *aj*

conjunctions

coordinating	coordinante *aj*

correlative	correlativo *aj*
disjunctive	disyuntivo *aj*
subordinating	subordinante *aj*
reciprocal	recíproco *aj*

TERMS IN SYNTAX

phrases

adjectival	adjetival *aj*
adverbial	adverbial *aj*
appositive	apositivo *aj*
infinitival *aj*	del infinitivo *nm*
periphrastic	perifrástico *aj*
prepositional	preposicional *aj*

clauses

concord	concordia *nf*
conditional	condicional *aj*
coordinate	coordinado *aj*
dependant, dependent	dependiente *aj*
independent	independiente *aj*
subordinate	subordinado *aj*
temporal *aj*	de tiempo *nm*

sentences

affirmative	afirmativo *aj*
complex	complejo *aj*
compound	compuesto *aj*
declarative	declarativo *aj*
declaratory	declaratorio *aj*
direct discourse	estilo directo *nm*
elliptical	elíptico *aj*
exclamatory	exclamatorio *aj*
grammatical	gramaticalmente correcto *aj*
imperative	imperativo *aj*
indirect discourse	estilo indirecto *nm*
interrogative	interrogativo *aj*
negative	negativo *aj*
predicate	predicado *nm*
simple	simple *aj*
subject	sujeto *nm*
ungrammatical	antigramatical *aj*

(*See also* **grammatical** *and* **semantic** under **DICTIONARIES**)

WRITING

GENERAL TERMS

alphabet	alfabeto *nm*
diacritic	signo diacrítico *nm*
graphic accent	acento ortográfico *nm*

manuscript	manuscrito *nm*
orthography	ortografía *nf*
punctuation	puntuación *nf*
script	escritura *nf*

SPECIALIZATIONS

calligraphy	caligrafía *nf*
cryptography	criptografía *nf*
decipherment	descifre *nm*
epigraphy	epigrafía *nf*
graphology	grafología *nf*
paleography Ⓐ	paleografía *nf*
philology	filología *nf*
stenotypy	estenotipia *nf*

ASPECTS OF WRITTEN LANGUAGE

forms

abbreviation	abreviatura *nf*
initials	iniciales *nfpl*
inscription	inscripción *nf*
monogram	monograma *nm*
text	texto *nm*

types of writing systems

alphabetic(al)	alfabético *aj*
cuneiform	cuneiforme *aj*
hieroglyphic	jeroglífico *aj*
ideography	ideografía *nf*
logography	logografía *nf*
pictography	pictografía *nf*
stenography	estenografía *nf*
syllabary	silabario *nm*

units

character	carácter *nm*
cryptogram, cryptograph	criptograma *nm*
digraph	dígrafo *nm*
grapheme	grafema *nm*
hieroglyph	jeroglífico *nm*
ideogram, ideograph	ideograma *nm*
letter	letra *nf*
phonogram	fonograma *nm*
pictogram, pictograph	pictograma *nm*
pictograph	pictografía *nf*
stenotype	estenotipo *nm*
symbol	símbolo *nm*

diacritical marks

cedilla	cedilla *nf*
dieresis Ⓑ	diéresis Ⓒ *nf*

tilde	tilde *nm or nf*
vowel point	punto vocálico *nm*

graphic accents

acute	agudo *aj*
breve	breve *nf*
circumflex	circunflejo *aj*
grave	grave *aj*

punctuation

apostrophe	apóstrofo *nm*
capital letter	letra capital *nf*
comma	coma *nf*
contraction	contracción *nf*
paragraph	párrafo *nm*
parenthesis ⓑ	paréntesis ⓒ *nm*
period	período, periodo *nm*
suspension	suspensión *nf*

handwriting

cursive script	cursiva *nf*
flourish	floreo *nm*
illegible	ilegible *aj*
legible	legible *aj*

other terms

ABC-book	abecedario *nm*
aleph	álef *nm*
aphaeresis	aféresis *nf*
homograph	homógrafo *nm*
insert (word)	insertar *vt*
lacuna ⓑ	laguna *nf*
obliteration	obliteración *nf*
palindrome	palíndromo *nm*
Romanization	romanización *nf*
spelling reform	reforma ortográfica *nf*
stylograph	estilógrafo *nf*
transliteration	trasliteración *nf*

ALPHABETS

Arabic	árabe *aj*
Cyrillic	cirílico *aj*
Greek	griego *aj*
Hebrew	hebreo *aj*
phonetic	fonético *aj*
Roman	romano *aj*

HISTORICAL TERMS

scripts

Cherokee	cheroquí *aj, nm*
Egyptian	egipcio, -a *aj, nm*

Gothic	gótico *aj, nm*
Phoenician	fenicio *aj, nm*
Semitic	semítico *aj, nm*
Ugaritic	ugarítico *aj, nm*

other terms

boustrophedon	bustrófedon *nm*
palimsest	palimsesto *nm*
Rosetta stone	piedra de Roseta *nf*
rune	runa *nf*
scribe	escriba *nm*

THE GREEK ALPHABET

alpha	alfa *nf(el)*
beta	beta *nf*
chi	ji *nf*
delta	delta *nf*
epsilon	epsilón *nf*
eta	eta *nf*
gamma	gamma *nf*
iota	iota *nf*
kappa	kappa *nf*
lambda	lambda *nf*
mu	my *nf*
omega	omega *nf*
omicron	ómicron *nf*
phi	phi, fi *nf*
pi	pi *nf*
psi	psi *nf*
rho	rho *nf*
sigma	sigma *nf*
tau	tau *nf*
theta	theta *nf*
upsilon	ípsilon *nf*
xi	xi *nf*
zeta	zeta *nf*

PERSONS

graphologist	grafólogo, -a *nmf*
calligrapher	calígrafo, -a *nmf*
copyist	copista *nmf*
cryptographer	criptógrafo, -a *nmf*
decipherer	descifrador, -a *nmf*
paleographer ⓐ	paleógrafo, -a *nmf*
philologist	filólogo *nmf*
stenographer	estenógrafo, -a *nmf*
stenotypist	estenotipista *nmf*

(*See also* **TERMS IN POETRY** under **LITERATURE**)

USING LANGUAGE

GENERAL TERMS

communication	comunicación *nf*
expression	expresión *nf*
fluency	fluidez *nf*
information	información *nf*
message	mensaje *nm*
rhetoric	retórica *nf*
semantics	semántica *nf*
use	uso *nm*

LANGUAGE FUNCTIONS

good purpose

clarification	aclaración *nf*
congratulations	congratulaciones *nfpl*
consultation	consulta *nf*
counsel	consejo *nm*
description	descripción *nf*
elaboration	elaboración *nf*
elucidation	elucidación *nf*
enumeration	enumeración *nf*
exhortation	exhortación *nf*
explication	explicación *nf*
felicitation	felicitación *nf*
hortative, hortatory	hortatorio *aj*
identification	identificación *nf*
interpretation	interpretación *nf*
interrogation	interrogación *nf*
iteration	iteración *nf*
notification	notificación *nf*
persuasion	persuasión *nf*
socialization	socialización *nf*
suggestion	sugerencia *nf*

bad purpose

accusation	acusación *nf*
denunciation	denuncia, denunciación *nf*
evasion	evasión *nf*
excuse	excusa *nf*
falsification	falsificación *nf*
fulmination	fulminación *nf*
insinuation	insinuación *nf*
invective	invectiva *nf*
malediction	maldición *nf*
obscenity	obscenidad *nf*
profanity	profanidad *nf*
vilification	vilipendio *nm*
vituperation	vituperio *nm*

SPECIFIC FORMS

written

addendum Ⓑ	adenda *nf*
annotation	anotación *nf*
bulletin	boletín *nm*
citation	citación *nf*
composition	composición *nf*
concordance	concordancia *nf*
correspondence	correspondencia *nf*
document	documento *nm*
gloss	glosa *nf*
list	lista *nf*
literature	literatura *nf*
manuscript	manuscrito *nm*
marginalia	notas marginales *nfpl*
memo, memorandum	memorándum *nm*
missive	misiva *nf*
note	nota *nf*
postscript	pos(t)data *nf*
printed matter *nsg*	impresos *nmpl*
publications	publicaciones *nfpl*
questionnaire	cuestionario *nm*

spoken

announcement	anuncio *nm*
colloquy	coloquio *nm*
comment, commentary	comentario *nm*
conversation	conversación *nf*
debate	debate *nm*
declamation	declamación *nf*
declaration	declaración *nf*
dialog(ue)	diálogo *nm*
dictation	dictado *nm*
dictum Ⓑ	dictamen *nm*
discourse	discurso *nm*
discussion	discusión *nf*
edict	edicto *nm*
eulogy	elogio *nm*
harangue	arenga *nf*
interlocution	interlocución *nf*
interpolation	interpolación *nf*
interruption	interrupción *nf*
mention	mención *nf*
monolog(ue)	monólogo *nm*
murmurrings	murmullos *nmpl*
observation	observación *nf*
oration (funeral)	oración *nf*
oratory	oratoria *nf*
peroration	peroración *nf*
promise	promesa *nf*
recital (poem)	recital *nm*

recitation	recitado, recitación *nm, nf*
response (question)	respuesta *nf*
rumor Ⓐ	rumor *nm*
salaam	zalema *nf*
salutation	saludo, salutación *nf*
sermon	sermón *nm*
tête-à-tête	tête-à-tête *nm*
verbalization	expresión verbalmente *nf*

written or oral

admonition	admonición, amonestación *nf*
anecdote	anécdota *nf*
blasphemy	blasfemia *nf*
calumny	calumnia *nf*
compliment	cumplido *nm*
diatribe	diatriba *nf*
falsehood	falsedad *nf*
insult	insulto *nm*
name	nombre *nm*
panegyric	panegírico *nm*
proclamation	proclama *nf*
proposal	propuesta *nf*
propaganda	propaganda *nf*
recapitulation	recapitulación *nf*
recommendation	recomendación *nf*
relate	relatar *vt*
repetition	repetición *nf*
retraction (statement)	retractación *nf*

restricted language use

argot	argot *nm*
jargon	jerga, jerigonza *nf*
legalese	jerga legal *nf*
nomenclature	nomenclatura *nf*
vernacular	vernáculo *nm*

DESCRIBING LANGUAGE USE

desirable

articulate	articulado *aj*
clear	claro *aj*
correct	correcto *aj*
eloquent	elocuente *aj*
expressive	expresivo *aj*
intelligible	inteligible *aj*
proper	propio *aj*
succinct	sucinto *aj*

undesirable

ambiguous	ambiguo *aj*

cryptic	críptico *aj*
equivocal (reply)	equívoco *aj*
expletive	palabra expletiva *nf*
grandiloquent	grandilocuente *aj*
improper	impropio *aj*
incoherent	incoherente *aj*
incorrect	incorrecto *aj*
inexpressive	inexpresivo *aj*
insinuating	insinuador *aj*
insulting	insultante *aj*
mordant	mordaz *aj*
obscene	obsceno *aj*
obscure	o(b)scuro *aj*
offensive	ofensivo *aj*
pejorative	peyorativo *aj, nm*
poisonous (fig)	ponzoñoso *aj*
redundant	redundante *aj*
repetitive	repetitivo *aj*
scabrous	escabroso *aj*
turgid	turgente *aj*
unclear	poco claro *aj*
unintelligible	ininteligible *aj*
vague	vago *aj*
vilifying	vilipendiador *aj*
vitriolic	vitriólico *aj*
vociferating	vociferante *aj*
vulgar	vulgar *aj*

incorrect language

barbarism	barbarismo *nm*
corruption	corrupción *nf*
hypercorrection	ultracorrección *nf*
locution	locución *nf*
neologism	neologismo *nm*
pleonasm	pleonasmo *nm*
solecism	solecismo *nm*
vulgarism	vulgarismo *nm*

special usages

acronym	acrónimo *nm*
cliché	cliché *nm*
colloquialism	expresión coloquial *nf*
euphemism	eufemismo *nm*
evasive statement	evasiva *nf*
localism	localismo *nm*
metaphrase	metáfrasis *nf*
palindrome	palíndromo *nm*
regionalism	regionalismo *nm*

other terms

abstract	abstracto *aj*
concrete	concreto *aj*

formal	formal *aj*
indescribable	indescriptible *aj*
ineffable	inefable *aj*
informal	informal *aj*
literal	literal *aj*
nontechnical	no técnico *aj*
onomatopoeic	onomatopéyico *aj*
poetic	poético *aj*
scientific	científico *aj*
technical	técnico *aj*

DESCRIBING LANGUAGE USERS

overusers

bombastic	bombástico *aj*
garrulous	gárrulo *aj*
loquacious	locuaz *aj*
pontificate	pontificar *vi*
repetitious	repetidor *aj*
sententious	sentencioso *aj*
tendentious	tendencioso *aj*
verbiage	verborragía, verborrea *nf*
verbose	verboso *aj*
vituperative	vituperioso *aj*
vociferous	vociferador *aj*

underusers

inarticulate	inarticulado *aj*
laconic	lacónico *aj*
mute	mudo *aj*
silent	silencioso *aj*
taciturn	taciturno *aj*
uncommunicative	poco comunicativo *aj*

other terms

emphatic	enfático *aj*
fluently *av*	con fluidez *nf*
humorous	humorístico *aj*
inoffensive	inofensivo *aj*
ironic(al)	irónico *aj*
sarcastic	sarcástico *aj*
vehement	vehemente *aj*

voice qualities

dulcet	dulce *aj*
mellifluous	melifluo *aj*
resonant	resonante *aj*
strident	estridente *aj*
vibrant	vibrante *aj*

TERMS IN SEMANTICS

kinds of meaning

connotative	connotativo *aj*
contextual *aj*	del contexto *nm*
denotative	denotativo *aj*
figurative	figurado *aj*
inferred	inferido *aj*
lexical	léxico *aj*
notional	nocional *aj*
referential *aj*	de referencia *nf*

other terms

antonym	antónimo *nm*
polysemy	polisemia *nf*
presupposition	presuposición *nf*
significance	significado, significación *nm, nf*
synonymy	sinonimia *nf*
synonym	sinónimo *nm*
term	término *nm*

TERMS IN RHETORIC

allusion	alusión *nf*
amplification	ampliación *nf*
antithesis Ⓑ	antítesis *nf*
apostrophe	apóstrofe *nm*
argumentation	argumentación *nf*
circumlocution	circunlocución *nf*
controvert	controvertir *vt*
diction	dicción *nf*
digression	digresión *nf*
disquisition	disquisición *nf*
dissuasion	disuasión *nf*
elocution	elocución *nf*
figure of speech	figura retórica *nf*
inversion	inversión *nf*
oxymoron	oxímoron *nm*
paraphrase	paráfrasis Ⓒ *nf*
periphrasis Ⓑ	perífrasis Ⓒ *nf*
polemic	polémica *nf*
qualification	calificación *nf*
redefine	redefinir *vt*
refutation	refutación *nf*
reiteration	reiteración *nf*
syllogism	silogismo *nm*
synecdoche	sinécdoque *nm*

PERSONS

annotator	anotador(a) *nmf*
announcer	anunciador(a) *nmf*
arguer	argumentador(a) *nmf*

commentator	comentarista *nmf*
conversationalist	conversador(a) *nmf*
correspondent	correspondiente *nmf*
declaimer	declamador(a) *nmf*
fulminator	fulminador(a) *nmf*
interlocutor	interlocutor(a) *nmf*
interpreter	intérprete *nmf*
lexicographer	lexicógrafo, -a *nmf*
orator	orador(a) *nmf*
pamphleteer	panfletista *nmf*
polemicist	polemista *nmf*
fluency	fluidez *nf*

(*See also* usage labels under **DICTIONARIES**; word games under **GAMES**; **LITERATURE**)

LANGUAGES OF THE WORLD

KINDS OF LANGUAGES

artificial	artificial *aj*
international	internacional *aj*
lingua franca **B**	lengua franca *nf*
modern	moderno *aj*
national	nacional *aj*
native language	lengua materna *nf*
official	oficial *aj*
regional	regional *aj*
second	segundo *aj*

LANGUAGE FAMILIES

major language families

Afro-Asiatic	afroasiático *aj*
Dravidian	dravidiano, dravida *aj*
Indo-European	indoeuropeo *aj*
Malayo-Polynesian	malayopolinesio *aj*
Sino-Tibetan	sinotibetano *aj*
Uralic-Altaic	uralo-altaico, uraloaltaico *aj, nm*

other language families

Altaic	altaico *aj*
Aryan	ario *aj*
Austro-Asiatic	austroasiático *aj*
Austronesian	austronesio *aj*
Bantu	bantú *aj*
Caucasian	caucasiano, caucásico *aj*
Indo-Aryan	indoario *aj*
Indo-Germanic	indogermánico *aj*
Mayan	maya *aj*
Semitic	semítico *aj*
Teutonic	teutónico *aj*

branches of Indo-European

Albanian	albanés *nm*
Armenian	armenio *nm*
Baltic	báltico *nm*
Celtic	celta *nm*
Germanic	germánico *nm*
Greek	griego *nm*
Indo-Iranian	indoiranés *nm*
Romance	romance *nm*
Slavic **A**	eslavo *nm*

LANGUAGE NAMES

major world languages

Arabic	árabe *nm*
Bengali	bengalí *nm*
Chinese	chino *nm*
English	inglés *nm*
French	francés *nm*
Hindi	hindi *nm*
Indonesian	indonesio *nm*
Japanese	japonés *nm*
Korean	coreano *nm*
Portuguese	portugués *nm*
Punjabi	penjabi *nm*
Russian	ruso *nm*
Spanish	español *nm*
Tamil	tamil *nm*
Urdu	urdu *nm*

other European languages

Bulgarian	búlgaro *nm*
Byelorussian	bielorruso *nm*
Castilian	castellano *nm*
Catalan	catalán *nm*
Croatian	croata *nm*
Czech	checo *nm*
Danish	danés, dinamarqués *nm*
Estonian	estonio *nm*
Finnish	finlandés *nm*
Gaelic	gaélico *nm*
Hungarian	húngaro *nm*
Icelandic	islandés *nm*
Irish	irlandés *nm*
Italian	italiano *nm*
Lappish	lapón *nm*
Latvian	latvio *nm*
Lett, Lettish	letón *nm*
Lithuanian	lituano *nm*
Norwegian	noruego *nm*
Polish	polaco *nm*
Rumanian, Romanian	rumano *nm*

Scottish	escosés *nm*
Serbo-Croatian	servocroata *nm*
Swedish	sueco *nm*
Turkish	turco *nm*
Ukranian	ucraniano *nm*
Yiddish	yid(d)ish *nm*

other Asian languages

Burmese	birmano *nm*
Cambodian	camboyano *nm*
Cantonese	cantonés *nm*
Hawaiian	hawaiano *nm*
Hebrew	hebreo *nm*
Hindu	hindú *nm*
Hindustani	indostaní *nm*
Javanese	javanés *nm*
Khmer	kmer *nm*
Malay	malayo *nm*
Manchu B	manchú, manchuriano *nm*
Mandarin	mandarín *nm*
Mongolian	mongol *nm*
Nepali	nepalés *nm*
Persian	persa *nm*
Sinhalese, Singhalese	cingalés *nm*
Tagalog	tagalo *nm*
Thai	tailandés *nm*
Tibetan	tibetano *nm*
Vietnamese	vietnamita *nm*

American Indian languages

Eskimo	esquimal *nm*
Guarani	guaraní *nm*
Navaho, Navajo	navajo *nm*
Quechua	quechua, quichua *nm*

African languages

Afrikaans	africaans *nm*
Amharic	amhárico *nm*
Berber	beréber *nm*
Coptic	copto *nm*
Hausa	hausa *nm*
Swahili	swahili, suajili *nm*
Yoruba	yoruba *nm*
Zulu	zulú *nm*

historical languages

Akkadian	acadio *nm*
Anglo-Saxon	anglosajón *nm*
Aramaic	arameo *nm*
Assyrian	asirio *nm*
Babylonian	babilonio *nm*
Cornish	córnico *nm*
Etruscan	etrusco *nm*
Gothic	gótico *nm*
Hamitic	camita *nm*
Hittite	hitita *nm*
Latin	latín *nm*
Mayan	maya *nm*
Phoenician	fenicio *nm*
Phrygian	frigio *nm*
Sanskrit	sánscrito *nm*
Sumerian	sumerio *nm*

regional languages

Basque	vascuence, vasco *nm*
Breton	bretón *nm*
Malagasy	malgache *nm*
Maldivian	maldivo *nm*
Romansch, Romansh	romanche *nm*

mixed and artificial languages

Basic English	inglés básico *nm*
Creole	criollo *nm*
Esperanto	esperanto *nm*
Franglais	franglés *nm*
Spanglish	espanglés *nm*

BORROWINGS

Americanism	americanismo *nm*
Anglicism	anglicismo *nm*
Arabic expression	arabismo *nm*
Argentinian expression	argentinismo *nm*
calque	calco *nm*
Cubanism	cubanismo *nm*
Gallicism	galicismo *nm*
Hebraism	hebreaísmo *nm*
Italianism	italianismo *nm*

PERSONS

Africanist	africanista *nmf*
Arabist	arabista *nmf*
Hebraist	hebraísta *nmf*
Hispanist	hispanista *nmf*
interpreter	intérprete *nmf*
Sinologist	sinólogo, -a *nmf*

(*See also* **ETHNIC GROUPS AROUND THE WORLD** under **ANTHROPOLOGY AND ARCHEOLOGY**; **PLACE NAMES II: POLITICAL**)

Our Planet and Its Peoples

GEOGRAPHY

GENERAL TERMS

area	área *nf(el)*
climate	clima *nm*
direction	dirección *nf*
distance	distancia *nf*
elevation	elevación *nf*
formation	formación *nf*
geography	geografía *nf*
global	global *aj*
hemisphere	hemisferio *nm*
horizon	horizonte *nm*
hydrosphere	hidrósfera *nf*
isometric	isométrico *aj*
line	línea *nf*
location	localización *nf*
map	mapa *nm*
pole	polo *nm*
region	región *nf*
zone	zona *nf*

SPECIALIZATIONS

biological geography

biogeography	biogeografía *nf*
ecology	ecología *nf*
oceanography	oceanografía *nf*
phytogeography	fitogeografía *nf*
zoogeography	zoogeografía *nf*

physical geography

climatology	climatología *nf*
cosmography	cosmografía *nf*
geochemistry	geoquímica *nf*
geodesy	geodesia *nf*
geomorphology	geomorfología *nf*
hydrography	hidrografía *nf*
hydrology	hidrología *nf*
oceanology	oceanología *nf*
orography	orografía *nf*
physiography	fisiografía *nf*

other fields

cartography	cartografía *nf*
geopolitics	geopolítica *nf*
meteorology	meteorología *nf*
photogrammetry	fotogrametría *nf*

topography	topografía *nf*
toponymy	toponimia *nf*

ASPECTS OF GEOGRAPHY

physical formations

abyss	abismo *nm*
archipelago B	archipiélago *nm*
atoll	atolón *nm*
bank	banco *nm*
bay	bahía *nf*
canyon	cañón *nm*
cape	cabo *nm*
cascade	cascada *nf*
cataract	catarata *nf*
cave	cueva *nf*
cavern	caverna *nf*
cay	cayo *nm*
channel	canal *nm*
continent	continente *nm*
delta	delta *nm*
desert	desierto *nm*
divide	divisoria *nf*
dune	duna *nf*
estuary	estuario *nm*
fiord	fiordo *nm*
grotto B	gruta *nf*
gulf	golfo *nm*
iceberg	iceberg *nm*
island, isle	isla *nf*
islet	isleta *nf*
isthmus B	istmo *nm*
jungle	jungla *nf*
lagoon	laguna *nf*
lake	lago *nm*
massif	macizo *nm*
mountain	monte, montaña *nm, nf*
oasis B	oasis *nm*
ocean	océano *nm*
peak	pico *nm*
peninsula	península *nf*
point	punta *nf*
precipice	precipicio *nm*
promonotory	promonotorio *nm*
rapids	rápidos *nmpl*
reef	arrecife *nm*
river	río *nm*
sandbank	banco de arena *nm, nf*

sandbar	barra de arena *nf*
tributary	tributario *nm*
vale	valle *nm*
valley	valle *nm*
virgin forest	bosque virgen *nm*
volcano 🅑	volcán *nm*

regions and zones

agricultural	agrícola *aj*
alpine	alpestre, alpino *aj*
Antarctic	antártico *aj, nm*
Arctic	ártico *aj, nm*
coastal	costero *aj*
desert-like	desértico *aj*
inhabited	habitado *aj*
littoral	litoral *aj, nm*
mountainous	montañoso *aj*
northland	tierra del norte *nf*
overpopulated	superpoblado *aj*
pampa	pampa *nf*
pelagic	pelágico *aj*
populated	poblado *aj*
riverside	ribera *nf*
savanna(h)	sabana *nf*
steppe	estepa *nf*
subcontinent	subcontinente *nm*
taiga	taiga *nf*
tropics	zona tropical *nf*
tundra	tundra *nf*
unexplored	inexplorado *aj*
uninhabited	inhabitado *aj*

directions and locations

antipodes	antípodas *nfpl*
cardinal point	punto cardinal *nm*
east	este *nm*
eastbound	con rumbo al este
easterly	desde/hacia el este
eastern	del este, oriental
easternmost	más al este
eastward	hacia el este
magnetic pole	polo magnético *nm*
midcontinent	medio del continente *nm*
north	norte *nm*
northeast	nordeste *nm*
northeasterly	del nordeste
northeastern	del nordeste
northerly	desde/hacia el norte
northern	del norte
northward	hacia el norte
northwards	hacia el norte
northwest	noroeste *aj, nm*
northwestern	hacia el noroeste
orientation	orientación *nf*
southeast	sudeste *nm*
west	oeste *nm*
westbound	con rumbo al oeste
westerly	del oeste
western	del oeste
westward	hacia el oeste

climates

arid	árido *aj*
continental	continental *aj*
equatorial	ecuatorial *aj*
glacial	glacial *aj*
insular	insular *aj*
oceanic	oceánico *aj*
polar	polar *aj*
subtropical	subtropical *aj*
temperate	templado *aj*
torrid	tórrido *aj*
tropical	tropical *aj*

other terms

confluence	confluencia *nf*
corridor	corredor *nm*
crest (wave)	cresta *nf*
current	corriente *nf*
declivity	declive *nm*
denude	desnudar *vt*
enclave	enclave *nm*
erosion	erosión *nf*
exploration	exploración *nf*
fluvial	fluvial *aj*
frontier	frontera *nf*
geostrophic	geostrófico *aj*
habitat	habitat *nm*
meander	meandro *nm*
territorial	territorial *aj*
turbid (water)	túrbio *aj*
vegetation	vegetación *nf*

CARTOGRAPHY

kinds of maps

aerial map	aeromapa *nm*
celestial	celeste *aj*
contour	contorno *nm*
inventory	inventario *nm*
mobility	movilidad *nf*
nautical	náutico *aj*
physical	físico *aj*
political	político *aj*
population	población *nf*

projection	proyección *nf*
reference	referencia *nf*
relief	relieve *nm*
terrestrial	terrestre *aj*
thematic	temático *aj*
transit	tránsito *nm*
transportation	tra(n)sportación *nf*
world map	mapamundi *nm*

forms of maps

atlas	atlas *nm*
globe	globo *nm*
homolosine	homolosenoidal *aj*
photomap	fotomapa *nm*
plane	plano *aj, nm*
planisphere	planisferio *nm*
terrain	terreno *nm*

imaginary lines

circle	círculo *nm*
equator	ecuador *nm*
latitude	latitud *nf*
longitude	longitud *nf*
meridian	meridiano *nm*
parallel	paralelo *nm*
tropic	trópico *nm*

isometric lines

isobar	isobara *nf*
isogonic	isogónico, isógono *aj*
isogram	isograma *nm*
isotherm	isoterma *nf*

other terms

altitude	altitud *nf*
azimuth	acimut, azimut *nm*
chart	carta *nf*
color Ⓐ	color *nm*
distortion	distorsión *nf*
graphic	gráfico *aj*
index Ⓑ	índice *nm*
scale	escala *nf*
symbol	símbolo *nm*

TOOLS AND MEASUREMENTS

compass	compás *nm*
geocentric	geocéntrico *aj*
inclinometer	inclinómetro *nm*
pantograph	pantógrafo *nm*
theodolite	teodolito *nm*

PERSONS
famous explorers

Columbus	Colón
Magellan	Magallanes
Vespucci	Vespucio

other persons

cartographer	cartógrafo, -a *nmf*
discoverer	descubridor(a) *nmf*
explorer	explorador(a) *nmf*
geographer	geógrafo, -a *nmf*
topographer	topógrafo, -a *nmf*

(*See also* **GEOLOGY**; **METEOROLOGY**)

PLACE NAMES I: PHYSICAL
GLOBAL TERMS
hemispheres

Eastern Hemisphere	hemisferio oriental *nm*
Northern Hemisphere	hemisferio boreal *nm*
Southern Hemisphere	hemisferio austral *nm*
Western Hemisphere	hemisferio occidental *nm*

inhabitants

Easterner	habitante del este *nmf*
Northerner	norteño, -a *nmf*
Southerner	sureño, -a *nmf*
Westerner	habitante del oeste *nmf*

CONTINENTS
names

Africa	África
Antarctica	Antártida
Asia	Asia
Australia	Australia
Europe	Europa
North America	Norteamérica
South America	Sudamérica

inhabitants

African	africano, -a *aj, nmf*
Asian	asiático, -a *aj, nmf*
Australian	australiano, -a *aj, nmf*
European	europeo, -a *aj, nmf*
North American	norteamericano, -a *aj, nmf*
South American	sudamericano, -a *aj, nmf*

PENINSULAS

Arabia	Arabia
Asia Minor	Asia Menor
Balkans	Balcanes
Crimea	Crimea
Iberia	Iberia
Indo-China	Indochina
Sinai	Sinai
Yucatan	Yucatán

ISLANDS

single islands

Bali	Bali
Barbados	Barbados
Borneo	Borneo
Corfu	Corfú
Corsica	Córcega
Crete	Creta
Cuba	Cuba
Curaçao	Curazao
Cyprus	Chipre
Elba	Elba
Fiji	Fiji, Fiyi
Greenland	Groenlandia
Grenada	Granada
Guadeloupe	Guadalupe
Guam	Guam
Ireland	Irlanda
Jamaica	Jamaica
Java	Java
Jersey	Jersey
Madagascar	Madagascar
Majorca	Mallorca
Minorca	Menorca
Puerto Rico	Puerto Rico
Rhodes	Rodas
Sardinia	Cerdeña
Sicily	Sicilia
Singapore	Singapur
Tahiti	Tahití
Taiwan	Taiwan
Tasmania	Tasmania
Tobago	Tobago
Trinidad	Trinidad
Zanzibar	Zanzíbar

island groups

Antilles	Antillas
Azores	Azores
Bahamas	Bahamas
Balearics	Baleares
Bermuda	Bermudas
Canaries	Canarias
Caymans	Caimanes
Faeros	Feroes
Filipines	Filipinas
Galapagos	Galápagos
Grenadines	Granadinas
Hebrides	Hébrides
Maldives	Maldivas
Melanesia	Melanesia
Micronesia	Micronesia
Polynesia	Polinesia
Samoa	Samoa
Virgins	Vírgenes

inhabitants

Aleutian	Aleuta *aj, nmf*
Balinese Ⓑ	balinés, -esa *aj, nmf*
Barbadian	barbadense *aj, nmf*
Bermudian	bermudeño, -a *aj, nmf*
Canarian	canario, -a *aj, nmf*
Corsican	corso, -a *aj, nmf*
Cretan	cretense *aj, nmf*
Cuban	cubano, -a *aj, nmf*
Cypriot	chipriota *aj, nmf*
Fijian	fidjiano, -a, fiyiano, -a *aj, nmf*
Filipino	filipino, -a *aj, nmf*
Greenlander	groenlandés, -esa *nmf*
Grenadian	granadino, -a *aj, nmf*
islander	isleño, -a *nmf*
Jamaican	jamaiciano, -a, jamaiquino, -a *aj, nmf*
Javanese Ⓑ	javanés, -esa *aj, nmf*
Majorcan	mallorquín, -ina *aj, nmf*
Maldivian	maldivo, -a *aj, nmf*
Melanesian	melanesio, -a *aj, nmf*
Micronesian	micronesio, -a *aj, nmf*
Polynesian	polinesio, -a *aj, nmf*
Puerto Rican	puertorriqueño, -a *aj, nmf*
Samoan	samoano, -a *aj, nmf*
Sardinian	sardo, -a *aj, nmf*
Sicilian	siciliano, -a *aj, nmf*
Tahitian	tahitiano, -a *aj, nmf*
Taiwanese Ⓑ	taiwanés, -esa *aj, nmf*

WATER FORMATIONS

oceans

Antarctic	Antártico

Arctic	Ártico
Atlantic	Atlántico
Indian	Índico
Pacific	Pacífico

seas

Adriatic	Adriático
Aegean	Egeo
Arabian	Arábigo
Baltic	Báltico
Caribbean	Caribe
Caspian	Caspio
Ionian	Jónico
Mediterranean	Mediterráneo
North Sea	Mar del Norte
	nm

rivers

Amazon	Amazonas
Congo	Congo
Danube	Danubio
Ebro	Ebro
Elbe	Elba
Euphrates	Eufrates
Ganges	Ganges
Jordan	Jordán
Mississippi	Misisipí
Moselle	Mosela
Niger	Níger
Nile	Nilo
Rhine	Rin
Seine	Sena
Thames	Támesis
Tiber	Tíber
Yangtze	Yang-Tsé
Yukon	Yukón
Zambezi	Zambeze

gulfs

Aden	Adén
Bothnia	Botnia
Mexico	Méjico, México
Persian	Pérsico

straits and channels

Bosphorus	Bósforo
Dardanelles	Dardanelos
Magellan	Magallanes

bays and capes

Biscay	Vizcaya
Canaveral	Cañaveral
Horn	Hornos

MOUNTAINS
single mountains

Fuji, Fujiyama	Fujiyama
Kilimanjaro	Kilimanjaro
Olympus	Olimpo
Parnassus	Parnaso
Sinai	Sinai
Vesuvius	Vesubio

mountain ranges

Alps	Alpes
Andes	Andes
Apennines	Apeninos
Appalachians	Apalaches
Carpathians	Carpatos
Himalayas	Himalaya
Pyrenees	Pirineos
Rockies	Rocosas
Urals	Urales

PLACE NAMES II: POLITICAL

(*Note:* Island countries are listed in **PLACE NAMES I: PHYSICAL**)

COUNTRIES

names

Afghanistan	Afganistán
Albania	Albania
Algeria	Argelia
Angola	Angola
Argentina	La Argentina
Armenia	Armenia
Australia	Australia
Austria	Austria
Azerbaijan	Azerbaiyán, Azerbaiján
Bahamas	Bahamas
Bangladesh	Bangladesh
Barbados	Barbados
Belgium	Bélgica
Belize	Belice
Bhutan	Bután
Bolivia	Bolivia
Bosnia	Bosnia
Botswana	Botsuana
Brazil	Brasil
Bulgaria	Bulgaria
Burundi	Burundi
Byelorus, Bielorus	Bielorrusia
Cambodia	Camboya
Cameroon	Camerún
Canada	El Canadá

Chile	Chile	Lithuania	Lituania
China	La China	Luxemb(o)urg	Luxemburgo
Colombia	Colombia	Malawi	Malawi
Costa Rica	Costa Rica	Malaysia	Malasia
Croatia	Croacia	Mali	Malí
Cuba	Cuba	Malta	Malta
Czech Republic	República Checa	Mauritania	Mauritania
Denmark	Dinamarca	Mexico	Méjico, México
Dominican Republic	La República	Monaco	Mónaco
	Dominicana	Morocco	Marruecos
Ecuador	El Ecuador	Mozambique	Mozambique
Egypt	Egipto	Myanmar	Mianmar
El Salvador	El Salvador	Namibia	Namibia
England	Inglaterra	Nepal	Nepal
Estonia	Estonia	New Zealand	Nueva Zeland(i)a
Ethiopia	Etiopía	Nicaragua	Nicaragua
Fiji	Fiji, Fiyi	Nigeria	Nigeria
Finland	Finlandia	Norway	Noruega
France	Francia	Oman	Omán
Gambia	Gambia	Pakistan	Paquistán
Georgia	Georgia	Panama	Panamá
Ghana	Ghana	Papua New Guinea	Papua Nueva Guinea
Great Britain	Gran Bretaña	Paraguay	Paraguay
Greece	Grecia	Peru	Perú
Guatemala	Guatemala	Phillipines	Filipinas
Guinea	Guinea	Poland	Polonia
Guyana	Guyana	Portugal	Portugal
Haiti	Haití	Rumania, Romania	Rumania
Holland	Holanda	Russia	Rusia
Honduras	Honduras	Rwanda	Rwanda
Hungary	Hungría	Saudi Arabia	Arabia Saudita
Iceland	Islandia	Senegal	Senegal
India	La India	Serbia, Servia	Serbia
Indonesia	Indonesia	Sierra Leone	Sierra Leona
Iran	Irán	Slovakia	Eslovaquia
Iraq	Iraq	Somalia	Somalia
Ireland	Irlanda	Spain	España
Israel	Israel	Sri Lanka	Sri Lanka
Italy	Italia	Sudan	Sudán
Jamaica	Jamaica	Surinam	Surinam
Japan	Japón	Swaziland	Suazilandia
Jordan	Jordania	Sweden	Suecia
Kenya	Kenya	Switzerland	Suiza
Kirghizia, Kirghizistan	Kirguizistán	Syria	Siria
Korea	Corea	Tadzhikistan	Tayiquistán
Kuwait	Kuwait	Tanzania	Tanzania
Laos	Laos	Thailand	Tailandia
Latvia	Latvia	Togo	Togo
Lebanon	Libano	Tunisia	Túnez
Lesotho	Lesotho	Turkey	Turquía
Liberia	Liberia	Turkmenistan	Turkmenistán
Libya	Libia	Uganda	Uganda
Liechtenstein	Liechtenstein	Ukraine	Ucrania

United Kingdom	Reino Unido
United States	Estados Unidos
Uruguay	Uruguay
Uzbekistan	Uzbekistán
Venezuela	Venezuela
Vietnam	Vietnam
Yemen	Yemen
Zaire	Zaire
Zambia	Zambia
Zimbabwe	Zimbabwe

inhabitants

Afghan	afgano, -a *aj, nmf*
Albanian	albanés, -esa *aj, nmf*
Algerian	argelino, -a *aj, nmf*
Angolan	angoleño, -a *aj, nmf*
Argentine,	argentino, -a *aj, nmf*
Argentinean	
Armenian	armenio, -a *aj, nmf*
Australian	australiano, -a *aj, nmf*
Austrian	austríaco, -a *aj, nmf*
Azerbaijani	Azerbaiyáni *aj, nmf*
Bahamian	bahameño, -a, bahamés, -esa *aj, nmf*
Bangladeshi	bangladesí *aj, nmf*
Barbadian	barbadense *aj, nmf*
Belgian	belga *aj, nmf*
Belizean	beliceño, -a *aj, nmf*
Bhutanese Ⓑ	butanés, -esa *aj, nmf*
Bolivian	boliviano, -a *aj, nmf*
Bosnian	bosnio, -a *aj, nmf*
Botswanan	botsuano, -a *aj, nmf*
Brazilian	brasileño, -a *aj, nmf*
Bulgarian	búlgaro, -a *aj, nmf*
Burundian	burundés, -esa *aj, nmf*
Byelorussian	bielorruso, -a *aj, nmf*
Cambodian	camboyano, -a *aj, nmf*
Camerounian	camerunés, -esa *aj, nmf*
Canadian	canadiense *aj, nmf*
Chilean	chileno, -a *aj, nmf*
Chinese Ⓑ	chino, -a *aj, nmf*
Colombian	colombiano, -a *aj, nmf*
Costa Rican	costarricense, costarriqueño, -a *aj, nmf*
Croat, Croatian	croata *aj, nmf*
Cuban	cubano, -a *aj, nmf*
Czech	checo, -a *aj, nmf*
Dane	danés, -esa, dinamarqués, -esa *nmf*
Dominican	dominicano, -a *aj, nmf*
Ecuadorean	ecuatoriano, -a *aj, nmf*

Egyptian	egipcio, -a *aj, nmf*
Englishman Ⓑ	inglés *nm*
Englishwoman Ⓑ	inglesa *nf*
Estonian	estonio, -a *aj, nmf*
Ethiopian	etíope *aj, nmf*
Fijian	fidjiano, -a, fiyiano, -a *aj, nmf*
Finn	finlandés, -esa *nmf*
Frenchman Ⓑ	francés *nm*
Frenchwoman Ⓑ	francesa *nf*
Gambian	gambiano, -a *aj, nmf*
Georgian	georgiano, -a *aj, nmf*
Ghanaian	ghanés, -esa *aj, nmf*
Greek	griego, -a *aj, nmf*
Guatemalan	guatemalteco, -a *aj, nmf*
Guinean	guineo, -a *aj, nmf*
Guyanese Ⓑ	guyanés, -esa *aj, nmf*
Haitian	haitiano, -a *aj, nmf*
Hollander	holandés, -desa *nmf*
Honduran	hondureño, -a *aj, nmf*
Hungarian	húngaro, -a *aj, nmf*
Icelander	islandés, -esa *nmf*
Indian	indio, -a *aj, nmf*
Indonesian	indonesio, -a *aj, nmf*
Iranian	iraní, iranio, -a *aj, nmf*
Iraqui	iraquí *aj, nmf*
Irishman Ⓑ	irlandés *nm*
Irishwoman Ⓑ	irlandesa *nf*
Israeli	israelí *aj, nmf*
Italian	italiano, -a *aj, nmf*
Jamaican	jamaiciano, -a, jamaiquino, -a *aj, nmf*
Japanese Ⓑ	japonés, -esa *aj, nmf*
Jordanian	jordano, -a *aj, nmf*
Kenyan	keniano, -a *aj, nmf*
Korean	coreano, -a *aj, nmf*
Kuwaiti	kuwaití *aj, nmf*
Lao, Laotian	laosiano, -a *aj, nmf*
Latvian	latvio, -a, letón, -ona *aj, nmf*
Lebanese Ⓑ	libanés, -esa *aj, nmf*
Liberian	liberiano, -a *aj, nmf*
Libyan	libio, -a *aj, nmf*
Lithuanian	lituano, -a *aj, nmf*
Luxemb(o)urger	luxemburgués, -esa *aj, nmf*
Malawian	malawiano, -a *aj, nmf*
Malay, Malaysian	malayo, -a *aj, nmf*
Malian	maliense *aj, nmf*
Maltese Ⓑ	maltés, -esa *aj, nmf*
Mauritanian	mauritano, -a *aj, nmf*

Mexican	mejicano, -a *aj, nmf*
Monacan, Monegasque	monagesco, -a *aj, nmf*
Moroccan	marroquí *aj, nmf*
Mozambican	mozambiqueño, -a *aj, nmf*
Namibian	namibio, -a *aj, nmf*
Nepalese, Nepali Ⓑ	nepalés, -esa *aj, nmf*
Netherlander	neerlandés, -esa *nmf*
New Zealander	neocelandés, -esa *nmf*
Nicaraguan	nicaragüense *aj, nmf*
Nigerian	nigeriano, -a *aj, nmf*
Norwegian	noruego *aj, nmf*
Omani	omaní *aj, nmf*
Pakistani	pakistaní, paquistaní *aj, nmf*
Panamanian	panameño, -a *aj, nmf*
Papuan	Papú *aj, nmf*
Paraguayan	paraguayo, -a *aj, nmf*
Peruvian	peruano, -a *aj, nmf*
Phillipine, Filipino	filipino, -a *aj, nmf*
Pole	polaco, -a *nmf*
Portuguese Ⓑ	portugués, -esa *aj, nmf*
Rumanian, Romanian	rumano, -a *aj, nmf*
Russian	ruso, -a *aj, nmf*
Rwandan	rwandés, -esa *aj, nmf*
Salvadoran, Salvadorian	salvadoreño, -a *aj, nmf*
Saudi, Saudi-Arabian	saudita, saudí *aj, nmf*
Senegalese Ⓑ	senegalés, -esa *aj, nmf*
Serb	serbio, -a, servio, -a *nmf*
Serbian	serbio, servio *aj, nm*
Slovak, Slovakian	eslovaco, -a *aj, nmf*
Somali, Somalian	somalí *aj, nmf*
Spaniard	español(a) *nmf*
Sri Lankan	esrilanqués, -esa *aj, nmf*
Sudanese Ⓑ	sudanés, -esa *aj, nmf*
Swede	sueco, -a *nmf*
Swiss	suizo, -a *aj, nmf*
Syrian	sirio, -a *aj, nmf*
Tanzanian	tanzaniano, -a *aj, nmf*
Thai	tailandés, -esa *aj, nmf*
Togolese Ⓑ	togolés, -esa *aj, nmf*
Tunisian	tunecino, -a *aj, nmf*
Turk	turco, -a *nmf*
Ugandan	ugandés, -esa *aj, nmf*
Ukranian	ucrani(a)no, -a *aj, nmf*
Uruguayan	uruguayo, -a *aj, nmf*
Uzbek	uzbeko, -a *aj, nmf*
Venezuelan	venezolano, -a *aj, nmf*
Vietnamese Ⓑ	vietnamita *aj, nmf*
Yemeni, Yemenite	yemení *aj, nmf*

Zairian	zaireño, -a *aj, nmf*
Zambian	zambiano, -a *aj, nmf*
Zimbabwean	zimbabwense *aj, nmf*

CITIES

names

Addis Ababa	Addis-Abeba
Alexandria	Alejandría
Algiers	Argel
Amman	Amán
Astrakhan	Astracán
Athens	Atenas
Avignon	Aviñón
Baghdad	Bagdad
Bangkok	Bangkok
Barcelona	Barcelona
Basel, Basle	Basilea
Bayonne	Bayona
Beijing	Beijing
Belgrade	Belgrado
Berlin	Berlín
Bern, Berne	Berna
Bogota	Bogotá
Bologna	Bolonia
Bruges	Brujas
Brussels	Bruselas
Bucharest	Bucarest
Budapest	Budapest
Cairo	El Cairo
Calcutta	Calcuta
Canton	Cantón
Caracas	Caracas
Cologne	Colonia
Copenhagen	Copenhague
Cordova	Córdoba
Crakow	Cracovia
Damascus	Damasco
Dublin	Dublín
Dunkirk	Dunquerque
Edinburgh	Edimburgo
Frankfort	Francfort
Gaza	Gaza
Geneva	Ginebra
Genoa	Génova
Ghent	Gante
Gibraltar	Gibraltar
Hague, The	La Haya
Havana	La Habana
Hong Kong	Hong-Kong
Honolulu	Honolulú
Istanbul	Estambul
Jakarta	Yakarta

Jerusalem	Jerusalén
Kabul	Kabul
Khartoum	Jartum
Koblenz	Coblenza
Krakow	Cracovia
Lima	Lima
London	Londres
Madrid	Madrid
Marseille	Marsellas
Mecca	La Meca
Milan	Milán
Moscow	Moscú
Naples	Nápoles
Nazareth	Nazaret
New Delhi	Nueva Delhi
New Orleans	Nueva Orleáns
New York	Nueva York
Nice	Niza
Paris	París
Philadelphia	Filadelfia
Prague	Praga
Rangoon	Rangún
Rio de Janeiro	Río de Janeiro
Riyadh	Riad, Riyad
Rome	Roma *nf*
Saint Petersburg	San Petersburgo
Seoul	Seúl
Stockholm	Estocolmo
Strasbourg	Estrasburgo
Taipei	Taipeh
Tangiers	Tánger
Teheran, Tehran	Teherán
Timbuktu	Tombuctú, Timbuctú
Tokyo	Tokio
Tripoli	Trípoli
Tunis	Túnez
Valencia	Valencia
Venice	Venecia
Versailles	Versalles
Warsaw	Varsovia
Washington	Washington

inhabitants

Athenian	ateniense *aj, nmf*
Berliner	berlinés, -esa *nmf*
Cantonese Ⓑ	cantonés, -esa *aj, nmf*
Cordovan	cordobés, -esa *aj, nmf*
Dubliner	dublinés, -esa *nmf*
Florentine	florentino, -a *nmf*
Genevan	ginebrino, -a, ginebrés, -esa *nmf*
Genoese Ⓑ	genovés, -esa *aj, nmf*
Havanan	habanero, -a *nmf*

Londoner	londinense *nmf*
Madrilenian	madrileño, -a *nmf*
Muscovite	moscovita *nmf*
Neapolitan	napolitano, -a *nmf*
New Yorker	neoyorquino, -a *nmf*
Parisian	parisiense *nmf*
Roman	romano, -a *nmf*
Tangerine	tangerino, -a *aj, nmf*
Venetian	veneciano, -a *aj, nmf*

GEOGRAPHICAL REGIONS OF THE WORLD

names

America	América
Asia Minor	Asia Menor
Australasia	Austrolasia
Balkans	Balcanes *nmpl*
Central America	Centroamérica
Eurasia	Eurasia
Hispano-America	Hispanoamérica *nf*
Latin America	Latinoamérica
Occident	Occidente *nm*
Oceania	Oceanía
Orient	Oriente *nm*
Scandinavia	Escandinavia

inhabitants

American	americano, -a *aj, nmf*
Australasian	australasiático, -a *aj, nmf*
Balkan	balcánico, -a *aj, nmf*
Central American	centroamericano, -a *aj, nmf*
Eurasian	eurasiático, -a *aj, nmf*
Latin-American, Latino	latinoamericano, -a *aj, nmf*
Occidental	occidental *aj, nmf*
Oriental	oriental *aj, nmf*
Scandinavian	escandinavo, -a *aj, nmf*

PARTS OF COUNTRIES

names

Alsace	Alsacia
Andalusia	Andalucía
Appalachia *nsg*	los Apalaches *nmpl*
Aragon	Aragón
Arcadia	Arcadia
Balkans	Balcanes
Barbary	Berbería
Bavaria	Baviera
Benelux	Benelux

241

Bengal	Bengala
Bohemia	Bohemia
Brittany	Bretaña
Burgandy	Borgoña
Castile	Castilla
Catalonia	Cataluña
Caucasus	Cáucaso
Cornwall	Cornualles
Dalmatia	Dalmacia
Flanders	Flandes
Galicia	Galicia
Galilee	Galilea
Gascony	Gascuña
Gaza Strip	franja de Gaza *nf*
Hindustan	Indostán
Kashmir	Cachemira
Lapland	Laponia
Levant	Levante
Lombardy	Lombardía
Macedonia	Macedonia
Manchuria	Manchuria
Moldavia, Moldava	Moldavia, Moldava
Mongolia	Mongolia
Moravia	Moravia
Normandy	Normandía
North Korea	Corea del Norte
Palestine	Palestina
Provence	Provenza
Prussia	Prusia
Punjab	Pendjab
Quebec	Quebec
Saar	Sarre
Savoy	Saboya
Saxony	Sajonia
Scotland	Escocia
Siberia	Siberia
Slovenia	Eslovenia
Tibet	Tibet
Transylvania	Transilvania
Tuscany	Toscana
Tyrol, Tirol	Tirol
Wales	Gales

inhabitants

Alsatian	alsaciano, -a *aj, nmf*
Andalusian	andaluz(a) **C** *aj, nmf*
Arcadian	árcade, arcadio, -a *aj, nmf*
Balkan	balcánico, -a *aj, nmf*
Bavarian	bávaro, -a *aj, nmf*
Bengali, Bengalese **B**	bengalí *aj, nmf*
Bohemian	bohemio, -a *aj, nmf*

Breton	bretón, -a *nmf*
Burgundian	borgoñón, -ona *aj, nmf*
Castilian	castellano, -a *aj, nmf*
Catalan, Catalonian	catalán, -lana *aj, nmf*
Caucasian	caucásico, -a *aj, nmf*
Dalmatian	dálmata *aj, nmf*
French-Canadian	francocanadiense *aj, nmf*
Galician	gallego, -a *aj, nmf*
Gascon	gascón, -ona *aj, nmf*
Hindustani	indostanés, -esa, indostano, -a *aj, nmf*
Lapp, Laplander	lapón, -ona *nmf*
Manchu	manchú, manchuriano, -a *aj, nmf*
Moldavian	moldavo, -a *aj, nmf*
Mongol, Mongolian	mongol *aj, nmf*
Moravian	moravo, -a *aj, nmf*
Norman	normando, -a *aj, nmf*
North Korean	norcoreano, -a *aj, nmf*
Palestinian	palestino, -a *aj, nmf*
Provençal	provenzal *aj, nmf*
Prussian	prusiano, -a *aj, nmf*
Punjabi	penjabo, -a *nmf*
Savoyard	saboyano, -a *aj, nmf*
Saxon	sajón, -ona *aj, nmf*
Scotsman **B**	escosés *nm*
Scotswoman **B**	escosesa *nf*
Siberian	siberiano, -a *aj, nmf*
Slovene, Slovenian	esloveno, -a *aj, nmf*
Tibetan	tibetano, -a *aj, nmf*
Transylvanian	transilvano, -a *aj, nmf*
Tuscan	tuscano, -a *aj, nmf*
Tyrolean	tirolés, -esa *aj, nmf*

U.S. STATES

names

Hawaii	Hawai
Louisiana	Luisiana
Missouri	Misuri
New Hampshire	Nueva Hampshire
New Jersey	Nueva Jersey
New Mexico	Nuevo México
Pennsylvania	Pensilvania
Texas	Tejas

inhabitants

Floridian	floridense *aj, nmf*
Hawaiian	hawaiano, -a *aj, nmf*
Texan	tejano, -a *aj, nmf*

OBSOLETE NAMES

name changes

Abyssinia = Ethiopia	Abisinia
Burma = Myanmar	Birmania
Cathay = China	Catay
Ceylon = Sri Lanka	Ceilán
Congo = Zaire	Congo
Constantinople = Istanbul	Constantinopla
Erin = Ireland	Erín
Gold Coast = Ghana	Costa de Oro
Helvetia = Switzerland	Helvecia
Kampuchea = Cambodia	Kampuchea
Leningrad = St. Petersburg	Leningrado
Malagasy = Madagascar	Malgache
Peking = Beijing	Pekín
Persia = Iran	Persia
Rhodesia = Zimbabwe	Rodesia
Siam = Thailand	Siam

former 20th-century countries

Austria-Hungary	Austria-Hungría
Czechoslovakia	Checoslovaquia
Soviet Union	Unión Soviética
Yugoslavia	Yugo(e)slavia

inhabitants

Abyssinian	abisinio, -a *aj, nmf*
Burmese	birmano, -a *aj, nmf*
Ceylonese	ceilañes, -nesa *aj, nmf*
Congolese	congoleño, -a *aj, nmf*
Czechoslovak(ian)	checoslovaco, -a *aj, nmf*
Helvetian	helvecio, -a *aj, nmf*
Kampuchean	kampucheano, -a *aj, nmf*
Persian	persa *aj, nmf*
Siamese	siamés, -esa *aj, nmf*
Yugoslav(ian)	yugo(e)slavo, -a *aj, nmf*

poetic names

Araby = Arabia	Arabia
Babylon = Babilonia	Babylonia
Eire = Ireland	Eire

(*See also* **geographical names** under **ANCIENT CIVILIZATIONS**; *ETHNIC GROUPS AROUND THE WORLD* under **ANTHROPOLOGY AND ARCHEOLOGY**)

Times Past

HISTORY

GENERAL TERMS

archaic	arcaico *aj*
civilization	civilización *nf*
decay	decaer *vi*
epoch	época *nf*
era	era *nf*
extinct	extinto *aj*
history	historia *nf*
past	pasado *aj, nm*
period	período, periodo *nm*
remembrance	remembranza *nf*

SPECIALIZATIONS

kinds of history

chronological	cronológico *aj*
comparative	comparativo *aj*
cultural	cultural *aj*
diplomatic	diplomático *aj*
economic	económico *aj*
intellectual	intelectual *aj*
political	político *aj*
social	social *aj*

allied fields

anthropology	antropología *nf*
archeology Ⓐ	arqueología *nf*
demography	demografía *nf*
Egyptology	egiptología *nf*
glottochronology	glotocronología *nf*
historiography	historiografía *nf*
linguistics	lingüística *nf*
numismatics	numismática *nf*
paleography	paleografía *nf*
philology	filología *nf*

ASPECTS OF HISTORY

time divisions

ancient	muy antiguo *aj*
antediluvian	antediluviano *aj*
antiquity	antigüedad *nf*
classical	clásico *aj*
colonial	colonial *aj*
contemporary	contemporáneo *aj*
feudal	feudal *aj*

medieval	medieval *aj*
modern	moderno *aj*
postcolonial	postcolonial *aj*
prehistoric	prehistórico *aj*
present-day *aj*	de hoy día *nm*

historical periods

Byzantine	bizantino *aj*
Edwardian	eduardiano *aj*
Elizabethan	elisabetiano *aj*
Greco-Roman	grecorromano *aj*
Hellenistic	helenístico *aj*
Mycenaen	micénico *aj*
Napoleonic	napoleónico *aj*
Renaissance	Renacimiento *nm*
Victorian	victoriano *aj*

sources

annals	anales *nmpl*
autobiography	autobiografía *nf*
Bible	Biblia *nf*
biography	biografía *nf*
chronicle	crónica *nf*
diary	diario *nm*
document	documento *nm*
exploration	exploración *nf*
folklore	folklore, folclore *nm*
genealogy	genealogía *nf*
historical record	historial *nm*
legend	leyenda *nf*
myth	mito *nm*
narrative	narrativa *nf*
publication	publicación *nf*
registry	registro *nm*
reminiscence	reminiscencia *nf*

preservation

antiquary	anticuario *nm*
antique	antigualla *nf*
archives *npl*	archivo *nm*
attic	ático *nm*
film	filme *nm*
museum	museo *nm*
relic	reliquia *nf*
reliquary	relicario *nm*
repository	repositorio *nm*
restoration	restauración *nf*
tomb	tumba *nf*

remembrance

anniversary	aniversario *nm*
candle	candela *nf*
commemoration	conmemoración *nf*
homage	homenaje *nm*
memorial	memorial *nm*
monument	monumento *nm*
oration	oración *nf*
plaque	placa *nf*
retrospective	retrospectiva *nf*

PERSONS

historians

archeologist 🅰	arqueólogo, -a *nmf*
chronicler	cronista *nmf*
historian	historiador(a) *nmf*
historiographer	historiógrafo, -a *nmf*
medievalist	medievalista *nmf*
paleographer	paleógrafo, -a *nmf*
social scientist	científico, -a social *nmf*

persons of the past

beatnik	beatnik *nmf*
buccaneer	bucanero *nm*
cave dweller	cavernícola *nmf*
colonialist	colonialista *aj, nmf*
consul (Roman)	cónsul *nm*
crusader	cruzado *nmf*
damsel	damisela *nf*
epicure	epicúreo, -a *nmf*
galley slave	galeote *nm*
herald	heraldo *nm*
legate	legado *nm*
patrician	patricio *aj, nm*
peon	peón *nm*
pioneer	pionero, -a *nmf*
pirate	pirata *nmf*
plebeian	plebeyo, -a *aj, nmf*
preceptor	preceptor *nm*
prefect	prefecto *nm*
proconsul	procónsul *nm*
procurator	procurador *nm*
restorer	restaurador(a) *nmf*
scribe	escriba *nm*
slave	esclavo, -a *nmf*
sophist	sofista *nmf*
suffragette	sufragista *nf*
vassal	vasallo, -a *nmf*

(*See also* TERMS IN ARCHEOLOGY under **ANTHROPOLOGY AND ARCHEOLOGY**; *HISTORICAL TERMS* under **CHEMISTRY**;

historical clothing under **CLOTHING**; *historical dances* under **DANCING**; *HISTORICAL TERMS* under **POLITICS AND GOVERNMENT**; *historical languages* under **LANGUAGES OF THE WORLD**; *historical* under **LAW**; *HISTORICAL TERMS* under **MEDICAL PRACTICE**; *historical and obsolete* under **MONEY AND FINANCE**; *OBSOLETE AND HISTORICAL TERMS* under **MUSIC**; *OBSOLETE NAMES* under **PLACE NAMES II: POLITICAL**; *HISTORICAL TERMS* under **RELIGION**; *HISTORICAL TERMS* under **THE MILITARY ESTABLISHMENT**; *historical* under **TITLES**; *HISTORICAL TERMS* under **WRITING**)

THE BIBLE

GENERAL TERMS

apostle	apóstol *nm*
canticle	cántico *nm*
commandment	mandamiento *nm*
covenant	convenio *nm*
deity	deidad *nf*
disciple	discípulo, -a *nmf*
epistle	epístola *nf*
exegesis 🅱	exégesis 🅲 *nf*
exile	exilio *nm*
jubilee	jubileo *nm*
matriarch	matriarca *nf*
miracle	milagro *nm*
New Testament	Nuevo Testamento *nm*
Old Testament	Antiguo Testamento *nm*
parable	parábola *nf*
patriarch	patriarca *nm*
plague	plaga *nf*
prophecy	profecía *nf*
prophet	profeta *nm*
psalm	salmo *nm*
publican	publicano *nm*
synagog(ue)	sinagoga *nf*
tabernacle	tabernáculo *nm*
temple	templo *nm*
tribe	tribu *nf*
verse	versículo *nm*
Vulgate	Vulgata *nf*

NAMES IN THE OLD TESTAMENT

Pentateuch

Deuteronomy	Deuteronomio *nm*
Exodus	Éxodo *nm*
Genesis	Génesis *nm*

Leviticus	Levítico *nm*
Numbers	Números *nmpl*

Prophets

Amos	Amós *nm*
Elijah	Elías *nm*
Elisha	Elíseo *nm*
Ezekiel	Ezequiel *nm*
Ezra	Esdras *nm*
Habakkuk	Habacuc *nm*
Hosea	Oseas *nm*
Isaiah	Isaías *nm*
Jeremiah	Jeremías *nm*
Malachi	Malaquías *nm*
Micah	Miqueas *nm*
Nahum	Nahum *nm*
Zechariah	Zacarías *nm*

other books

Chronicles	Crónicas *nfpl*
Daniel	Daniel *nm*
Ecclesiastes	Eclesiastés *nm*
Esther	Éster *nf*
Job	Job *nm*
Jonah	Jonás *nm*
Judges	Jueces *nmpl*
Lamentations	Lamentaciones *nfpl*
Nehemiah	Nehemías *nm*
Proverbs	Proverbios *nmpl*
Psalms	Salmos *nmpl*
Ruth	Rut *nf*
Samuel	Samuel *nm*

patriarchs

Abraham	Abrahán *nm*
Isaac	Isaac *nm*
Jacob	Jacob *nm*

matriarchs

Leah	Lía *nf*
Rachel	Raquel *nf*
Rebecca	Rebeca *nf*
Sarah	Sara *nf*

other women

Bathsheba	Betsabé *nf*
Deborah	Debora *nf*
Delilah	Dalila *nf*
Eve	Eva *nf*
Jezebel	Jezabel *nf*
Judith	Judit *nf*

other men

Aaron	Arón *nm*

Abel	Abel *nm*
Adam	Adán *nm*
Benjamin	Benjamín *nm*
Cain	Caín *nm*
David	David *nm*
Emmanuel, Immanuel	Emanuel, Imanuel *nm*
Esau	Esaú *nm*
Gideon	Gedeón *nm*
Goliath	Goliat *nm*
Hezekiah	Esequías *nm*
Ishmael	Ismail *nm*
Joseph	José *nm*
Joshua	Josué *nm*
Josiah	Josías *nm*
Lot	Lot *nm*
Methuselah	Matusalén *nm*
Moses	Moisés *nm*
Nathan	Natán *nm*
Noah	Noé *nm*
Pharaoh	faraón *nm*
Samson	Sansón *nm*
Saul	Saúl *nm*
Seth	Set *nm*
Solomon	Salomón *nm*

peoples and tribes

Amalekites	amalecitas *nmpl*
Assyrians	asirios *nmpl*
Babylonians	babilonios *nmpl*
Canaanites	cananeos *nmpl*
Hamites	hamitas, camitas *nmpl*
Hittites	hititas *nmpl*
Israelites	israelitas *nmpl*
Levites	levitas *nmpl*
Maccabees	macabeos *nmpl*
Philistines	filisteos *nmpl*
Samaritans	samaritanos *nmpl*
Semites	semitas *nmpl*

NAMES IN THE NEW TESTAMENT

Gospels

John	Juan *nm*
Luke	Lucas *nm*
Mark	Marcos *nm*
Matthew	Mateo *nm*

Epistles

Colossians	Colosenses *nm*
Corinthians	Corintios *nmpl*
Ephesians	Efesios *nmpl*
Galatians	Gálatas *nmpl*
Hebrews	Hebreos *nmpl*

James	Jaime *nm*
Jude	Judas *nm*
Peter	Pedro *nm*
Philemon	Filemón *nm*
Philippians	filipenses *nmpl*
Romans	Epístola a los romanos *nf, nmpl*
Thessalonians	tesalonicenses *nmpl*

other books

Acts	Hechos de los Apóstoles *nmpl*
Apocrypha	libros apócrifos *nmpl*
Revelation	Revelación *nf*

disciples

Andrew	Andrés *nm*
Bartholomew	Bartolomé *nm*
James	Jaime *nm*
John	Juan *nm*
Judas	Judas *nm*
Matthew	Mateo *nm*
Matthias	Matías *nm*
Philip	Felipe *nm*
Simon	Simón *nm*
Thaddeus	Tadeo *nm*
Thomas	Tomás *nm*

other men and women

Barabbas	Barrabás *nm*
Barnabas	Barnabás *nm*
Ephraim	Efraín *nm*
Gamaliel	Gamaliel *nm*
Herod	Herodes *nm*
Jesus	Jesús *nm*
Lazarus	Lázaro *nm*
Mary	María *nf*
Nathanael	Natánael
Paul	Pablo *nm*
Salome	Salomé *nf*
Timothy	Timoteo *nm*
Titus	Tito *nm*

sects and groups

Christians	cristianos *nmpl*
Essenes	esenios *nmpl*
Jews	judíos *nmpl*
Magi	los Reyes Magos *nmpl*
Nazarenes	nazareos *nmpl*
Pharisees	fariseos *nm*
Sadducees	saduceos *nmpl*
Sanhedrin	sanedrín *nm*
Scribes	escribas *nmpl*
Zealots	zelotes *nm*

DEITIES AND DEVILS

Antichrist	Anticristo *nm*
Baal	Baal *nm*
Beelzebub	Belcebú *nm*
Christ	Cristo *nm*
Gabriel	Gabriel *nm*
Jehovah	Jehová *nm*
Lucifer	Lucifer *nm*
Mammon	Mammón *nm*
Messiah	Mesías *nm*
Michael	Miguel *nm*
Redeemer	Redentor *nm*
Satan	Satanás *nm*
Savior Ⓐ	Salvador *nm*
Yahweh, Yaheh	Jahvé *nm*
Raphael	Rafael

PLACES AND EVENTS

places

Armageddon	Armagedón *nm*
Babel	Babel *nm or nf*
Babylon	Babilonia *nf*
Bethlehem	Belén *nm*
Calvary	Calvario *nm*
Canaan	Canaán *nm*
Corinth	Corinto *nf*
Damascus	Damasco *nf*
Eden	Edén *nm*
Egypt	Egipto *nm*
Ephesus	Éfeso *nf*
Galilee	Galilea *nf*
Gehenna	Gehena *nm*
Gethsemane	Getsemaní *nm*
Golgotha	Gólgota *nm*
Gomorrah	Gomorra *nf*
Israel	Israel *nm*
Jericho	Jericó *nf*
Jerusalem	Jerusalén nm
Jordan (river)	Jordán *nm*
Judah	Judá *nm*
Judea	Judea *nf*
Nazareth	Nazaret
Nineveh	Nínive *nf*
Palestine	Palestina *nf*
Samaria	Samaria *nf*
Sinai	Sinaí *nm*
Sodom	Sodoma *nf*
Tarsus	Tarso *nf*
Ur	Ur *nm*
Zion	Sión *nm*

events

Annunciation	Anunciación *nf*
Apocalypse	Apocalipsis *nm*
Assumption	Asunción *nf*
Beatitudes	Beatitudes *nm*
Creation	Creación *nf*
Crucifixion	Crucifixión *nf*
Decalogue	Decálogo *nm*
Deluge	Diluvio *nm*
Incarnation	Encarnación *nf*
Nativity	Natividad *nf*
Resurrection	Resurrección *nf*
Transfiguration	Transfiguración *nf*

OTHER BIBLICAL VOCABULARY

creatures

angel	ángel *nm*
archangel	arcángel *nm*
behemoth	behemot *nm*
cherub Ⓑ	querubín *nm*
devil	diablo *nm*
dragon	dragón *nm*
leviathan	leviatán *nm*
scorpion	escorpión *nm*
seraph Ⓑ	serafín *nm*

things

ark	arca *nf(el)*
cross	cruz *nf*
manna	maná *nm*
myrrh	mirra *nf*
stigmata	estigmas *nmpl*
apocalyptic	apocalíptico *aj*
apocryphal	apócrifo *aj*

(*See also* **RELIGION**)

MYTHOLOGY

GENERAL TERMS

anthropomorphism	antropomorfismo *nm*
fable	fábula *nf*
incarnation	encarnación *nf*
legend	leyenda *nf*
myth	mito *nm*
mythology	mitología *nf*

GREEK MYTHOLOGY

gods

Aeolus	Eolo *nm*
Apollo	Apolo *nm*
Ares	Ares *nm*
Boreas	Bóreas *nm*
Cronus	Cronos *nm*
Dionysus	Dionisos *nm*
Eros	Eros *nm*
Helios	Helios *nm*
Hephaestus	Hefestos *nm*
Hermes	Hermes *nm*
Hypnos	Hipnos *nm*
Morpheus	Morfeo *nm*
Pan	Pan *nm*
Phoebus	Febo *nm*
Pluto	Plutón *nm*
Plutus	Pluto *nm*
Poseidon	Poseidón *nm*
Triton	Tritón *nm*
Uranus	Urano *nm*
Zeus	Zeus *nm*

goddesses

Aphrodite	Afrodita *nf*
Artemis	Artemisa *nf*
Athena	Atena, Atenea *nf*
Demeter	Démeter *nf*
Eos	Eos *nf*
Furies	Furias *nfpl*
Gaea, Gaia	Gea, Ge *nf*
Graces	Gracias *nfpl*
Hebe	Hebe *nf*
Hecate	Hécate *nf*
Hera	Hera *nf*
Hestia	Hestia *nf*
Hygeia	Higía *nf*
Hymen	Himeneo *nm*
Iris	Iris *nf*
Muse	musa *nf*
Nemesis	Némesis *nf*
Phoebe	Febe *nf*

minor deities

Alpheus	Alfeo *nm*
Chloris	Cloris *nf*
oracle	oráculo *nm*
Proteus	Proteo *nm*

muses

Calliope	Calíope *nf*
Clio	Clío *nf*
Erato	Erato *nf*
Euterpe	Euterpe *nf*
Melpomene	Melpómene *nf*
Polyhymnia, Polymnia	Polimnia *nf*
Terpsichore	Terpsícore *nf*

Thalia	Talía *nf*
Urania	Urania *nf*

Homeric heroes and characters

Achilles	Aquiles *nm*
Agamemnon	Agamenón *nm*
Ajax	Áyax *nm*
Calypso	Calipso *nm*
Cassandra	Casandra *nf*
Circe	Circe *nf*
Clytemnestra	Clitemnestra *nf*
Electra	Electra *nf*
Hecuba	Hécuba *nf*
Helen	Helena *nf*
Iphigenia	Ifegenia *nf*
Menelaus	Menelao *nm*
Orestes	Orestes *nm*
Paris	Paris *nm*
Penelope	Penélope *nf*
Priam	Príam *nm*
Scylla	Escila *nf*

other Greek characters

Adonis	Adonis *nm*
Amazon	amazona *nf*
Andromeda	Andrómeda *nf*
Antigone	Antígona *nf*
Arachne	Aracne *nf*
Argonaut	Argonauta *nm*
Ariadne	Ariadna *nf*
Atlas	Atlas *nm*
Baucis	Baucis *nf*
Cadmus	Cadmo *nm*
Castor	Cástor *nm*
Charon	Carón, Caronte *nm*
Chronos	Cronus *nm*
Daedalus	Dédalo *nm*
Daphne	Dafne *nf*
Echo	Eco *nm*
Endymion	Endimión *nm*
Europa	Europa *nf*
Eurydice	Eurídice *nf*
Galatea	Galatea *nf*
Ganymede	Ganimedes *nm*
Hercules	Hércules *nm*
Hesperides	Hespérides *nfpl*
Hyperion	Hiperión *nm*
Icarus	Icaro *nm*
Io	Io *nf*
Jason	Jasón *nm*
Medea	Medea *nf*
Memnon	Memnón *nm*

Mentor	Mentor *nm*
Midas	Midas *nm*
Minos	Minos *nm*
Narcissus	Narciso *nm*
Nereid	Nereida *nf*
Nereus	Nereo *nm*
Niobe	Níobe *nf*
Odysseus	Odiseo *nm*
Oedipus	Edipo *nm*
Orion	Orión *nm*
Orpheus	Orfeo *nm*
Pandora	Pandora *nf*
Persephone	Perséfone *nf*
Perseus	Perseo *nm*
Phaedra	Fedra *nf*
Phaeton	Faetón *nm*
Pleiades	Pléyades *nmpl*
Pollux	Pólux *nm*
Prometheus	Prometeo *nm*
Pygmalion	Pigmalión *nm*
Rhea	Rea *nf*
Semele	Semele, Sémele *nf*
Sisyphus	Sísifo *nm*
Tantalus	Tántalo *nm*
Thanatos	Tánatos *nm*
Theseus	Teseo *nm*
Titan	Titán *nm*

places

Acheron	Aqueronte *nm*
Atlantis	Atlántida *nf*
Augean Stables	establos de Augías *nmpl*
Delphi	Delfos *nm*
Elysium	Elíseo *nm*
Erebus	Erebo *nm*
Hades	Hades *nm*
Lethe	Lete, Leteo *nm*
Olympia	Olimpia *nf*
Olympus	Olimpo *nm*
Parnassus	Parnaso *nm*
Styx	Estigio *nm*
Tartarus	Tártaro *nm*
Thebes	Tebas *nf*
Troy	Troya *nf*

creatures

Argus	Argos *nm*
centaur	centauro *nm*
Cerberus	Cerbero *nm*
Chimera	Quimera *nf*
Chiron	Quirón *nm*
Cyclops Ⓑ	Cíclope *nm*

dryad	dríada, dríade *nf*
faun	fauno *nm*
giant	gigante *nmf*
Gorgon	Gorgona *nf*
griffin, griffon	grifo *nm*
hamadryad	hamadríada *nf*
Harpy	arpía *nf*
Hydra B	Hidra *nf*
Medusa	Medusa *nf*
Minotaur	Minotauro *nm*
naiad	náyade *nf*
nymph	ninfa *nf*
oread	oréade, oréada *nf*
Pegasus	Pegaso *nm*
phoenix	fénix *nm*
Polyphemus	Polifemo *nm*
Python	Pitón *nm*
satyr, Satyr	sátiro *nm*
Silenus	Sileno *nm*
siren	sirena *nf*
Sphinx	Esfinge *nf*

things

aegis	égida *nf*
ambrosia	ambrosía *nf*
baccanal	bacanal *nm*
caduceus	caduceo *nm*
cornucopia	cornucopia *nf*
Gordian knot	nudo gordiano *nm*
labyrinth	laberinto *nm*
nectar	néctar *nm*
nepenthe	nepente *nm*
Palladium	paladión *nm*
trident	tridente *nm*

ROMAN MYTHOLOGY

gods

Aesculapius	Esculapio *nm*
Apollo	Apolo *nm*
Bacchus	Baco *nm*
Cupid	Cupido *nm*
Janus	Jano *nm*
Jupiter	Júpiter *nm*
Mars	Marte *nm*
Mercury	Mercurio *nm*
Neptune	Neptuno *nm*
Pluto	Plutón *nm*
Saturn	Saturno *nm*
Vulcan	Vulcano *nm*

goddesses

Aurora	Aurora *nf*
Ceres	Ceres *nf*
Diana	Diana *nf*
Flora	Flora *nf*
Fortuna	Fortuna *nf*
Juno	Juno *nf*
Luna	Luna *nf*
Minerva	Minerva *nf*
Venus	Venus *nf*
Vesta	Vesta *nf*

other Roman characters

Androcles	Androcles *nm*
Dido	Dido *nf*
Furies	Furias *nfpl*
Proserpina	Proserpina *nf*
Psyche	Psiquis *nf*
Remus	Remo *nm*
Romulus	Rómulo *nm*
sibyl	sibila *nf*
Ulysses	Ulises *nm*

EGYPTIAN GODS AND GODDESSES

Ammon	Amón *nm*
Horus	Horus *nm*
Isis	Isis *nf*
Osiris	Osiris *nm*
Ra, Re	Ra *nm*

OTHER ANCIENT DIETIES

Baal	Baal *nm*
Cybele	Cibeles *nf*
Mithras	Mitra *nm*
Semiramis	Semíramis *nf*

NORSE AND GERMANIC MYTHOLOGY

Brunhild	Brunilda *nf*
Frey	Freyr *nm*
Freya	Freya *nf*
Nibelung	nibelungo *nm*
Norn	Norna *nf*
Odin	Odín *nm*
Siegfried	Sigfrido *nm*
Thor	Tor *nm*
Valhalla	Valhala *nm*
Valkyrie	Valquiria *nf*
Yggdrasil	Ygdrasil *nm*

(*See also* **animals in myth and folklore** under **ANIMALS**; *DEITIES AND DEVILS* under **THE BIBLE**; *folklore and legend* under **LITERATURE**)

ANCIENT CIVILIZATIONS

FAMOUS NAMES

writers and artists

Aeschylus	Esquilo *nm*
Aesop	Esopo *nm*
Aristophanes	Aristófanes *nm*
Euripides	Eurípides *nm*
Homer	Homero *nm*
Horace	Horacio *nm*
Ovid	Ovidio *nm*
Plautus	Plauto *nm*
Plutarch	Plutarco *nm*
Praxiteles	Praxíteles *nm*
Sappho	Safo *nf*
Sophocles	Sófocles *nm*
Virgil	Virgilio *nm*

philosophers

Aristotle	Aristóteles *nm*
Cicero	Cicerón *nm*
Confucius	Confucio *nm*
Plato	Platón *nm*
Seneca	Séneca *nm*
Socrates	Sócrates *nm*

physicians

Galen	Galeno *nm*
Hippocrates	Hipócrates *nm*
Imhotep	Imhotep *nm*
Maimonides	Maimónides *nm*

historians

Cato	Catón *nm*
Herodotus	Heródoto *nm*
Josephus	Josefo *nm*
Thucydides	Tucídides *nm*

scientists

Archimedes	Arquímedes *nm*
Euclid	Euclides *nm*
Hipparchus	Hiparco *nm*
Ptolemy	Tolomeo *nm*
Pythagoras	Pitágoras *nm*

statesmen and generals

Brutus	Bruto *nm*
Caesar	César *nm*
Cassius	Casio *nm*
Demosthenes	Demóstenes *nm*
Draco	Dracón *nm*
Hannibal	Aníbal *nm*
Scipio	Escipión *nm*
Solon	Solón *nm*

emperors and kings

Alexander	Alejandro *nm*
Augustus	Augusto *nm*
Caligula	Calígula *nm*
Claudius	Claudio *nm*
Cleopatra	Cleopatra *nf*
Constantine	Constantino *nm*
Croesus	Creso *nm*
Cyrus	Ciro *nm*
Darius	Dario *nm*
Hammurabi	Hamurabi *nm*
Herod	Herodes *nm*
Julian	Juliano *nm*
Nero	Nerón *nm*
Ramses	Ramsés *nm*
Titus	Tito *nm*
Tutankhamen	Tutankamen, Tutankamón *nm*
Vespasian	Vespasiano *nm*
Xerxes	Jerjes *nm*

PLACES AND THINGS

geographical names

Antioch	Antioquía *nf*
Assyria	Asiria *nf*
Babylon	Babilonia *nf*
Babylonia	Babilonia *nf*
Bethlehem	Belén *nm*
Byzantium	Bizancio *nm*
Carthage	Cartago *nf*
Chaldea	Caldea *nf*
Corinth	Corinto *nf*
Egypt	Egipto *nm*
Ephesus	Éfeso *nf*
Gaul	Galia *nf*
Greece	Grecia *nf*
Herculaneum	Herculano *nf*
Judea	Judea *nf*
Marathon	Maratón *nm*
Memphis	Menfis *nf*
Mesopotamia	Mesopotamia *nf*
Mycenae	Micenas *nf*
Olympia	Olimpia *nf*
Phoenicia	Fenicia *nf*
Phrygia	Frigia *nf*
Pompeii	Pompeya *nf*
Rhodes	Rodas *nf*
Rome	Roma *nf*
Rubicon	Rubicón *nm*

Sparta	Esparta *nf*
Syracuse	Siracusa *nf*
Thebes	Tebas *nf*
Thermopylae	Termópilas *nfpl*
Troy	Troya *nf*
Vesuvius	Vesubio *nm*

buildings and monuments

Acropolis	Acrópolis *nf*
Colosseum	Coliseo *nm*
Colossus Ⓑ	Coloso *nm*
Parthenon	Partenón *nm*
Sphinx	Esfinge *nf*

other places

basilica	basílica *nf*
forum Ⓑ	foro *nm*
hippodrome	hipódromo *nm*
lyceum	liceo *nm*
pyramid	pirámide *nf*
ziggurat	zigurat *nm*

objects and materials

cartouche	cartucho *nm*
mummy	momia *nf*
papyrus	papiro *nm*
pylon	pilón *nm*
sarcophagus Ⓑ	sarcófago *nm*
scarab	escarabajo *nm*

EVENTS

festivals and celebrations

Bacchanalia	bacanales *nfpl*
hecatomb	hecatombe *nf*
lustrum	lustro *nm*
Saturnalia	saturnales *nfpl*

wars

Peloponnesian	peloponense *aj*

Punic	púnico *aj*
Trojan *aj*	de Troya *nf*

dates and keeping time

calends	calendas *nfpl*
century	centuria *nf*
Ides	idus *nmpl*
Olympiad	olimpiada, olimpíada *nf*

PERSONS

Assyrian	asirio, -a *aj, nmf*
Babylonian	babilonio, -a *aj, nmf*
Breton	bretón, -a *nmf*
Byzantine	bizantino, -a *aj, nmf*
Carthaginian	cartaginense *aj, nmf*
Celt	celta *nmf*
Corinthian	corintio, -a *aj, nmf*
Druid, druid	druida *nm*
Egyptian	egipcio, -a *aj, nmf*
Etruscan	etrusco, -a *aj, nmf*
Gaul (person)	galio, -a *nmf*
Greek	griego, -a *aj, nmf*
Judean	judío, -a *aj, nmf*
Mycenaen	micénico, -a *aj, nmf*
Phoenician	fenicio, -a *aj, nm*
Phrygian	frigio, -a *aj, nmf*
Pict	picto, -a *nmf*
Roman	romano, -a *aj, nmf*
Saxon	sajón, -ona *aj, nmf*
Spartan	espartano, -a *aj, nmf*
Sumerian	sumerio, -a *aj, nmf*
Theban	tebano, -a *aj, nmf*
Trojan	troyano, -a *aj, nmf*
Vandal	vándalo *nm*

(*See also* **peoples and tribes** under **THE BIBLE**; *historical terms* under **DEATH**; *founders of religions* under **RELIGION**)

Appendix A
British Spellings

aerogram : aerogramme
aluminum : aluminium
amphitheater : amphitheatre
analyze : analyse
anemia : anaemia
anemic : anaemic
anesthesia : anaesthesia
anesthesiologist : anaesthetist
anesthesiology : anaesthesiology
anesthetic : anaesthetic
anesthetist : anaesthetist
anesthetize : anaesthetize
apnea : apnoea
arbor : arbour
archeological : archaeological
archeologist : archaeologist
archeology : archaeology
ardor : ardour
armor : armour
armored : armoured
armory : armoury
artifact : artefact
ax : axe
behaviorism : behaviourism
behaviorist : behaviourist
caldron : cauldron
caliber : calibre
calisthenics : callisthenics
carburetor : carburettor
center : centre
centiliter : centilitre
centimeter : centimetre
cesium : caesium
check : cheque
checkbook : chequebook
chlorophyl : chlorophyll
clamor : clamour
color : colour
coloration : colouration
colored : coloured
colorful : colourful
colorfully : colourfully
coloring : colouring
colorist : colourist
colorless : colourless
connection : conexion

counselor : counsellor
cryoanesthesia : cryoanaesthesia
defense : defence
diopter : dioptre
discolor : discolour
discoloration : discolouration
discolored : discoloured
disfavor : disfavour
dishonor : dishonour
dishonorable : dishonourable
dishonored : dishonoured
dramatize : dramatise
enamor : enamour
enamored : enamoured
enologist : oenologist
enology : oenology
epicenter : epicentre
esophagus : oesophagus
estrogen : oestrogen
estrus : oestrus
fa : fah
favor : favour
favorable : favourable
favored : favoured
favorite : favourite
favoritism : favouritism
fecal : faecal
feces : faeces
fetal : foetal
fetus : foetus
fiber : fibre
flutist : flautist
garrote : garrotte
genuflection : genuflexion
gram : gramme
gynecological : gynaecological
gynecologist : gynaecologist
gynecology : gynaecology
hectogram : hectogramme
hectoliter : hectolitre
hectometer : hectometre
hematic : haematic
hematology : haematology
hematoma : haematoma
hemoglobin : haemoglobin
hemolysis : haemolysis

hemophilia : haemophilia
hemophiliac : haemophiliac
hemoptysis : haemoptysis
hemorrhage : haemorrhage
hemorrhoidal : haemorrhoidal
hemorrhoids : haemorrhoids
hemostasis : haemostasis
hemostat : haemostat
hemostatic : haemostatic
honor : honour
honorable : honourable
honors : honours
humor : humour
humorist : humourist
humorless : humourless
hydrolyze : hydrolyse
hyena : hyaena
inflection : inflexion
inquire : enquire
inquiring : enquiring
inquiry : enquiry
intellectualize : intellectualise
ketchup : catsup
kilogram : kilogramme
kiloliter : kilolitre
kilometer : kilometre
la : lah
labor : labour
leukocyte : leucocyte
license : licence
litchi : lychee
liter : litre
luster : lustre
maneuver : manoeuvre
maneuverable : manoeuverable
marvelous : marvellous
medalist : medallist
meter : metre
milligram : milligramme
millimeter : millimetre
miter : mitre
modeler : modeller
modeling : modelling
mold : mould
molding : moulding
mommy : mummy
multicolored : multicoloured
niter : nitre
ocher : ochre
odor : odour
odorless : odourless
offcenter : offcentre
offense : offence

omelet : omelette
organdy : organdie
orient : orientate
orthopedic : orthopaedic
orthopedics : orthopaedics
orthopedist : orthopaedist
pajamas : pyjamas
paleographer : palaeographer
paleography : palaeography
Paleolithic : Palaeolithic
paleontologist : palaeontologist
paleontology : palaeontology
paneling : panelling
panelist : panellist
pediatric : paediatrics
pediatrician : paediatrician
pediatrics : paediatrics
pedophile : paedophile
pedophilia : paedophilia
pharmacopeia : pharmacopoeia
philter : philtre
pickax : pickaxe
practice : practise
practiced : practised
practicing : practising
pretense : pretence
preterit : preterite
program : programme
pyorrhea : pyorrhoea
racism : racialism
racist : racialist
rancor : rancour
reflection : reflexion
rigor : rigour
rose-colored : rose-coloured
ruble : rouble
rumor : rumour
saber : sabre
savior : saviour
savor : savour
savory : savoury
scepter : sceptre
self-defense : self-defence
septicemia : septicaemia
sepulcher : sepulchre
skeptic : sceptic
skeptical : sceptical
skepticism : scepticism
Slavic : Slavonic
somber : sombre
specter : spectre
succor : succour
sulfate : sulphate

sulfide : sulphide
sulfite : sulphite
sulfonamide : sulphonamide
sulfur : sulphur
sulfuric : sulphuric
sulfurous : sulphurous
theater : theatre
toxemia : toxaemia
tranquility : tranquillity
tranquilize : tranquillize
tranquilizer : tranquillizer

tumor : tumour
TV : telly
unequaled : unequalled
unfavorable : unfavourable
unsportsmanlike : unsporting
valor : valour
vapor : vapour
vaporization : vapourization
vaporize : vapourize
vaporizer : vapourizer
vigor : vigour

Appendix B
Irregular English Plurals

abacus : abacuses or abaci
abscissa : abscissas or abscissae
addendum : addenda
aide-de-camp : aides-de-camp
albatross : albatrosses or albatross
alga : algae
alkali : alkalis or alkalies
alluvium : alluviums or alluvia
ameba : amebas or amebae
amoeba : amoebas or amoebae
ampulla : ampullae
amygdala : amygdalae
analysis : analyses
angioma : angiomas or angiomata
antelope : antelope or antelopes
antenna : antennae
antihero : antiheroes
antiserum : antiserums or antisera
antithesis : antitheses
anus : anuses or ani
aorta : aortas or aortae
apex : apexes or apices
apotheosis : apotheoses
apparatus : apparatus or apparatuses
appendix : appendixes or appendices
aquarium : aquariums or aquaria
archipelago : archipelagos or archipelagoes
areola : areolas or areolae
Ashkenazi : Ashkenazim
auditorium : auditoriums or auditoria
automaton : automatons or automata
bacillus : bacilli
Balinese : (the) Balinese
barracuda : barracuda or barracudas
basis : bases
biceps : biceps or bicepses
bison : bison
bongo : bongos or bongoes
bonito : bonitos or bonito
branchia : branchiae
bregma : bregmata
brontosaurus : brontosauruses or brontosauri
bubo : buboes
buffalo : buffalo, buffalos or buffaloes
bus : buses or busses
cactus : cactuses or cacti

caesura : caesuras or caesurae
calculus : calculi
calculus : calculuses
calico : calicos or calicoes
calix : calices
calyx : calyxes or calyces
cameraman : cameramen
candelabrum : candelabrums or candelabra
Cantonese : (the) Cantonese
carcinoma : carcinomas or carcinomata
cargo : cargos or cargoes
caribou : caribou
caries : caries
carp : carps or carp
carpus : carpi
catharsis : catharses
cavalryman : cavalrymen
cerebellum : cerebellums or cerebella
cerebrum : cerebrums or cerebra
cervix : cervixes or cervices
chassis : chassis
cherub : cherubim
chiasma : chiasmata
Chinese : (the) Chinese
chrysalis : chrysalises or chrysalides
ciborium : ciboria
cicatrix : cicatrices
cicerone : cicerones or ciceroni
cilium : cilia
clergyman : clergymen
clergywoman : clergywomen
coagulum : coagula
coccus : cocci
coccyx : coccyxes or coccyges
codex : codices
colloquium : colloquiums or colloquia
colon : colons or cola
colossus : colossuses or colossi
commando : commandos or commandoes
compendium : compendiums or compendia
congressman : congressmen
congresswoman : congresswomen
consortium : consortiums or consortia
copula : copulas or copulae
corona : coronas or coronae
corps : corps

corpus : corpuses or corpora
cortex : cortices
costa : costae
councilman : councilmen
councilwoman : councilwomen
cranium : craniums or crania
crisis : crises
criterion : criterions or criteria
cumulonimbus : cumulonimbuses
    or cumulonimbi
cumulus : cumuli
curriculum : curriculums or curricula
Cyclops : Cyclopes
dado : dados or dadoes
datum : data
delirium : deliriums or deliria
diagnosis : diagnoses
dialysis : dialyses
dictum : dictums or dicta
dieresis : diereses
dingo : dingoes
directrix : directrixes or directrices
divertimento : divertimentos or divertimenti
dodecahedron : dodecahedrons or dodecahedra
dodo : dodos or dodoes
dogma : dogmas or dogmata
domino : dominoes
duodenum : duodenums or duodena
echo : echoes
ellipsis : ellipses
embargo : embargoes
embolus : emboli
emphasis : emphases
emporium : emporiums or emporia
encomium : encomiums or encomia
epenthesis : epentheses
ephemeris : ephemerides
epiglottis : epiglottises
epithelium : epitheliums or epithelia
erratum : errata
esophagus : esophagi
exegesis : exegeses
facies : facies
fauna : faunas or faunae
femur : femurs or femora
fetus : fetuses
fez : fezzes
fiasco : fiascos or fiascoes
fibula : fibulas or fibulae
flamingo : flamingos or flamingoes
flora : floras or florae
focus : focuses or foci
forceps : forceps

formula : formulas or formulae
forum : forums or fora
frenum : frenums or frena
fresco : frescos or frescoes
fulcrum : fulcrums or fulcra
fungus : fungi or funguses
ganglion : ganglions or ganglia
gastrula : gastrulas or gastrulae
gecko : geckos or geckoes
generatrix : generatrices
genesis : geneses
genie : genies or genii
genius : geniuses or genii
Genoese : (the) Genoese
gens : gentes
genus : genuses or genera
ghetto : ghettos or ghettoes
ginkgo : ginkgoes
giraffe : giraffes or giraffe
gladiolus : gladioluses or gladioli
glans : glandes
glioma : gliomas or gliomata
glottis : glotisses or glottides
goby : gobies or goby
gonococcus : conococci
grotto : grottos or grottoes
guanaco : guanacos or guanaco
gym : gymnasiums or gymnasia
halo : halos or haloes
helix : helixes or helices
hematoma : hematomas or hematomata
herbarium : herbariums or herbaria
hernia : hernias or herniae
hero : heroes
hertz : hertz
hiatus : hiatuses
hibiscus : hibiscuses or hibiscus
hippopotamus : hippopotamuses
    or hippopotami
honorarium : honorariums or honoraria
humerus : humeri
hydra : hydras or hydrae
hyperbola : hyperbolas or hyperbolae
hypnosis : hypnoses
hypothesis : hypotheses
ibex : ibexes or ibices
ibis : ibises or ibis
ilium : ilia
imago : imagoes or imagines
incubus : incubi or incubuses
index : indexes or indices
indigo : indigos or indigoes
intermezzo : intermezzos or intermezzi

interregnum : interregnums or interregna
isthmus : isthmuses
Japanese : (the) Japanese
Javanese : (the) Javanese
jejunum : jejuna
jinn : jinns or jinn
kangaroo : kangaroos or kangaroo
kibbutz : kibbutzim
kilohertz : kilohertz
kohlrabi : kohlrabies
krona : kronor
krone : kroner
lacuna : lacunae
lamina : laminas or laminae
larva : larvae
larynx : larynges or larynxes
lasso : lassos or lassoes
Lebanese : (the) Lebanese
lens : lenses
leu : lei
lev : leva
lexicon : lexicons or lexica
libretto : librettos or libretti
lingua : lingua francas or linguae francae
lipoma : lipomas or lipomata
lobelia : lobelias or lobelia
locus : loci
lumen : lumens or lumina
lux : luxes or luces
lymphoma : lymphomas or lymphomata
lynx : lynxes or lynx
maestro : maestros or maestri
Mafioso : Mafiosi
magma : magmas or magmata
magus : magi
malleolus : malleoli
mango : mangos or mangoes
manifesto : manifestos or manifestoes
mantis : mantises or mantes
marten : martens or marten
matrix : matrices
maximum : maximums or maxima
medium : media
medulla : medullas or medulae
megahertz : megahertz
melanoma : melanomas or melonamata
memorandum : memorandums or memoranda
meniscus : meniscusus or menisci
metamorphosis : metamorphoses
metatarsus : metatarsi
metathesis : metatheses
midrash : midrashim
militiaman : militiamen

millenium : millenniums or millennia
minimum : minimums or minima
modulus : moduli
mongoose : mongooses
moratorium : moratoriums or moratoria
mosquito : mosquitos or mosquitoes
mucosa : mucosas or mucosae
mulatto : mulattos or mulattoes
narcissus : narcissuses or narcissi
nautilus : nautiluses or nautili
nebula : nebulas or nebulae
neurosis : neuroses
nexus : nexuses or nexus
nimbus : nimbuses or nimbi
nobleman : noblemen
noblewoman : noblewomen
nova : novas or novae
nucleus : nucleuses or nuclei
oasis : oases
obbligato : obbligatos or obbligati
octahedron : octahedrons or octahedra
ovum : ova
paramecium : paramecia
parenthesis : parentheses
parhelion : parhelia
partridge : partridges or partridge
paterfamilias : paterfamiliases
pathogenesis : pathogeneses
peccadillo : peccadillos or peccadilloes
pelvis : pelvises or pelves
penicillium : penicilliums or penicillia
penis : penises or penes
penny : pence (British)
pentahedron : pentahedrons or pentahedra
penumbra : penumbres or penumbrae
perch : perches or perch
pericardium : pericardia
perineum : perinea
periosteum : periostea
periphrasis : periphrases
peritoneum : peritoneums or peritonea
persona : personae
phalanx : phalanxes or phalanges
phallus : phalluses or phalli
pharynx : pharynxes or pharynges
phenomenon : phenomena
phlox : phloxes or phlox
phylum : phyla
placebo : placebos or placeboes
placenta : placentas or placentae
plectrum : plectrums or plectra
pleura : plurae
plexus : plexuses or plexus

podium : podiums or podia
policeman : policemen
policewoman : policewomen
polyhedron : polyhedrons or polyhedra
pompano : pompanos or pompano
portico : porticos or porticoes
Portuguese : (the) Portuguese
potato : potatoes
presidium : presidiums or presidia
proboscis : proboscises or proboscides
prognosis : prognoses
prosthesis : prostheses
protozoan : protozoa
psychoneurosis : psychoneuroses
psychosis : psychoses
pupa : pupas or pupae
pyxis : pyxides
quantum : quanta
radius : radiuses or radii
rand : rand
rectum : rectums or recta
referendum : referendums or referenda
retina : retinas or retinae
retrovirus : retroviruses
rhino : rhinos or rhino
rhinoceros : rhinoceroses or rhinoceros
sacrum : sacra
salmon : salmon
salmonella : salmonella or salmonellae
salvo : salvos or salvoes
samba : sambas
samurai : samurais or samurai
sanatorium : sanatoriums or sanatoria
sarcoma : sarcomas or sarcomata
sarcophagus : sarcophaguses or sarcophagi
scapula : scapulas or scapulae
scherzo : scherzos or scherzi
scotoma : scotomas or scotomata
scrotum : scrotums or scrota
sequela : sequelae
seraph : seraphs or seraphim
series : series
serum : serums or sera
shako : shakos or shakoes
sinus : sinuses
Sioux : Sioux
solfeggio : solfeggios or solfeggi
spadix : spadices
species : species
spectrum : spectrums or spectra
speculum : speculums or specula
sputum : sputa
stadium : stadiums or stadia

statesman/stateswoman : statesmen/stateswomen
stela : stelae
sternum : sternums or sterna
stigma : stigmas or stigmata
stiletto : stilettos or stilettoes
stimulus : stimuli
stoma : stomata
stratocumulus : stratocumuli
stratum : stratums or strata
stratus : strati
streptococcus : streptococci
stria : striae
stylus : styluses or styli
substratum : substrata
superhero : superheroes
superstratum : superstrata
symbiosis : simbioses
symposium : symposiums or simposia
synapsis : synapses
synopsis : synopses
synthesis : syntheses
Taiwanese : (the) Taiwanese
tempo : tempos or tempi
terminus : terminuses or termini
terrarium : terrariums or terraria
testis : testes
tetrahedron : tetrahedrons or tetrahedra
thalamus : thalami
theca : thecae
thesaurus : thesauruses or thesauri
thesis : theses
thorax : thoraxes or thoraces
thrombosis : thrombosis
thrombus : thrombi
tibia : tibias or tibiae
tomato : tomatoes
tornado : tornados or tornadoes
torpedo : torpedoes
tournedos : tournedos
trachea : tracheas or tracheae
trauma : traumas or traumata
triceps : tricepses or triceps
trichina : trichinae
trout : trout or trouts
tympanum : tympanums or tympana
ultimatum : ultimatums or ultimata
urethra : urethras or urethrae
uterus : uteruses or uteri
uvula : uvulas or uvulae
vertebra : vertebras or vertebrae
vertex : vertexes or vertices
vertigo : vertigoes
veto : vetoes

Vietnamese : (the) Vietnamese
virtuoso : virtuosos or virtuosi
volcano : volcanos or volcanoes
vortex : vortexes or vortices
vulva : vulvas or vulvae
watchman : watchmen
whiskey : whiskeys or whiskies

xanthoma : xanthomas or
    xanthomata
yeti : yeti
zebra : zebras or zebra
zebu : zebu
zero : zeros or zeroes
zloty : zlotys or zloty

Appendix C
Irregular Spanish Plurals

abrebotellas : abrebotellas
análisis : análisis
andalúz : andaluces
apoteosis : apoteosis
archidiócesis : archidiócesis
arquidiócesis : arquidiócesis
bambú : bambúes or bambús
bestseller : bestsellers
bíceps : bíceps
brandy : brandys
bumerang : bumerangs
cárdigan : cárdigans
caribú : caribúes
caries : caries
cebú : cebús o cebúes
chasis : chasis
chip : chips
cicatriz : cicatrices
clic : clics
clímax : clímax
cocker : cockers
cortacircuitos : cortacircuitos
cowboy : cowboys
crisis : crisis
diéresis : diéresis
diócesis : diócesis
dosis : dosis
epéntesis : epéntesis
escáner : escáners
espécimen : especímenes
espray : sprays
esprint : esprints
esquí : esquís or esquíes
exégesis : exégesis
fan : fans
fez : feces

flashback : flashbacks
floppy : floppys
forceps : forceps
foul : fouls
gag : gags
glotis : glotis
gong : gongs
gurú, guru : gurús or gurúes
hipótesis : hipótesis
ítem : ítems
jockey : jockeys
manatí : manatíes
metáfrasis : metáfrasis
metamorfosis : metamorfosis
metátesis : metátesis
microchip : microchips
modem : modems
neurosis : neurosis
paráfrasis : paráfrasis
paréntesis : paréntesis
pelvis : pelvis
perífrasis : perífrasis
psiconeurosis : psiconeurosis
psicosis : psicosis
show : shows
siconeurosis : siconeurosis
sicosis : sicosis
simbiosis : simbiosis
sinopsis : sinopsis
síntesis : síntesis
sobredosis : sobredosis
sprint, esprint : sprints
tabú : tabúes or tabús
tesis : tesis
yogur, yogurt : yogurts
yupi : yupis

Appendix D
Supplementary Vocabulary

abandon	abandonar *vt*	admissibility	admisibilidad *nf*
abhor	aborrecer *vt*	admit	admitir *vt*
abominable	abominable *aj*	adopt	adoptar *vt*
abominate	abominar *vt*	adoptable	adoptable *aj*
aboriginal	aborigen *aj*	adore	adorar *vt*
abort	abortar *vi*	adoring	adorador *aj*
abound	abundar *vi*	adorn	adornar *vt*
abrogation	abrogación *nf*	adsorb	adsorber *vt*
absence	ausencia *nf*	adulate	adular *vt*
absolve	absolver *vt*	adulterate	adulterar *vt*
absolved	absuelto *aj*	adulterous	adúltero *aj*
absorb	absorber *vt*	advance	avanzar *vti*
absorbable	absorbible *aj*	advance(d)	avanzado *aj*
absorbency	absorbencia *nf*	advantageous	ventajoso *aj*
abstain	abstenerse *vr*	advocate	abogar *vi*
abstinent	abstinente *aj*	Aeolian	eolio, eólico *aj*
abstract	abstraer *vt*	aerial	aéreo *aj*
abstracted	abstraído *aj*	aerodynamic	aerodinámico *aj*
absurdity	absurdidad, absurdo *nf, nm*	aerostatic	aerostático *aj*
		aesthetic, esthetic	estético *aj*
abundance	abundancia *nf*	affectionate	afectuoso *aj*
accelerate	acelerar(se) *vt(r)*	affective	afectivo *aj*
accelerating	acelerador *aj*	affiliate	afiliar(se) *vt(r)*
accent, accentuate	acentuar *vt*	affirmation	afirmación *nf*
accessible	accesible *aj*	affricative	fricativo *aj*
accidental	accidental *aj*	agglomerate	aglomerarse *vr*
acclaim	aclamar *vt*	agglutinate	aglutinar(se) *vt(r)*
acclimate, acclimatize	aclimatizar(se) *vt(r)*	aggravating	agravador *aj*
accompany	acompañar *vt*	aggravation	agravación, agravamiento *nf, nm*
accredit	acreditar *vt*		
accreditation	acreditación *nf*	agile	ágil *aj*
accumulation	acumulación *nf*	agitate	agitar *vt*
accuse	acusar *vt*	agrarianism	agrarismo *nm*
acidify	acidificar(se) *vt(r)*	air-condition	acondicionar *vt*
acidulous	acídulo *aj*	air-conditioned	con aire condicionado
act	actuar *vi*	airy	airoso *aj*
acuity	agudeza *nf*	alabastrine	alabastrino *aj*
adapt	adaptar(se) *vt(r)*	alarm	alarmar *vt*
add (join)	adicionar *vt*	albuminous	albuminoso *aj*
addicted	adicto *aj*	alcohol-poisoned	alcoholizado *aj*
adenoidal	adenoideo *aj*	alert	alertar *vt*
adhere	adherirse *vr*	algebraic	algebraico *aj*
adjust	ajustar *vt*	algorithmic	algorítmico *aj*
administer	administrar *vt*	alienable	alienable *aj*
admire	admirar *vt*	align, aline	alinear *vt*
admiring	admirativo *aj*	alkalinize	alcalinizar(se) *vt(r)*

alkalize	alcalizar(se) *vt(r)*
allege	alegar *vt*
alleged	alegado *aj*
allegoric(al)	alegórico *aj*
allegorize	alegorizar *vt*
allergic	alérgico *aj*
alleviate	aliviar *vt*
alleviating	aliviador *aj*
allied	aliado *aj*
alliterate	aliterar *vt*
allopathic	alopático *aj*
allotropic	alotrópico *aj*
alloy	alear *vt*
allude	aludir *vi*
allusive	alusivo *aj*
alluvial	aluvial *aj*
alphabetization	alfabetización *nf*
alphabetize	alfabetizar *vt*
alternate	alternar *vti*
alternation	alternancia *nf*
amalgamate	amalgamar(se) *vt(r)*
Amazonian	amazónico *aj*
ambassadorial	de embajador(a)
ambiguity	ambigüedad *nf*
ambivalent	ambivalente *aj*
amble	amblar *vi*
ambulate	ambular *vi*
ambush	emboscar *vt*
amebic, amoebic	amébico *aj*
amend	enmendar *vt*
Americana *nsg*	cosas americanas *nfpl*
Americanize	americanizar *vt*
amoral	amoral *aj*
amortize	amortizar *vt*
amplify	ampliar *vt*
amputate	amputar *vt*
anabolic	anabólico *aj*
anachronistic	anacrónico *aj*
anaerobic	anaerobio *aj*
analogical	analógico *aj*
analogize	hacer analogías *vi*
anaphylactic	anafiláctico *aj*
anarchic(al)	anárquico *aj*
anatomical	anatómico *aj*
anchor	anclar *vt*
androgynous	andrógino *aj*
anecdotal	anecdótico *aj*
anemic Ⓐ	anémico *aj*
anesthetic Ⓐ	anestésico *aj, nm*
anesthetize Ⓐ	anestesiar *vt*
angelic	angélico, angelical *aj*
Anglicize	anglicanizar *vt*
anguish	angustiar *vt*
anhydrous	anhidro *aj*
animate	animar *vt*
annex	anexar *vt*
annexed	anexo *aj*
annotate	anotar *vt*
announce	anunciar *vt*
annul	anular *vt*
anonymous	anónimo *aj*
antagonistic	antagónico *aj*
antagonize	antagonizar *vt*
anthropometric	antropométrico *aj*
anti-American	antiamericano *aj*
anti-imperialism	antiimperialismo *nm*
anti-imperialist	antiimperialista *aj*
anti-Semitic	antisemítico *aj*
anti-Soviet	antisoviético *aj*
anticipate	anticipar *vt*
anticlerical	anticlerical *aj*
anticlericalism	anticlericalismo *nm*
antifeminist	antifeminista *aj*
antilabor	antiobrero *aj*
antiprotectionist	antiproteccionista *aj*
antiquarian	anticuario *aj*
antiquated	anticuado *aj*
antirevolutionary	antirrevolucionario *aj*
antitank	antitanque *aj*
antiterrorism	antiterrorismo *nm*
antiterrorist	antiterrorista *aj*
antitheft	antirrobo *aj*
antitoxic	antitóxico *aj*
antitrust	antimonopolista *aj*
apathetic	apático *aj*
aphonic	afónico *aj*
apolitical	apolítico *aj*
apoplectic	apoplético *aj*
appeal	apelar *vti*
appetizing	apetitoso *aj*
apposition	aposición *nf*
appreciate	apreciar *vt*
apprentice	poner de aprendiz
approximate	aproximar(se) *vt(r)*
approximation	aproximación *nf*
arbitrable	arbitrable *aj*
arbitrate	arbitrar *vti*
arboreal	arbóreo *aj*
arch	arquear(se) *vtr*
archaism	arcaísmo *nm*
arched	arqueado *aj*
archeological Ⓐ	arqueológico *aj*
archetypal	arquetípico *aj*
arching	arqueo *nm*
arguable	argumentable *aj*
argue	argüir *vti*

aristocratic	aristocrático *aj*	audit	auditar *vt*
arithmetic	aritmético *aj*	augment	aumentar *vt*
arm	armar(se) *vt(r)*	aural	aural *aj*
armed	armado *aj*	auricular	auricular *aj*
aromatize	aromatizar *vt*	auscultate	auscultar *vt*
arrest	arrestar *vt*	Austro-Hungarian	austro-húngaro *aj*
arrhythmic	arrítmico *aj*	authenticate	autenticar *vt*
arrive	arribar *vi*	authentication	autenticación *nf*
arterial	arterial *aj*	authenticity	autenticidad *nf*
arthritic	artrítico *aj*	authorization	autorización *nf*
articulate	articular *vt*	authorize	autorizar *vt*
articulated	articulado *aj*	authorship	autoría *nf*
artistic	artístico *aj*	autistic	autista *aj*
arty, artsy-craftsy	pseudo-artístico *aj*	autobiographical	autobiográfico *aj*
ascend	ascender *vti*	autocratic	autocrático *aj*
ascetic	ascético *aj*	autograph	autografiar *vt*
aspectual	aspectivo *aj*	automate	automatizar(se) *vt(r)*
asphalt	asfaltar *vt*	automatic	automático *aj*
asphalting	asfaltado *nm*	autonomous	autónomo *aj*
asphyxiate	asfixiar(se) *vt(r)*	autopsy	autopsiar *vt*
asphyxiating	asfixiador, asfixiante *aj*	ax Ⓐ	cortar con hacha *vt*
aspirate	aspirar *vt*	axial	axial *aj*
aspirated	aspirado *aj*	axillary	axilar *aj*
assassinate	asesinar *vt*	axiomatic	axiomático *aj*
assault	asaltar *vt*	bacchanalian	bacanal, báquico *aj*
assay	ensayar *vt*	bacillar	bacilar *aj*
assent	asentir *vi*	bacillary	baciliforme *aj*
assign	asignar *vt*	banana	bananero *aj*
assimilate	asimilar(se) *vt(r)*	bandage	vendar *vt*
associate	asociar *vt*	banking	bancario *aj*
assonant	asonante *aj*	banquet	banquetear *vi*
assonate	asonantar *vt*	baptismal	bautismal *aj*
astigmatic	astigmático *aj*	baptize	bautizar *vt*
astrological	astrológico *aj*	barometric	barométrico *aj*
astronautical	astronáutico *aj*	baronial	baronial *aj*
asymmetrical	asimétrico *aj*	barricade	poner barricadas
atavistic	atávico *aj*	base	basar *vt*
atheistic	ateo *aj*	bastardize	bastardear *vt*
athletic	atlético *aj*	bastardy	bastardía *nf*
atmospheric	atmosférico *aj*	bat	batear *vti*
atomization	atomización *nf*	battle	batallar *vi*
atomize	atomizar *vt*	battling	batallador *aj*
atonal	atonal *aj*	bayonet	herir con bayoneta
atrophied	atrofiado *aj*	beastly	bestial *aj*
atrophy	atrofiarse *vr*	beatific	beatífico *aj*
attack	atacar *vti*	beatify	beatificar *vt*
attacking	atacante *aj*	benefit	beneficiar(se) *vt(r)*
attempt (to kill)	atentado *nm*	bestial	bestial *aj*
attend (take care of)	atender *vt*	Biblical	bíblico *aj aj*
attenuate	atenuar(se) *vt(r)*	bibliographic	bibliográfico *aj*
attest	atestiguar *vt*	bicycle, bike	ir en bicicleta *vi*
attract	atraer(se) *vt(r)*	bidirectional	bidireccional *aj*
attribute	atribuir *vt*	bifurcate	bifurcar(se) *vt(r)*

bigamous	bígamo *aj*
biliary	biliar *aj*
bilingualism	bilingüismo *nm*
bilious	bilioso *aj*
biochemical	bioquímico *aj*
biodegrade	biodegradarse *vr*
biogenetic	biogenético *aj*
bionic	biónico *aj*
biotic	biótico *aj*
bipartite	bipartito *aj*
bivouac	vivaquear *vi*
blaspheme	blasfemar *vi*
blasphemous	blasfemo *aj*
blockade	bloquear *vt*
blockading	bloqueador *aj*
bomb, bombard	bombardear *vt*
bore	aburrir *vt*
botanical	botánico *aj*
bottle	embotellar *vt*
box	boxear *vi*
boycott	boicotear *vt*
boycotting	boicoteo *nm*
brevity	brevedad *nf*
bridle	embridar *vt*
brilliance	brillantez *nf*
bronchial	bronquial *aj*
bronze	broncear *vt*
bronzed	bronceado *aj*
bulbous	bulboso *aj*
buoyant	boyante *aj*
bus *vt*	llevar en autobús *vt, nm*
button	abotonar *vt*
buttoning	botonadura *nf*
Byzantinism	bizantinismo *nm*
cabalistic	cabalístico *aj*
cable	cablegrafiar *vt*
cadaverous	cadavérico *aj*
Caesarean, Cesarean	cesáreo *aj*
calamitous	calamitoso *aj*
calcic	cálcico *aj*
calcify	calcificar(se) *vt(r)*
calculable	calculable *aj*
calculate	calcular *vti*
calibrate	calibrar *vt*
calligraphic	caligráfico *aj*
calm	calmar *vt*
caloric	calórico *aj*
calorific	calorífico *aj*
camouflage	camuflar *vt*
camp, encamp	acampar *vi*
campaign *vt*	hacer una campaña *vi, nf*
camphorate	alcanforar *vt*

cancelled	cancelado *aj*
cancerous	canceroso *aj*
candidacy	candidatura *nf*
cannibalistic	caníbal *aj*
cannonade	cañonear *vt*
canoe *vi*	ir en canoa *vi, nf*
canonize	canonizar *vt*
capillary	capilar *aj*
capital	capitalino *aj*
capitalistic	capitalista *aj*
capitalization	capitalización *nf*
capitalize	capitalizar *vt*
capitulate	capitular *vi*
capsular	capsular *aj*
captain	capitanear *vt*
caramelize	acaramelar, caramelizar(se) *vti*
caravansary	caravanera *nf*
carbonic	carbónico *aj*
carbonize	carbonizar *vt*
carburization	carburación *nf*
card	carda, cardencha *nf*
card (wool)	cardar *vt*
careen	carenar *vt*
caress	acariciar *vt*
caricature	caricaturizar *vt*
carnival	carnavalesco *aj*
cartilaginous	cartilaginoso *aj*
cascade *vi*	caer en cascadas *vi, nfpl*
castrate	castrar *vt*
casuistry	casuística *nf*
cat-like	gateado, gatuno *aj*
catabolic	catabólico *aj*
catalytic	catalítico *aj*
catalyze	catalizar *vt*
catapult	catapultar *vt*
catatonic	catatónico *aj*
catechize	catequizar *vt*
categorical	categórico *aj*
categorization	categorización *nf*
categorize	categorizar *vt*
cathartic	catártico *aj, nm*
causal	causal *aj*
cause	causar *vt*
cauterize	cauterizar *vt*
caution	cautela, precaución *nf*
cavernous	cavernoso *aj*
ceaseless	incesante *aj*
celebrate	celebrar(se) *vt(r)*
cellular	celular *aj*
Celtic	celta *aj, nm*
cement	cementar *vt*
censor	censurar *vt*

censure	censurar *vt*
center **A**	centrar *vt*
centralization	centralización *nf*
centralize	centralizar *vt*
centric	céntrico *aj*
ceramic	cerámico *aj*
cerebral	cerebral *aj*
certifiable	certificable *aj*
certification	certificación *nf*
certify	certificar *vt*
cervical	cervical *aj*
cessation	cesación *nf*
cession	cesión *nf*
chaotic	caótico *aj*
characteristic	característico *aj*
characterize	caracterizar *vt*
charge	cargar *vt*
chase	cazar *vt*
chauvinism	chovinismo *nm*
cherubic	querúbico *aj*
chimeric(al)	quimérico *aj*
chisel	cincelar *vt*
chlorinate	clorinar *vt*
choral	coral *aj*
choreograph	coreografiar *vt*
choreographic	coreográfico *aj*
chrome-like	acromado *aj*
chromic	crómico *aj*
chronicity	cronicidad *nf*
ciliary	ciliar *aj*
cinematographic	cinematográfico *aj*
cipher	cifrar *vt*
circuitry	circuitería *nf*
circulate	circular *vti*
circumcise	circuncidar *vt*
circumnavigate	circunnavegar *vt*
circumscribe	circunscribir *vt*
circumstantial	circunstancial *aj*
circus	circense *aj*
cite	citar *vt*
civic	cívico *aj*
civilize	civilizar *vt*
clamoring	clamoreo *nm*
clarify	aclarar *vt*
clarifying	aclaratorio *aj*
clarity	claridad *nf*
classic	clásico *nm*
classless	sin clases
claustrophobic	claustrofóbico *aj*
clavicular	clavicular *aj*
clear	clarearse *vr*
clerical	clerical *aj*
click	hacer clic *vi*
climatic	climático *aj*
climatological	climatológico *aj*
cloister	enclaustrar *vt*
clonal	clónico *aj*
clone	clonar *vt*
cluck	cloquear, clocar *vi*
coachhouse	cochera *nf*
coagulate	coagular(se) *vt(r)*
coccygeal	coccígeo *aj*
code, encode	codificar *vt*
coeducation	coeducación *nf*
coexistent, coexisting	coexistente *aj*
coffee	cafetelero *aj*
coffee-colored *aj*	de color de café *nm*
cognitive	cognitivo, cognoscitivo *aj*
cognitive	cognoscitivo *aj*
cognizant	conocedor *aj*
cohabit	cohabitar *vi*
coincidence	coincidencia *nf*
collaborate	colaborar *vi*
collaborative	colaborativo *aj*
collect	coleccionar *vt*
collectivist	colectivista *aj*
collectivization	colectivización *nf*
collectivize	colectivizar *vt*
collegiate	colegiado *aj*
colloidal	coloidal *aj*
colloquialism	expresión coloquial *nf*
colonic	colónico *aj*
colonization	colonización *nf*
colonize	colonizar *vt*
color **A**	colorear(se) *vt(r)*
comatose	comatoso *aj*
combat	combatir *vt*
combination	combinación *nf*
combustible	combustible *aj*
comedic *aj*	de la comedia *nf*
comical	cómico *aj*
command (army)	comandar *vti*
command (give order)	mandar *vt*
commemorate	conmemorar *vt*
commemorative	conmemorativo *aj*
commencement	comienzo *nm*
comment	comentar *vt*
commercialism	comercialismo *nm*
commercialization	comercialización *nf*
commercialize	comercializar *vt*
commission	comisionar *vt*
commune	comuna *nf*
communicate	comunicar(se) *vt(r)*
communicating	comunicador *aj*
communistic	comunista *aj*

commute	conmutar *vt*
compact	compactar *vt*
comparable	comparable *aj*
compartmentalize	compartimentar *vt*
compensate	compensar *vti*
compete	competir *vi*
competing	competidor *aj*
competitive	competitivo *aj*
compile	compilar, recopilar *vt*
complement	complementar *vt*
complete (make whole)	completar *vt*
comply	cumplir *vi*
compose	componer *vt*
composed	compuesto *aj*
comprehend	comprender *vti*
compress	comprimir *vt*
computable	computable *aj*
compute	computar *vt*
computerize	computarizar *vt*
concatenate	concatenar *vt*
conceive	concebir *vti*
conceptual	conceptual *aj*
conceptualize	conceptuar *vt*
concertize *vi*	dar conciertos *nmpl*
conciliate	conciliar *vt*
conclude	concluir(se) *vt(r)*
concupiscent	concupiscente *aj*
concurrence	concurrencia *nf*
condemn	condenar *vt*
condemnatory	condenatorio *aj*
condense	condensar(se) *vt(r)*
conduct	conducir *vt*
confess	confesar(se) *vti(r)*
confessed	confeso *aj*
confide	confiar *vti*
configure	configurar *vt*
confine	confinar *vt*
confirm	confirmar *vt*
confiscate	confiscar *vt*
confluent	confluente *aj*
conform	conformar(se) *vt(r)*
confound	confundir *vt*
confute	confutar *vt*
congested	congestionado *aj*
congestive	congestivo *aj*
conglomerate	conglomerar(se) *vt(r)*
conglomeration	conglomeración *nf*
congratulate	congratular *vt*
congressional	congresional *aj*
conjecture	conjeturar *vi*
conjugate	conjugar *vt*
connect	conectar *vt*
connotation	connotación *nf*

connote	connotar *vt*
conquer	conquistar *vt*
consanguineous	consanguíneo *aj*
consecrate	consagrar *vt*
consent	consentir *vi*
consequent	consecuente *nm*
conserve	conservar *vt*
consider	considerar *vt*
consign	consignar *vt*
consist	consistir *vi*
consolidate	consolidar(se) *vt(r)*
consonantal	consonántico *aj*
conspire	conspirar *vi*
constancy	constancia *nf*
constitute	constituir *vt*
constitutionality	constitucionalidad *nf*
construct	construir *vt*
constructive	constructivo *aj*
consular	consular *aj*
consulting	consultivo, consultor *aj*
consume	consumir *vt*
consummate	consumar *vt*
contact *vt*	ponerse en contacto con *vr, nm*
contaminate	contaminar *vt*
contemplate	contemplar *vt*
contemplative	contemplativo *aj*
contend	contender *vi*
context	contexto *nm*
contextualize	contextualizar *vt*
contingent	contingente *aj*
continuation	continuación *nf*
continue	continuar *vt*
continuity	continuidad *nf*
continuum	continuo *nm*
contort (one's body)	contorsionarse *vt*
contortion	contorsión *nf*
contract	contratar(se) *vt(r)*
contracting	contratante *aj*
contradict	contradecir *vt*
contradictory	contradictorio *aj*
contrast	contrastar *vi*
contravention	contravención *nf*
control	controlar *vt*
controversial	controvertido *aj*
controversy	controversia *nf*
convalesce	convalecer *vi*
convenient	conveniente *aj*
converge	convergir *vi*
conversational	conversacional *aj*
converse	conversar *vi*
convert	convertirse *vr*
convertibility	convertibilidad *nf*

convicted	convicto *aj*	cruciform	cruciforme *aj*
convoke	convocar *vt*	crucify	crucificar *vt*
convoy	convoyar *vt*	cruise	cruzar *vi*
convulsive	convulsivo *aj*	cruising	de crucero
coordinate	coordinar(se) *vt(r)*	cryogenic	criogénico *aj*
coppery,	cobrizo, cobreño *aj*	cryptographic	criptográfico *aj*
copper-colored		crystalline	cristalino *aj*
copulate	copularse *vr*	crystallize	cristalizar(se) *vt(r)*
copy	copiar(se) *vt(r)*	cube	cubicar *vt*
coral	coralino *aj*	cubic volume	cubicaje *nm*
cordon off	acordonar *vt*	culminate	culminar *vi*
Cornish	de Cornualles *aj*	culpable	culpable *aj*
corporate	corporativo *aj*	cultivable	cultivable *aj*
corpulent	corpulento *aj*	cultivate	cultivar *vt*
corpuscular	corpuscular *aj*	culture	cultivar *vt*
corral	acorralar, encorralar *vt*	cupric	cúprico *aj*
correct	corregir *vt*	cupriferous	cuprífero *aj*
correlate	correlacionar *vt*	cuprous	cuproso *aj*
correspond (with)	corresponderse (con) *vr*	curative	curativo *aj*
corroborate	corroborar *vt*	cure	curar *vt*
corroborative	corroborativo *aj*	curtain *vt*	poner cortinas *vt, nfpl*
corrode	corroer(se) *vt(r)*	curtains *npl*	cortinaje *nm*
corroded	corroído *aj*	curve *vi*	describir una curva *vt,*
corrosive	corrosivo *aj, nm*		*nf*
corrupted	corrompido *aj*	cushioned	acojinado *aj*
cortical	cortical *aj*	custodial *aj*	de la custodia *nf*
cost	costar *vi*	cutaneous	cutáneo *aj*
costly	costoso *aj*	cyanotic	cianótico *aj*
counsel	aconsejar *vt*	cybernetic	cibernético *aj*
counterattack	contraatacar *vti*	cystic	cístico *aj*
countermarch	contramarchar *vi*	cytotoxic	citotóxico *aj*
counterrevolution	contrarrevolución *nf*	daily	diariamente *av*
counting	cuenta *nf*	damage	dañar *vt*
countless	incontable *aj*	damask	damasquino *aj*
couple	acoplar *vt*	dance	danzar *vti*
court	cortejar *vt*	dancing	danzante *aj*
covalence	covalencia *nf*	Danish	danés, dinamarqués *aj*
covalent	covalente *aj*	date	datilero *aj*
covariant	covariante *aj*	debate	debatir *vt*
cranial	craneal, craneano *aj*	debilitate	debilitar *vt*
credit	acreditar *vt*	debit	debitar *vt*
credit	crediticio *aj*	debut	debutar *vi*
credulity	credulidad *nf*	debut, début	debut *nm*
credulous	crédulo *aj*	decadence	decadencia *nf*
Creolized	creolizado *aj*	decalcify	descalcificar *vt*
crepitate	crepitar *vi*	decapitate	decapitar *vt*
cretinous	cretino *aj*	decarbonize	descarbonizar *vt*
criminality	criminalidad *nf*	decelerate	decelerar *vi*
croak	croar *vi*	decentralization	descentralización *nf*
crochet *vi*	hacer crochet *vi, nm*	decipher	descifrar *vt*
crochet *vt*	tejer a crochet *vt, nm*	decipherable	descifrable *aj*
cross	cruzar(se) *vt(r)*	declaim	declamar *vt*
crown	coronar *vt*	declamatory	declamatorio *aj*

declare	declarar *vti*
declinable	declinable *aj*
decline	declinar *vt*
decoding	descodificación *nf*
decompose	descomponer(se) *vt(r)*
decontaminate	descontaminar *vt*
decorate	condecorar *vt*
decorate	decorar *vt*
decorative	decorativo *aj*
decree	decretar *vt*
decrepit	decrépito *aj*
dedicate	dedicar *vt*
deductible	deducible *aj*
deductive	deductivo *aj*
deescalate	desescalar(se) *vt(r)*
defame	difamar *vt*
defecate	defecar *vi*
defect	defeccionar *vi*
defend	defender *vt*
defenseless	indefenso *aj*
defensible	defendible *aj*
deficiency	deficiencia *nf*
definable	definible *aj*
define	definir *vt*
deflate	desinflar(se) *vt(r)*
deflation	desinflación *nf*
deflower	desflorar *vt*
defoliate	defoliar *vt*
deforest	deforestar *vt*
defraud	defraudar *vt*
degenerate	degenerar *vi*
dehumanize	deshumanizar *vt*
dehumidify	deshumedecer *vt*
dehydrate	deshidratar *vt*
deify	deificar *vt*
delegate	delegar *vt*
deliberate	deliberar *vi*
deliberately	deliberadamente *av*
deliberative	deliberativo *aj*
delicacy	delicadeza *nf*
delight	deleitar(se) *vt(r)*
delimit	delimitar *vt*
delineate	delinear *vt*
delinquent	delincuente *aj*
delirious	delirante *aj*
Delphic	délfico *aj*
deltoid	deltoideo *aj*
demagogic	demagógico *aj*
demagogy,	demagogia,
demagoguery	demogogismo *nf,*
	nm
demarcate	demarcar *vt*
demented	demente *aj*

demilitarize	desmilitarizar *vt*
demobilize	desmovilizar(se) *vt(r)*
democratic	democrático *aj*
democratization	democratización *nf*
demographic	demográfico *aj*
demolish	demoler *vt*
demonic	demoníaco *aj*
demonstrable	demostrable *aj*
demoralize	desmoralizar *vt*
denationalization	desnacionalización *nf*
denature	desnaturalizar *vt*
denigrate	denigrar *vt*
denotation	denotación *nf*
denote	denotar *vt*
denounce	denunciar *vt*
dense	denso *aj*
deodorize	desodorizar *vt*
deoxidize	desoxidar *vt*
departmental	departamental *aj*
depersonalize	despersonalizar *vt*
deplume	desplumar *vt*
depolarize	despolarizar *vt*
depopulate	despoblar *vt*
depopulation	despoblación *nf*
depose	deponer *vt*
deposed	depuesto *aj*
deposit	depositar *vt*
depreciate	depreciar(se) *vt(r)*
depress	deprimir *vt*
deprive	privar *vt*
deputation	deputación *nf*
deputize	diputar *vt*
derive	derivar *vt*
desalinate	desalin(iz)ar *vt*
descent	descendencia *nf*
describable	descriptible *aj*
desensitize	desensibilizar *vt*
desert	desertar *vt*
design	diseñar *vt*
designate	designar *vt*
desirable	deseable *aj*
desire	desear *vt*
desirous	deseoso *aj*
desolate	desolar *vt*
despair	desesperarse *vr*
despotism	despotismo *nm*
destined	destinado *aj*
destroy	destruir *vt*
destructive	destructivo *aj*
detach	destacar *vt*
detail	detallar *vt*
detain	detener *vt*
detect	detectar *vt*

deteriorate	deteriorarse *vr*
determine	determinar *vt*
detest	detestar *vt*
detonate	detonar *vt*
detonating	detonante *aj*
detoxify	desintoxicar *vt*
devaluate	devaluar, desvalorizar *vt*
devastate	devastar *vt*
deviate	desviarse *vr*
diacritical	diacrítico *aj*
diagnose	diagnosticar *vt*
dialectical	dialéctico *aj*
diametric(al)	diametral *aj*
diaphragmatic	diafragmático *aj*
diastolic	diastólico *aj*
diatomic	diatómico *aj*
dichogamous	dicógamo *aj*
dictate	dictar *vt*
differ	diferir *vi*
differentiate	diferenciar *vt*
diffract	difractar(se) *vt(r)*
diffuse	difundir(se) *vt(r)*
diffuse	difuso *aj*
digest	digerir *vt*
digestible	digerible *aj*
dilate	dilatar(se) *vt(r)*
dilute	diluir *vt*
dilution	dilución *nf*
dimensional	dimensional *aj*
diminish	disminuir(se) *vt(r)*
diminution	disminución *nf*
diphthongize	diptongar *vt*
direct	dirigir *vt*
disadvantageous	desventajoso *aj*
disappear	desaparecer *vi*
disapprove	desaprobar *vi*
disarm	desarmar(se) *vt(r)*
disarmed	desarmado *aj*
disastrous	desastroso *aj*
discern	discernir *vt*
discernible	discernible *aj*
discharge	descargar(se) *vt(r)*
disciplinary	disciplinario *aj*
discipline	disciplinar *vt*
discolor Ⓐ	descolorar(se) *vt(r)*
disconcert	desconcertar *vt*
disconnect	desconectar *vt*
disconnected	desconectado, inconexo *aj*
discontinuance	descontinuación *nf*
discontinue	descontinuar *vt*
discontinuous	descontinuo *aj*
discount	descontar *vt*
discountable	descontable *aj*
discover	descubrir *vt*
discredit	desacreditar *vt*
discuss	discutir *vt*
disdain	desdeñar(se) *vt(r)*
disembarcation	desembarco *nm*
disenchant	desencantar *vt*
disfigure	desfigurar *vt*
dishonor	deshonrar *vt*
disillusion	desilusionar *vt*
disinfect	desinfectar *vt*
disinfecting	desinfectante *aj*
disintegrate	desintegrar(se) *vt(r)*
disinter	desenterrar *vt*
disinterred	desenterrado *aj*
dislocate	dislocar *vt*
disorganize	desorganizar *vt*
disorient	desorientar *vt*
disparate	dispar *aj*
dispatch	despachar *vt*
disperse	dispersar(se) *vt(r)*
displace	desplazar *vt*
dispose	disponer *vi*
dispossess	desposeer *vt*
dispute	disputar *vt*
disqualify	descalificar *vt*
disquiet	inquietar *vt*
dissatisfy	no satisfacer *vt*
dissect	disecar *vt*
disseminate	diseminar *vt*
dissent	disentir *vi*
dissimilate	disimilar *vt*
dissipate	disipar(se) *vt(r)*
dissociate	disociar(se) *vt(r)*
dissolve	disolver(se) *vt(r)*
dissolved	disuelto *aj*
dissuade	disuadir *vt*
distant	distante *aj*
distend	distenderse *vr*
distill	destilar *vt*
distinct	distinto *aj*
distinguishable	distinguible *aj*
distract	distraer *vt*
distraction	distracción *nf*
distribute	distribuir *vt*
disunite	desunir(se) *vt(r)*
disunited	desunido *aj*
disuse	desuso *nm*
diverge	divergir *vi*
diverse	diverso *aj*
diversification	diversificación *nf*
diversify	diversificar(se) *vt(r)*

divert	divertir *vt*
diverting	divertido *aj*
divine	adivinar *vt*
divine	divino *aj*
divorce	divorciar(se) *vt(r)*
doctrinaire	doctrinario *aj*
document	documentar *vt*
dogmatism	dogmatismo *nm*
domesticate	domesticar *vt*
domiciled	domiciliado *aj*
domiciliary	domiciliario *aj*
dominate	dominar *vt*
donate	donar *vt*
dose	dosificar *vt*
double	doblar(se) *vt(r)*
doubt	dudar *vti*
douche	ducharse *vr*
Draconian	draconiano *aj*
drain	drenar *vt*
dramatize	dramatizar *vt*
dribble	driblar *vti*
drug	drogar *vt*
drugged	drogado *aj*
ductile	dúctil *aj*
duelling	el batir en duelo *nm*
duodenal	duodenal *aj*
duplicate	duplicar *vt*
dynamite	dinamitar *vt*
dynastic	dinástico *aj*
dysfunctional	disfuncional *aj*
dyslexic	disléxico *aj*
dyspeptic	dispéptico *aj*
dystrophic	distrófico *aj*
ecclesiastic(al)	eclesiástico *aj*
echo *vi*	hacer echo *vt, nm*
echoic	ecoico *aj*
eclipse	eclipsar *vt*
ecological	ecológico *aj*
ecstatic	extático *aj*
ectodermic	ectodérmico *aj*
ectomorphic	ectomórfico *aj*
ectopic	ectópico *aj*
ecumenical	ecuménico *aj*
edify	edificar *vt*
editorialize	editorializar *vi*
educable	educable *aj*
educate	educar *vt*
effective	efectivo *aj*
effectiveness	efectividad *nf*
effectuate	efectuar *vt*
efficacy	eficacia *nf*
efflorescent	eflorescente *aj*
effortless *aj*	sin esfuerzo *nm*

ejaculate	eyacular *vti*
eject	eyectar *vi*
elaborate	elaborar *vt*
elasticized	elastizado *aj*
elect	elegir *vt*
elected	elegido *aj*
electrify	electrificar *vt*
electrocute	electrocutar *vt*
electrolytic	electrolítico *aj*
electrothermal	electrotermal *aj*
electrotonic	electrotónico *aj*
electrovalence	elecrovalencia *nf*
elevate	elevar *vt*
elide	elidir *vt*
eligibility	eligibilidad *nf*
eliminate	eliminar *vt*
elitist	elitista *aj*
ellipsis Ⓑ	elipsis *nf*
eloquence	elocuencia *nf*
elucidate	elucidar *vt*
emanate	emanar *vi*
emancipate	emancipar *vt*
emasculate	emascular *vt*
embalm	embalsamar *vt*
embarcation	embarco, embarque *nm*
emblematic	emblemático *aj*
embrace	abrazar *vt*
embryonic	embrionario *aj*
emend	enmendar *vt*
emerge	emerger *vi*
emigrant	emigrante *aj*
eminent	eminente *aj*
emit	emitir *vt*
emphasis Ⓑ	énfasis *nm*
emphasize	enfatizar *vt*
employ	emplear *vt*
employed	empleado *aj*
emulation	emulación *nf*
emulsify	emulsionar *vt*
enamor Ⓐ	enamorar *vt*
enchant	encantar *vt*
encode	codificar *vt*
encounter	encontrar *vt*
encyclopedic	enciclopédico *aj*
endodermic	endodérmico *aj*
endorse	endosar *vt*
endothermic	endotérmico *aj*
enemy	enemigo *aj*
energetic (physics)	energético *aj*
engender	engendrar *vt*
English	inglés, inglesa *aj*
engrave	grabar *vt*
enigmatic	enigmático *aj*

enlist	alistarse *vr*	evanescence	evanescencia *nf*
enormity	enormidad *nf*	evangelical	evangélico *aj*
enrage	enrabiar *vi*	evangelize	evangelizar *vt*
enrich	enriquecer *vt*	evaporate	evaporarse *vr*
enslave	esclavizar *vt*	evasive	evasivo *aj*
entertain	entretener *vt*	evident	evidente *aj*
entertaining	entretenido *aj*	evocative	evocador *aj*
enthuse	entusiasmar *vt*	evoke	evocar *vt*
enthusiastic	entusiasta,	evolutionary	evolutivo *aj*
	entusiasmado *aj*	evolve	evolucionar *vi*
entrance	poner en trance *vt*	exacerbate	exacerbar *vt*
entrench	atrincherar *vt*	exaggerate	exagerar *vt*
entrenchment	atrincheramiento *nm*	exaggeration	exageración *nf*
enumerate	enumerar *vt*	exalt	exaltar *vt*
enunciate	enunciar *vt*	examine	examinar *vt*
envy	envidiar *vt*	exasperate	exasperar *vt*
eolithic	eolítico *aj*	excavate	excavar *vt*
epenthetic	epentético *aj*	exceed	exceder *vt*
epic	épico *aj*	excellence	excelencia *nf*
epidermal	epidérmico *aj*	excitable	excitable *aj*
episcopal	episcopal *aj*	excite	excitar *vt*
epistolary	epistolar *aj*	exciting	excitante *aj*
epitomize	epitomar *vt*	exclaim	exclamar *vt*
epochal	que hace época	exclamation	exclamación *nf*
equalize	igualar(se) *vt(r)*	exclude	excluir *vt*
equate *vt*	poner en ecuación *vt,*	exclusive	exclusivo *aj*
	nf	excommunicate	excomulgar *vt*
equip	equipar *vt*	excoriate	excoriar *vt*
equipped	equipado *aj*	excrete	excretar *vt*
equitable	equitativo *aj*	excretory	excretorio *aj*
equivalence,	equivalencia *nf*	exculpate	exculpar *vt*
equivalency		excuse	excusar *vt*
erosive	erosivo *aj*	execute	ejecutar *vt*
eroticize	erotizar *vt*	exercise *vi*	hacer ejercicios *vt,*
erudite	erudito *aj*		*nmpl*
erupt *vi*	hacer erupción *vt, nf*	exhale	exhalar *vti*
escalate	escalar(se) *vt(r)*	exhibit	exhibir *vt*
escape	escapar(se) *vt(r)*	exhort	exhortar *vt*
escapist	escapista *aj*	exhortative	exhortativo *aj*
eschatological	escatológico *aj*	exhume	exhumar *vt*
establish	establecer *vt*	existential	existencial *aj*
esteem	estimar *vt*	exonerate	exonerar *vt*
esthetic, aesthetic	estético *aj*	exorcize	exorcizar *vt*
estimate	estimar *vt*	expansible	expansible *aj*
ethereal	etéreo *aj*	expansionary	expansionista *aj*
ethical	ético *aj*	expansive	expansivo *aj*
ethnocentric	etnocéntrico *aj*	expect	esperar *vt*
ethnographic	etnográfico *aj*	expectorate	expectorar *vti*
eugenic	eugenésico *aj*	experiment	experimentar *vti*
eulogize	elogiar *vt*	experimentation	experimentación *nf*
euphemistic	eufemístico *aj*	expiate	expiar *vt*
Europeanize	europeizar *vt*	expiatory	expiatorio *aj*
evacuate	evacuar *vt*	expire	espirar *vi*

expire	expirar *vi*
expletive	expletivo *aj*
explicate	explicar *vt*
explode	explosionar, explotar *vi*
explore	explorar *vt*
explosive	explosivo *aj*
exponential	exponencial *aj*
export	exportar *vt*
expose	exponer *vt*
exposed	expuesto *aj*
express	expresar *vt*
expressiveness	expresividad *nf*
expropriate	expropiar *vt*
exterminate	exterminar *vt*
extort	extorsionar *vt*
extradite	extradicionar *vt*
extrapolate	extrapolar *vti*
extraterritorial	extraterritorial *aj*
extravagance	extravagancia *nf*
extremely	extremadamente *av*
extroverted	extrovertido *aj*
extrude	extrudir *vt*
exudate	exudado *nm*
exult	exultar *vi*
fabricate	fabricar *vt*
fabulous	fabuloso *aj*
factionalism	faccionalismo *nm*
factor *vt*	dividir en factores *vt, nmpl*
factored	factorializado *aj*
fallacious	falaz *aj*
falsify	falsear, falsificar *vt*
familiar	familiar *aj*
familiarity	familiaridad *nf*
familiarize	familiarizar *vt*
fantasize	fantasear *vti*
fantastic	fantástico *aj*
farinaceous	farináceo *aj*
fascinate	fascinar *vt*
fatigue	fatigar *vt*
favor	favorecer *vt*
favorable	favorable *aj*
fax	faxear *vt*
feast	festejar *vt*
fecal Ⓐ	fecal *aj*
fecund	fecundo *aj*
fecundate	fecundar *vt*
feminize	afeminar *vt*
ferment	fermentar *vt*
fertilize	fertilizar *vt*
fervent	ferviente *aj*
festive	festivo *aj*
feverish, febril	febril, afiebrado *aj*
fibrous	fibroso *aj*
fictional, fictitious	ficticio *aj*
fiduciary	fiduciario *aj*
figurative	figurativo *aj*
filigree	afiligranar *vt*
film	filmar *vt*
film	fílmico *aj*
filter	filtrar(se) *vt(r)*
finance	financiar *vt*
finances	finanzas *nfpl*
finesse	fineza, finura *nf*
Finnish	finlandés *aj*
fix	fijar *vt*
flaccid	fláccido *aj*
flagellate	flagelar *vt*
flame	flamear *vi*
flank	flanquear *vt*
flatulent	flatulento *aj*
flirt	flirtear *vi*
float	flotar *vi*
floral	floral *aj*
flow	fluir *vi*
flower	florear, florecer *vi*
flowery	floreado *aj*
fluency	fluidez *nf*
flutelike	flautado *aj*
focus	enfocar(se) *vt(r)*
focussed	enfocado *aj*
focussing	enfoque *nm*
foment	fomentar *vt*
football-crazy	futbolero *aj*
forage	forrajear *vt*
forest	forestal *aj*
forge	forjar *vt*
form	formar(se) *vt(r)*
formality	formalidad *nf*
formalize	formalizar *vt*
formulaic	formulaico *aj*
formulate	formular *vt*
fornicate	fornicar *vi*
fortifiable	fortificable *aj*
fortify	fortificar *vt*
fossilized	fosilizado *aj*
found	fundir *vt*
fractional	fraccionario *aj*
fractionate	fraccionar *vt*
fracture	fracturar(se) *vt(r)*
fragment	fragmentar *vt*
fragment	fragmento *nm*
fragmentary	fragmentario *aj*
fragrant	fragante *aj*
franchise *vt*	conceder en franquicia *vt, nf*

fraternize	fraternizar, confraternizar *vi*	germinate	germinar *vi*
		gestate	gestar *vi*
fraudulence	fraudulencia *nf*	gesticulate	gesticular *vi*
French	francés *aj*	giant-sized *aj*	de tamaño gigante *aj, nm*
fricative	fricativo *aj*		
fried	frito *aj*	gigantic size	gigantez *nf*
frontier	fronterizo *aj*	glamorous	glamoroso *aj*
fructiferous	fructífero *aj*	glandular	glandular *aj*
fructify	fructificar *vi*	glorify	glorificar *vt*
fruit	frutal *aj*	glorious	glorioso *aj*
fruit	frutal, frutero *aj*	glory	gloriarse *vr*
frustrate	frustrar *vt*	gluteal	glúteo *aj*
fulminate	fulminar *vt*	glutinous	glutino *aj*
fulminating	fulminante *aj*	glyptic	glíptico *aj*
fumigate	fumigar *vt*	glyptics	glíptica *nf*
funeral	funerario, fúnebre *aj*	gnostic	gnóstico, nóstico *aj*
funereal	fúnebre *aj*	golf	jugar golf
fungous	fungoso *aj*	gouty	gotoso *aj*
furuncular	furúnculo *aj*	governable	gobernable *aj*
fuse	fusionar(se) *vt(r)*	governance	gobernación, gobierno *nf, nm*
futile	fútil *aj*		
futuristic	futurista *aj*	governmental	gubernamental, gubernativo *aj*
futurity	futuridad *nf*		
futurology	futurología *nf*	grade *vt*	ordenar por grado *vt, nm*
galactic	galáctico *aj*		
gallop	galop(e)ar *vi*	gradually	gradualmente *av*
galloping	galopante *aj*	graduate	graduar(se) *vt(r)*
galvanic	galvánico *aj*	grandeur	grandeza *nf*
gangrenous	gangrenoso *aj*	grandiloquence	grandilocuencia *nf*
garden *vi*	trabajar en el jardín *vi, nm*	grandiose	grandioso *aj*
		granite	granítico *aj*
gargle	gargarizar *vi*	granular	granular *aj*
garnish	guarnición *nf*	granulate	granular(se) *vt(r)*
garrulity	garrulidad *nf*	gratify	gratificar *vt*
gaseous	gaseoso *aj*	gratuitous	gratuito *aj*
gasiform	gaseiforme *aj*	gravid	grávido *aj*
gasify	gasificar *vt*	gravitate	gravitar *vi*
gastric	gástrico *aj*	gravitational	gravitacional *aj*
gastronomic	gastronómico *aj*	grease	engrasar *vt*
gel	gelificarse *vr*	Grecian	griego *aj*
genealogical	genealógico *aj*	guarantee	garantizar *vt*
generality	generalidad *nf*	guard	guardar *vt*
generalize	generalizar(se) *vt(r)*	gubernatorial	gubernativo *aj*
genital	genital *aj*	guide	guiar *vt*
genocidal	genocida *aj*	gummed	engomado *aj*
genuflect *vi*	hacer una genuflexión *vi, nf*	gutteralize	guteralizar *vt*
		gymnastic	gimnástico *aj*
geodesic	geodésico *aj*	gynecological Ⓐ	ginecológico *aj*
geodetic	geodésico *aj*	habitual	habitual *aj*
geomagnetic	geomagnético *aj*	hallucinate	alucinar *vti*
geopolitical	geopolítico *aj*	hallucinating	alucinante *aj*
germicidal	germicida *aj*	hallucinatory	alucinador, alucinatorio *aj*
germinal	germinal *aj*		

hallucinogenic	alucinógeno *aj*	hydrocephalous	hidrocéfalo,
harangue	arengar *vt*		hidrocefálico *aj*
harlequinesque	arlequinesco *aj*	hydrogenate	hidrogenar *vt*
harmonize	armonizar *vti*	hydrolyze Ⓐ	hidrolizar(se) *vt(r)*
harpoon	arponear *vt*	hydrophobic	hidrofóbico *aj*
harpooning	arponeo *nm*	hydroponic	hidropónico *aj*
hedonistic	hedonista *aj*	hydrotropic	hidrotrópico *aj*
heliacal	helíaco *aj*	hygienic	higiénico *aj*
heliocentric	heliocéntrico *aj*	hyperactive	hiperactivo *aj*
hemiplegic	hemipléjico *aj*	hypertensive	hipertenso *aj*
hemispheric	hemisférico *aj*	hypertrophic	hipertrófico *aj*
hemorrhoidal Ⓐ	hemorroidal *aj*	hypertrophy	hipertrofiarse *vr*
hemostatic Ⓐ	hemostático *aj*	hyperventilate	hiperventilarse *vr*
hepatic	hepático *aj*	hypnotize	hipnotizar *vt*
heraldic	heráldico *aj*	hypodermic	hipodérmico *aj*
herbaceous	herbáceo *aj*	hypoglycemic	hipoglicémico *aj, nm*
herbal	herbario *aj*	hypotensive	hipotensivo *aj*
herbivorous	herbívoro *aj*	hypothesize	formar una hipótesis
heretic(al)	herético *aj*	hypothetical	hipotético *aj*
heritable	heredable *aj*	hysterical	histérico *aj*
heterodox	heterodoxo *aj*	iambic	yámbico *aj*
heterologous	heterólogo *aj*	Icelandic	islandés *aj*
heuristic	heurístico *aj*	iconoclastic	iconoclasta *aj*
hibernate	hibernar *vi*	identify (oneself)	identificar(se) *vt(r)*
hierarchical	jerárquico *aj*	ideographic	ideográfico *aj*
hilarious	hilarante *aj*	ideological	ideológico *aj*
hirsute	hirsuto *aj*	idiom	idiotismo *nm*
Hispanicize	hispanizar *vt*	idolatrous (person)	idolatra *aj*
histological	histológico *aj*	idolatrous (practice)	idolátrico *aj*
histrionic	histriónico *aj*	idolize	idolatrar *vt*
holographic	holográfico *aj*	idyllic	idílico *aj*
holography	holografía *nf*	iliac	iliaco, ilíaco *aj*
homeopathic	homeopático *aj*	illegality	ilegalidad *nf*
homeostatic	homeostático *aj*	illegitimate	ilegítimo *aj*
Homeric	homérico *aj*	illicit	ilícito *aj*
homicidal	homicida *aj*	illuminate	iluminar *vt*
hominoid	hominoideo *aj*	illustrate	ilustrar *vt*
homogenize	homogeneizar *vt*	imitate	imitar *vt*
homographic	homógrafo *aj*	immanent	inmanente *aj*
homologous	homólogo *aj*	immediacy	inmediatez *nf*
homonymous	homónimo *aj*	immensity	inmensidad *nf*
homophobic	homofóbico *aj*	immolate	inmoler *vt*
homophony	homofonía *nf*	immortal	inmortal *aj*
Horatian	horaciano *aj*	immortalize	inmortalizar *vt*
horrify	horrorizar *vt*	immune	inmune *aj*
horticultural	hortícola *aj*	immunize	inmunizar *vt*
hospitalize	hospitalizar *vt*	impede	impedir *vt*
hotel	hotelero *aj*	impel	impeler *vt*
humid	húmedo *aj*	imperfection	imperfección *nf*
humidify	humedecer *vt*	imperial	imperial *aj*
humiliate	humillar *vt*	imperialist(ic)	imperialista *aj*
hybridize	hybrid(iz)ar *vti*	impious	impío *aj*
hydrate	hidratar(se) *vt(r)*	implant	implantar *vt*

implicate	implicar *vt*
implode	implosionar *vt*
impolitic	impolítico *aj*
import	importar *vti*
importable	importable *aj*
impose	imponer(se) *vt(r)*
impossible	imposible *aj*
impoverish	empobrecer *vt*
impoverished	empobrecido *aj*
imprecision	imprecisión *nf*
impregnate (permeate)	impregnar *vt*
impress	impresionar *vt*
impressionistic	impresionista *aj*
improbability	improbabilidad *nf*
impropriety	impropiedad *nf*
improvise	improvisar *vti*
impulsion	impulsión *nf*
impure	impuro *aj*
impurity	impureza *nf*
inadmissibility	inadmisibilidad *nf*
inattentive	desatento *aj*
inaugural	inaugural *aj*
inaugurate	inaugurar *vt*
incalculable	incalculable *aj*
incapacitate	incapacitar *vt*
incarcerate	encarcelar *vt*
incessant	incesante *aj*
incidental	incidente *aj*
incinerate	incinerar *vt*
incite	incitar *vt*
incline	inclinar(se) *vt(r)*
including	incluso *prep*
inclusion	inclusión *nf*
inclusive	inclusivo *aj*
incombustible	incombustible *aj*
incomplete	incompleto *aj*
incongruent	incongruente *aj*
incongruity	incongruencia *nf*
incongruous	incongruo *aj*
incontinent	incontinente *aj*
incorrectness	incorrección *nf*
incriminate	incriminar *vt*
incriminating	incriminador *aj*
incriminatory	incriminatorio *aj*
incubate	incubar(se) *vt(r)*
inculcate	inculcar *vt*
indebted	adeudado, endeudado *aj*
indecisive	indeciso *aj*
indeclinable	indeclinable *aj*
indefinable	indefinible *aj*
indemnification	indemnización *nf*
indemnify	indemnizar *vt*

index *vt*	poner índice a *vt, nm*
indicate	indicar *vt*
indication	indicación, indicio *nf, nm*
indigence	indigencia *nf*
indigestible	indigestible, indigesto *aj*
indisposed	indispuesto *aj*
indoctrinate	adoctrinar *vt*
inductive	inductivo *aj*
industrialization	industrialización *nf*
industrialize	industrializar *vt*
ineducable	ineducable *aj*
ineligibility	inelegibility *nf*
ineligible	inelegible *aj*
inexact	inexacto *aj*
inexplicable	inexplicable *aj*
inexpressible	inexpresable *aj*
infamous	infame *aj*
infect	infectar *vt*
infer	inferir *vt*
infest	infestar *vt*
infiltrate	infiltrar(se) *vt(r)*
infirm	enfermo *aj*
inflame	inflamar *vt*
inflationary	inflacionario, inflacionista *aj*
influence	influenciar *vt*
infrequency	infrecuencia *nf*
infuriate	enfurecer *vt*
ingest	ingerir *vt*
inhabit	habitar *vt*
inhale	inhalar *vti*
inherent	inherente *aj*
inherit	heredar *vt*
inhibit	inhibir *vt*
initial *vt*	poner iniciales *vt, nfpl*
initiation	iniciación *nf*
inject	inyectar *vt*
innocent	inocente *aj*
innovate	innovar *vt*
inoculate	inocular *vt*
inscribe	inscribir *vt*
inscribed	inscrito *aj*
insectivorous	insectívoro *aj*
inseminate	inseminar *vt*
insensitive	insensible *aj*
insignificance	insignificancia *nf*
insinuate	insinuar *vt*
insist	insistir *vi*
insoluble	insoluble *aj*
insolvent	insolvente *aj*
inspect	inspeccionar *vt*

inspection	inspección *nf*
inspirational	inspirador *aj*
inspire	inspirar *vt*
instantly *av*	al instante *nm*
instigate	instigar *vt*
instinctive	instintivo *aj*
institute	instituir *vt*
institutional	institucional *aj*
institutionalize	institucionalizar *vt*
instructive	instructivo *aj*
instrumental	instrumental *aj*
insulate	aislar *vt*
insult	insultar *vt*
insuperable	insuperable *aj*
insurrectionary	insurreccional *aj*
intact	intacto *aj*
integrate	integrar *vt*
intensely	intensamente *av*
intensify	intensificar(se) *vt(r)*
intentional	intencional *aj*
interact	interaccionar *vi*
interaction	interacción *nf*
intercalation	intercalación *nf*
interconnection	interconexión *nf*
intercontinental	intercontinental *aj*
interdependence	interdependencia *nf*
interdependent	interdependiente *aj*
interest	interesar *vt*
interfere	interferir *vti*
intergovernmental	intergubernamental *aj*
intern	internar *vt*
interpolate	interpolar *vt*
interpose	interponer(se) *vt(r)*
interpret	interpretar *vt*
interpret *vi*	servir de intérprete *vi, nmf*
interpretive	interpretivo *aj*
interred	enterrado *aj*
interrelate	interrelacionar *vt*
interrelation(ship)	interrelación *nf*
interrogate	interrogar *vt*
interrupt	interrumpir *vt*
intersect	intersecarse *vr*
interview	entrevistar *vt*
intimate	íntimo *aj*
intimidate	intimidar *vt*
intoxicate	intoxicar *vt*
intrigue	intrigar *vti*
intriguing	intrigante *aj*
introverted	introvertido *aj*
intrusive	intruso *aj*
inundate	inundar *vt*
invade	invadir *vt*
invading	invasor *aj*
invalidate	invalidar *vt*
invalidation	invalidación *nf*
invariable	invariable *aj*
invariant	invariable *aj*
invent	inventar *vt*
inventory	inventariar *vt*
invert	invertir *vt*
investigate	investigar *vt*
invigorate	vigorizar *vt*
inviolable	inviolable *aj*
inviolate	inviolado *aj*
invite	invitar *vt*
invoke	invocar *vt*
iodize	yodar *vt*
ionic	iónico *aj*
ionize	ionizar *vti*
Irish	irlandés *aj*
irradiate	irradiar *vt*
irredeemable	irredimible *aj*
irreducible	irreduc(t)ible *aj*
irrefutable	irrefutable *aj*
irreligious	irreligioso *aj*
irremediable	irremediable *aj*
irreparable	irreparable *aj*
irrevocable	irrevocable *aj*
irrigate	irrigar *vt*
irritate	irritar *vt*
isolate	aislar *vt*
isolation	aislación *nf*
iterate	iterar *vt*
iterative	iterativo *aj*
jingoism	jingoísmo *nm*
join	juntar *vt*
judge	juzgar *vti*
judicious	juicioso *aj*
juridical	jurídico *aj*
jurisdictional	jurisdiccional *aj*
justify	justificar *vt*
juxtapose	yuxtaponer *vt*
juxtaposed	yuxtapuesto *aj*
keel-shaped	aquillado *aj*
keratinous	queratinoso *aj*
knock out	noquear *vt*
knot	anudar *vt*
labialization	labialización *nf*
labialize	labializar *vt*
lacerate	lacerar *vt*
lachrymose	lagrimoso *aj*
laconism	laconismo *nm*
lacquer	laquear *vt*
lament	lamentar(se) *vt(r)*
laminate	laminar *vt*

lance *vt*	abrir con lanceta *vt, nf*	macrocosmic	macrocósmico *aj*
lapidary	lapidario *aj*	magic(al)	mágico *aj*
lard	lardear *vt*	magnetize	magnetizar *vt*
larval	larvario, larval *aj*	magnificence	magnificencia *nf*
lasciviousness	lascivia *nf*	maintain	mantener *vt*
latitudinal	latitudinal *aj*	majesty	majestuosidad *nf*
launch	lanzar *vt*	majority	mayoritario *aj*
launder	lavar *vt*	maltreat	maltratar *vt*
lay	laico *aj*	manage	manejar(se) *vt(r)*
leaven	leudar *vt*	maneuver	maniobrar *vti*
legalism	legalismo *nm*	maniacal	maniático *aj*
legalistic	legalístico *aj*	manic	maníaco *aj*
legality	legalidad *nf*	manicure *vt*	hacer la manicura *vt, nf*
legalize	legalizar *vt*	manifest	manifestar(se) *vt(r)*
legendary	legendario *aj*	manipulate	manipular *vt*
legibility	legibilidad *nf*	manufacture	manufacturar *vt*
legitim(iz)ation	legitimación *nf*	manufacturing	manufacturero *aj*
legitimacy	legitimidad *nf*	manumit	manumitir *vt*
legitimize	legitimar *vt*	map	trazar el mapa de *vt*
leguminous	leguminoso *aj*	marbled *aj*	revestido de mármol *aj,*
lepidopterist	lepidóptero *aj*		*nm*
lethargic	letárgico *aj*	march	marchar *vi*
leukemic	leucémico *aj*	marching	marchando *aj*
lexicographic	lexicográfico *aj*	marginal	marginal *aj*
liberalization	liberalización *nf*	marginalize	marginar *vt*
liberate	libertar *vt*	mark	marcar *vt*
limit	limitar *vt*	marketable	mercadeable *aj*
liquefy	licuar(se) *vt(r)*	marmoreal,	marmóreo *aj*
liquidate	liquidar *vt*	marmorean	
liquidation	liquidación *nf*	martyr	martirizar *vt*
liquidity	liquidez *nf*	marvel	maravilla *nf*
lithographic	litográfico *aj*	marvel	maravillarse *vr*
litigate	litigar *vti*	masculinize	masculinizar *vt*
litigious	litigioso *aj*	mask	enmascarar *vt*
liturgical	litúrgico *aj*	masonic	masónico *aj*
localize	localizar *vt*	massacre	masacrar *vt*
locate	localizar *vt*	massage	masajear *vt*
lochial	loquial *aj*	mastery	maestría *nf*
locomotion	locomoción *nf*	masticate	masticar *vt*
locomotor	locomotor, locomotriz *aj*	mastoid	mastoideo, mastoidal *aj*
		masturbate	masturbarse *vr*
lodge	alojar(se) *vt(r)*	materiality	materialidad *nf*
logarithmic	logarítmico *aj*	materialize	materializar(se) *vt(r)*
logistic(al)	logístico *aj*	maternal (motherly)	maternal *aj*
longevity	longevidad *nf*	matriculate	matricularse *vr*
longitudinal	longitudinal *aj*	matronly	matronal *aj*
loquacity	locuacidad *nf*	mature	madurarse *vr*
lubricate	lubricar *vt*	mature	maduro *aj*
lucidity	lucidez *nf*	maturing	maduramiento *nm*
luxurious	lujoso *aj*	measurable	mensurable *aj*
lynch	linchar *vt*	mechanistic	mecanicista *aj*
Machiavellian Ⓐ	maquiavélico *aj*	mechanize	mecanizar *vt*
macrocephalous	macrocéfalo *aj*	mediate	mediar *vti*

medicate	medicar *vt*
meditate	meditar *vi*
melodic	melódico *aj*
melodramatic	melodramático *aj*
memorable	memorable *aj*
menace	amenazar *vt*
Mendelian	mendeliano *aj*
menstrual	menstrual *aj*
menstruate	menstruar *vi*
mention	mencionar *vt*
mercurial	mercurial *aj*
mercuric	mercúrico *aj*
mercurous	mercurioso *aj*
merely	meramente *av*
meridional	meridiano, meridional *aj*
merit	merecer *vt*
merit	mérito *nm*
merited	merecido *aj*
mesomorphic	mesomórfico *aj*
messianic	mesiánico *aj*
metabolize	metabolizar *vt*
metacarpal	metacarpiano, metacarpeo *aj*
metalloid	metaloideo *aj*
metaphysical	metafísico *aj*
metastasize	estenderse por metástasis
metastatic	metastático *aj*
metatarsal	metatarsiano *aj*
meteoric	meteórico *aj*
meteorological	meteorológico *aj*
methodological	metodológico *aj*
metropolitan	metropolitano *aj*
microfilm	microfilmar *vt*
migrate	migrar *vi*
militaristic	militarista *aj*
militarize	militarizar *vt*
mime *vi*	hacer la mímica *vt, nf*
mimetic	mimético *aj*
mine	minar *vt*
miniaturize	miniaturizar *vt*
minimally *av*	en grado mínimo *nm*
minimize	minimizar *vt*
mining	minero *aj*
minister	ministrar *vi*
ministerial	ministerial *aj*
Minoan	minoico *aj*
minority	minoritario *aj*
minuteness	minuciosidad *nf*
minutiae	minucias *nfpl*
miraculous	milagroso *aj*
misanthropy	misantropía *nf*
miscalculate	calcular mal *vi*
miscount	contar mal *vi*
misinterpret	interpretar mal *vt*
misinterpretation	mala interpretación *nf*
misogynous	misógino *aj*
missile	misilístico *aj*
mistreat	maltratar *vt*
mnemonic	mnemotécnico, nemónico *aj*
mobilize	movilizar(se) *vt(r)*
model	modelar(se) *vt(r)*
modeling Ⓐ	profesión de modelo *nf*
moderately	moderadamente *av*
modernity	modernidad *nf*
modernization	modernización *nf*
modernize	modernize(se) *vt(r)*
modify	modificar *vt*
modish *aj*	de moda *nf*
modulate	modular *vt*
molar	molar *aj*
mold Ⓐ	moldear *vt*
monarchical	monárquico *aj*
monastic	monástico, monacal *aj*
monatomic	monatómico *aj*
monaural	monaural, monoaural *aj*
monetize	monetizar *vt*
monitor	monitorear *nm*
monogamous	monógamo *aj*
monolingualism	monolingüismo *nm*
monolithic	monolítico *aj*
monomeric	monómero *aj*
monomorphic	monomórfico *aj*
monopolistic	monopolizador *aj*
monopolize	monopolizar *vt*
monosyllabic	monosílabo *aj*
monotheistic	monoteísta *aj*
monotonous	monótono *aj*
monovalent	monovalente *aj*
moral	moraleja *nf*
moralize	moralizar *vt*
morals (npl)	moral *nf*
morphological	morfológico *aj*
mortify	mortificar *vt*
mossy	musgoso *aj*
motionless	inmóvil *aj*
motivate	motivar *vt*
motorcycle *vi*	ir en motocicleta *vi, nf*
motorize	motorizar *vt*
movable	movible, móvil *aj*
multicultural	multicultural *aj*
multilingualism	multilingüismo *nm*
multiplicity	multiplicidad *nf*

multiply	multiplicar(se) *vt(r)*	noncombatant	no combatiente *aj*
multiracial	multirracial *aj*	noncombustible	anticombustible *aj*
multitudinous	multitudinario *aj*	noncommercial	no comercial *aj*
multivalent	multivalente *aj*	nondiscriminatory	no discriminatorio *aj*
mummification	momificación *nf*	nonexistent	inexistente *aj*
mummify	momificar(se) *vt(r)*	nonflammable	no inflamable *aj*
murmur	murmurar *vti*	nongovernmental	no gubernamental *aj*
murmurring	murmurante *aj*	nonpolitical	apolítico *aj*
muscular	musculoso *aj*	nonproductive	improductivo *aj*
(muscle-bound)		nonresponsive	no respondiente *aj*
muscular (of muscles)	muscular *aj*	nonsectarian	no sectario *aj*
musicality	musicalidad *nf*	nonsexist	no sexista *aj*
musicianship	maestría musical *nf*	nontoxic	atóxico *aj*
mutate	mudar(se) *vt(r)*	nontransferable	intransferible *aj*
mutilate	mutilar *vt*	normally	normalmente *av*
mutinous	amotinador *aj*	nostalgic	nostálgico *aj*
mutiny	amotinarse *vr*	notarized	notariado *aj*
myopic	miope *aj*	note	notar *vt*
mysterious	misterioso *aj*	notify	notificar *vt*
mystic(al)	místico *aj*	notion	noción *nf*
mystification	mistificación *nf*	novelistic	novelístico *aj*
mythical	mítico *aj*	novelize	novelar *vti*
mythological	mitológico *aj*	nudism	nudismo, desnudismo *nm*
name (appoint)	nombrar *vt*		
name (give name to)	ponerle nombre a *vt, nm*	nudity	desnudez *nf*
		nullity	nulidad *nf*
narcotize	narcotizar *vt*	number	numerar *vt*
narrate	narrar *vt*	numbering,	numeración *nf*
nasality	nasalidad *nf*	numeration	
nasalize	nasalizar *vt*	numismatic	numismático *aj*
nationalistic	nacionalista *aj*	nuptial	nupcial *aj*
nationalize	nacionalizar *vt*	nutritious	nutricio, nutritivo *aj*
native	nativo, -a *aj*	nutritive	nutritivo *aj*
naturalistic	naturalista *aj*	obese	obeso *aj*
naturalize	naturalizar *vt*	obey	obedecer *vt*
nauseate	nausear *vt*	object	objetar *vi*
nauseating, nauseous	nauseabundo *aj*	obliterate	obliterar *vt*
navigable	navegable *aj*	obscure	oscurecer *vt*
navigate	navegar *vti*	obscurity	oscuridad *nf*
nebulous	nebuloso *aj*	observable	observable *aj*
negative	negativa *nf*	observe	observar *vt*
negligent	negligente *aj*	obsess	obsesionar *vt*
negotiability	negociabilidad *nf*	obstetric	obstétrico *aj*
negotiate	negociar *vti*	obstruct	obstruir *vt*
nephritic	nefrítico *aj*	occasion	ocasionar *vt*
neural	neural *aj*	occlude	ocluir *vi*
neuralgic	neurálgico *aj*	occluded	ocluído *aj*
neurotoxic	neurotóxico *aj*	occupied	ocupado *aj*
neutral	neutral *aj*	occur	ocurrir *vi*
neutralize	neutralizar *vt*	octuple	octuplicar *vt*
nihilistic	nihilista *aj*	odoriferous	odorífero, odorífico *aj*
nomadic	nómada *aj*	odorless Ⓐ	inodoro *aj*
nominate	nominar *vt*	odorous	oloroso *aj*

offend	ofender(se) *vt(r)*
offending	ofensor *aj*
offer	ofrecer *vt*
offer	ofrender *vt*
officiating	oficiante *aj*
oleaginous	oleaginoso *aj*
oligarchic	oligárquico *aj*
Olympian	olímpico *aj*
Olympic	olímpico *aj*
omit	omitir *vt*
omnipotent	omnipotente *aj*
omnipresence	omnipresencia *nf*
omnipresent	omnipresente *aj*
omniscience	omnisciencia *nf*
omnivorous	omnívoro *aj*
oncogenic	oncogénico *aj*
onomastic	onomástico *aj*
ontological	ontológico *aj*
operable	operable *aj*
operatic	operístico *aj*
operational	operacional *aj*
operative	operatorio *aj*
opine	opinar *vt*
oppose	oponer *vt*
opposed	opuesto *aj*
oppressed	oprimido *aj*
opt	optar *vi*
optimize	optim(iz)ar *vt*
optional	opcional *aj*
opulence	opulencia *nf*
oratorical	oratorio *aj*
orbit	orbitar *vti*
orbital	orbital *aj*
orchestral	orquestal *aj*
orchestrate	orquestar *vt*
ordain	ordenar *vt*
order	ordenar *vt*
orderly	ordenado *aj*
ordinarily	ordinariamente *av*
orgiastic	orgiástico *aj*
orient	orientar *vt*
originate	originar(se) *vt(r)*
ornament	ornamentar *vt*
orphanhood	orfandad *nf*
oscillate	oscilar *vt*
oscillating	oscilador *aj*
osseus	óseo *aj*
ossify	osificarse *vr*
ostentation	ostentación *nf*
ostracize	condenar al ostracismo *vt*
otalgic	otálgico *aj*
overabundance	sobreabundancia *nf*
overabundant	superabundante *aj*
overconsumption	superconsumo *nm*
overestimate	sobreestimado *nm*
overestimate	sobreestimar *vt*
overexcite	sobr(e)excitar *vt*
overexcitement	sobr(e)excitación *nf*
overexpose	sobreexponer *vt*
overpopulation	superpoblación *nf*
overproduce	sobreproducir *vt*
overproduction	sobreproducción *nf*
oversimplification	sobresimplificación *nf*
oversimplified	simplificado demasiado *aj*
overvalue	sobrevalorar *vt*
ovoid(al)	ovoide, ovoideo aj
ovulate	ovular *vi*
oxidize	oxidar(se) *vt(r)*
oxygenate, oxygenize	oxigenar *vt*
oxytocic	oxitócico *aj*
pacify	pacificar *vt*
page, paginate	paginar *vt*
paint	pintar *vti*
pair off	aparearse *vr*
palatal	palatal *aj*
palatalize	palatalizar *vt*
palatine	palatino *aj*
pale	palidecer *vi*
pale, pallid	pálido *aj*
palliate	paliar *vt*
palpable	palpable *aj*
palpate	palpar *vt*
palpitate	palpitar *vi*
palpitating	palpitante *aj*
Pan-American	panamericano *aj*
panel	poner paneles a *vt*
panic *vi*	sobrecogerse de pánico *vi, nm*
panoramic	panorámico *aj*
pantheistic	panteístico *aj*
papal	papal *aj*
paradigmatic	paradigmático *aj*
paradoxical	paradójico *aj*
paralytic	paralítico *aj*
paralyze	paralizar *vt*
paramedical	paramédico *aj*
paraphrase	parafrasear *vt*
parcel out (land)	parcelar *vt*
pardon	perdonar *vt*
parenthetical	parentético *aj*
parliamentary	parlamentario *aj*
parochial	parroquial *aj*
parody	parodiar *vt*
partially	parcialmente *av*

participate	participar *vi*	pertinent	pertinente *aj*
participating	participante *aj*	perturb	perturbar *vt*
participatory	partícipe *aj*	pestiferous	pestífero *aj*
participial	participial *aj*	petition	peticionar *vt*
particularity	particularidad *nf*	petrifying	petrificante *aj*
partisan	partidista *aj*	petroleum	petrolero *aj*
pasteurize	paste(u)rizar *vt*	phallic	fálico *aj*
pastoral	pastoral *aj*	phantasmagoric	fantasmagórico *aj*
pasture	pastar *vti*	pharmacological	farmacológico *aj*
pasty	pastoso *aj*	pharyngeal	faríngeo *aj*
patent	patentar *vt*	phenomenon Ⓑ	fenómeno *nm*
paternal (fatherly)	paternal *aj*	philological	filológico *aj*
paternalistic	paternalista *aj*	philosophize	filosofar *vi*
pathogenic	patógeno *aj*	phonemic	fonémico *aj*
patriotic	patriótico *aj*	phonic	fónico *aj*
patrol	patrullar *vti*	phonological	fonológico *aj*
patronize (sponsor)	patrocinar *vt*	phosphoresce	fosforecer *vi*
pauperization	pauperización *nf*	photic	fótico *aj*
pauperize	pauperizar, depauperar *vt*	photoactinic	fotoactínico *aj*
		photoelectric	fotoeléctrico *aj*
pause	pausar *vi*	photograph	fotografiar *vt*
pave	pavimentar *vt*	photographic	fotográfico *aj*
pedagogical	pedagógico *aj*	photophobic	fotófobo *aj*
penalize	penalizar *vt*	photosensitive	fotosensible *aj*
penetrable	penetrable *aj*	photovoltaic	fotovoltaico *aj*
penetrate	penetrar *vti*	phrase	frasear *vt*
peninsular	peninsular *aj*	phraseology	fraseología *nf*
penitential	penitencial *aj*	phytotoxic	fitotóxico *aj*
pension	pensionar *vt*	picket	piquetear *vti*
pentasyllabic	pentasílabo *aj*	picnic *vi*	ir de picnic *vi, nm*
perceive	percibir *vt*	pictorial	pictórico *aj*
perceptible	perceptible *aj*	pile	apilar *vt*
perceptive	perceptivo *aj*	pillage	pillar *vt*
perfect	perfeccionar *vt*	pilot	pilot(e)ar *vt*
perforate	perforar *vt*	pioneering	pionero *aj*
perfume	perfumar *vt*	pious	piadoso, pío *aj*
periodicity	periodicidad *nf*	pirate	piratear *vt*
periscopic	periscópico *aj*	piratical	pirático *aj*
permanence	permanencia *nf*	pirouette	piruetar *vi*
permissible	permisible *aj*	plagiarize	plagiar *vt*
permission	permiso *nm*	plan	planificar *vt*
permute	permutar *vt*	planetary	planetario *aj*
perorate	perorar *vi*	planting	plantío *nm*
perpetrate	perpetrar *vt*	Platonic	platónico *aj*
perpetuate	perpetuar *vt*	please	complacer *vt*
perpetuation	perpetuación *nf*	plethoric	pletórico *aj*
perplex *vt*	dejar perplejo *vt, aj*	pluralistic	pluralista *aj*
perplexity	perplejidad *nf*	pluralize	pluralizar *vt*
persecute	perseguir *vt*	Plutonian, Plutonic	plutoniano *aj*
persist	persistir *vi*	pneumonic	neumónico *aj*
personalize	personalizar *vt*	poison (fig)	ponzoña *nf*
personify	personificar *vt*	polarity	polaridad *nf*
persuade	persuadir *vt*	polarize	polarizar(se) *vt(r)*

polemic(al)	polémico *aj*	prefabricate	prefabricar *vt*
polemicize	polemizar *vi*	preferential	preferencial, preferente *aj*
police	policial, policíaco *aj*	preferred	preferido *aj*
Polish	polaco *aj*	pregnancy	preñez *nf*
politicize	politizar *vt*	prehistory	prehistoria *nf*
polivalent	polivalente *aj*	prejudice	perjudicar *vt*
pollinate	polinizar *vt*	premedical	premédico *aj*
polyandrous	poliandro *aj*	premeditate	premeditar *vt*
polymeric	polimérico *aj*	premeditation	premeditación *nf*
polymerize	polimerizar(se) *vt(r)*	premenstrual	premenstrual *aj*
polymorphic	polimórfico *aj*	prenatal	antenatal *aj*
polynomial	polinómico *aj*	preordain	preordinar *vt*
polysyllabic	polisílabo *aj*	presage	presagiar *vt*
polytheistic	politeísta *aj*	presbyopic	presbiápico *aj*
polyvalent	polivalente *aj*	prescient	presciente *aj*
pomp	pompa *nf*	prescribe	prescribir *vt*
pontifical	pontifical *aj*	prescribed	prescrito *aj*
popery	papismo *nm*	present	presentar *vt*
popularize	popularizar *vt*	preserve	preservar *vt*
populate	poblar *vt*	presidential	presidencial *aj*
populous	populoso *aj*	presiding *aj*	que preside *vi*
pornographic	pornográfico *aj*	press	prensar *vt*
porous	poroso *aj*	pressurize	presurizar *vt*
pose	hacer posar *vi*	primacy	primacía *nf*
possess	poseer *vt*	primarily	primariamente *av*
possessed (by demon)	poseído *aj*	primitivism	primitivismo *nm*
possibility	posibilidad *nf*	primordial	primordial *aj*
post	apostar *vt*	princely	principesco *aj*
posterity	posteridad *nf*	principally	principalmente *av*
postulate	postular *vt*	print	imprimir *vt*
potential	potencial *aj*	printable	imprimible *aj*
powerful	poderoso *aj*	printed	impreso, imprimido *aj*
practicable	practicable *aj*	privatize	privatizar *vt*
practicing	practicante *aj*	privileged	privilegiado *aj*
pragmatic	pragmático *aj*	pro-American	proamericano *aj*
precede	preceder *vti*	probity	probidad *nf*
precedence	precedencia *nf*	problematic(al)	problemático *aj*
precipitate	precipitar *vt*	proceed	proceder *vi*
preconceived	preconcebido *aj*	process	procesar *vt*
predestine	predestinar *vt*	processional	procesional *aj*
predetermine	predeterminar *vt*	proclaim	proclamar *vt*
predicate	predicativo *aj*	procreate	procrear *vti*
predicative	predicativo *aj*	procreative	procreador *aj*
predict	predecir *vt*	producing	productor *aj*
predispose	predisponer *vt*	productive	productivo *aj*
predisposed	predispuesto *aj*	profane	profanar *vt*
predominance	predominio *nm*	profane	profano *aj*
predominate	predominar *vi*	professionalism	profesionalismo *nm*
preeminence	preeminencia *nf*	professorial	profesoral *aj*
preeminent	preeminente *aj*	profundity	profundidad *nf*
preexist	preexistir *vi*	profusely	profusamente *av*
preexistence	preexistencia *nf*	profusion	profusión *nf*
preexistent	preexistente *aj*		

prognosticate	pronosticar *vti*	puncture	punzar *vt*
program **A**	programar *vti*	purify	purificar *vt*
progress	progresar *vi*	purulent	purulento *aj*
prohibit	prohibir *vt*	pustular	pustuloso *aj*
project	proyectar *vt*	putrescent	putrescente *aj*
prolong	prolongar *vt*	pyrotechnic	pirotécnico *aj*
prolongation	prolongación *nf*	Pyrrhic	pírrica *aj*
promise	prometer *vti*	Pythian	pítico *aj*
promising	prometedor *aj*	quadratic	cuadrático *aj*
promote	promocionar *vt*	quadripartite	cuadripartido *aj*
promotional	promovedor *aj*	quadruple	cuadruplicar(se) *vt(r)*
promulgate	promulgar *vt*	quadruplicate	cuadruplicar *vt*
pronounce	pronunciar *vt*	qualify	calificar *vt*
pronounceable	pronunciable *aj*	quantifiable	cuantificable *aj*
proofread	corregir pruebas *vt*	quantify	cuantificar *vt*
propagandize *vi*	hacer propaganda *vt, nf*	quarantine	poner en cuarentena *vt*
prophesy	profetizar *vt*	quarter (divide)	cuartear *vt*
prophetic	profético *aj*	quarter (troops)	acuartelar *vt*
prophylactic	profiláctico *aj, nm*	quartic	cuártico *aj*
proportional	proporcional *aj*	quasijudicial	cuasijudicial *aj*
propose	proponer *vt*	question	cuestionar *vt*
proposed	propuesto *aj*	quintuple	quintuplicar(se) *vt(r)*
prorate	prorratear *vt*	quintuplicate	quintuplicar *vt*
prosaic	prosaico *aj*	quote	cotizar *vt*
proscribe	proscribir *vt*	rabbinic(al)	rabínico *aj*
proscribed	proscrito *aj*	racial	racial *aj*
prosodic	prosódico *aj*	radiate	radiar *vti*
prostitute oneself	prostituirse *vt*	radio	radiofónico *aj*
protect	proteger *vt*	radio *vt*	enviar por radio *vt, nf*
protective	protectivo *aj*	rage	rabiar *vi*
protest	protestar *vti*	ramify	ramificar(se) *vt(r)*
protuberant	protuberante *aj*	rarefy	enrarecer *vt*
proven	probado *aj*	rasp	raspar *vt*
provide	proveer *vt*	ration	racionar *vt*
providential	providencial *aj*	rationalize	racionalizar *vt*
provision	aprovisionar *vt*	rationing	racionamiento *nm*
provoke	provocar *vt*	react	reaccionar *vi*
pseudoscientific	(p)seudocientífico *aj*	realignment	realineamiento *nm*
psychedelic	(p)sicodélico *aj*	realistic	realista *aj*
psychiatric	(p)siquíatrico *aj*	realize (profits)	realizar *vt*
psychoanalytic	(p)sicoanalítico *aj*	rearm	rearmar(se) *vt(r)*
psychoneurotic	(p)siconeurótico *aj*	rearmament	rearme *nm*
psychopathic	(p)sicopático *aj*	reason	razonar *vi*
pubescent	pubescente *aj*	recapitulate	recapitular *vti*
publicize	publicitar *vt*	recharge	recargar(se) *vt(r)*
publish	publicar *vt*	rechargeable	recargable *aj*
publishable	publicable *aj*	recite	recitar *vt*
pulverization	pulverización *nf*	recommend	recomendar *vt*
pulverize	pulverizar *vt*	recompense	recompensar *vt*
pump	bombear *vt*	reconcile	reconciliar(se) *vt(r)*
pumping	bombeo *nm*	reconquer	reconquistar *vt*
punctuality	puntualidad *nf*	reconsider	reconsiderar *vt*
punctuate	puntuar *vt*	reconsideration	reconsideración *nf*

reconstitute	reconstituir *vt*	repeat (oneself)	repetir(se) *vt(r)*
recount	recontar *vt*	repeatable	repetible *aj*
recover (consciousness)	recobrar *vt*	repent (vti)	arrepentirse *vr*
recriminate	recriminar *vt*	repentant	arrepentido *aj*
recruit	reclutar *vt*	replace	reemplazar *vt*
rectify	rectificar *vt*	replant	replantar *vt*
recuperate	recuperarse *vr*	repose	reposar *vi*
recuperative	recuperativo *aj*	repose	reposo *nm*
recyclable	reciclable *aj*	representative	representativo *aj*
redecorate *vt*	cambiar el decorado *vt,* *nm*	repress	reprimir *vt*
		reprimand	reprender *vt*
redeemable	redimible *aj*	reprint	reimprimir *vt*
redeeming, redemptive	redentor *aj*	reproach	reprochar *vt*
reducing	reductor *aj*	reproduce	reproducir(se) *vt(r)*
reduction	reducimiento *nm*	reproducing	reproductor *aj*
reeducate	reeducar *vt*	republican	republicano *aj*
reeducation	reeducación *nf*	repudiate	repudiar *vt*
reelection	reelección *nf*	repulse	repulsar *vt*
refine	refinar *vt*	require	requerir *vt*
reflect	reflejar(se) *vt(r)*	requirement	requirimiento *nm*
reforest	reforestar *vt*	requisite	requisito *nm*
reform	reformar(se) *vt(r)*	requisition	requisición *nf*
reformat	reformatear *vt*	resent	resentirse *vt*
refract	refractar *vt*	reserve	reservar *vt*
refresh	refrescar *vt*	reside	residir *vi*
refrigerant	refrigerante *nm*	resign oneself	resignarse *vr*
refutable	refutable *aj*	resigned	resignado *aj*
refute	refutar *vt*	resist	resistir(se) *vt(r)*
regenerate	regenerar(se) *vt(r)*	resonate	resonar *vi*
regiment	regimentar *vt*	respect	respetar *vt*
regularity	regularidad *nf*	respire	respirar *vi*
regulate	regular *vt*	resplendence	resplandor *nm*
regurgitate	regurgitar *vti*	respond	responder *vi*
rehabilitate	rehabilitar *vt*	restore	restaurar *vt*
reimbursable	reembolsable *aj*	restrict	restringir *vt*
reimburse	reembolsar *vt*	restrictive	restrictivo *aj*
reincarnate	reincarnar *vt*	result	resultar *vi*
reiterate	reiterar *vti*	resurgence	resurgimiento *nm*
rejuvenate	rejuvenecer(se) *vt(r)*	resuscitate	resucitar *vt*
relate (x to y)	relacionar(se) *vt(r)*	resuscitative	resucitador *aj*
relativistic	relativista *aj*	retain	retener *vt*
relax	relajar *vt*	reticular	reticular, reticulado *aj*
relaxed	relajado *aj*	retinal	retinal *aj*
relieve	relevar *vt*	retire	retirarse *vr*
remodel	remodelar *vt*	retract	retractar(se) *vt(r)*
remunerate	remunerar *vt*	retraction (claws)	retracción *nf*
renascent	renaciente *aj*	retrospective	retrospectivo *aj*
renounce	renunciar *vt*	reunification	reunificación *nf*
renovate	renovar *vt*	reunified	reunificado *aj*
reorganize	reorganizar *vt*	reunify	reunificar(se) *vt(r)*
repaint	repintar *vt*	reunite	reunirse *vr*
repair	reparar *vt*	revengeful	revanchista *aj*
reparable	reparable *aj*	reverberate	reverberar *vi*

reverberating	reverberante *aj*	satiate	saciar *vt*
revert	revertir *vi*	satiny	satinado *aj*
review	revistar *vt*	satirical	satírico *aj*
revocable	revocable *aj*	satirize	satirizar *vt*
revoke	revocar *vt*	satisfy	satisfacer *vti*
revolt	revuelta *nf*	saturant	saturante, saturativo *aj*
rhapsodic	rapsódico *aj*	saturate	saturar *vt*
rheumatoid	reumatoideo *aj*	Saturnalian	saturnal *aj*
rhyme	rimar *vti*	savor Ⓐ	saborear(se) *vt(r)*
rhythmic(al)	rítmico *aj*	scale (mountain)	escalar *vt*
ridicule	ridiculizar *vt*	scandalize	escandalizar *vt*
rigidity	rigidez *nf*	scapular	escapular, escapulario *aj*
rigorous	riguroso *aj*		
risk	arriesgar *vt*	scatological	escatológico *aj*
risky	arriesgado, riesgoso *aj*	scepter Ⓐ	cetro *nm*
ritualistic	ritualista *aj*	schematic	esquemático *aj*
rob	robar *vt*	schismatic	cismático *aj*
robust	robusto *aj*	scholastic	escolástico *aj*
Romanize	romanizar *vt*	schooling	escolaridad *nf*
romantic	romántico *aj*	Scottish, Scotch	escosés *aj*
rotate	rotar *vt*	sculpt	esculpir *vti*
rudimentary	rudimentario *aj*	seal	sellar *vt*
ruin (financially)	arruinar *vt*	secession	secesión *nf*
ruination	arruinamiento *nm*	secondarily	segundariamente *av*
ruinous	ruinoso *aj*	secondly *av*	en segundo lugar *nm*
ruminate	rumiar *vi*	secrete	secretar *vt*
rumination	rumia *nf*	sectarian	sectario *aj*
rumor	rumorear(se) *vt(r)*	secular	secular *aj*
runic	rúnico *aj*	secularize	secularizar *vt*
sabotage	sabotear *vt*	secure	asegurar *vt*
sacerdotal	sacerdotal *aj*	sedate	sedar *vt*
sack	saquear *vt*	seditious	sedicioso *aj*
sacramental	sacramental *aj*	seduce	seducir *vt*
sacrifice	sacrificar(se) *vt(r)*	segment	segmentar *vt*
sacrificial	sacrificatorio *aj*	select	seleccionar *vt*
sacrilegious	sacrílego *aj*	selectivity	selectividad *nf*
sacrosanct	sacrosanto *aj*	self-government	autogobierno *nm*
sainted	santo *aj*	self-medicate	automedicarse *vr*
sainthood	santidad *nf*	semester	semestral *aj*
saintly	santo *aj*	semiautomatic	semiautomático *aj*
salaciousness	salacidad *nf*	semiconscious	semiconsciente *aj*
saline	salino *aj*	semifinal	semifinal *nf*
salinize	salinizar *vt*	senatorial	senatorial *aj*
salivate	salivar *vi*	senescent	senescente *aj*
salubrious	salubre *aj*	senile	senil *aj*
salutary	saludable *aj*	sensational	sensacional *aj*
salute	saludar *vti*	sensitize	sensibilizar *vt*
salvage	salvar *vt*	sentence	sentenciar *vt*
sanctify	santificar *vt*	sentimentalize *vt*	imbuir de sentimiento *vt, nm*
sanctimony	santurronería *nf*		
sanction	sancionar *vt*	separate	separarse *vr*
sanitize	sanear *vt*	septic	séptico *aj*
sapphire	zafirino *aj*	sepulchral	sepulcral *aj*

sequential	secuencial *aj*
sequester	secuestrar *vt*
serialize	serializar *vt*
sermonize	sermonear *vi*
serpentine	serpentino *aj*
serve	servir *vti*
severity	severidad *nf*
sex	sexar *vt*
sexed	sexuado *aj*
sexiness	atractivo sexual *nm*
sexless	asexuado *aj*
sextuple	sextuplicar(se) *vt(r)*
sexual	sexual *aj*
signal	señalar(se) *vt(r)*
signify	significar *vt*
silence	silenciar *vt*
simian	simiesco *aj*
simplicity	simplicidad *nf*
simplify	simplificar *vt*
simulate	simular *vt*
simulator	simulador *nm*
simultaneity	simultaneidad *nf*
singularity	singularidad *nf*
sinter	sinterizar *vt*
skeptical 🅐	escéptico *aj*
ski	esquiar *vi*
sniff (glue)	esnifar *vt*
sober	sobrio *aj*
socialistic	socialista *aj*
socialize	socializar *vt*
societal *aj*	de la sociedad *nf*
sociocultural	sociocultural *aj*
sociological	sociológico *aj*
sociopolitical	sociopolítico *aj*
solace	solazar *vt*
solder	soldar *vt*
solemn	solemne *aj*
solemnize	solemnizar *vt*
solicit (help)	solicitar *vt*
solidarity	solidaridad *nf*
solidify	solidificar(se) *vt(r)*
soliloquize	soliloquiar *vi*
solo	solista *aj*
soluble	soluble *aj*
solve	solucionar *vt*
solvent	solvente *aj*
somatic	somático *aj*
sonority	sonoridad *nf*
sordid	sórdido *aj*
sound	sondear *vt*
sovereignty	soberanía *nf*
space	espaciar *vt*
Spanish	español *aj*

spatial	espacial *aj*
specialize	especializar(se) *vt(r)*
specify	especificar *vt*
speculate	especular *vi*
speculative	especulativo *aj*
spermicidal	espermaticida *aj*
spiny, spinose	espinoso *aj*
spiritualistic	espiritualista *aj*
spirituality	espiritualidad *nf*
spongy	esponjoso *aj*
sportsmanlike *aj*	de buen deportista *nmf*
sprint	esprintar *vi*
spume	espuma *nf*
spy	espiar *vi*
spying	espionaje *nm*
stabilization	estabilización *nf*
stabilize	estabilizar(se) *vt(r)*
stake	estacar *vt*
stampede *vi*	salir de estampida *vi, nf*
standardization	estandar(d)ización *nf*
standardize	estandarizar(se) *vt(r)*
station	estacionar *vt*
stationary	estacionario *aj*
statistical	estadístico *aj*
statutory	estatutario *aj*
stenographic	estenográfico *aj*
stereotype	estereotipar *vt*
stereotyping	estereotipado *nm*
sterile	estéril *aj*
stigmatize	estigmatizar *vt*
stimulate	estimular *vt*
stipulate	estipular *vt*
stoical	estoico *aj*
strangle	estrangular *vt*
stratify	estratificar(se) *vt(r)*
stressful	estresante *aj*
striated	estriado *aj*
stridence	estridencia *nf*
structure	estructurar *vt*
stucco	estucar *vt*
stuccowork	estucado *nm*
student	estudiantil *aj*
studious	estudioso *aj*
stupefy *vt*	dejar estupefacto *vt, aj*
Stygian	estigio *aj*
stylistic	estilístico *aj*
stylize	estilizar *vt*
styptic	estíptico *aj, nm*
subcontract	subcontratar *vt*
subdivide	subdividir(se) *vt(r)*
subject	sujeto *aj, nm*
subjection	sujeción *nf*
sublimate	sublimar *vt*

subliminal	subliminal *aj*	synaptic	sináptico *aj*
submerge	sumergir(se) *vt(r)*	synchronism	sincronismo *nm*
suborbital	suborbital *aj*	synchronize	sincronizar(se) *vt(r)*
suborn	sobornar *vt*	synclinal	sinclinal *aj*
subroutine	subrutina *nf*	syncopate	sincopar *vt*
subscribe	suscribir(se) *vt(r)*	synonymous	sinónimo *aj*
subsist	subsistir *vi*	syntactic	sintáctico *aj*
substitute	sustituir *vti*	synthesize	sintetizar *vt*
substitution	substitución *nf*	syphilitic	sifilítico *aj*
substructure	infraestructura *nf*	system(at)ize	sistematizar *vt*
subsystem	subsistema *nm*	systematic	sistemático *aj*
subtitle	subtitular *vt*	tabulate	tabular *vt*
subtract	sustraer *vt*	tabulator	tabulador *nm*
subtype	subtipo *nm*	tacit	tácito *aj*
suburban	suburbano *aj*	tardiness	tardanza *nf*
subversion	subversión *nf*	tarsal	tarsal, tarsiano *aj*
succulence	suculencia *nf*	tattoo	tatuar *vt*
sudorific	sudorífero *aj*	technocratic	tecnocrático *aj*
suffer	sufrir *vti*	telecast	teledifusión *nf*
sufficiency	suficiencia *nf*	telegraph	telegrafiar *vt*
suffixed	sufijo *aj*	telegraphic	telegráfico *aj*
suffocating	sofocante *aj*	teleological	teleológico *aj*
sugar	azucarar *vt*	telepathic	telepático *aj*
suggest	sugerir *vt*	telephone	telefonear *vt*
suicidal	suicida *aj*	telephonic	telefónico *aj*
sum	sumar *vt*	telescopic	telescópico *aj*
superhuman	sobrehumano *aj*	teletype *vt*	enviar por teletipo *vt, nm*
superstitious	supersticioso *aj*		
supervise	supervisar *vt*	televize	televisar *vt*
supplicate	suplicar *vt*	telex *vt*	enviar por télex *vt, nm*
suppose	suponer *vt*	temper	templar *vt*
suppress	suprimir *vt*	tempered	templado *aj*
supranational	supranacional *aj*	temporality	temporalidad *nf*
surgical	quirúrgico *aj*	temporarily	temporalmente *av*
surprise	sorprender *vt*	tempt	tentar *vt*
surprising	sorprendente, sorpresivo *aj*	tend to	tender *vi*
		tense	tensar *vt*
surrealistic	surrealista *aj*	terminological	terminológico *aj*
surrender	rendirse *vr*	terrible	terrible *aj*
survive	sobrevivir *vti*	terrify	aterrar *vt*
suspect	sospechar *vt*	terrifying	aterrorizador *aj*
suspicious (person)	suspicaz *aj*	terrorize	aterrorizar *vt*
sustain	sostener *vt*	testamentary	testamentario *aj*
sustainable	sostenible *aj*	testicular	testicular *aj*
suture	suturar *vt*	testify	testificar *vt*
syllabic	silábico *aj*	testimonial	testimonial *aj*
syllabify	silabear *vt*	tetravalent	tetravalente *aj*
syllogize	silogizar *vi*	textual	textual *aj*
symbiotic	simbiótico *aj*	theatricality	teatralidad *nf*
symbolic	simbólico *aj*	theistic	teísta *aj*
symbolize	simbolizar *vt*	theological	teológico *aj*
symphonic	sinfónico *aj*	theorize	teorizar *vi*
symptomatic	sintomático *aj*	theorizing	teorizante *aj*

theosophical	teosófico *aj*	tripartite	tripartito *aj*
therapeutic	terapéutico *aj*	triple	triplicar(se) *vt(r)*
thermoplastic	termoplástico *aj*	triplicate	triplicar *vt*
tint	tinturar *vt*	trisect	trisecar *vt*
title	titular *vt*	trisyllabic	trisílabo *aj*
titled (book)	titulado, intitulado *aj*	triumph	triunfar *vi*
titled (person) *aj*	con título de nobleza *nm, nf*	triumphal	triunfal *aj*
		trivalent	trivalente *aj*
tolerate	tolerar *vt*	trivia	trivialidades *nfpl*
tonal	tonal *aj*	triviality	trivialidad *nf*
tonic (note)	tónico *aj*	trivialize	trivializar *vt*
topographic(al)	topográfico *aj*	trot	trotar *vi*
torment	atormentar *vt*	truncation	truncamiento *nm*
torpedo	torpedear *vt*	tubercular	tuberculoso *aj*
torrential	torrencial *aj*	tuberous	tuberoso *aj*
torture	torturar *vt*	tubular	tubular *aj*
total	totalizar *vt*	tumble	tumbar *vt*
totalitarian	totalitario *aj*	tumid	túmido *aj*
touch	tocar *vt*	turbidity	turbiedad *nf*
touch	tocar(se) *vt(r)*	turgidity	turgencia *nf*
touch-sensitive *aj*	sensible al tacto *aj, nm*	tutelage	tutela *nf*
touchable	tocable *aj*	tutor	tutelar *vt*
toxic	tóxico *aj*	tympanic	timpánico *aj*
traffic	traficar *vi*	typify	tipificar *vt*
tragicomic	tragicómico *aj*	typographic	tipográfico *aj*
train	entrenar(se) *vt(r)*	tyranny	tiranía *nf*
transatlantic	tra(n)satlántico *aj*	ubiquity	ubicuidad *nf*
transcend	tra(n)scender *vti*	ulcerate	ulcerarse *vr*
transcendent	tra(n)scendente *aj*	ulcerous	ulceroso *aj*
transcontinental	tra(n)scontinental *aj*	un-American	antiamericano *aj*
transfer	tra(n)sferir *vt*	unabbreviated	sin abreviar
transform	tra(n)sformar *vt*	unanimity	unanimidad *nf*
transgress	transgredir *vt*	unappealable	inapelable *aj*
transistorize *vt*	equipar con transistores *vt, nmpl*	unappetizing	poco apetitoso
		unarmed	inerme *aj*
transitional *aj*	de transición *nf*	unbandage	desvendar *vt*
translucence	tra(n)slucidez *nf*	unbutton	desabotonar *vt*
transmit	tra(n)smitir *vt*	unceasing	incesante *aj*
transplant	tra(n)splantar *vt*	uncensored	no censurado
transport	tra(n)sportar *vt*	uncertain	incierto *aj*
transpose	tra(n)sponer *vt*	unconditional	incondicional *aj*
trap	atrapar *vt*	unconfessed	inconfeso *aj*
trapped	atrapado *aj*	unconnected	inconexo *aj*
traumatic	traumático *aj*	unconquerable	inconquistable *aj*
traumatize	traumatizar *vt*	unconstitutional	anticonstitucional *aj*
treat	tratar *vt*	uncontaminated	incontaminado *aj*
tremble	temblar *vi*	uncountable	incontable *aj*
trepan	trepanar *vt*	undecipherable	indescifrable *aj*
triacid	triácido *aj, nm*	undefended	indefenso *aj*
triatomic	triatómico *aj*	undemocratic	antidemocrático *aj*
tribalism	sistema tribal	underconsumption	infraconsumo *nm*
trigonometric	trigonométrico *aj*	underexpose	subexponer *vt*
trimolecular	trimolecular *aj*	underpopulated	subpoblado *aj*

undulate	ondular *vi*	vacation *vi*	tomar las vacaciones *vt*, *nfpl*
undulation	ondulación *nf*	vaccinate	vacunar *vt*
uneconomic	antieconónomico *aj*	vacillate	vacilar *vi*
uneconomical	antieconómico *aj*	vaginal	vaginal *aj*
unemployed	desempleado *aj*	vagueness	vaguedad *nf*
unequal	desigual *aj*	valid	válido *aj*
unexpected	inesperado *aj*	validate	convalidar *vt*
unfocus(s)ed	desenfocado *aj*	valuation	valoración *nf*
unhygienic	antihigiénico *aj*	value	avaluar, valorar *vt*
unidimensional	unidimensional *aj*	valvular	valvular *aj*
uniformed	uniformado *aj*	vaporize Ⓐ	vaporizar(se) *vt(r)*
uniformity	uniformidad *nf*	vaporous	vaporoso *aj*
unify	unificar *vt*	variability	variabilidad *nf*
uninhabitable	inhabitable *aj*	varnish	barnizar *vt*
unisex	unisexo *aj*	vary	variar *vti*
unitary	unitario *aj*	varying	variante, variable *aj*
united	unido *aj*	vectorial	vectorial *aj*
univalent	univalente *aj*	veer	virar *vi*
universality	universalidad *nf*	vegetate	vegetar *vi*
university	universitario *aj*	vegetating	vegetante *aj*
unlimited	ilimitado *aj*	vegetative	vegetativo *aj*
unoccupied	desocupado *aj*	vehicular	vehicular *aj*
unofficial	extraoficial *aj*	veil	velar *vt*
unpack	desempacar(se) *vt(r)*	veined	venoso *aj*
unpatriotic	antipatriótico *aj*	velar	velar *aj*
unpopular	impopular *aj*	velarize	velarizar *vt*
unpopulated	no poblado *aj*	vend	vender *vt*
unpremeditated	impremeditado *aj*	vending	vendedor *aj*
unpronounceable	inpronunciable *aj*	venerate	venerar *vt*
unpunished	impune *aj*	venous	venoso *aj*
unquestionable	incuestionable *aj*	ventilate	ventilar *vt*
unreal	irreal *aj*	ventricular	ventricular *aj*
unredeemable	irredimible *aj*	Venusian *aj*	del planeta Venus *nm*
unrepentant	impenitente *aj*	verbalize	verbalizar *vt*
unsaturated	no saturado	verbosity	verbosidad *nf*
unscientific	no científico	verdant	verde *aj*
unsystematic	no sistemático *aj*	verifiable	verificable *aj*
uranic	uránico *aj*	verify	verificar *vt*
urbanize	urbanizar(se) *vt(r)*	vermicidal	vermicida *aj*
urinary	urinario *aj*	versatility	versatilidad *nf*
urinate	orinar *vi*	versification	versificación *nf*
use	usar *vt*	versify	versificar *vi*
usufructuary	usufructuario *nm*	vertebral	vertebral *aj*
usurious	usurero *aj*	vertiginous	vertiginoso *aj*
uterine	uterino *aj*	vesicular	vesicular *aj*
utilitarian	utilitario *aj*	vestigial	vestigial *aj*
utility	utilidad *nf*	veterinary	veterinario *aj*
utilization	utilización *nf*	viability	viabilidad *nf*
utilize	utilizar *vt*	victimize	victimar *vt*
uveitic	uveítico *aj*	videotape *vt*	grabar en video *vt, nm*
uvular	uvular *aj*	vigorous	vigoroso *aj*
vacate	vaciar *vt*	vilify	vilipendiar *vt*

vindicate	vindicar *vt*	volley	volear *vt*
virulent	virulento *aj*	volumetric	volumétrico *aj*
visceral	visceral *aj*	vomit	vomitar *vti*
viscous	viscoso *aj*	voyage	viajar *vi*
visibility	visibilidad *nf*	voyeuristic	voyeurista *aj*
visionary	visionario *aj*	vulcanize	vulcanizar *vt*
visit	visitar *vt*	vulturine	buitrero *aj*
visiting	visitante *aj*	vulvar	vulvar *aj*
visualize	visualizar *vt*	widowed	viudo *aj*
vitalize	vitalizar *vt*	xenophobic	xenófobo *aj*
vitrify	vitrificar(se) *vt(r)*	xerophilious	xerófilo *aj*
vituperate	vituperar *vt*	xerophytic	xerofítico *aj*
vivacious	vivaz *aj*	zealous	celoso *aj*
vocalic	vocálico *aj*	zigzag	zigzaguear *vi*
vocalism	vocalismo *nm*	zigzagging	zigzagueo *nm*
vocalize	vocalizar *vti*	zonal	zonal *aj*
vociferate	vociferar *vi*	zone *vt*	dividir en zonas
volatile	volátil *aj*		*vt, nfpl*
volatilize	volatilizar(se) *vt(r)*	zoological	zoológico *aj*

Symbols and Abbreviations

A	=	Appendix A
B	=	Appendix B
C	=	Appendix C
D	=	Appendix D
(obs)	=	obsolete or historical word
aj	=	adjective
av	=	adverb
intj	=	interjection
nf	=	feminine noun
nf(el)	=	feminine noun used with masculine definite article in the singular
nfpl	=	feminine plural noun
nm	=	masculine noun
nmf	=	masculine or feminine noun
nmpl	=	masculine plural noun
npl	=	plural (English) noun
nsg	=	singular (English) noun
prep	=	preposition
vi	=	intransitive verb
vr	=	reflexive verb
vt	=	transitive verb
vti	=	transitive or intransitive verb
vt(r)	=	transitive or reflexive verb